SQL SERVER 2000

SQL Server™ 2000 Web Application Developer's Guide

CRAIG **UTLEY**

Osborne/**McGraw-Hill**

Berkeley New York St. Louis San Francisco
Auckland Bogotá Hamburg London Madrid
Mexico City Milan Montreal New Delhi Panama City
Paris São Paulo Singapore Sydney
Tokyo Toronto

Osborne/**McGraw-Hill**
2600 Tenth Street
Berkeley, California 94710
U.S.A.

For information on translations or book distributors outside the U.S.A., or to arrange bulk purchase discounts for sales promotions, premiums, or fund-raisers, please contact Osborne/**McGraw-Hill** at the above address.

SQL Server™ 2000 Web Application Developer's Guide

1234567890 DOC DOC 01987654321
ISBN 0-07-212619-1

Publisher
　Brandon A. Nordin

Vice President & Associate Publisher
　Scott Rogers

Editorial Director
　Wendy Rinaldi

Project Editor
　Mark Karmendy

Acquisitions Coordinator
　Tim Madrid

Technical Editor
　Doug Churchman

Copy Editor
　Marcia Baker

Proofreader
　Susie Elkind

Indexer
　Claire Splan

Computer Designers
　Lauren McCarthy
　Kelly Stanton-Scott

Illustrator
　Michael Mueller

Series Design
　Peter F. Hancik

Cover Design
　Amparo Del Rio

This book was composed with Corel VENTURA™ Publisher.

S ER 2000

™ 2000

lication

Developer's Guide

To Linda, whose understanding and
encouragement made this possible.
And to Alison, who always makes me proud.

ABOUT THE AUTHOR

Craig Utley is a Microsoft Certified Solutions Developer and Microsoft Certified Trainer with nine years of experience developing client/server and Web applications. He started building client/server applications with Access 1.0 and Visual Basic 2.0, and began developing n-tier systems as soon as Visual Basic 4.0 made COM components possible. Craig has been involved with Active Server Pages since they were in beta, having produced courseware about, and written applications using, Active Server Pages and SQL Server. Craig has also written data warehousing courseware focusing on Microsoft's Analysis Services. Craig is president of CIOBriefings LLC, a consulting and training company focusing on n-tier Web solutions and data warehousing. He is a regular speaker at the SQL Connections conference and is co-writing a series of articles about data warehousing for Pinnacle Publishing's *SQL Server Professional*.

AT A GLANCE

CONTENTS

Part I

Web Application Development with Active Server Pages

Part II

Server-Side Database Access

Part V

Appendixes

ACKNOWLEDGMENTS

I was 18 the first time I went skydiving. After seven hours of ground school, they suited us up with our jumpsuits and parachutes and put us on the plane. I knew the first jump was to be from 3,000 feet and, as I was seated by the window, I watched the ground recede as the airplane climbed. Once things on the ground looked impossibly small, I decided we must be at jump altitude and checked my jumpmaster's altimeter—it read 1,000 feet. I remember thinking, *"What have I gotten myself into?"*

I've asked myself that same question many times during the course of writing this book. Despite everyone warning me that it was a huge undertaking, I had no idea just what all was involved until I got started. Without a doubt, I never would have finished without the excellent staff at Osborne. Editorial Director Wendy Rinaldi was a voice of reassurance and reason, and kept me on track with nudges in the right direction. Acquisitions Coordinators Monika Faltiss and Timothy Madrid did a wonderful job coordinating the entire process. Project Editor Mark Karmendy, in addition to his regular job, was great at answering the stupid questions of a first-time author. Copy Editor Marcia Baker tried to make me live up to all those things I learned in English class over the years. Lauren McCarthy and Kelly Stanton-Scott took my text and created the layouts for the pages you now hold in your hands, and Michael Mueller adeptly translated my sketched concepts into clean, crisp graphics. Doug Churchman provided invaluable, and sometimes warmly critical, technical comments. And although many people had a hand in this book, please realize that any mistakes are solely the fault of the author.

As this is my first book, there are several others I'd like to thank. Michael Washington provided many hours of late-night support when the task seemed too large (the monkey comment still makes me laugh). Andrew McMahon bailed me out of a tight spot when a laptop decided to give up the ghost for good. Tammy Tilzey agreed to coauthor some articles with me to help relieve some of that pressure. My parents, sister, and brother all provided their support and words of encouragement, even when I was too busy writing to pay them a visit. My dogs, Torrey and Hailey, were great too, reminding me every two hours to go take a walk and clear my mind.

Finally, a book is ultimately about teaching, and I have been fortunate to have a number of great teachers in my life. Three stand out more than any others: Gene Todd, who taught me that firm, fair, and consistent are more than just words; the late Ora Nall, who never stopped believing that I could achieve great things; and Marilyn Simpson, whose humor and intelligence I still try to emulate.

INTRODUCTION

The purpose of this book is to discuss the development of Web applications with Microsoft SQL Server as the database engine. The idea of Web applications is a broad topic, and this book takes a high-level look at a variety of technology. Based on certain experience as a developer and consultant, I do go into extensive detail on some very important issues, such as the objects in Internet Information Server and ActiveX Data Objects.

THE ROADMAP

Given that the topic covered in this book is very broad, it helps to look at a roadmap of what you actually need to know in order to create Web applications. If you examine Figure 1, you will see the major areas or expertise and the rough order in which you have to learn them. First, you will notice that HTML is at the top of the list. The truth is, HTML is the language of the Internet. Despite what you hear about XML, you'll still want to know HTML in order to display pages to the end user.

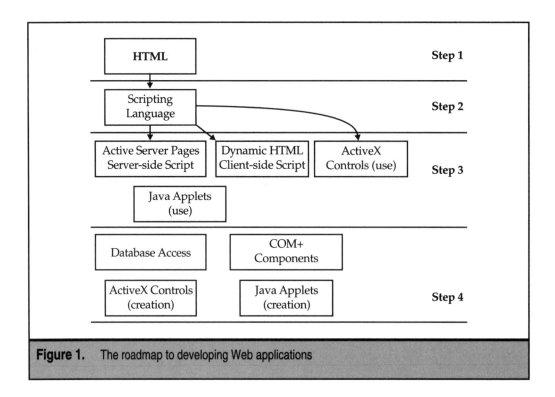

Figure 1.   The roadmap to developing Web applications

NOTE: XML can be used to display information as well. However, XML, like HTML, is all text, and it requires at least one extra step to display it to the user like HTML. Therefore, this book assumes that HTML is the format used to display text, while XML may be used to pass, or perhaps display, data.

After learning HTML, you have to learn a scripting language. This language is usually VBScript or JavaScript (also called JScript and ECMAScript). Many Web developers program in both VBScript and JavaScript. Adding the scripting language allows you to do several important things. First, it allows you to use client-side scripting and DHTML (Dynamic HTML, an "advanced form" of client-side scripting, in one sense). This allows you to actually run code on the client machine. This adds some powerful functionality, but can limit the reach of your applications to only particular browsers.

A scripting language also lets you create pages with server-side script. Server-side script is powerful because it runs on the server and does not rely on any of the capabilities of the client browser. This makes it a powerful approach with a broader reach than DHTML. Most of this book will focus on server-side scripting, using VBScript. This doesn't mean that VBScript is better than JavaScript, but it is more widely known and is commonly used on the server.

Adding scripting languages also makes the use of ActiveX Controls and Java Applets on the client more powerful. You can use ActiveX Controls or Java Applets without any client-side scripting, but generally you need client-side scripting in order to interact with these controls or applets.

Once you have mastered HTML and a scripting language, you will be able to create pages that use client-side and server-side scripting. Now, it is time to extend your applications by adding very powerful features, such as database access and the ability to call COM/COM+ Components. You can create your own components, and you can also use full languages (not scripting languages) to create your own ActiveX Controls or Java Applets.

How This Book Maps to the Roadmap

As you can see from the roadmap in Figure 1, creating Web applications covers a lot of territory. When this book was first started, I had to make several important decisions: Should I assume the reader already knows HTML? What about VBScript? Will the user be familiar with SQL Server 2000? Will the reader have ever created a COM Component?

Because the book is part of the Database Professional's Library, I had to assume some familiarity with SQL Server, but I tried to keep that to a minimum. I assume that you know how to use the SQL Server Enterprise Manager to navigate through the nodes, create databases, and set permissions. Beyond that, the use of SQL Server is surprisingly light; this book is about accessing SQL Server, and not so much about creating databases and tables.

As far as HTML, I had to assume that the reader was familiar with HTML. If you are not or have little experience with it, please check out Appendix E. While hardly a complete HTML reference, Appendix E serves as a crash course in the most important topics you need to understand: how HTML works, HTML forms, and HTML tables. This quick look at HTML should get you through most of the examples in the book.

Next, I had to assume a familiarity with VBScript. This is more of a stretch, but again I have provided a crash course, in Appendix F. VBScript can be a book unto itself, so Appendix F covers only the absolute basics needed to get you through this book.

Active Server Pages, on the other hand, takes up a large percentage of the book. Chapters 2 and 4 cover Active Server Pages in detail, while Chapter 3 covers Visual InterDev, the tool you will use to work with Active Server Pages. Almost every other chapter in the book deals with Active Server Pages.

Dynamic HTML is mentioned only briefly in Chapter 12. The reason the mention is brief is that the use of DHTML usually limits the reach of your application. Microsoft and Netscape both have different ways of implementing DHTML in their browsers, which makes writing DHTML for multiple browsers a challenge. Not only do you have to worry about the *brand* of browser, you have to worry about the *version* of the browser. I have seen DHTML that works in Internet Explorer 4.*x* but does not work properly in version 5.*x*.

Database access, not surprisingly, receives a tremendous amount of attention, most of which is concentrated in Chapters 5–9, and then mentioned again in Chapters 10–14 to varying degrees. COM+ Components are important for building scalable Web applications, both from a database access and general performance view, and these are covered in Chapters 13 and 14.

Finally, Chapter 15 covers security. This isn't mentioned on the roadmap, but it is a critical section nonetheless.

SOFTWARE

This book assumes that you will be building Web applications using Microsoft technology. If you are running SQL Server 2000, this means that you have Windows 2000, Windows NT, Windows 9*x*, or Windows Me. The book assumes Windows 2000, but most of this book will work on any of the above-mentioned operating systems.

None of what this book covers is unique to SQL Server 2000 Enterprise Edition, but this is the version used for this book. The engine was running on Windows 2000 Advanced Server. Using Windows 2000 means that I had Internet Information Services 5.0, Microsoft's built-in Web server. If you are using Windows 9*x* or Windows Me, some of the material in the book will require you to use a different management tool, because the Web server on Windows 9*x* and Windows Me is called Personal Web Server. The security portion of Chapter 15 will not be valid for users of Windows 9*x* or Windows Me.

Finally, this book uses Visual InterDev 6.0, with Service Pack 4. If you do not have this tool, you can still do almost all of the book, with the exception of

Chapters 2, 10, and 11. Still, it will be useful to read these chapters, and you should try to obtain a copy of Visual InterDev if you can.

Despite the fact that Visual Studio .NET is changing much of how Visual InterDev works, the ADO topics will not change, and understanding how ASPs work is still critical. Therefore, none of this book will be wasted effort if you are considering moving to Visual Studio .NET, which may be in beta by the time this book hits the shelves.

PART I

Web Application Development with Active Server Pages

CHAPTER 1

Introduction to Web Applications

This book will examine how to build Web applications using Microsoft's SQL Server 2000 as a back-end. First, we need to embark on a journey to understand what we mean by "Web application," and how we can use Microsoft technology to build Web applications. We will examine such topics as HTML, IIS, ASP, and n-tier development in this introductory chapter. This chapter assumes you are familiar with HTML; if not, you can refer to Appendix E.

WHAT ARE WEB APPLICATIONS?

Web applications are applications that run over the Web. If that sounds redundant, think about this: many Web sites are simply an online catalog, sometimes called "brochureware." They are just pages of pictures and descriptions. When we talk about building *applications,* we are talking about building sites that *do* something. They allow you to enter information, and they intelligently respond to your requests. If Web applications had never been developed, we would just have Web *pages* that would be no more interactive than the pages of a catalog or magazine.

Web applications include all the e-commerce sites that have become the rage. These sites allow you to browse the catalog, but you can also place items in your shopping basket, choose a shipping option, and then pay for the items, all without ever picking up the phone. Many sites offer real-time inventories, so you know if the items you want are in stock. Other applications include many business-to-business applications. For example, Company A may track demographic data on consumers. Other companies can log on to Company A's Web site and run reports to try to identify markets with their target demographic. This means these sites must have real-time access to a database and the ability not only to read the data, but also to build a page on the fly to reflect the values in the database. Building pages on the fly is at the heart of Web applications.

To build Web applications, we first need to understand how Web servers and static Web pages work. We will then move into how to build applications that are driven by the data in our SQL Server databases.

Web Servers and HTML

At their heart, Web servers can be very simple software. A client computer connected to the network requests a particular page from a particular Web server. On a Web server, a page is just a file stored on a physical drive. The server locates the page on some computer and sends a copy of the page (file) to the requesting client computer, as can be seen in Figure 1-1.

The request from the client to the Web server and the response from the server back to the client are done with a standard protocol

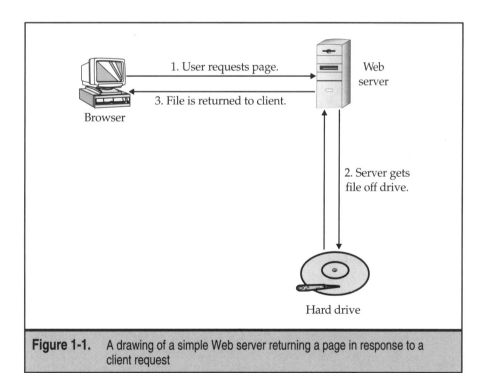

Figure 1-1.   A drawing of a simple Web server returning a page in response to a client request

of the Internet: HTTP (HyperText Transfer Protocol). HTTP takes the client request and packages it in a format that a standard Web server can understand. When the server responds, the page information is sent back to the client using the same HTTP protocol. HTTP rides on top of a well-known networking protocol, IP (Internet Protocol).

So, at the heart of their functionality, Web servers just send files to the requesting browser. And this is one of the important things to understand about static HTML (HyperText Markup Language) pages: the Web server doesn't process them in any way. In other words, Web servers are "dumb" concerning static Web pages. However, most Web servers do have the ability to perform processing before pages are sent to the client. This processing of the page requires some form of intelligence on the Web server and is what most of this book is about.

First, however, we need to understand what happens with simple, static HTML files. If the files are sent down to the client with no processing, how are they displayed? This is the job of the browser. The two most popular browsers are Microsoft's Internet Explorer (IE) and Netscape's Navigator, although there are a number of others available, such as Opera, WebTV, and AOL (America OnLine). Browsers are built with the express purpose of taking the HTML and interpreting it to display the page on the screen.

HTML was originally developed so that a document's content could be displayed on any hardware platform. This was to be achieved by marking content by meaning, and letting the browser handle display issues as they may be appropriate for that platform. If you use an application like Microsoft Word to create a document, Word stores that document in a binary format to preserve the text formatting. This binary format is not necessarily compatible with other applications on other platforms. Therefore, the creators of HTML wanted a format that could preserve text formatting but that was also portable to any platform. To do this meant that HTML needed to be all text, with no binary information.

NOTE: Many people get some credit for the concept of an HTML-like language, but Tim Berners-Lee and Robert Caillau actually created HTML. Berners-Lee and Caillau created HTML as a way to provide a platform-independent, linked information system on the various computers at CERN (European Organization for Nuclear Research), a physics research center in Geneva where they worked. In 1991, CERN created the Web that has grown into what we know today.

To accomplish this all-text requirement, HTML stores the document's formatting in *tags.* These tags are not processed by the Web server, but instead are interpreted by the browser on the client computer. The browsers are the platform-specific applications, but they are all written to interpret HTML in roughly the same way, based on the standards set forth by the World Wide Web Consortium in Boston, Massachusetts (http://www.w3.org). This means that each browser will interpret the <H1> tag as a command to render the text in a larger and bolder font.

Given that the purpose of HTML was simply to display text on the screen, preserve the formatting (boldfacing, italicizing, underlining, and so on) from one platform to another, and allow for linked information, I should point out something many people never think about: HTML is *not* a programming language. A programming language has certain elements, three of which are variables, loops, and decision-making structures (such as If statements). HTML does not have any of these three elements. HTML is a computer language, but its purpose is to store text-formatting information. It is not a programming language and therefore cannot perform the functions we would expect in an application. As you will see in later in this chapter, there are ways to add in some client-side script that allows our Web page to perform some processing. Realize, however, that this client-side script is going to be JavaScript or VBScript, and not HTML itself. Running code on the client requires a mix of HTML and a scripting language. Come to think of it, running code on the server with Active Server Pages requires HTML and a scripting language. More on all of this in Chapter 2.

> **NOTE:** Throughout this book, I will refer to JavaScript. Understand that JavaScript is a language created by Netscape. Microsoft created their version of it, called JScript. JavaScript and JScript are similar but not identical. In an attempt to address these differences, a third language called ECMAScript was developed, is endorsed by a standards body, and is supported on both platforms.
> Throughout this book, I will refer to the language as "JavaScript." Please realize that this is just a generic term and could be relating to JavaScript, JScript, or ECMAScript.

One thing that is important to understand is that the different browsers do not always render the same code in exactly the same way. First of all, computers may be in different resolutions. A page that looks good on an 800×600 screen may not appear as desired on a screen set to 640×480. In addition, the color depth may be set differently on various machines, which can lead to colors and graphics not being displayed as expected. Also, the default font on different systems can vary, which means that the page may display differently from one machine to another.

Not only can the same code render slightly differently from one browser to the next, but browser manufacturers also add their own proprietary extensions to standard HTML. This can result in code that only works on one browser and not another. For example, the <BGSOUND> tag is a tag added by Microsoft to play a background sound for a Web page. This tag only works in Internet Explorer. Instead of adding tags, the browser vendors sometimes just add their own attributes to existing tags.

This brings us to another important point about how browsers work: by design, they ignore any tags or attributes they do not understand. Take a look at the following code snippet:

```
<H1>Welcome to Northwind</H1>
    <CRAIG>This text is formatted with the Craig style</CRAIG>
```

Guess what? There *is* no <CRAIG> tag. A browser looking at this code will simply ignore the tag and print the text between the opening and closing tags as normal text. The browser expects the tags to tell it how to format the text, and if it sees a tag that it doesn't understand, it just ignores it and prints the text using the default font and size. You can see this text rendered in Figure 1-2.

Browsers are intentionally very forgiving. This has benefits and drawbacks. One benefit is that the clients do not see error messages. Let's face it, what could they do about it anyway? A major drawback, however, is that we, as developers, do not see any errors when we are trying to debug the pages. In addition, the fact that HTML is not case sensitive, and that some container tags do not have to be closed, leads to a very loosely structured language. Developers like structure,

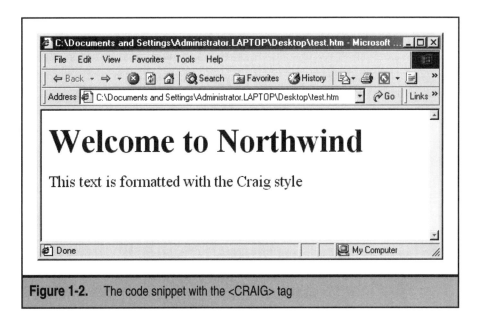

Figure 1-2. The code snippet with the <CRAIG> tag

but HTML does not enforce good, structured coding. There are some online validation tools available, such as the World Wide Web Consortium's HTML Validation Server (http://validator.w3.org) and Netscape's Web Site Garage (http://Websitegarage.netscape.com).

Another important point about HTML is that once it is rendered in the browser, it cannot be updated without performing a refresh, which means going back to the server and getting the page again. In other words, the text on the page can't change once it has been rendered. This is more evidence of the static nature of HTML. There are ways around this: the fields on a form can be updated with some client-side code, or you can turn sections of the code into programmable objects with Dynamic HTML (DHTML). However, both of these require some client-side scripting that was not originally available in HTML, and that is still not supported by all browsers.

Client-side Scripting

Let's take a moment to examine client-side scripting. Remember that HTML is not a programming language and therefore cannot natively perform any processing. We can, however, include some scripting on the client that allows us to perform some action. There are a couple of considerations when you look at client-side scripting:

- ▼ Can the client browser support client-side scripting at all?
- ▲ If so, what languages does it support?

The rule of thumb here is pretty simple: VBScript is known by far more developers, is generally considered easier to program, and only runs in Internet Explorer. JavaScript works in both IE and Navigator. Obviously, your broader reach will be with JavaScript.

NOTE: Do not confuse JavaScript with Java Applets. Java Applets are compiled components that get downloaded and executed in a Java Virtual Machine (VM) in the client browser. JavaScript and VBScript are not compiled, but are interpreted by the client browser.

When I teach people about HTML, I cover how to create HTML forms. Forms, of course, allow the user to enter some information and send it to the server, where we presumably perform some magic on it, such as adding it to a database. A question that almost always comes up, if the students are paying attention, is: "How can I validate the form input?" The answer with straight HTML is simple: "You can't." Standard HTML has no way to validate data in a form field. That means that if you are asking for the users' age, and they type "abc," they will send "abc" to the server in the age field, and you will have to perform your validation on the server. This isn't a bad thing, but consider what the users go through: they fill in the form, select the Submit button, and wait. The data goes across the Internet to your server, and then you perform the data validation. If a field value was incorrect, you have to build a page that tells them of the error and send that page back. Now the users get an error message and must select the Back button in the browser, return to the original form, and change the data. This whole process can take a number of seconds to perform.

With client-side scripting, however, we could validate some of the data at the client before it is sent to the server. This gives users immediate feedback on the data and keeps them on the same page so there is no need to select the Back button after receiving an error message. Not all data can be validated on the client, obviously. We may need access to a database to validate certain values, and we do not usually have direct database access from the client, although direct database access from the client is possible, as we will see in Chapter 12.

To see how client-side scripting can be used to validate form input, the following code shows an oversimplified Web page with a two-field form. If the data entered in both fields is valid, we will send it to the server. If not, we will notify the users of the problem and allow them to fix it. The checks will be simple, too: in the e-mail field, we will just make sure there is an "@" symbol somewhere in the field. In the date of birth field, we will simply make sure what they type is a valid date. The code is then responsible for submitting the form. To see the form in action, see Figure 1-3. Here, we do not actually submit the form, because we don't yet have anything on the server to handle the data. Notice too that the code is written in VBScript, which means this example will only work in IE.

```html
<HTML>
    <H1>Form Validation Example</H1>
    <FORM name="frmSignUp" method="post">
        Enter your e-mail address: <INPUT name="email"><br>
        Enter your date of birth: <INPUT name="dob"><br>
        <INPUT type="button" name="cmdSubmit" value="Submit">
    </FORM>
    <SCRIPT language="VBScript">
        <!--
        Sub cmdSubmit_onClick()
            If InStr(document.frmSignUp.email.value,"@")=0 Then
                alert "E-mail address must contain the @ symbol."
            Else
                If IsDate(document.frmSignUp.dob.value) then
                    alert "Data is fine, form will be submitted"
                Else
                    alert "Date of birth is not a valid date format." & _
                        " Please re-enter."
                End If
            End If
        End Sub
        -->
    </SCRIPT>
</HTML>
```

Clients can also be enhanced using other techniques. For example, we have ActiveX Controls and Java Applets. While these technologies are quite different, they have a similar end result: the client interface can do things you can't normally do with HTML. For now, the biggest difference between the two is that ActiveX Controls only run in IE. Java Applets work in both IE and Navigator, although not all Applets work equally well in both browsers.

ActiveX Controls are popular because they pervade the Windows world and they are easy to create in Visual Basic and Visual C++, among other tools. ActiveX Controls, however, depend on the

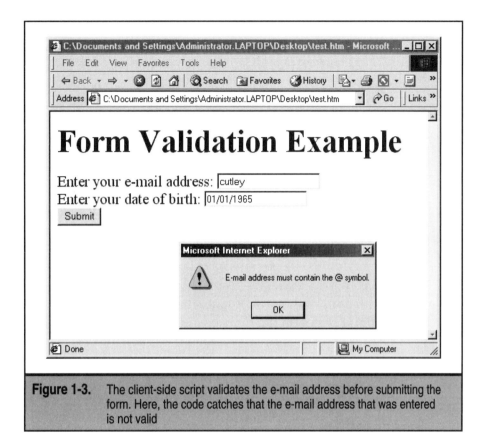

Figure 1-3. The client-side script validates the e-mail address before submitting the form. Here, the code catches that the e-mail address that was entered is not valid

capabilities of the client browser. The controls are downloaded and registered on the client machine, where they stay installed from then on. That way, when users visit the site again in the future, the control is already present on their local machine and does not have to be downloaded again. The control has all the capabilities you might associate with a Windows application: it is event driven, can access the machine's hardware, can read/write to the hard drive, and so on. This ability to access the computer's hard drive has led some people to worry about the security implications of ActiveX Controls. It is true that malicious ActiveX Controls could cause damage to a user's machine. There are some measures taken to try to prevent this, such as the Authenticode technology. We will examine Authenticode in more detail when we discuss security in Chapter 15.

Java Applets can be event driven and give the user a richer interface, but they cannot access the hardware as can ActiveX Controls. This makes many people feel more secure using Java Applets. In addition, they have a broader reach because they are supported by the current versions of both IE and Navigator. There are many Java Applets available, such as stock tickers, countdown timers, and calendars.

Server-side Scripting

Now that we've talked about how Web servers simply send streams of static HTML to a browser to be interpreted, let's examine the concept of Web servers that can build pages dynamically. The reasons for this are obvious: you may want to build pages that reflect data from a database, the results of a search, or time-sensitive information. Without the capabilities provided to us by Web servers that build pages on the fly, we would not have online shopping carts, inventories, or any other Web-based application.

The first Web servers that allowed us to build pages dynamically used CGI (Common Gateway Interchange). CGI is still very common today, and Microsoft's Internet Information Services (IIS) can use CGI as well as Active Server Pages, which we will use throughout this book. CGI is not a programming language. Instead, CGI is a technology that allows us to call compiled programs or scripts on the Web server. These programs or scripts can accept user input and then build pages dynamically based on those inputs. CGI is often seen on UNIX-based Web servers, and many of the CGI programs are Perl scripts (identifiable because they typically end with ".pl").

As previously mentioned, IIS can use CGI, but IIS uses another technology called Active Server Pages (ASP). ASP enables us to mix scripting right into the HTML page. This means that, unlike when using CGI, we are not starting a separate server process when we build a page dynamically. ASP also allows us to work with portions of the final HTML as we interlace the script directly into it. This approach has been so popular that there are now Java Server Pages that work much the same way.

Because ASPs are executed on the server, the choice of the scripting language is up to the developer. Remember that with client-side scripting, we have to know if the browser supports a scripting language, and if so, which one(s). With server-side scripting, we are not concerned about the capabilities of the client browser; we process all the code on the server and just send straight HTML to the client machine. This means that the client browser does not have to support any scripting language at all. In fact, if the clients view the source of the document in their browser, it looks like static HTML; they do not see any of the code that was used to create the page.

ASPs allow us to have a much more complex application environment than we could get with just HTML and client-side scripting. For example, we might need to access some data, or even programs, on a mainframe. These programs could crunch a significant amount of data and send us the results. We might then put this data into a database to further manipulate it before producing the final page that will be sent to the client. Such an application is shown in Figure 1-4. The abilities to run programs on

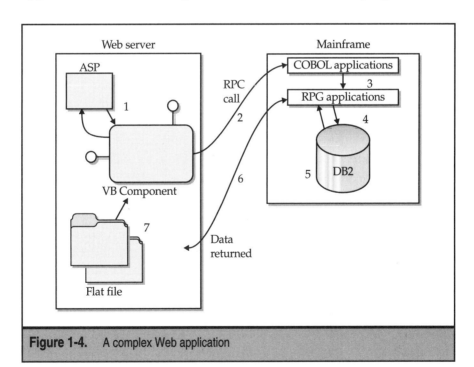

Figure 1-4.   A complex Web application

the mainframe, add and query data from a database, and build a page with the results are beyond the capabilities of standard HTML and client-side script. Intelligent Web servers that support server-side scripting, however, allow us to build these rich applications without a concern for the capabilities of the client browser.

If you've ever worked in a mainframe environment, this is all sounding very familiar. When computers were first created, they were huge machines that took up hundreds or thousands of square feet. Everything ran on that one computer, and people accessed it through dumb terminals. All these terminals could do was display information on the screen and accept user input. Around 1991, client/server began capturing the hearts and minds of the IT (information technology) world. This "power to the people" movement said that the power should be in the PCs sitting on each person's desktop. The data was stored in a central location (the *server)* and moved down to the PC (the *client)* where it was processed and displayed. The only thing that was shared was the data, with some business logic possibly being implemented in stored procedures on the database. This was the birth of *distributed processing.* This client/server architecture, which we now recognize as two-tier or fat-client, had some major advantages over traditional, monolithic systems. The display could be much richer and include things like mouse support, menus, buttons, graphs, animations, colors, and so on. No longer did the users have to type arcane command names and wait to have a report print on green-bar paper. Instead, they could select a few buttons and get the results back quickly, on screen, with graphs and colors and all other sorts of bells and whistles (which we call "features" when talking to management).

Client/server took us 180 degrees from the monolithic, mainframe environment into a distributed environment. While this was a boon for users, it led to some real IT headaches. Anyone who developed client/server applications in this period remembers the horrors of distribution: DLL conflicts, INI files, and ODBC data source names. These distribution issues led to maintenance issues as well. You were very concerned with the capabilities of the clients' machines: Did they have enough RAM? Did they have enough disk space? How would they connect to the server? Was the connection fast enough? All of these issues led IT shops to long for the days of monolithic applications with nothing more than dumb-terminal access.

Enter Web applications. Web applications took IT right back to the monolithic structure they had known and loved: all the functionality was on the Web server. The browser was nothing more than a dumb terminal. It allowed the user to enter text (via HTML forms) and it displayed text (via HTML). That was all a browser had to do, so it was in many respects a dumb terminal interface. Nothing had to be distributed to the client. As long as the clients had a browser capable of handling standard HTML, they were ideal

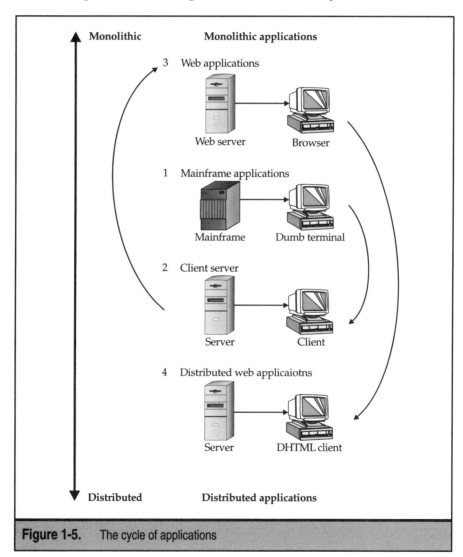

Figure 1-5.   The cycle of applications

candidates for using Web applications. In addition, connectivity for remote users no longer had to mean dedicated dial-up lines and modems. Remote users could now use any ISP, anywhere in the world, and connect to the application with ease. Figure 1-5 shows the cycle applications have gone through.

Before you monolithically-minded developers get too comfortable, realize that we are again moving to the distributed paradigm with technologies like Dynamic HTML (DHTML). DHTML is very browser specific at the moment, which means you are once again concerned about the client browser. In addition, some of the technology, such as Microsoft's data binding from the client, does require certain components to exist on the client machine. These enhancements lead us right back to the reach-versus-richness debate: the richer the user interface, the less reach it has. In other words, if we add all the bells and whistles, oops, features that are available to IE, the application won't work anymore with Netscape, Opera, and other browsers. If we keep it as just straight HTML, it will work with any browser, but won't have as rich a user interface. There is no right answer to the reach-versus-richness debate; it all depends on your client's needs. In fact, almost all questions in Web development can be answered with two words: "It depends."

Before we leave this discussion and take a closer look at Microsoft's offerings in this area, keep in mind the following points:

▼ Standard HTML is only for the display of data and the acceptance of user input.

■ Client-side script is usually used for form validation.

■ Client-side VBScript is only supported by Internet Explorer.

■ Client-side JavaScript is supported by both IE and Navigator.

■ Dynamic HTML is a mix of scripting and HTML that is often browser specific.

■ Server-side script is code that is executed by the Web server.

▲ Server-side script does not rely on capabilities of the client browser.

MICROSOFT'S IIS AND ASP

Microsoft's Web server is called Internet Information Services (IIS). IIS is built into the Windows NT and Windows 2000 operating systems. A subset of IIS, called Personal Web Server, is available for Windows 95 and Windows 98. IIS can act as a simple Web server, serving up static HTML pages like any other Web server. However, IIS has many other features that make it a popular platform on which to develop powerful Web applications. IIS enables such functionality as built-in state management, integration with the Windows 2000 security model, objects to ease Web application creation, and server-side scripting with Active Server Pages.

State management is important for developing Web applications. When you log on to a network or log in to a mainframe, there is a process that verifies you and then maintains an open session for you while you are logged in. On some systems, a period of inactivity will cause you to be logged out, which simply destroys your session on the network and removes your permissions from all network resources. This is an example of a *stateful* connection, in that it knows when you are and when you are not connected, and can maintain information about you while you are connected.

HTTP, on the other hand, is a *stateless* protocol. When a user requests a page from a Web server, the HTTP request is sent to the server, and the Web server sends the file back to the client. Once the file is sent to the client, the HTTP connection is closed. The users now have the HTTP document in their browser, so they do not care if the connection is closed. Now when the user requests the next page, the request goes to the server and the server sees it as a brand-new request. In other words, the Web server sees each request as a new request.

To understand the challenges of only having a stateless connection, imagine an online shopping cart. You are browsing around, looking at items, and find one you want to order. You choose the item and the system replies by saying that item is in your shopping cart. You now select the Check Out button, and it takes you to the checkout area. But your item is not in the shopping cart! In a stateless environment, that is exactly what would happen. A stateless application could not remember from one page to another whether something had been ordered. HTTP, then, presents a challenge when it comes to developing applications. Applications almost always require some form of state management, so developers have to find ways to handle state in what winds up being a disconnected environment. One of the strengths about IIS is that it can automatically maintain state for us even though we are using standard HTTP. The developer doesn't have to worry about creating cookies or passing hidden variables. We will examine how this IIS state management works in Chapter 4.

IIS is the hosting environment for the Active Server Pages engine. ASPs are files with a mix of HTML and a scripting language, and the file is processed on the server before the data is sent to the client. ASPs are a powerful way to create Web applications and can handle a number of different scripting languages. ASPs can easily call COM components that provide added functionality, including components that provide database access.

IIS provides a number of built-in objects that make building Web applications easier. These objects can be called from any scripting language used in an ASP. For example, there is an object that makes it simple to read the data sent from a client through an HTML form. Another object makes it simple to call COM components that allow us to extend the functionality of a Web application as far as it can go. We will examine the available IIS objects in Chapter 4.

When it comes to Active Server Pages, the ASP engine can handle a variety of scripting languages. In fact, any available interpreter for any language can be plugged into the engine. ASP natively supports VBScript and JavaScript. There are interpreters available for PerlScript, Python, and Rexx. This language-neutral position is made available because the Web server is handling the processing of the scripting. When the ASP engine finishes processing all the server-side script, the result that is sent back to the client is just standard HTML. The script is mixed inline with the HTML, and the page is processed within IIS. This means that, unlike when using CGI, a separate process is not started to build a dynamic page.

ASP is often called a "compile-free" technology. This is somewhat misleading and confuses many developers. The ASPs are not compiled by the developer. Instead, the files are merely placed into the appropriate directory on the Web server. When the client requests an ASP, it is interpreted by the ASP engine and then cached in memory in a compiled state. The page is cached for improved performance, since this means it does not have to be interpreted every time it is requested.

Caching the page in memory is a great performance-booster, but since this is a compile-free environment, how does it know when the page has changed? The simple answer is, IIS checks on every call. Say a page, called Order.asp, is cached in memory in its compiled state. When you, as the developer, make a change to Order.asp and save it, the old version is still what is cached in memory. However, when the next user calls Order.asp, IIS performs a check to see if the file on the disk has changed. Normally it has not, so it uses the version in memory. In this case, however, the file has changed, so the ASP engine goes through the interpretation process on the new file, and then stores the new compiled version in the cache. This way, the user is always getting the latest version of the ASP without you doing any more than just saving the file.

Active Server Pages are part of the IIS environment. However, a third-party product called Chili!Soft ASP (http://www.chilisoft.com) allows non-IIS servers to run ASPs. For example, a Lotus Domino or Netscape Enterprise Server could be the Web server used, but still allow ASPs to run. There is even a version for the popular Unix-based Apache Web server. This product allows ASP to extend beyond just the Microsoft platform, potentially making it a viable solution in mixed environments.

N-TIER WEB APPS

If you think back to the discussion on Web applications being similar to monolithic, mainframe applications, you'll remember that I talked about two-tier client/server applications instead of the more powerful n-tier solutions. N-tier, or three-tier, solutions involve pulling the business logic out of the user interface. You now have three logical layers: the *presentation* layer, the *business* layer, and the *data* layer. The presentation layer contains just the user interface (UI) components, such as the forms of your application. You don't want business logic at this level; you want to have just enough code to display the data and accept user input (sound familiar?). This approach is often called a "thin client" application.

The client is thin because it doesn't do much other than display data and accept some user input. Most of the work is done in the business layer. Here, you create a set of reusable components that implement your business rules. These components can then be used by any number of applications that need to perform the same functions.

The data layer sometimes includes just the database, and sometimes a set of components that lie between the business components and the database. This is a design decision that should be based on many factors. We will examine some of these factors later. Whether or not any components reside in this layer, the database may have some business logic implemented in stored procedures and triggers. This often leads to better performance at the cost of some ease of changing the back-end database in the future.

When we talk about components in the business or data layers, we are talking about COM components. COM is Microsoft's technology for allowing one application to create objects out of a separately compiled piece of code. There are a number of factors necessary for a COM component, and COM does a lot more than what I've just mentioned. But for now, let's just understand that COM will allow our front-end to call the business components we create.

Let's look at an example of an n-tier application. Hospitals keep patient information according to a specific data structure. Patients have some form of Patient ID, a name, an address, one or more insurance providers, one or more physicians looking after them, and so on. Each hospital may have a completely separate set of systems in-house to handle patients. Each one of these systems would need to look at the structure of a patient in exactly the same way. So, if the Patient ID were an alphanumeric value of ten characters, each system handling patients in any way would need this definition coded into it. Now comes the great problem of coding this way: what if the Patient

ID format were to change? With traditional systems, each application would have to be modified, tested, and placed back into production. Almost without fail, one system or another gets forgotten, and we now have systems that are out of sync with each other.

The answer to this is to build a Patient component. You build just one Patient component and store it physically in a central location. Every system that works with patients simply accesses the Patient component. The applications create objects from the component, and each object is identical in structure. If the Patient ID format needs to change, you can (in an ideal world) simply modify the component and be done. The applications using this component will automatically pick up the new structure the next time they create an object from the component.

If all of this is new to you, don't worry; we will examine n-tier application development in more detail in Chapters 13 and 14. For now, understand this important point: n-tier development allows us to create components that enforce our business rules, and our applications just call those components. Changes in business rules can be made independent of the presentation layer, which allows our applications to handle changing business conditions more easily and more quickly.

N-tier applications sound great, and they can be great, in both traditional Windows applications (Visual Basic, Visual C++, and so on) and in Web applications. IIS allows our ASPs to call COM components that implement our business rules for us. There is no reason why our Patient component mentioned earlier could not be used from a Web front-end. There are many reasons to build our Web applications using n-tier technology, and we will examine many of those throughout this book. We will describe how the use of components can make our applications more scalable, perform better, and support heterogeneous database transactions.

With n-tier Web applications, almost everything is under the control of the IT department: the ASPs, components, and database all reside in the computer room, safely under the control of the IT department. The only piece of the application on the client's machine is the browser. This gives IT the same control they enjoyed with monolithic systems and means that issues such as backups, distribution, and security are maintained within a department that (hopefully) has existing policies and resources to make sure things run smoothly.

SUMMARY

The World Wide Web is a popular platform for developing Web applications because the Web provides a number of important benefits: access from almost anywhere in the world, no distribution needed, and control by the IT department. To build Web applications, we need some method of dynamically creating pages, and Microsoft's Internet Information Services delivers with its support of the Active Server Pages engine.

Building large, robust Web applications is possible thanks to server-side scripting. We will use ASPs to access reusable COM components and SQL Server. We will examine how to make the application more scalable and perform better by use of COM+. If you are concerned that we haven't talked enough about databases yet, don't worry. We need to build some simple ASPs first to make sure we know how they work, but our Web application will end up being database driven.

CHAPTER 2

Your First Active Server Page

You've already learned about the benefits of server-side scripting which enables you to build complex, n-tier Web applications. Microsoft's technology for implementing server-side scripting is called *Active Server Pages* (*ASP*). To build data-driven Web applications, you need to examine how ASPs work. After you understand how ASPs are processed, you can begin working with the objects provided by the IIS environment. Then that functionality is extended with COM components, including data access components.

GETTING READY FOR ACTIVE SERVER PAGES

To understand how Active Server Pages work, you should first examine how you need to handle them differently from standard HTML pages. With HTML pages, the browser is doing the work. It interprets the HTML tags and renders the text accordingly. Therefore, you can open an HTML file directly from the hard drive without needing an actual Web server. If you store an HTML file on the desktop, you can double-click to open it in the browser and see the results.

NOTE: You can easily verify how HTML and ASP files work differently. Take a text file, put a line of text into it, and save it on the desktop with the filename Test.htm. If you then double-click it, it opens in Internet Explorer (or whatever happens to be your default browser). Now change the filename to Test.asp and double-click it again. Windows might ask you what application to use to open the file or it might launch Visual InterDev. If you actually try to open it in IE using IE's File | Open command, it either asks if you want to download the file or it opens Visual InterDev.

You aren't so lucky with ASPs. An ASP has server-side script, which means a Web server must process it before it is sent to the client browser. Therefore, to view an ASP file in your browser, you must have a Web server in place and request the ASP from the server. If you try to open the file directly from the hard drive, the browser may attempt to download the file or to open Visual InterDev. Either way, you don't get the desired result.

IIS and Virtual Directories

To use ASPs, you need to use a Web server to process the server-side script in the ASP. The Web server you will use is *Internet Information Services* (*IIS*), which has native support for ASPs. As mentioned earlier, IIS is Microsoft's Web server. IIS can serve up files requested with a standard HTTP request, but IIS only has access to certain directories. These directories, called *virtual directories,* are directories to which IIS has permissions and from which it can pull files to respond to HTTP requests.

As an experiment, if you are running Windows 2000 on your local machine, open Internet Explorer and, in the address field, type **http://localhost** and press ENTER. You should end up with a page that looks similar to Figure 2-1. "Localhost" is just a shortcut name for your computer. You can replace the word "localhost" with the name of your server, and you should see the same thing. If coworkers are running Windows 2000, you should be able to use the names of their machines to see the files on their machines, which are acting as Web servers, just like your machine. This server name is really no different than asking for http://www.microsoft.com. The only difference is you are issuing a request to your local machine instead of to some server located on the Internet. When you ask for a site on the Internet, you are entering the world where special machines look up the name of the site, such as www.Osborne.com, and convert it to an IP address. The request is then routed to the appropriate machine with that IP address, much like a letter gets sent to the proper street address.

NOTE: In this book, I assume you are running on a Windows 2000 platform. If you are instead using Windows 9*x*, you would be running Personal Web Server instead of IIS. Personal Web Server acts much like IIS; it will process Active Server Pages and it has the same concept of virtual directories. The management tool is slightly different, but the concepts are the same.

When you request http://localhost, what are you really asking for? The answer lies in what IIS sees as the root of your Web server. Your Web server has to reside *somewhere* and, in IIS, this is normally the directory C:\Inetpub\wwwroot. To verify the actual directory

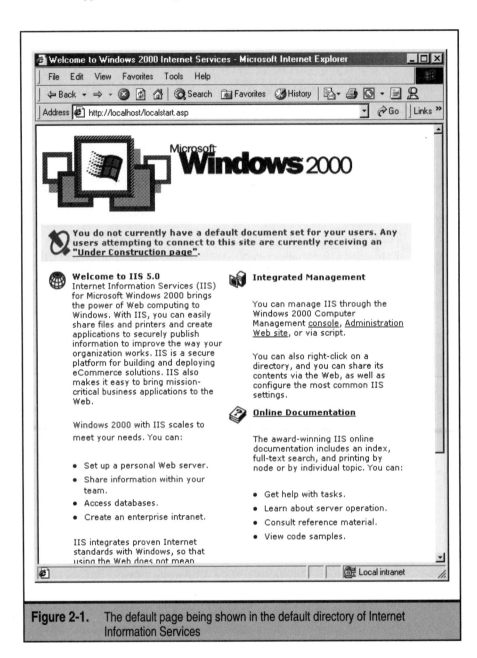

Figure 2-1. The default page being shown in the default directory of Internet Information Services

your copy of IIS is pointing to, open the Internet Services Manager by going to the Start button, and then Programs | Administrative Tools | Internet Services Manager. You should see the name of your machine there and, if you expand it, you see a list similar to Figure 2-2. Right-click Default Web Site and then select the Home Directory tab. In the Local Path text box, you see the physical path of the Home Directory for this Web server.

You didn't have to know the physical path of the directory to connect to the Web server. You only had to know the server name. When you visit Microsoft's site, do you know the physical directory in which the files you are viewing reside? Of course not, and you shouldn't have to worry about it. That is why IIS calls them *virtual* directories; you use a shortcut name to refer to a physical directory on the server.

You can manually create virtual directories using the IIS manager. First, you need to create a new physical directory for your files. Using the Windows Explorer, create a new directory called C:\WebDevSQL. (You can choose another name, but this is how I refer to this directory from now on.) Once you create the physical directory, you can create a virtual directory that points to it. Right now, IIS doesn't know

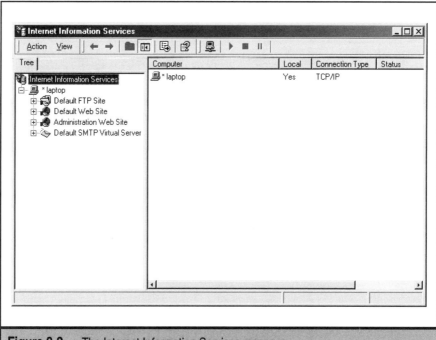

Figure 2-2. The Internet Information Services manager

anything about this new directory you have created and it won't have permissions for any files in this directory. Therefore, you need to set up a virtual directory so IIS can locate the files you place there. If you go back to the IIS manager, you simply right-click Default Web Site and then choose New | Virtual Directory. This brings up the Virtual Directory Creation Wizard. After you select Next, the first screen asks for the alias for this virtual directory. The alias is the name you use to reference the files in this directory. As you can see, this name represents your Web application, but I discuss that later in this chapter.

For now, just use the alias WebDev. Again, you can choose another name, but this is what this directory is called throughout this chapter. The next screen asks for the physical directory referenced by this virtual directory. Type **C:\WebDevSQL** or use the Browse button to locate the physical directory. Notice the alias and physical directory names are different. This is intentional, to show you the virtual names and the physical directory names needn't be the same.

After you fill in the physical directory and select the Next button, the next screen asks about the Access Permissions. Figure 2-3 shows the available options for Access Permissions. The options are as follows:

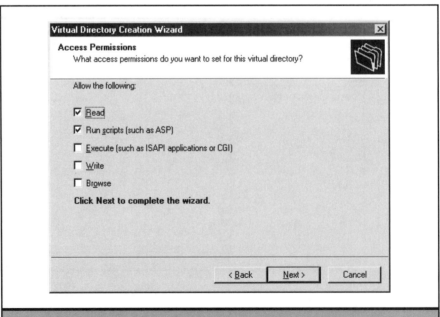

Figure 2-3. The Access Permissions dialog box for a virtual directory

▼ **Read**   Read permissions simply determine whether Web users have the ability to view files in this directory. Some directories contain executable files that are called by scripts on the Web server. Those scripts need permissions to execute files in these special directories, but you don't want clients to be able to read files in the directory. With read permissions, all files in the directory can be downloaded to the client. If the file extension is .htm or .html, the file is sent to the client and rendered in the browser. If the file isn't an HTML page, the browser asks if you want to save the file.

■ **Run scripts (such as ASP)**   This permission setting enables the client to call files with server-side script in them. This means IIS will process any script in the ASPs in this directory. Without this permission, your ASPs won't run. In fact, if someone tries to view an ASP, it will attempt to download the ASP to the client machine. This is an undesirable result; a downloaded ASP would enable the client to view all the server-side script within it.

■ **Execute (such as ISAPI applications or CGI)**   Execute permissions are necessary when a compiled program needs to be executed. Use execute permissions with care; if you place a self-extracting executable file in a directory with execute permissions, when the user selects a link to download it, it will actually execute on the server, instead of being downloaded. Having execute permissions for a directory is not a common occurrence.

■ **Write**   Write permissions mean the user can actually upload files to this directory. If you think of some of the e-mail sites, such as HotMail or Yahoo! Mail, they enable you to upload attachments to your e-mails. You can get the same functionality with IIS. To do this, it's still necessary to have some sort of component that allows uploading, such as Microsoft's Posting Acceptor.

▲ **Browse**   Browse permissions enable a user to see a list of the files in a directory. This is great for a development environment, but terrible for a production environment. You will see why later in this chapter.

As you can see, read and run scripts are the only default permissions. These are by far the most common permissions you need, so you should accept these default settings and select the Next button.

After selecting the Finish button, you wrap up the wizard. You have now created a virtual directory, called WebDev, that points to the physical directory C:\WebDevSQL. This directory has read and run scripts permissions on it, and will be where you place your ASPs to run them. As you will later see in this chapter, this virtual directory represents the boundary of an ASP application.

CREATING YOUR FIRST ACTIVE SERVER PAGE

Now that you have set up the virtual directory and given it the proper permissions, you need to create an Active Server Page to put in it. Let's start with a simple Active Server Page. Using Notepad, enter the following code:

```
<% @Language="VBScript" %> <HTML>
    <H1> Welcome to my first ASP </H1>
    <H2> The date is: <% =Date() %> </H2>
    <H2> The time is: <% =Time() %> </H2>
</HTML>
```

After typing the code, save it in the C:\WebDevSQL directory in a file called MyFirst.asp. Once the file has been saved, open Internet Explorer and, in the address box, type **http://localhost/WebDev/ MyFirst.asp**. You must open the file in this manner because it must be pulled from a Web server that can process the ASP in it. Once you open it, you should see a file that welcomes you to your first ASP, and prints the date and time on the page, as in Figure 2-4.

Now, in the browser, select View | Source. The source code for the page pops up in Notepad. The code should resemble this:

```
<HTML>
    <H1> Welcome to my first ASP </H1>
    <H2> The date is: 1/30/2000 </H2>
    <H2> The time is: 5:38:36 PM </H2>
</HTML>
```

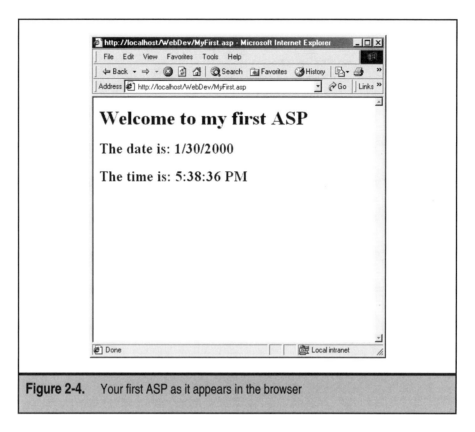

Figure 2-4. Your first ASP as it appears in the browser

Notice the code in the browser doesn't have any of the Active Server Pages code in it. In fact, it looks just like a hard-coded, static HTML page. This is one of the main points to remember with ASPs: because the code executes on the server, only HTML is sent to the client browser. This means your ASPs work with any browser, not just Internet Explorer. When you do client-side scripting, you worry about the brand and version of the client browser. With server-side scripting, you needn't worry about the client browser.

Let's make the page a little more complex, and then walk through an example of how the page is actually processed to create the "static" HTML the client sees. Modify MyFirst.asp to look like this:

```
<% @Language="VBScript" %>
<HTML>
    <H1> Welcome to my first ASP </H1>
    <FONT Color=<%
```

```
    Select Case WeekDay(Date())
       Case 1
          Response.Write "Red>"
       Case 2
          Response.Write "Orange>"
       Case 3
          Response.Write "Yellow>"
       Case 4
          Response.Write "Green>"
       Case 5
          Response.Write "Blue>"
       Case 6
          Response.Write "Purple>"
       Case 7
          Response.Write "Black>"
    End Select
    %>
    <H2> The date is: <% =Date() %> </H2>
    <H2> The time is: <% =Time() %> </H2>
    </FONT>
</HTML>
```

Once you have saved your changes, go back and select the Refresh button in your browser. Your output should have changed from before, unless it happens to be Saturday. The two lines with the date and time should now have a color other than black, except on Saturday, where they remain black. If this is the case, feel free to swap the "6" and "7" in the last two cases in the code.

You've added a large block of code, but if you select View | Source in the browser again, you don't see any of the ASP code. Once again, it looks like a static HTML page. How did the ASP get processed to produce this static-looking HTML?

How the ASP Engine Processes Code

Let's play the role of the ASP engine for a moment and see how it works. When the user requests an ASP, IIS picks up that file and the ASP engine starts processing the code in it. As the engine runs through a file, it builds the results in what I call the *HTML stream.* This stream is what gets sent to the client browser.

An ASP page is a mix of HTML and script, so when the ASP engine hits a line of HTML, it writes that line to the HTML stream without processing it in any other way. When the ASP engine hits the first line of code, it sees by the server-side script tags (the <% symbol) that this line needs to be processed on the server side. This first line tells the ASP engine which language interpreter to load (in this case, it is the interpreter for VBScript). Because this first line is only an instruction to the ASP engine, nothing is written to the HTML stream. The next line, however, is just a line of static HTML, so it is written, unchanged, to the HTML stream:

```
<HTML>
```

The next line is also straight HTML, so it is also written out to the HTML stream. Notice the leading spaces are considered part of the line and are included in the HTML stream.

```
<HTML>
   <H1> Welcome to my first ASP </H1>
```

Now you reach an interesting line. This line has a mix of HTML and script. The part that is only HTML is written to the HTML stream, so the stream looks (temporarily) like this:

```
<HTML>
   <H1> Welcome to my first ASP </H1>
   <FONT Color=
```

You are now in server-side script. In this case, you have a Select Case statement, which is like a nested If…Then statement. You use the WeekDay function, which returns a 1–7 for Sunday–Saturday, respectively. Therefore, if you run this code on Sunday, the function returns 1. This means you drop into the code for Case 1, and this code says Response.Write "Red>". Response.Write is discussed in more detail in Chapter 4 but, for now, just understand it takes a string and writes it to the HTML stream. In this case, you are going to write "Red>" to the HTML stream, minus the quotes. Now, your HTML stream will look like this:

```
<HTML>
   <H1> Welcome to my first ASP </H1>
   <FONT Color=Red>
```

You now have a fully formed Font tag. You are also down to the next line of the ASP, which also has a mix of HTML and VBScript. The line is static HTML up to the point where the server-side script tag opens. Once again, your HTML stream looks (temporarily, again) like this:

```
<HTML>
    <H1> Welcome to my first ASP </H1>
    <FONT Color=Red>
    <H2> The date is:
```

Now, enter server-side script and you have the following code: <% =Date() %>. The equal sign is a shortcut for the Response.Write you saw a moment ago. You can't always use the equal sign shortcut, but this is discussed in more detail in Chapter 4 as well. For the time being, realize it prints the date from the current system. So, your HTML stream now looks like this:

```
<HTML>
    <H1> Welcome to my first ASP </H1>
    <FONT Color=Red>
    <H2> The date is: 1/30/2000
```

Following the same logic, the next line gets printed with the static HTML at the beginning, and then the system time is printed to the HTML stream. Finally, the last two lines (the closing Font and HTML tags) are printed to the HTML stream. When done, the HTML stream looks like this:

```
<HTML>
    <H1> Welcome to my first ASP </H1>
    <FONT Color=Red>
    <H2> The date is: 1/30/2000
    <H2> The time is: 5:38:36 PM
    </FONT>
</HTML>
```

If this looks familiar, it should. This is the same code you see if you select View | Source in the browser. This makes sense, because this HTML stream is the only thing ever sent to the client. This is why ASPs are called *browser neutral* (or *browser independent* or *browser agnostic*); the code is executed on the server, and only static HTML is sent to the client browser.

In all your code so far, you have been using the server-side scripting tags, "<%" and "%>", to enclose your server-side script. This is the more common approach, but an alternative is to use the standard HTML script tag, with an attribute to tell the code to run on the server. Create a file called MySecond.asp and add the following code:

```
<% @Language="VBScript" %>
   <H1> Welcome to my first ASP </H1>
   <SCRIPT Language="VBScript" Runat="Server">
      Response.Write "<FONT Color="
      Select Case WeekDay(Date())
      Case 1
         Response.Write "Red>"
      Case 2
         Response.Write "Orange>"
      Case 3
         Response.Write "Yellow>"
      Case 4
         Response.Write "Green>"
      Case 5
         Response.Write "Blue>"
      Case 6
         Response.Write "Purple>"
      Case 7
         Response.Write "Black>"
      End Select
      Response.Write("<H2> The date is: " & Date() & "</H2>")
      Response.Write("<H2> The time is: " & Time() & "</H2>")
   </SCRIPT>
```

The preceding code produces the same output as you saw before. However, I took out some of the HTML. The code in the script block doesn't execute like you might expect; if you leave in the closing HTML tag, all the Response.Write code ends up after the ending HTML tag. That is, the HTML on the page is processed first, and then the ASP code places its output at the end of the file.

Directory Browsing and Default Documents

Before moving on, pointing out something about how the previous file was opened might be useful. When the virtual directory was created, the box for Browse permissions was left turned off. I mentioned before that directory browsing is good for a development environment but, generally, not good for a production environment. When you loaded this MyFirst.asp, you had to specify the address as http://localhost/WebDev/MyFirst.asp. When you go to most external sites, however, you don't have to specify a filename. You just enter the name of the server and it loads a page by default.

IIS can also load a default page. Back in the Internet Services manager, you can right-click the WebDev virtual directory and choose Properties. If you select the second tab, Documents, you see that IIS enables you to have a default document. In fact, it already has three in the list: Default.htm, Default.asp, and iisstart.asp. Figure 2-5

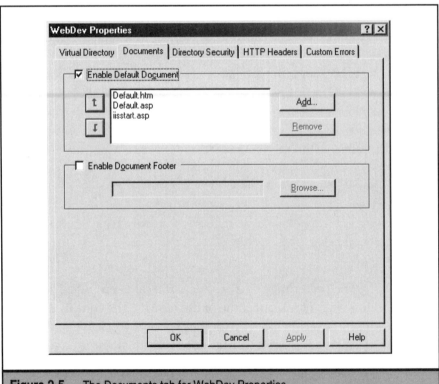

Figure 2-5. The Documents tab for WebDev Properties

shows this form. When someone comes into the WebDev virtual directory without specifying a filename, IIS looks through this list to see if any matching files are in the directory. For example, if you type http://localhost/WebDev, IIS first looks for a file in that directory named Default.htm. If it finds such a file, it loads it and is done. If it doesn't find Default.htm, it drops to the next one in the list. As soon as it finds a file to match what is in the list, it loads it and stops.

I can hear you asking now about what happens if no matches are found. This is exactly what will happen if we only type http://localhost/WebDev. No files in this directory match what we have in the list of default documents. At this point, one of two things happens:

▼   If directory browsing is turned off, the user gets a message stating, "You are not authorized to view this page," or some similar message, depending on your browser.

▲   If directory browsing is turned on, the user sees a list of all the files in the directory.

Previously, I mentioned that allowing this directory browsing might not be such a good idea in a production environment. The reason is that any user could now right-click a file, choose Save As, and then download the file, server-side script and all. As you will see later, placing user IDs and passwords in a file on the server is not unusual. You certainly wouldn't want users to be able to download a file with user IDs and passwords.

In a development environment, however, directory browsing makes life easier. You don't have to type the filename every time you go to the site. Instead, you just select the filename from the list.

Finally, in a production environment, you almost always want a default document. Not many people will want to visit your site if they have to know a filename to type on the address line. Therefore, you want to make sure you have a file that will load by default if someone types in just our application name. You can make a file called Default.htm, Default.asp, or Iisstart.asp. Or, you can add any other filename to the list by simply selecting the Add button you saw in Figure 2-5. We can then add any file in your directory and even use the arrows to change the order in which IIS searches for a file to load.

ACTIVE SERVER PAGES APPLICATIONS

Earlier in this chapter, you created a virtual directory that pointed to a physical directory. This virtual directory represents the boundaries of a Web application. All the files you place in that directory share the same security and permission settings by default. In addition, these files can share data and state maintenance. I discuss this in more detail in Chapter 4 but, for now, understand that the virtual directory represents the application boundary.

But what else makes up a Web application? With a client/server application, it's easy to understand an application: you compile an executable and distribute it, along with what seems like 400 DLLs. With Web applications, there is no single executable that you can point to and say, "This is the application." Instead, Web applications are made up of:

▼ One or more ASP files

■ Zero or more HTML files

■ The Global.asa file

■ Zero or more include files

▲ Zero or more COM components

All these files, with the exception of the COM components, are stored in a single directory tree. This doesn't mean a single directory, but a directory and all the directories below it. The physical directory to which the virtual directory is pointed is known as the *root directory*. This virtual directory represents the boundaries of an application. That is, all the pages in this directory structure share the same security context and, as you see in Chapter 4, they can share data.

Include Files

The preceding list also mentions include files. *Include files* are similar to include or header files in other languages; they are files that enable you to insert their code into any other file. Include files give you some reusability, and they enable you to change the look of all the files on a site just by changing the include file. In your current file, MyFirst.asp, you have a header at the top, but you don't have any copyright information along the bottom. With a page this good, you should certainly copyright it! You could just go into the ASP and add some text along the bottom that states this file is copyrighted. However, if you want that exact copyright on all your files, why don't you break that out and make it an include file? This will simplify life.

In the C:\WebDevSQL directory, create a file called incCopyright.asp. Some people name all their include files with the extension "inc" so they can easily be identified as include files. This has a disadvantage, however: if you are working with these files in Visual InterDev, which you will do starting in Chapter 3, you lose the color coding and IntelliSense if you end them with the .inc extension. Therefore, saving them with the .asp extension has some benefits. I like to use "inc" as the prefix so I know they are include files. I also like to save them with the "asp" extension so I get VI's color coding (and, sometimes, the syntax-checking).

Inside of incCopyright.asp, put this text in it (feel free to substitute your name for mine):

```
<FONT Size="-2">Copyright &copy;2000 Craig Utley - All rights reserved</FONT>
```

Save the file. That's all you'll put in it right now. You have created your first include file. It isn't very complex, but you can work on that later. Next, you need to include the file into MyFirst.asp. The code for include files looks a little strange. It's the standard HTML comment tag, but you then put "#Include" inside it. This tells the Web server to include a file in it while it is rendering the page. In fact, the file is inserted into the page before it is processed. This is an important point because it means the include files can pick up variables that are defined on the page. The code to use an include file looks like this:

```
<!-- #Include File="incCopyright.asp" -->
```

NOTE: Having an include file inserted into the page before the page is interpreted on the server is important. You can have code in the include file access data on the main page and vice versa. If you think about it, the process flows like this: the page is opened, the include files have their content added to the page, and then the ASP starts processing the whole page, including the code from the include file.

To include this file, open MyFirst.asp, and insert the include file after the closing Font tag. Your final code should look like this:

```
<% @Language="VBScript" %>
<HTML>
    <H1> Welcome to my first ASP </H1>
    <FONT Color=<%
    Select Case WeekDay(Date())
        Case 1
            Response.Write "Red>"
        Case 2
            Response.Write "Orange>"
        Case 3
            Response.Write "Yellow>"
        Case 4
            Response.Write "Green>"
        Case 5
            Response.Write "Blue>"
        Case 6
            Response.Write "Purple>"
        Case 7
            Response.Write "Black>"
    End Select
    %>
    <H2> The date is: <% =Date() %> </H2>
    <H2> The time is: <% =Time() %> </H2>
    </FONT>
    <!-- #Include File="incCopyright.asp" -->
</HTML>
```

Now, view the page in your browser. You should end up with something similar to Figure 2-6.

Now, of course, you can include incCopyright.asp on as many pages as you want. In fact, you can modify this one file, and all the pages that use it are automatically updated. Modify incCopyright.asp to look like this:

```
<FONT Size="-1">
    Copyright &copy;2000 Craig Utley - All rights reserved<BR>
    Created <% =Now() %>
</FONT>
```

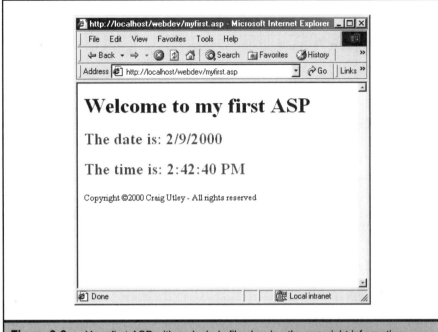

Figure 2-6.   Your first ASP with an include file showing the copyright information

After saving this new change to incCopyright.asp, reload MyFirst.asp, and you see it now includes the date and time the page was rendered. This may seem redundant for a page that displays the date and time already, but not all your ASPs will be so simple, and most certainly won't display the date and time.

NOTE: Remember the advantages of include files—they lead to reusable code, they are inserted into a page before any code is processed, and a change to one include file can update all the ASPs that use it.

Another file that's often part of an ASP application is the Global.asa file. For those of you who are roughly my age or older, think back to the old days of DOS. Remember when you had hair and weighed 20 pounds less? More important, remember the file on DOS machines called Autoexec.bat? This file ran every time the machine booted and was used to help set up some environment variables and start any necessary programs. The Global.asa file isn't much different.

It may contain code that executes for each new user to your Web application. You will work with the Global.asa file in upcoming chapters and it will end up holding a significant amount of code for you.

Recall from the previous chapter that HTTP is a stateless protocol. However, I also said IIS has built-in state management for your application. This means IIS knows when users are new users or if they have been using the site. This state management isn't for tracking users over a long period but, instead, is for tracking users during the use of the application. In other words, if users use your application and then return the next day, they are considered new users. When I discuss the Session object in Chapter 4, you will understand how IIS maintains state information.

SUMMARY

In this chapter, you have built your first Active Server Page. The ASP was simple, but the intent is to make sure you understand how the ASPs are processed on the Web server. The key point is that all the code is executed on the server and it just builds static HTML that is sent to the client. With ASP, it's easy to build dynamic pages that work in any browser.

We also talked about what makes up an ASP application. Web applications are different from traditional applications because nothing gets compiled. When dealing with IIS, your applications are just collections of ASPs, HTML files, include files, a global ASA, and any COM components they call. All the files, except for the COM components, are stored in a single directory structure.

If you are disappointed that you still haven't done anything with databases, hang on a little bit more. We need to examine more about the IIS environment and see how to interact with it. Once you learn how to call COM components, you can call your components that give you access to SQL Server and to any other database.

CHAPTER 3

Introduction to Visual InterDev

In the last chapter, you wrote your first *Active Server Page* (*ASP*). You wrote this ASP with Notepad, because an ASP is only text. You could do almost everything in this book with just Notepad, but using Visual InterDev can make your Web development much easier. Visual InterDev not only provides color-coding and line numbers, it also can enable you to debug your applications interactively and it can even write code for you.

VISUAL INTERDEV

Visual InterDev (*VI*) is Microsoft's tool for professional Web development. This contrasts with *FrontPage*, which is targeted at home users building static Web sites. InterDev includes most of the features found in FrontPage, but it also includes a number of features designed to support building server-side script into your Web application. Most of these features are examined throughout the book, but I start by examining how to install VI and set up your development environment.

Installing Visual InterDev

Visual InterDev can be a stand-alone product, but most people install it from the Visual Studio 6.0 CDs. VI can be installed on Windows 95/98, Windows NT 4.0, or Windows 2000. Where it installs depends on the operating system you are using, and the default installation directory can be changed.

A Web server is required to run VI. The Web server can be on a different machine, such as a development server. To run VI in local mode, however, a Web server must be on the local, or client, machine. What is meant by "local operations" is described in more detail later. To use the power of local operations, you want to have a Web server on the local machine, if at all possible. In fact, VI tries to install a Web server if it doesn't find one. On Windows 95/98 machines, this means installing *Personal Web Server* (*PWS*). On NT machines, this means installing Service Pack 3 or higher, which includes Internet Information Server 3 or 4. Windows 2000, which is the target operating system for this book, already includes *Internet Information Server 5*, which I call simply *IIS*.

Installing Visual InterDev from the Visual Studio CDs is fairly simple. In Figure 3-1, I simply start the setup program and remove the options for Visual C++ and Visual FoxPro. I am leaving the default installation directories alone and, on clicking the Next button, the installation proceeds.

After installing Visual InterDev (and, in my case, Visual Basic as well) the program asks if you want to install the MSDN Library. This enables you to install all the documentation for the products in Visual Studio. I highly recommend you install the documentation if you have the disk space.

After the installation program finishes with the MSDN Library, you are shown the screen you see in Figure 3-2. This screen asks you about the server components you want to install. These components are important if you want certain server-side capabilities, such as debugging your ASPs. Because debugging ASPs is an important feature, you can choose to launch the BackOffice Installation Wizard. Let's continue the installation while talking about what components to choose to enable server-side debugging.

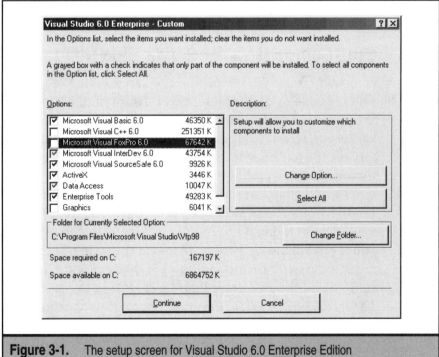

Figure 3-1. The setup screen for Visual Studio 6.0 Enterprise Edition

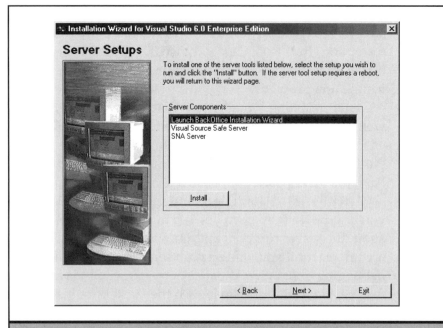

Figure 3-2.   The BackOffice Installation Wizard. Make sure you click BackOffice Installation Wizard, and then click the Install button, not the Next button

Installing the Components for Server-Side Debugging

VI installs on the client machine and can use the Web server on the local machine or on a remote server. Additional components must be installed to enable some of the advanced features of VI, such as server-side script debugging. If you are installing with the default options, the tools needed to be able to debug server-side script are not installed.

One of the biggest problems with the previous version of VI was it didn't support any kind of server-side debugging. The best you could do was to include a number of statements to print out the values of variables at various places in the script. This meant the only way to debug your application was by placing lines that said things like "About to enter loop" and "Ready to read records from database." With VI 6, however, you can actually debug both client-side and server-side script in the same application, even if the server-side script is running on a remote server. This is one of the most powerful features of VI, but it isn't installed by default. Installing the server-side debugging can be fairly simple or fairly complex, depending on your configuration.

> **NOTE:** Server-side debugging is only available with Windows NT or Windows 2000. It is unavailable with Windows 95 or Windows 98. While most of what we do in this book can be done on Windows9x, server-side debugging is one of the exceptions.

If you are using a local Web server, as is most often the case, setting up server-side debugging is not too difficult. You can set up the local server debugging by installing four components that come on the Visual Studio CDs: Remote Machine Debugging, Visual InterDev Server, Front Page Server Extensions, and *Microsoft Data Access Components* (*MDAC*). If you are already running Windows 2000, you already have the MDAC installed. These components enable you to debug server-side pages on the local machine—in other words, using the local Web server.

> **NOTE:** To install these components, you must have administrator privileges on your local machine. If you don't, have an administrator log in and install the components.

You are still sitting at the screen you see in Figure 3-2. After selecting Launch BackOffice Installation Wizard, press the Install button, not the Next button! This is confusing. Many people think by pressing the Next button, the installation of the server-side components begins. This isn't true. You must press the Install button to launch the setup.

After pressing the Install button, the setup shows a screen that asks what kind of installation you want. At this point, choose Custom, as shown in Figure 3-3. Next, you are shown a bizarre screen that displays the components, how big they are, and how much free disk space you have. You can't do anything from this screen other than click the Next button. This bizarre screen is shown in Figure 3-4—only so you know what it looks like and so you know you shouldn't expect it to do anything.

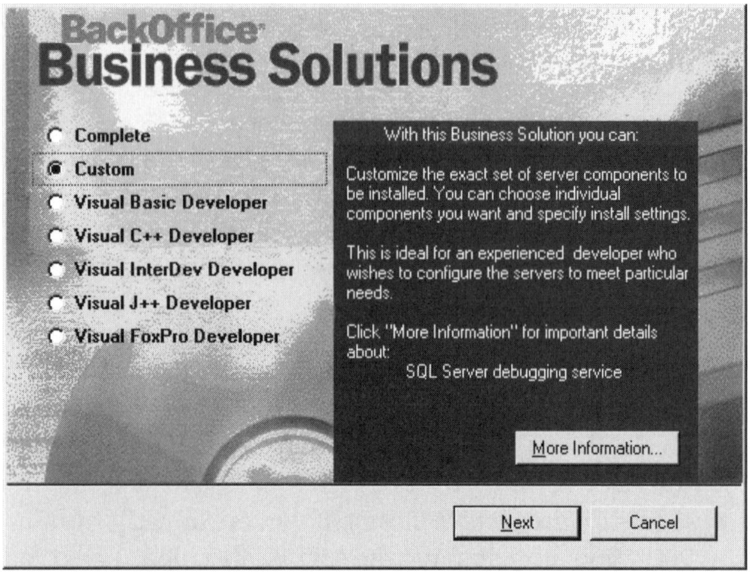

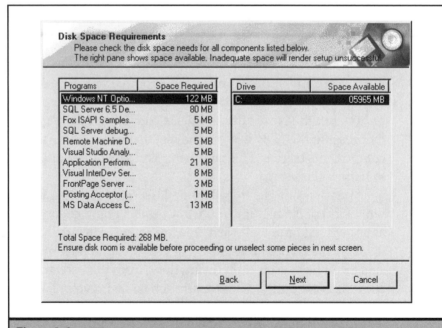

Figure 3-3. The setup screen for the BackOffice Server setup

Figure 3-4. This bizarre screen doesn't enable you to do anything. The purpose is to let you make sure you have enough disk space

Finally, you reach the screen that asks which components you want installed. Previously, I mentioned the four components you need to have installed: Remote Machine Debugging, Visual InterDev Server, Front Page Server Extensions, and Microsoft Data Access Components. Figure 3-5 shows these options chosen in the installation screen. After choosing these four options, click Next, and the installation proceeds.

If you wonder how you are supposed to know what four components to install to enable server-side debugging, two answers are

1. You are smart enough to read this book.

2. You have read a particular article on Microsoft's site.

Obviously, you are smart enough to read this book. However, an article on Microsoft's site talks about setting up server-side debugging with Visual InterDev. This article is long—42 printed pages! The article is so long because setting up server-side debugging on a remote server is much more challenging. This is something I

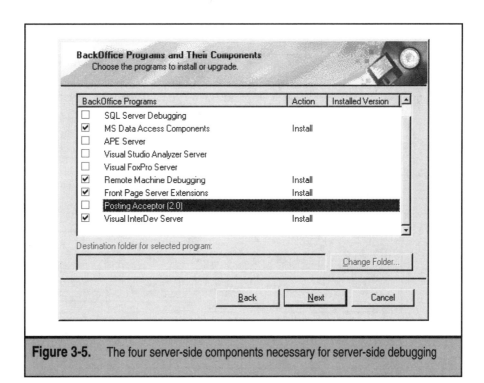

Figure 3-5. The four server-side components necessary for server-side debugging

won't do in this book, but it involves setting up some special user permissions using the Distributed COM Configuration Properties. The article title is "Microsoft Visual InterDev 6.0 Debugging" and can be found at http://msdn.microsoft.com/library/techart/msdn_videbugging.htm. Please note, the address changes occasionally, so you might have to search for the article title.

Visual InterDev is now installed and set up for local machine server-side debugging. Now it's time to create your first project and start creating both HTML and ASP files within InterDev.

USING VISUAL INTERDEV

Visual InterDev is only a tool. It's a good tool and it enables you to create Web applications easily but, at the end of the day, it is only a tool. As previously mentioned, most of what you do in this book could be done with just Notepad. However, VI makes your life much easier in many respects. Let's start by loading VI for the first time. You can find VI under Program, Microsoft Visual Studio 6.0. When you first load VI, you get a New Project dialog box, as shown in Figure 3-6.

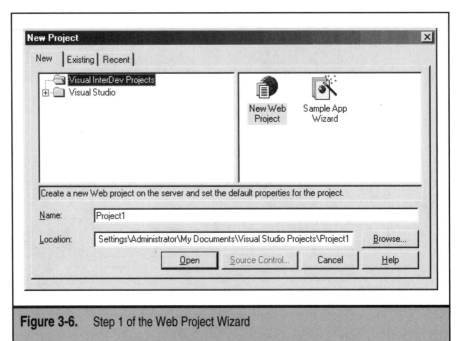

Figure 3-6. Step 1 of the Web Project Wizard

In the left-hand window, it asks what kind project you are creating. As shown, you want to have Visual InterDev Projects chosen. In the right-hand window, you have the choice between New Web Project and Sample App Wizard. For now, leave the choice as New Web Project.

Below these two windows are two text boxes. The first is the name of the project. This will be the name of the Web project you are creating. The physical directory is identified in the box below, labeled Location. This is where things start to get strange, however. The Location box is only the location of what I will call the local, or working, copy of the Web application. For now, notice the default directory is C:\Documents and Settings\Administrator\My Documents\Visual Studio Projects\ Project1. This seems rather long and involved, but let's leave it as the default for now. Project1 seems like a great name for a project (at least for testing) so, for now, leave this as the project name.

After clicking the Open button, you are running the Web Project Wizard, as seen in Figure 3-7. The combo box wants to know the

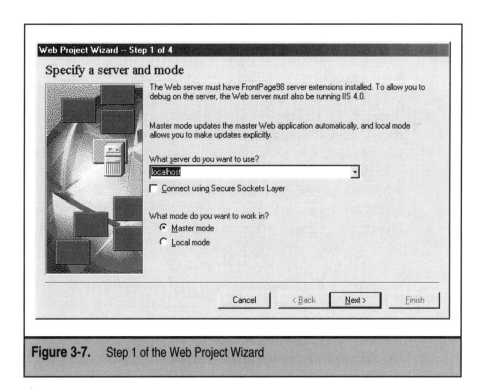

Figure 3-7. Step 1 of the Web Project Wizard

name of your Web server. At this point, you have several choices: you could put in the name of our local machine, you could use the name "localhost" to point to your location machine, or you could type in the name of a different server located anywhere in the world. That's right: this could be a machine located somewhere over the Internet. If you are connecting to a server and need encryption on your communications, click the Connect using Secure Sockets Layer check box. This requires the server you are contacting to have SSL installed and configured properly. This is discussed further when security is addressed.

Finally, you have two radio buttons asking which mode you prefer: Master mode or Local mode. For now, keep the mode as Master, and let's examine exactly what this means in a moment. After typing in the server name (or localhost), click the Next button. VI attempts to contact the Web server and, if successful, moves to Step 2 of the wizard.

In Step 2 of the wizard, VI asks if you want to create a new Web application or to use an existing one. What you have created so far is a project, but this will be the name of the actual Web application. Remember, in the last chapter the virtual directory and the application names are one and the same. Guess what? The name here is the virtual directory name. It points to the physical directory that holds the project. Now, here's another interesting point: the physical directory for this project is *not* the one you created in Step 1! Again, that directory is only for the local copy of the files. As you will see, another copy will be created that is the real Web application. For now, leave the name as Project1. Under that box is a checkbox asking whether you want to create a search.htm file. You can uncheck this box because you won't use this functionality now. If you leave this box checked, it will create an additional file in the project, but the project won't suffer any adverse affects. Figure 3-8 shows the choices you've made before moving forward.

Step 3 of the wizard asks you to choose a layout for the project. At this point, you don't want to choose a layout (we'll examine layouts shortly, but right now, understand that adding a layout moves a number of confusing elements into your project and I want to keep this simple). Therefore, when you see the screen shown in Figure 3-9, leave "<none>" selected in the list box.

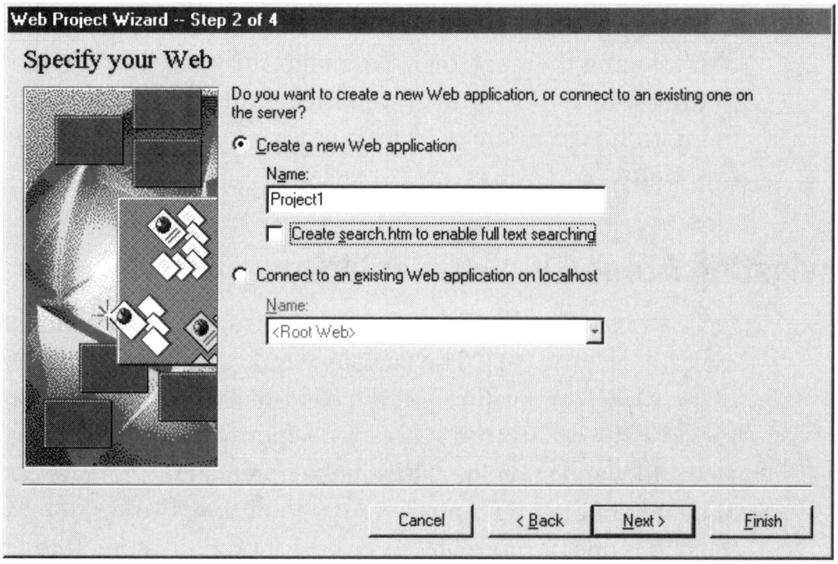

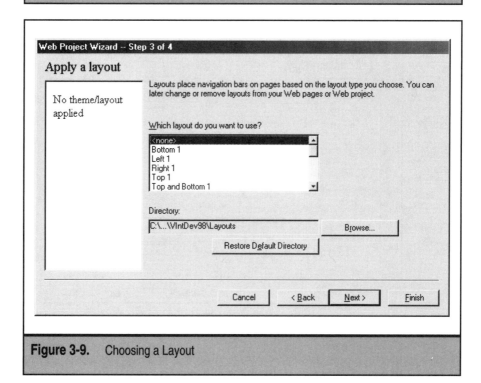

Figure 3-8.   Step 2 of the Web Project Wizard

Figure 3-9.   Choosing a Layout

Finally, you reach Step 4, as shown in Figure 3-10. This step asks if you want to apply a theme. Just as you don't want a layout yet, you don't want a theme, either. So, make sure "<none>" is the selection in the list box. Now, press the Finish button, sit back, and relax. VI is many things to many people, but it isn't generally considered fast, especially at creating new projects.

Navigating Around in Visual InterDev

Once VI is done creating the project, you should have something that looks like Figure 3-11. The various windows represent different facets of your Web application. On the right-hand side are two windows: the Project Explorer and the Properties windows. The Project Explorer shows all the files and subfolders that make up your current application. Note, at the top of the tree control, it says "Solution 'Project1' (1 project)." A *solution* is one or more projects. A solution is not something that gets created on the Web server; instead, it is something InterDev uses to group multiple projects. The line below says in bold "localhost/Project1."

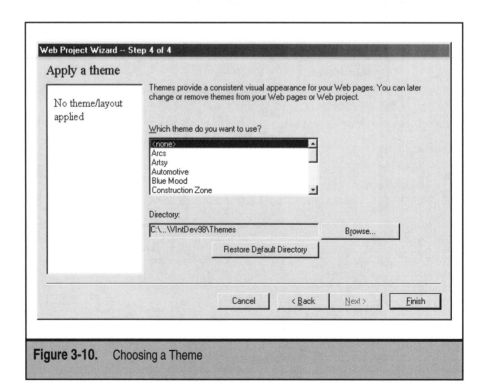

Figure 3-10.   Choosing a Theme

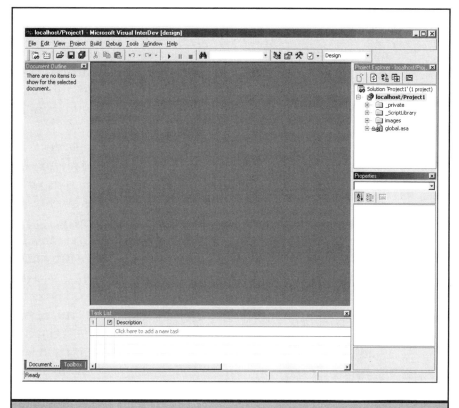

Figure 3-11.   Visual InterDev after creating a new project

This tells you the server name and application (or project) name. This is what you should type in your browser to load this application, just as in the previous chapter. If you think you need a virtual directory to do that, you're correct, but Visual InterDev has actually already created a virtual directory for you. You can open the Internet Services Manager to verify this.

If you are using a separate machine as your Web server, as is the case when you have a development server set up separate from your desktop machine, the virtual directory is created on the development server, and the local working copy is created on your desktop. Files are copied onto both machines. To see the Web application on the server, you must type the name of the development server in your browser, such as "//DevServer/Project1."

Below the project name is a list of subfolders, and then the actual files. Currently, you have three subfolders (_private, _ScriptLibrary, and images) and you have only one file: the global.asa. If you expand the _private and images directories, you can see that they are empty. The _ScriptLibrary directory, however, is full of ASP and HTM files. Don't worry about those right now; you'll work with them later when you start creating data-driven Web pages.

Below the Project Explorer window is the Properties window. If it's blank right now, it means you haven't clicked anything yet. As you will see, this box enables you to change properties when you start working with pages. Changing properties is an easy way to write some HTML code, as you will see in a moment.

At the bottom of VI is the Task List window. You can add notes to yourself about what work needs to be done. This way, you can keep track of steps you need to complete in your project. If you don't have enough to do, never fear: some of the tools in VI add tasks to the list automatically. Think of it as a built-in boss, except you never have to complete the tasks it recommends. While the task list can come in handy, many people close it to get more space in the main working area.

Along the left-hand side of VI is a long window that has two tabs at the bottom. Right now, in Figure 3-11, the Toolbox tab is active. This tab contains a number of controls you can place on your ASP and HTML pages. If you look at the Document Outline, it is blank right now, but it will be filled with information as you progress through your projects. These tabs come and go, and VI includes an auto-docking feature, which can be as much an exercise in frustration as it can be useful. If you don't see a tab you want, go to the View menu. All the possible windows are listed there.

The large gray area in the middle is your working area, where you have your open files and do your editing. On systems that run in low resolutions, such as 640 × 480 pixels, this area can be about the size of a postage stamp. Any of the windows can be resized, undocked, or closed. If you close a window, you can reopen by clicking the View menu. Most of the windows are listed under the Other Windows option. In most of my screenshots, I close the Task List, but leave the rest of them as you see them in Figure 3-11.

Creating Your First Page in Visual InterDev

Now that you have seen the windows in Visual InterDev, you can create your first page in it. You can add a new page to your project in five ways: four of them are the "right" way and one is the "wrong" way. Unfortunately, the "wrong" way is one of the most obvious. The right ways to add a file are

1. Right-click the project name and choose Add | Add Item.
2. Click the second button on the toolbar.
3. Choose Project | Add Item.
4. Press CTRL-D.

The *wrong* way to add a new file to the project is to choose File | New File. This might seem like the logical way to add a new file, and it does appear to add a file to the project, but it doesn't accomplish exactly what you want. I examine this in more detail shortly.

For now, use one of the four "right" methods to open the Add Item dialog box. As you can see in Figure 3-12, Add Item lets you

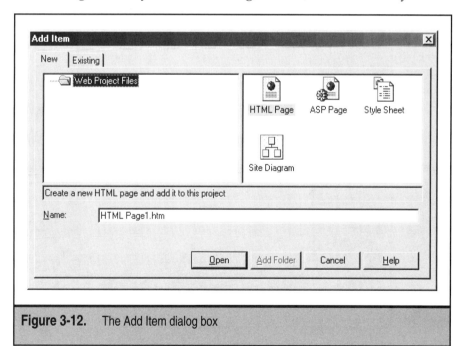

Figure 3-12.   The Add Item dialog box

choose one of four types of files to add: HTML Page, ASP Page, Style Sheet, and Site Diagram. There's also a tab to add existing items instead of creating new ones. For now, add a new HTML file. In the Name box, name it HomePage.htm, and then click Open.

Figure 3-13 shows the newly created HomePage.htm file loaded into VI. This looks like a blank page and, right now, it is. If you look along the bottom, you can see three tabs: Design, Source, and Quick View. The Design tab is what you see right now: a blank page. This enables you to work with your HTML documents as if they were Word documents. You can start typing in the white area. In this case, I'm going to type "Welcome to my Home Page" on the document. After I type this, I will highlight this text, click the drop-down list box that says "Normal," and change it to "Heading 1." What VI does, at this point, is insert the <H1> and </H1> tags around the highlighted text. To see this, click the Source tab.

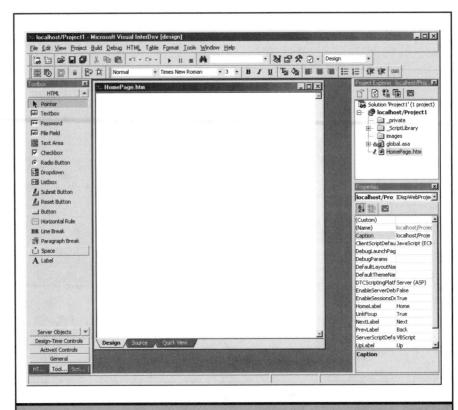

Figure 3-13.   HomePage.htm loaded into VI and shown in Design view

The Source tab shows your HTML source and, sure enough, you see the following line:

```
<H1>Welcome to my Home Page</H1>
```

Now, for fun, click back on the Design tab, select the text again, and press the Center button on the toolbar. When you go back to the Source tab, notice the code now looks like this:

```
<H1 align=center>Welcome to my Home Page</H1>
```

The point of this exercise is to let you create your HTML pages by treating them like a Word document. This enables you to make choices off the menu and toolbar and have VI write code for you. The Source view gives you several advantages over Notepad. First, your text is color-coded. Second, line numbers are in the status bar of VI, so you know what line you are on. This is helpful when you're creating ASPs, because the error messages returned by IIS tell you the line number of the error.

Back in VI, switch back to Design view, make sure you are at the end of the "Welcome to my Home Page" line, and press the enter key twice. Then press the Align Left button to return to the left-hand side of the page. Now, type the word "Osborne" and then select it. After highlighting the word, click the HTML menu and then Link (or press the link button on the toolbar). This brings up the Hyperlink dialog box, shown here:

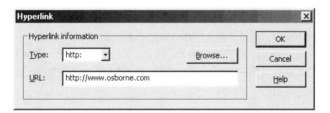

Type the Web site for Osborne, as shown in the illustration: **www.osborne.com**. Once you click OK, the word Osborne now looks like a standard HTML link. If you go into the Source view, you can see VI just inserted the standard anchor tag, <A>, around the word.

Switch back to Design view. Notice if you click Osborne, you move the cursor into the word. This means you can still edit it. In fact, you can change the word, but the anchor tag is unaffected. What if you want to click the link to test it? The third tab, Quick View, is for this. Quick View is a simple HTML browser. It interprets the HTML and renders it for you. The page is not editable in the Quick View tab, just as HTML pages viewed in Internet Explorer are not editable. Click the Quick View tab and then click the word Osborne. The Osborne/McGraw-Hill Web site should load into the window. Let me warn you about Quick View, though: it cannot process ASP code. Quick View acts as a browser, parsing HTML. It doesn't pull the file through the Web server, so the ASP code is not run!

Understanding How Visual InterDev Handles Files

You have now created a simple HTML file and viewed it with the Quick View tab. However, Quick View is only a browser that interprets the code within the page you have in Visual InterDev. If you want to see your page in a "real" browser, you can do this by being in either Design or Source view, and right-clicking anywhere on the page. One of the choices you see in the list is "View in Browser." Choosing this option launches Internet Explorer and loads the page in it. Try this now and you'll notice when the page comes up in IE, the address is http://laptop/Project1/HomePage.htm, where "laptop" is the name of my Web server. This means when you ask for the file in IE, it pulls the file from whatever Web server you specified when you created the project.

Now, let's make a change to the page. Close your browser and return to VI. In VI, look at the Properties window. Drop down the list at the top and make sure it says Document. One of the properties is bgColor. Click the button in the bgColor box and VI pops up a Color Picker dialog box. Choose a different color background and then press OK. The background color of the page is now different. If you look at the Source tab, you can see VI has just added a bgColor attribute to the <BODY> tag. Now, if you save the file, right-click it, and choose View in Browser again, you see the page with the new color background.

NOTE: The reason to close the browser between changes is to make sure you are seeing the latest version of the file. If you leave the browser open, make a change to the file, and then right-click on it and choose View in Browser, the browser doesn't show the latest version of the page; it shows the cached version you previously viewed. You need to hit the Refresh button in the browser to see the changes. To avoid this confusion, close the browser before making changes to the file. In fact, close *all* the open browser windows. Caching issues are a major cause of people saying "I know I just made that change, but it isn't showing up." Also, don't forget to save the file before trying to view your changes!

Notice that as soon as you made this change, it appeared on the Web server. In other words, if someone on another computer had been viewing the page, they would have seen the change as soon as you saved the file. This is because when you created the project, you said you wanted to run in Master mode. Master mode says that whenever you save a file, it saves that file to the master Web server, which was the server name used when you created the project. Obviously, this isn't always what you want. You might want to make changes and test them before they get moved to the master Web server. To do this, right-click on the project name (in this case, laptop/Project1) and you will see an option for Working Mode. Choose this option, and then choose Local. This switches the project into Local mode. Changes you make are no longer copied to the Web server. Instead, the changes are kept in the local working directory. Don't worry, though, you can get those changes back to the server in a moment, once you've tested them and are satisfied.

To test this, go back to the page in VI and change the background color to a different color. Now, save the page, right-click it, and view it in the browser. When you do, you see the new background color and think the author has completely lost his mind. However, look up at the address line. You can see the address line is http://laptop/Project1_Local/HomePage.htm. That's right: we're pointing to some local copy of the project. In IE, change the address back to http://laptop/Project1/HomePage.htm, and then you see the "old" version of the page. In other words, the changes haven't made it to the Web server.

How does this work? It all comes down to how VI handles projects. VI actually creates two copies of everything: a local (working) copy and a master (server) copy. The local copy is stored where you created the project earlier, in this case, C:\Documents and Settings\ Administrator\My Documents\Visual Studio Projects\Project1. (Actually, VI makes a directory under that, called Project1_Local, where it actually stores the files.) The second copy of the files is placed on the machine declared as the Web server when you set up the application. In these examples, the server and client machines are the same, but VI still makes two copies of everything. In my case, the server is called "laptop" and VI places the files on the server in the \Inepub\wwwroot\Project1 directory. All VI projects have their master copies put in the \Inetput\wwwroot directory. A subdirectory is created with the project name. This is the directory pointed to by a virtual directory. Figures 3-14 and 3-15 show the two different directories both containing the same files.

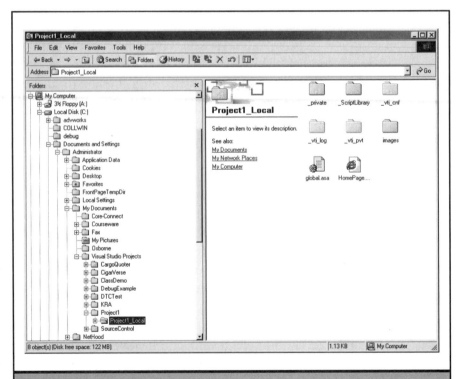

Figure 3-14.   The local copy of the files

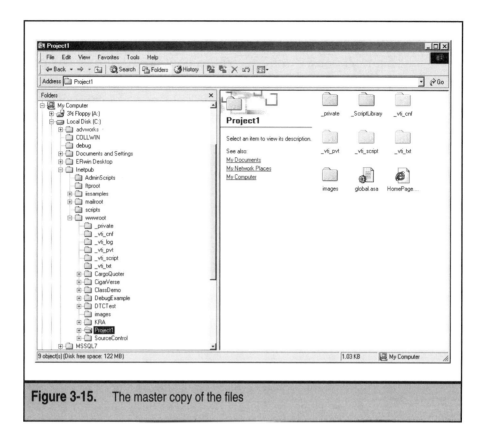

Figure 3-15. The master copy of the files

In this case, the server and client machine are the same. If the server was a different machine, VI would still keep the local copy on our machine, but would place the master copy of the files on the server. This can even be done over the Internet, provided the proper permissions are set up on the remote server, but this is beyond the scope of this book.

When working in Local mode, you can make changes to the Web site without updating the files on the Web server. You can test them with the View in Browser option and see them pulled through your local Web server. When you finish with your changes, all you need to do is change the working mode back to Master mode. This automatically copies all changed files up to the master Web server.

Adding Existing Content to Your Project

So far, all you've done is create a new HTML file. In the previous chapter, you created an ASP file that showed you the date and time on the server. You can add this to your project using several methods. Again, one of the ways to add it doesn't produce the intended results, just as when you create a new file. Now I'll discuss why.

First, let's add the file from the previous chapter into the project. The two main ways of doing this are to use the Add Item dialog box you saw earlier or to use drag-and-drop. To use the Add Item dialog box, open it with one of the four previously described methods. Notice the dialog box has a tab named Existing, which you saw back in Figure 3-12. If you choose the Existing tab, you can navigate to the C:\WebDevSQL directory, select MyFirst.asp, and then click Open. You also need to add incCopyright.asp, which you can do at the same time by selecting multiple files before clicking Open, or you can add them separately.

CAUTION: Dragging-and-dropping the file into the project requires some special care. You drop the file into the Project Explorer window, but you must drop it on the project name. If you drop it anywhere else in the Project Explorer, it shows up as seen in Figure 3-16: under a new folder called "Miscellaneous Files." Now, here's the kicker: the files under the Miscellaneous Files folder are part of your VI project, but they are *not* copied up to the Web server! In other words, they don't become part of the Web site. This is the same thing that happens if you use the File menu and then select New File. Why New File doesn't add a new file into the Web site is beyond me, but Bill didn't call me and ask my opinion while VI was in beta.

If you do happen to get files in the Miscellaneous Files folder, you can drag-and-drop them onto the project name. This creates copies of them. You must still right-click the ones in Miscellaneous Files and choose Remove From Project.

In Figure 3-17, I added MyFirst.asp and incCopyright.asp to the project. Notice the lock next to the filenames. This indicates the files in the working (local) directory are read-only. Double-clicking one of

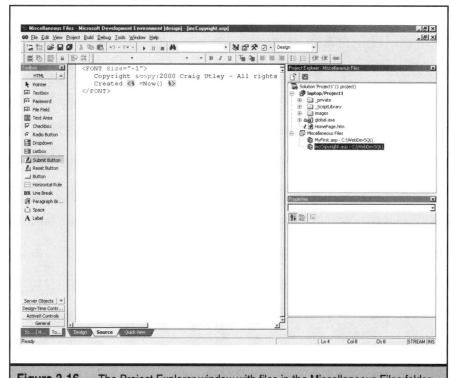

Figure 3-16.   The Project Explorer window with files in the Miscellaneous Files folder

the files pops up a box that asks if you want to get a working copy or if you want to open a read-only copy. Be careful. VI lets you edit files you have opened as read-only. A good habit to get into is always to ask for a working copy when you open a file. Remember, you can't switch to Quick View with an ASP, because Quick View doesn't run server-side script.

Debugging a Web Application

One of the greatest benefits of VI is it enables you to debug both client-side and server-side code at the same time. This means you can set breakpoints in code that run both on the client and the server, and you can examine variable values, change variable values, step through code, and, in general, interactively debug your applications. To demonstrate this functionality, let's create a couple of new files and

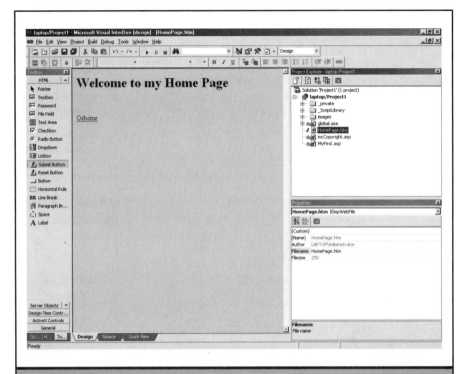

Figure 3-17. Files in the Project Explorer window showing they are currently read-only

then perform the necessary steps to begin the debugging process. In your project, add an HTML page using your favorite method for creating new files. Name the HTML file AddNumbers.htm. Switch to Source view and make your page look like this:

```
<HTML>
    <HEAD>
        <TITLE>Add Numbers</TITLE>
    </HEAD>
    <BODY>
        <FORM Name="frmAdd" Method="post" Action="AddItUp.asp">
            First Number: <INPUT Name="txtFirstNum"><BR>
            Second Number: <INPUT Name="txtSecondNum"><BR>
            <INPUT Type="button" Name="cmdSubmit" Value="Add Numbers">
        </FORM>
```

```
    </BODY>
    <SCRIPT Language="VBScript">
       Sub cmdSubmit_onClick()
          If Not IsNumeric(document.frmAdd.txtFirstNum.value) Then
             alert "First Number field must be numeric"
          Else
             If Not IsNumeric(document.frmAdd.txtSecondNum.value) Then
                alert "Second Number field must be numeric"
             Else
                document.frmAdd.submit
             End If
          End If
       End Sub
    </SCRIPT>
</HTML>
```

This HTML page provides a form with two text boxes. Each text box is expecting a number. The page runs some client-side code to make sure the user actually enters numbers in the text boxes before you submit the values to an ASP on the server.

Next, add an ASP to your project and name it AddItUp.asp. Make your ASP code look like this:

```
<%@ Language=VBScript %>
<HTML>
    <BODY>
       <%
       Dim iFirstNum
       Dim iSecondNum

       iFirstNum=Request.Form("txtFirstNum")
       iSecondNum=Request.Form("txtSecondNum")
       %>
       <H1>The Answer is: <% =(iFirstNum+iSecondNum) %></H1>
    </BODY>
</HTML>
```

Now, it's time to try out your two new pages. First, view AddNumbers.htm in the browser. If you enter alpha characters in one or both boxes, you receive a warning. For the sake of the first test, enter 25 in the first box and 50 in the second box. Press the Add Numbers button and the ASP then fires up. Sure enough, you get the answer: 2,550. If you know VBScript, you can probably guess why you got 2,550 instead of what you might expect when you add 25 and 50, which is usually 75.

This is an overly simplified example, but let's debug it to determine why the total isn't as expected. In VI, open AddNumbers.htm and place a breakpoint in the client-side script. To place a breakpoint in the code, you can click within the gray border on the left-hand side of the window that holds the code. Figure 3-18 shows the code window with a breakpoint placed at the appropriate point. The text box you see is a tooltip from placing the mouse pointer over the breakpoint.

Next, open AddItUp.asp and add a breakpoint, as shown in Figure 3-19. You now have breakpoints in both the client-side and the server-side code, and you are almost ready to debug. You have one

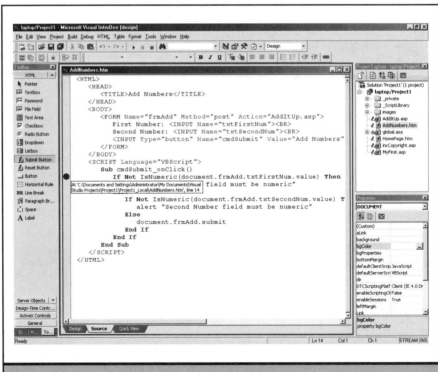

Figure 3-18. The breakpoint in the client-side code

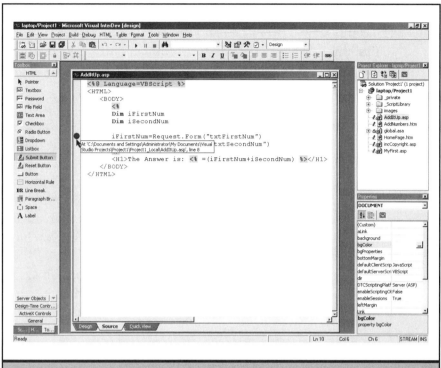

Figure 3-19.   The breakpoint in the server-side code

more step to perform, however. With regular Windows applications, you can set a form to display at startup. With Web applications, though, people can start on any page. To start a debugging session, you have to notify VI which form to start up when you start your debugging session. Do this by right-clicking the filename in the Project Explorer window and choosing Set as Start Page. This doesn't change anything about the page; it just notifies VI what your first page will be when you start debugging. In this case, right-click AddNumbers.htm and choose Set as Start Page. Now, from the Debug menu, choose Start. Or, you can click the Start button on the menu along the top. Simply viewing the page in the browser does *not* start the debugging session.

After choosing Start, VI usually notifies you that the project isn't set up for ASP debugging. A dialog box enables you to choose whether you want to debug only HTML files or also to debug ASPs. Obviously, you want to debug ASPs, which include HTML debugging.

Next, VI asks you to log in to the server. Log in with an account with Administrator privileges and the debugging session will start. The first thing to happen is the AddNumbers.htm is loaded in IE. Go ahead and type **25** in the first box, type **50** in the second box, and then click the button.

Figure 3-20 shows the debugging process in action. The highlighted line is the current line of execution. The highlighted line has not yet executed. At this point, you can step through the code one line at a time and check variable values as you go. You can place watches on variables and change variable values. You can step through the file by choosing Step Into from the Debug menu or by using the appropriate button from the toolbar. For this file, just step through the file and follow the code logic. Keep choosing Step Into until you have gone through the file.

Next, the server-side script hits the breakpoint. This now appears in the VI debugging session. Again, the highlighted line hasn't been executed yet. If you step through the file to the next line, iFirstNum

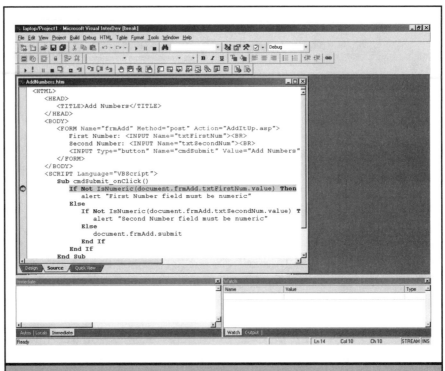

Figure 3-20.   The debugging process in action

has a value. If the mouse cursor is placed over the variable name, a tooltip pops up showing the value in the variable, as seen in Figure 3-21. Notice the value of iFirstNum is in double quotes. This means the value is not really a number, but a string. All values passed up from an HTML form are strings. This means the line of code that should be adding the numbers is only concatenating two strings together. You can continue stepping through the code until it is done. To end the debugging session, choose End from the Debug menu.

Just in case you want to fix AddItUp.asp, modify the line that does the calculation to look like this:

```
<H1>The Answer is: <% =(cint(iFirstNum)+cint(iSecondNum)) %></H1>
```

The debugger has many more features and learning to use it effectively is one of the most important tools to building Web applications.

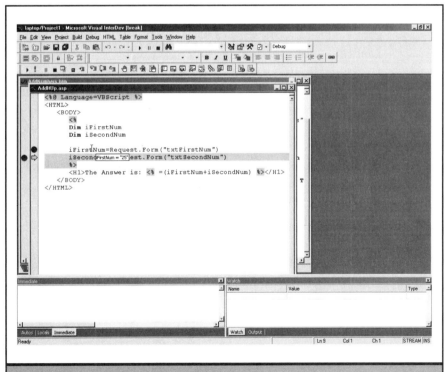

Figure 3-21.   A tooltip showing a variable value in the debugger

Using the Site Designer, Layouts, and Themes

When this project was first created, you walked through the four steps of the Web Project Wizard. On the last two steps, I said we didn't want a theme or a layout. Now, however, you want to add these in and see how they affect the look of this application. Let's start back at the beginning. In VI, click New Project on the File menu. Name the new project LayoutTest. Accept the defaults in Steps 1 and 2 of the wizard. In Step 3, choose "Left 1" as the layout and press the Next button. For now, leave Step 4 as "<none>." You can choose a theme in a moment. After clicking finish, VI creates the new project.

After the project has been created, open the Add Item dialog box. This time, create a new Site Diagram. The name is unimportant, as it will be the only one you create. When you create a Site Diagram, VI automatically creates a home page for you. In the diagram, right-click anywhere on the background and choose New ASP Page. A page called Page1 is then created. Using the mouse, drag Page1 under the Home page. As Page1 gets close, a connector automatically appears that connects Page1 to the Home page. Add two more ASP pages and connect them to the Home page. Figure 3-22 shows what the Site Diagram should look like.

Save the Site Diagram and then double-click on Page1. This opens Page1.asp for editing. Notice that when Page1.asp appears, it is different from what you were seeing before. Figure 3-23 shows the source view of the file, but now a number of graphical elements are in the Source view. This might appear confusing, which is why it was left out of the first project you did. When you get to the VI database tools later in the book, you'll examine these graphical elements. At this point, just view Page1 in the browser, saving it if necessary. Figure 3-24 shows that, when the page loads in the browser, it already has links to Page2 and Page3. You didn't write any of the code to add these links; they are handled by the layout you added when you created the project. The links work. Feel free to click them and see the pages change.

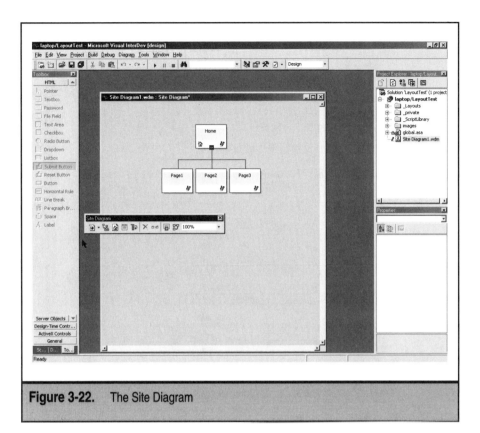

Figure 3-22. The Site Diagram

Now, go back to VI and open the site diagram. Grab the Page3 icon and move it until the connector between it and the Home page disappears. Save the diagram and then open Page1 in the browser again. Notice the link to Page3 is gone (if it isn't, don't forget to refresh the page). The site diagram is a way not only to document the layout of the site, but if you use a Layout in VI, it also maintains these links for you.

Finally, you want your page to look better. This is what the Themes are all about. You could have chosen a theme when you created the project or you can add (or remove) one at any time. In VI, right-click the project name in the Project Explorer window and choose Apply

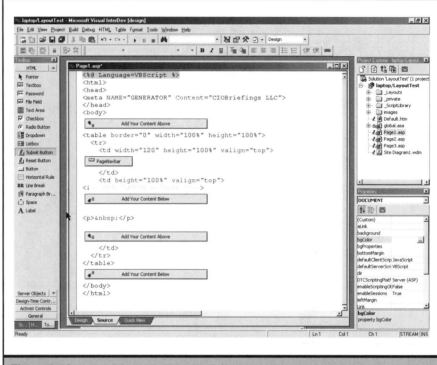

Figure 3-23.   Page1.asp with the graphical elements in it to enable the layout capabilities of VI

Theme and Layout. On the Theme tab, choose Automotive. VI copies a number of files into your project. When VI finishes copying files, view Page1.asp in the browser again. The links are still there, but the page now appears as you see in Figure 3-25.

Your First Data-Driven Web Page

You have spent a tremendous amount of time so far in this book, but you haven't yet touched SQL Server. It's time to change that, but understand one thing: At first, I'm going to take a 60 mile-per-hour drive past the topic. Then, I'll turn around and I won't just drive by slowly, but I'll actually get out of the car and examine these topics in great detail. For now, I'll use one of the more generic (non-VI specific) techniques for getting to the database.

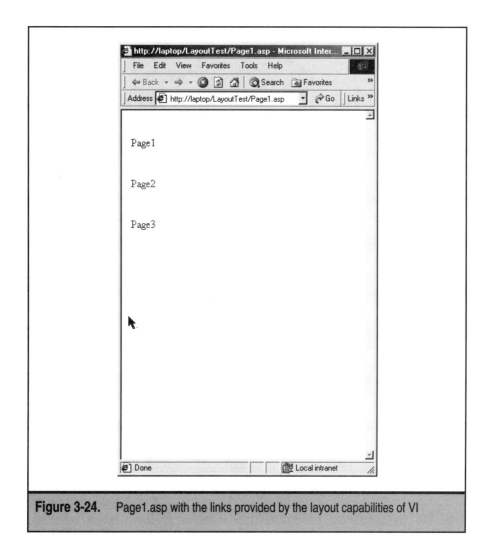

Figure 3-24.   Page1.asp with the links provided by the layout capabilities of VI

Once again, let's create a new project. In VI, click New Project on the File menu, and name the project DataDriven. Accept the defaults in Steps 1 and 2 of the wizard and leave both Steps 3 and 4 as "<none>". Once inside the project, add a new ASP and name it CustomerData.asp.

The next thing you need to do is make a database connection. This is the tricky part, as you must modify the actual connection string to make the connection. Depending on your situation, you may only

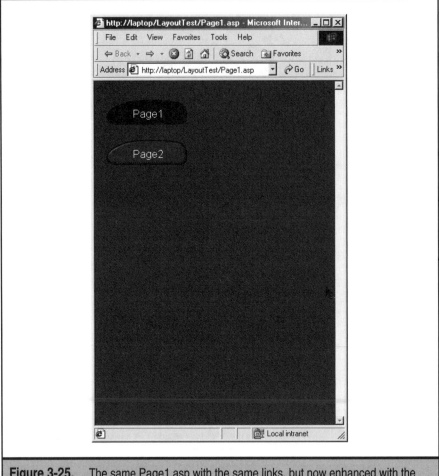

Figure 3-25. The same Page1.asp with the same links, but now enhanced with the Themes in VI

have to change the server name, or you may also have to change the user name and password. The server name is specified by the "Data Source" attribute.

Please understand you can connect to SQL Server 2000 in two ways: using Window NT authentication (integrated security) or using SQL Server authentication. If you are using SQL Server authentication, you must specify the User ID and Password arguments in the connection string. If you are using NT authentication, you don't have to specify the User ID or Password arguments. However, you must go into SQL Server and give permissions for that specific database to a user on your system called IUSR_<servername>, where <servername> is the name of your Web server. This is a special account used for IIS, and you will see ways around this in Chapter 15 when security is discussed.

The code for CustomerData.asp should look like this:

```
<%@ Language=VBScript %>
<HTML>
    <BODY>
        <H1>Customer Phone List</H1>
        <%
        dim cn
        dim rs
        set cn=server.CreateObject("adodb.connection")
        cn.Open "Provider=SQLOLEDB;User ID=sa;Initial Catalog=" & _
            "northwind;Data Source=laptop;Password=;"
        set rs=cn.Execute("select CompanyName, ContactName, " & _
            "Phone from Customers")
        Response.Write "<table border=1 cellpadding=2 cellspacing=2>"
        do until rs.eof
            Response.Write "<tr>"
            Response.Write "<td>" & rs("CompanyName") & "</td>"
            Response.Write "<td>" & rs("ContactName") & "</td>"
            Response.Write "<td>" & rs("Phone") & "</td>"
            Response.Write "</tr>"
            rs.movenext
        loop
        Response.Write "</table>"
        %>
    </BODY>
</HTML>
```

Once you have typed in this code and saved the file, you are almost ready to view the file. To view the file, however, you can't just switch to Quick View. The Quick View tab acts like a client browser, so it processes HTML, but it can't process server-side script any more than IE can. Therefore, to view the file you have to pull it through a Web server. To do this, right-click the file and choose View in Browser. This opens the file through the Web server and runs the code. Opening the file produces a result like that seen in Figure 3-26.

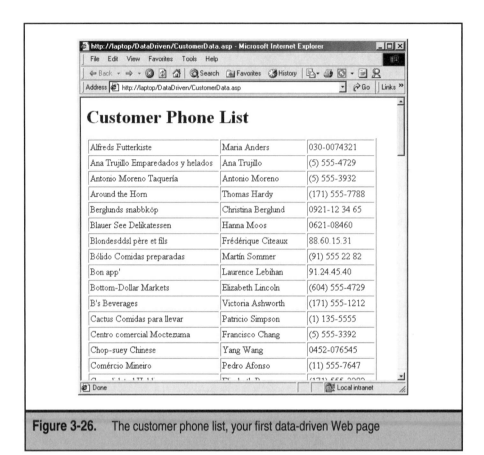

Figure 3-26. The customer phone list, your first data-driven Web page

If the code doesn't make much sense to you, don't worry. You examine this code in coming chapters. For now, just understand that you have produced an ASP that is built off live data in your database. If you modify one of the records in the table, and then press the refresh button in the browser, you can see the updates immediately. Recall from Chapter 2 that if you view the source in your Web browser, you only see the resulting HTML, not the actual ASP code, which was processed on the server.

SUMMARY

Visual InterDev is Microsoft's tool for building professional Web applications. VI enables you to debug both client-side and server-side code interactively, make your applications look better with themes, and automatically maintains links using layouts.

VI makes two copies of all of your Web files. The files are located in a local working directory and in a master directory on the Web server. You can work in Master mode, where you update the Web server with every change, or you can work in Local mode where you simply update the local copy until you are ready to update the master copy.

You are now almost ready to start working with data in your Web pages. Before you do, though, one critical topic is left to cover: the objects provided to you by IIS. These objects make it easy for you to interact with the values passed in from forms, to insert output to the HTML stream, and to call COM components.

CHAPTER 4

Using the ASP Objects

A t this point, you've created a few simple Active Server Pages and have begun using Visual InterDev to make your Web application development easier. Before you move into the heart of building data-driven pages, it's imperative for you to understand how you will work with the objects provided to you by the ASP engine that enable you to leverage the full power of IIS Web applications.

One of the most important aspects of the ASP objects for you is the capability to maintain state transparently. Maintaining state is critical for building Web applications, and this will be part of many of your solutions. These objects are also important because they provide the mechanism for you to use COM components, including ADO, which you use for all your database access.

The objects examined in this chapter are provided to you by the ASP engine. While your examples are written in VBScript, these objects are part of the environment, which means they are available to any scripting language you choose. Therefore, don't mistake these as being VBScript functions.

MAINTAINING STATE—THE APPLICATION AND SESSION OBJECTS

Maintaining state is one of the most important elements in building Web applications. Remember, HTTP is a stateless protocol. If you request a page from a Web server, you make an HTTP connection, the Web server returns the page to you via HTTP, and then the connection is broken. When you request the second page, the server has no idea you have been there before. The server sees every request as coming from a new user. IIS, however, gives you a built-in mechanism to maintain state.

Maintaining state is important because you must remember a person from page-to-page if you want to build in functionality such as an accurate page counter, a shopping cart, or an application driven by user permissions. Using some of the built-in objects given to you by the ASP engine enables you to maintain this state on the server, with no additional programming on your part. How this works and

how you can incorporate these built-in state components into your
Web applications are both examined here.

The Application Object

Technically, you have already written a Web application. All it takes
to create an application under IIS is to have a virtual directory defined
and to call an ASP in that directory. This creates an Application object
in memory on the server. If you haven't rebooted your machine since
the last chapter, you still have an Application object running in memory.

> **NOTE:**   Calling an ASP starts the application, but calling an HTML page does
> not. This is an important distinction because it means the processing that runs
> when an application starts doesn't run until the user requests an ASP.

So, what exactly is this Application object? The *Application object*
is the object that holds the application state. This means it maintains
information across time and across users. Variables held in the
Application object are visible to all users—a concept examined in
more detail soon. The Application object can store information across
time because it never shuts down. In fact, it stays in memory as long
as IIS is up and running, which is forever, theoretically. Only one
Application object exists per application, no matter how many people
are using the application.

Having only one Application object per application means the
Application object is created only when the first user gets into the
application. Subsequent users will not start an Application object
because it is already running.

You can capture an event when an Application object starts: the
OnStart event. This event fires when the Application object first starts,
which theoretically is only one time. This means the event should fire
one time only. In reality, you can shut down IIS or the entire server
(which shuts down IIS), or the machine can crash. When the server
restarts, the first person who comes in to the Web application restarts
the application, and then the OnStart event fires all over again.

Just as there is an OnStart event, there is an OnEnd event that fires when the Application object terminates. You can't guarantee this will ever occur, because the Application object only shuts down when the Web server is shut down gracefully, and most people try to avoid ever shutting down a production Web server. If the Web server is shut down in an orderly manner, however, the Application objects closes, and the OnEnd event will run. This can be used to save certain values you want to restore when the application restarts.

To see how to use the Application object, and where to put the code for the OnStart and OnEnd events, you need to examine the Session object first. Then you learn how the Application and Session objects work together to provide state maintenance.

The Session Object

Unlike the Application object, one Session object exists for each user of a Web application. This means if you have 10,000 simultaneous users of your Web application, one Application object exists, but 10,000 Session objects are in memory. Each user gets his own Session object, so the session is the place to store user-specific variables, such as a user name. When the user makes her first request, a Session object is created for her. On subsequent trips, she is returned to the same Session object.

Both the Application and Session objects can store variables. If you think of a "regular" or non-Web application, you have the concept of global (or public) variables and private variables. If you wrote a Visual Basic program and put in a *global variable,* that variable is visible anywhere in the application. If you run that application on your machine and someone else is running a copy on another machine, however, his copy of the program cannot see the variables on your machine. In other words, global variables are global only for each user. In a Web environment, though, application variables are accessible to all users. Session variables are accessible only to the user who owns that session, so they are more like traditional global variables in other languages. Private variables are those that have a scope limited to just the procedure to which they are defined. You still have those in ASPs as well.

There is, in fact, a third level of variable scope: *page level* variables, which are local to a page running in a session for a particular application. An individual page can see the session variables for the session in which that page is executing, and they can also see the application variables for that application. Not only can they "see" or read these variables, but any page can create or modify application or session variables.

Figure 4-1 shows how the application, session, and page variables work together. The drawing represents the logical, not physical, view of how applications, sessions, and pages work. When the application is first called, the Application object is created. That first user also gets her own Session object, which runs under that application's

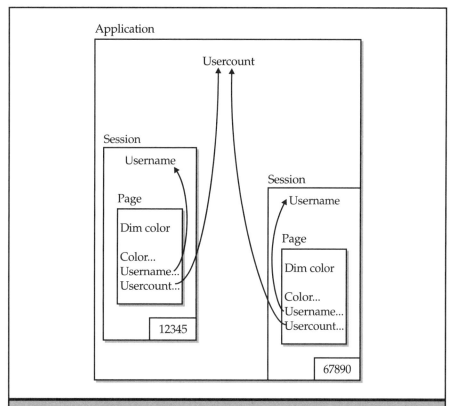

Figure 4-1.   The application and session objects, and how pages access the variables

context. The second user to request an ASP gets a new Session object, but it is also under that Application object's context. The individual pages requested then run under the user's Session object's context. This means if a page requests a session variable, it will read the one for only that user.

At this point, you are probably saying to yourself, "Fine. Each user gets a Session object for himself. How in the world does he get back into it? How do I know who owns which session object if HTTP is stateless?" The answer is fairly simple and elegant: with the SessionID. When each session is created, it is given a number that uniquely identifies it within that Application object.

When the user makes her first request into the application, she asks for a page but does not send up a SessionID. IIS, seeing that SessionID is not part of the request, creates a new Session object and assigns it a unique SessionID. When the page is rendered and returned to the user, the SessionID is sent along with it "under the covers." The user doesn't see this number and is usually not aware of its existence. When the user makes the request for the next page, however, the request goes to the server, along with the SessionID. When the request reaches the server, IIS receives the call and sees that the request does have a SessionID with it, and routes the request (and thus, the user) back to the same Session object she had before. In this way, any user-specific variables, such as UserID, can be stored in the Session object and returns users into that Session object for all future requests. In this way, you can maintain state, even though you are using a disconnected protocol like HTTP. Even better, you can achieve this without any programming on our part! Figure 4-2 shows this SessionID passing in action.

While knowing about the SessionID is helpful, you usually don't have anything to do with it. SessionID is read-only, so you cannot change it in any way. You might be tempted to store it in a database, but be careful: Session objects, unlike Application objects, do *not* stay around forever. The Application object can stay in memory forever because only one exists per application, so memory use is minimal. With Session objects, on the other hand, one per user exists. If you

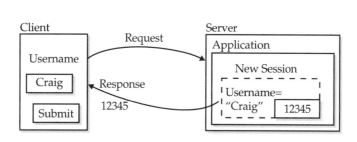

Step 1. On the first request, the user does not pass up a SessionID. A new session is created, given a SessionID, and that SessionID is returned to the client as part of the response. You have also created a session variable called Username.

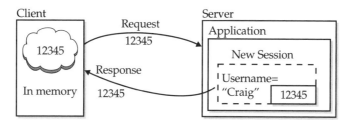

Step 2. Subsequent requests from client include SessionID, so user is returned to same session object. State is maintained!

Figure 4-2. The SessionID is passed between the server and the client to ensure user state is maintained

have 10,000 simultaneous users, you can imagine that over time you would end up with millions of Session objects in memory. Because most people would agree this isn't really a good thing, Microsoft has made it so Session objects time out. The default value in IIS 5.0 is twenty minutes, but you can change this as wanted.

Session objects timing out can obviously affect your program. Let's look at several scenarios, but do it with code. First, fire up

Visual InterDev and create a new project. Let's call this application Objs, because this application will be used for all your object demonstrations in this chapter. After creating the project, create an ASP called SessionTest and type in the following code:

```
<%@ Language=VBScript %>
<HTML>
<HEAD>
<TITLE>Maintaining State</TITLE>
</HEAD>
<BODY>
Your current SessionID is: <% =Session.SessionID %>
</BODY>
</HTML>
```

When you run this ASP, you see something similar to Figure 4-3. Your number will most likely be different, of course, but you should have some number in that window. This is the number the server sent to your client when you requested the page. If you hit the refresh button on the browser, the number stays the same.

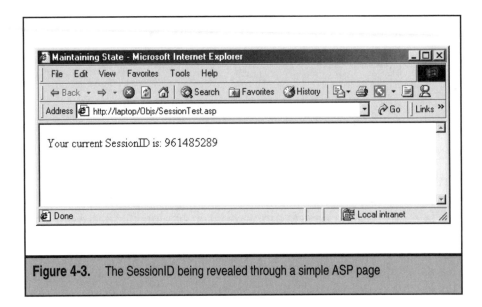

Figure 4-3.   The SessionID being revealed through a simple ASP page

Right now, your browser has this SessionID cached in memory (on the client side) and the number is stored in the Session object on the server. On the client, the SessionID is stored in memory, not written to disk. If you shut down the browser, you will lose this SessionID from the client. The Session object on the server continues to run. Why? Because the server doesn't know you've closed your browser. Remember, HTTP is stateless, so the server doesn't know if the client closes the browser. If you close your browser, therefore, the session remains in memory on the server for twenty minutes by default. The session times out after twenty minutes of inactivity; any request you make restarts this twenty-minute clock, including hitting the refresh button.

Note the SessionID shown in your browser and close the browser. Immediately reopen the browser and reopen SessionTest.asp. The SessionID should have changed; usually it only increments by one, but the change can vary. You got a new Session object and, therefore, a new SessionID because your request to SessionTest.asp didn't send along a SessionID. When you closed your browser, you cleared out the memory where the previous SessionID was kept. So when you requested the page, IIS had to start a new Session object. The old session is still around and will be for twenty minutes after your last request. The SessionID is stored on the client using cookies, which are examined later in this chapter. Just understand two important points here:

▼   The cookie used to store the SessionID is never written to the client's hard drive; it is only stored in memory.

▲   If the client turns off the capability to accept cookies, you won't be able to maintain state using this mechanism.

Now, let's take a different approach. You have the SessionID cached on the client machine. If you sit for twenty minutes after requesting the page and do nothing, the session will time out on the server. If you wait 21 minutes from your last request and then make a new request, you will send up the SessionID you have cached. However, IIS will look for a Session object with a matching

SessionID, but it won't find it. So, IIS then creates a new Session object, but it creates this new session using the SessionID you just sent. Some code will be examined shortly that will run anytime a new session is started. Using this, you will be able to see just when a session is being created. Because the new Session object is given the old SessionID, you might think everything is fine. However, understand the Session object has dropped out of memory on the server and you have lost any variables you have stored there. You can see this by creating a second file and modifying the original file. Create a new ASP called SetName.asp and add the following code:

```
<%@ Language=VBScript %>
<%
session("UserName")="Craig"
Response.Redirect "SessionTest.asp"
%>
```

This page sets a session variable called UserName to the value "Craig", and then runs the SessionTest page. Feel free to substitute your name for mine, of course. You should also modify SessionTest to look like this:

```
<%@ Language=VBScript %>
<HTML>
<HEAD>
<TITLE>Maintaining State</TITLE>
</HEAD>
<BODY>
<% Session.Timeout=1 %>
Your current SessionID is: <% =Session.SessionID %><br>
Your UserName is: <% =session("UserName") %>
</BODY>
</HTML>
```

NOTE: In my testing, the 1 I used here, which should have timed out the session in one minute, sometimes took 1:15 or 1:30 to close the session. You can see the number of sessions running using the Performance Monitor and choosing the Active Server Pages object and the Sessions Current counter.

This added line of code, <% Session.Timeout=1 %>, tells the session to timeout after only one minute instead of twenty. Save the page, but now open SetName.asp in your browser. It will run, and then run SessionTest.asp for you. If you hit refresh within 60 seconds of opening the page, you see the UserName set to whatever value you specified in SetName.asp. This is because SetName.asp creates a session variable and that value stays in memory during the lifetime of the Session object. If you wait more than one minute and hit refresh, you get a new Session object. It has the same SessionID as before, but the UserName variable no longer exists. Figure 4-4 demonstrates what is happening.

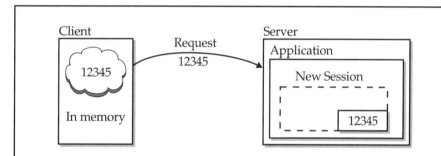

If the session has timed out on the server, a subsequent request will re-create a session with the same ID, but session variables are gone.

Figure 4-4.   A session variable is placed in memory in a session. If the session times out, the new session will have the same SessionID as the old one, but the variables will be gone

Global.asa

Now that we've started examining how IIS maintains state for you, you need to learn the items that go in Global.asa. You already know the Application object has OnStart and OnEnd events. The Session object also has OnStart and OnEnd events. The code for these events goes in the Global.asa file. When you create a new project in VI, it creates a Global.asa file for you. This file is examined every time an Application or Session object starts or ends.

In the case of Objs, you already have an Objs Application object running in memory. Therefore, if you now write some code to run on the Application_OnStart event, it won't get executed unless the Application object is first taken out of memory.

For now, let's use Global.asa to build a site counter. On many Web sites, a *site counter* is a graphic image placed on the page. A CGI application is called, which generates a new graphic for each request. The problem is, with HTTP, each request is seen as a new user. You can go to a site with such a counter, keep hitting the refresh button, and watch the number increment. This is obviously not an accurate count. The same user may jump from your home page to other pages and back ten times during a session, but this shouldn't count as ten different users.

NOTE: This discussion gets into the whole argument of the number of visitors versus the number of page views. You can count both if you want. Just understand the difference.

In your application, you only want to count the number of unique visitors. Therefore, you want to set up a variable that increments only when a new person arrives, not each time a page is viewed. In IIS terms, you want to increment this variable when the Session_OnStart event fires. To do this, you need to modify Global.asa and add in some code. VI automatically puts in a lot of comments; you are free to leave those in or to delete them. When done, your code (minus any comments) should look like this:

```
<SCRIPT LANGUAGE=VBScript RUNAT=SERVER>

Sub Application_OnStart
    application("UserCount")=0
End Sub

Sub Session_OnStart
    Application.lock
    application("UserCount")=application("UserCount") + 1
    session("UserNumber")=application("UserCount")
    Application.unlock
End Sub
```

First, create the routine to run when the Application_OnStart event fires. This routine contains only one line of code: it creates an application variable named UserCount and sets its value to 0. This means if the application is ever stopped, the count will go back to zero. This isn't ideal and, in the real world, you would periodically save the value to a file, and on restarting the application, you would read that value from the file. For now, you start with a UserCount of zero, and then assign the current UserCount to a session variable called UserNumber. This user number remains constant for this person, even if UserCount is changing often, as it would on a busy system.

A new user requesting a page forces IIS to create a new Session object, which fires the Session_OnStart code. In this code, you first lock the Application object. This is no different from locking a row or page in a database: you don't want multiple people changing the same value at the same time. Because application variables are accessible to all users, you must make sure you lock them when you need to make a change. In this case, you apply your lock, add one to it, and then issue your unlock. Notice you are locking the Application object, not individual variables. This means you should apply your locks as late as possible and remove them as early as possible. This won't come as any surprise to SQL Server developers and DBAs.

You need to modify one of your ASPs to show the new value. Make SessionTest look like this:

```
<%@ Language=VBScript %>
<HTML>
<HEAD>
<TITLE>Maintaining State</TITLE>
</HEAD>
<BODY>
<% Session.Timeout=1 %>
Your current SessionID is: <% =Session.SessionID %><br>
Your UserName is: <% =session("UserName") %><br>
The total UserCount is: <% =application("UserCount") %><br>
Your UserNumber is: <% =session("UserNumber") %>
</BODY>
</HTML>
```

Now, run the SessionTest.asp. Don't worry about the UserName in this instance. Notice the first time you run it, the UserCount and UserNumber are the same, each with a value of 1. Now, open a second browser, but be careful: do *not* use File | New Window from within IE. If you do, it will have the same SessionID and the server will see both browsers as one. Instead, open the second browser from the Start button and navigate through the menus. In this second browser, open SessionTest.asp and notice that now the UserCount and UserNumber are both 2. Refresh the first browser, and it will show you UserCount is now 2, but UserNumber is still 1 for that user. This is what you should expect. You can see this behavior explained in Figure 4-5.

A final word on application and session variables: they are defined with the words "application" or "session" in front of them. In other words, just saying "session"("UserName") creates a session-level variable accessible to any page within that session. In your Global.asa, you can put variables that are local to those routines. In other words,

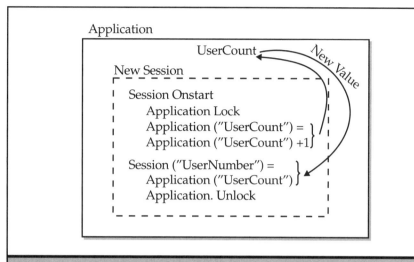

Figure 4-5.   The application and session objects work together with variables to keep count of unique visitors to the site and give each user a visitor number

they are not application or session variables. In this code snippet, the variable sFileName is not an application variable. It is private to Application_OnStart and will fall out of memory as soon as Application_OnStart finishes processing.

```
Sub Application_OnStart
    Dim sFileName
    sFileName="c:\UserCount.txt"
...
```

WORKING WITH USERS AND THE ENVIRONMENT AROUND YOU

Maintaining state is critical, but other objects need to be used to build Web applications. You must be able to send information to users and retrieve information from them. This is true of any data-driven Web application. Using the Response and Request objects can accomplish these tasks.

You also need a way to interact with your environment. For this, you can use the Server object. This enables you to gather details about the environment around you, which includes launching COM components, such as the *ActiveX Data Objects* (*ADO*). ADO is what enables you to get access to SQL Server.

The Response Object

When it comes to building applications, one of the most important things you have to do is send output to the user. This is pretty obvious, but how do you send the values of variables, or fields from a database, to the HTML stream? If you remember from your first ASP, you used Response.Write. The Response object is what the ASP engine gives you so you can send output to the HTML stream, write cookies on the client machine, and send directives to the client browser.

While the Response object can perform many tasks, by far the most common task is to write output to the HTML stream. This is what you have done on almost every ASP so far. Take the following code snippet:

```
<% Response.Write Now() %>
```

This simply prints the current date and time into the HTML stream. You saw a similar line of code in Chapter 2 when you created your first ASP. Back then, though, it looked like this:

```
<% =Now() %>
```

Response.Write is so common Microsoft created a shortcut for it: the equal sign. While this sounds great, be aware that you cannot always use the equal sign as a shortcut. The rule is this: you can only use the equal sign as the shortcut for Response.Write if it is the first command after an open server-side script tag. Notice in the previous code that you have the open server-side script tag (<%) and the next thing is the equal sign (spaces don't count). This means, in this case, the equal sign is a perfectly acceptable substitute for the words Response.Write.

Response.Write sends output to the HTML stream. In the previous example, the output is a VBScript function that returns the current date and time. You can also return a literal string, or a combination of a literal string and a variable or function, as in this example:

```
The time is <% =Time() %> on <% =Date() %>
```

While the Response object is most often used to write output to the HTML stream, it can also be used for a variety of other functions. One of the common methods of the Response object is used to call another page, and is called Redirect. Response.Redirect causes execution in that page to stop and another page to load. For example, look at this code snippet:

```
<%
If sPassword="pass" Then
    Response.Redirect "Account.asp"
Else
    Response.Redirect "LoginFailed.asp"
End If
%>
```

In this code block, you examine the value of the variable sPassword. If the value of the variable is "pass", then you run the page Account.asp. If the value is anything else, you execute the page LoginFailed.asp.

Be aware of three things with Response.Redirect:

▼ Response.Redirect won't work if anything has been written out to the HTML stream. In other words, the following code snippet produces an error because the text "<HTML>" has been written out to the HTML stream before the redirect command was issued.

```
<HTML>
<% Response.Redirect "Account.asp" %>
```

■ Response.Redirect ends all execution of the script at that point. It won't process any code after the Response.Redirect statement. The code in the first file must be valid, however, meaning it must compile correctly. Because the whole page is parsed and stored in memory in a compiled state, the entire page must be valid code.

▲ Response.Redirect actually sends a command to the client, telling it to request a new page. This causes a server round-trip, which you can imagine isn't efficient. As you see later, Server.Transfer may be a better solution, especially from a performance standpoint.

The Response object is also used to write out cookie information to the client browser. This is discussed in more detail in the section on handling cookies found in "The Request Object" section.

The Request Object

While the Response object is used to output information to the client browser, the Request object is used to retrieve information from the client. One of the most common events in Web applications is the retrieval of information from HTML forms. In an HTML form, the data can be sent to the server in one of two ways: using the Post or the Get method. The *Post* method is more commonly used because it allows more data to be passed to the server (although the actual amount is browser-dependent). The Get method usually only allows 1,024 or 2,048 characters to be passed to the server. Under the covers, the data passed by the Post method is sent in the HTTP header, which means the data is sent as part of the request. The Get method appends all the data to the address line of the site. If you pass the data from a form with the Get method and call a form called Test.asp, the address line might look like this:

```
http://localhost/test.asp?Name=Craig+Utley&Address=123+Main+Street
```

All the information after the question mark is called the *query string*. Not surprising, there is a Request.QueryString collection. If you assume you are using the call previously shown, the code inside Test.asp to retrieve the values would look like this:

```
Full Name: <% =Request.QueryString("Name") %>
Address: <% =Request.QueryString("Address") %>
```

This code snippet retrieves the Name and Address values from the query string and displays them on the page. If the data is passed with the Post method, however, the values don't appear on the address line. Instead, the values are passed up in the HTTP header and are invisible to the end user. However, the values are still accessible to you in the ASP that receives the call. In this example, if the calling HTML form was set to use Post instead of Get, you would retrieve the data this way:

```
Full Name: <% =Request.Form("Name") %>
Address: <% =Request.Form("Address") %>
```

The Form collection is used to retrieve data coming from HTML forms that use the Post method. The same data is passed to the server, but isn't visible to the end user.

The collection name with the Request object is optional. This means, in either of the two previous code snippets, you could have typed Request("Name") and had the data retrieved. If you leave off the collection name, the various collections of the Request object are searched until a match is found. This means an ASP can be written without knowing how the data will be passed from the HTML form. Because the ASP engine has to search through the various collections if you don't specify one, however, giving the collection name is more efficient, if you know it. In general, the time needed to search through the other collections is short, but it's all a matter of scale. If you can save $1/100^{th}$ of a second, it doesn't sound like much. But if you have 100,000 hits per hour and save $1/100^{th}$ of a second for each user, you can see that saving time everywhere you can is a good idea.

Cookies

Cookies are a way of storing information on the client computer. Most browsers support cookies, although some browsers enable you to turn off cookies. The way IIS passes the SessionID to the client and brings it back to the server, however, is by using the cookie mechanism: if the user turns off cookies you won't be able to maintain state using the Session object. The cookie used for storing the SessionID on the client is only stored in memory and is not written to the hard drive. However, you may want to write cookies to the user's hard drive to remember information about them over time. A session is a great place to store information during a single use of the application, but the Session object drops out of memory after a certain period of inactivity, and any information in it is lost.

To use cookies, you must write to cookies—using the Response object—and read from cookies—using the Request object. A single cookie can store multiple values, depending on how you write the code. A cookie with multiple values is called an *indexed cookie* and is commonly used to store multiple pieces of data about the same person.

NOTE: The browser is in charge of managing cookies on the client. Developers needn't worry about where cookies are stored or what name is given to them. When you request information from a cookie, it is up to the browser to locate the appropriate cookie and return the information to you.

Cookies are only written to the hard drive on the client if they are given an expiration date. This may sound strange, but cookies are only stored in memory until an expiration date is given.

To write out cookie information, examine the following lines of code:

```
<%
    Response.Cookies("UserName")="Craig"
    Response.Cookies("UserName").Expires="January 1, 2002"
%>
```

The first line looks for a cookie called UserName on the client. If the cookie doesn't exist, it is created. If the cookie does exist, the browser puts the value "Craig" in it. You then set an expiration date for the cookie, so the browser writes the cookie to the hard drive. Note, just because you say the cookie will be named "UserName" doesn't mean this will be the physical filename; in fact, the physical filename usually has the Web site's domain name in it. If you open the cookie in a text editor, however, you see the "UserName" cookie in it.

To write out an indexed cookie, the code looks like this:

```
<%
   Response.Cookies("MyCookie")("UserName")="Craig"
   Response.Cookies("MyCookie")("Address")="123 Main Street"
   Response.Cookies("MyCookie").Expires="January 1, 2002"
%>
```

This code creates an indexed cookie called MyCookie. Inside the cookie are two keys: UserName and Address. The value for UserName is "Craig" and the value of Address is "123 Main Street." The cookie is written to the hard drive because you set an expiration date for it.

Retrieving the cookie information from an ASP is just as easy. If you wrote out the first, nonindexed cookie, retrieving the data would be this simple:

```
<% =Request.Cookies("UserName") %>
```

To pull the information from an indexed cookie, the code would look like this:

```
<%
   Response.Write Request.Cookies("MyCookie")("UserName")
   Response.Write Request.Cookies("MyCookie")("Address")
%>
```

The Server Object

The *Server object* enables you to interact with IIS. The most commonly used feature of the Server object is the CreateObject method, which enables you to instantiate COM components. Server.CreateObject is examined in a moment.

In IIS 5.0, methods exist that enable you to transfer control to other pages. This is similar to the Response.Redirect examined earlier, however, Response.Redirect actually sends a command to the client browser, telling it to load a new page. Some browsers can warn the user they are being redirected to another page. This is also slow because the request for the new page must be sent to the client, which then sends the request for the new page back to the server, and the new page is then sent to the browser.

The Server object has two methods to alleviate these problems: Execute and Transfer. *Server.Execute* doesn't really transfer you to another page; instead, it lets you execute another page and then return control to the calling page. In other words, Server.Execute is an alternative to using server-side include files, similar to a call to a function in another file, common in many languages.

Server.Transfer truly transfers control from the calling page to the called page. This called page is processed and sends the response to the client. This means the client is redirected to a new page, but you don't have the time delay associated with the round-trip from the server to client and back associated with Response.Redirect. In addition, if PageOne.asp is called and it does a Server.Transfer to PageTwo.asp, PageTwo.asp has access to any of the Request collections that were originally sent to PageOne.asp.

Much of the time, you use the CreateObject method of the Server object to instantiate COM components, including the ADO objects used to access SQL Server. Because both VBScript and JavaScript use only late binding, you cannot create objects using the New keyword. Therefore, you use Server.CreateObject and pass in the program ID (ProgID) to instantiate the object.

The following block of code instantiates the ADO Connection and RecordSet objects:

```
<%
   Dim cn
   Dim rs
   Set cn=Server.CreateObject("ADODB.Connection")
   Set rs=Server.CreateObject("ADODB.Recordset")
%>
```

In both cases, the objects are instantiated with Server.CreateObject and are now available for use in the script. Let's examine how these objects can be used in a sample application.

PUTTING IT ALL TOGETHER

Now it's time to apply all you've learned about the different objects and how ASP works to start building a "real" application. This application stores a cookie to remember a user from one session to another. This functionality requires the Request and Response objects. In addition, it is data driven using the Server object and ADO. The application tracks the number of users using an application variable and the FileSystemObject.

To get started, go into Visual InterDev and create a new project. Call this project RealApp. Make your Global.asa look like this:

```
<SCRIPT LANGUAGE=VBScript RUNAT=Server>
Sub Application_OnStart
      Dim fso
      Dim File
      Dim lCurrentUserCount
      'Create the FileSystemObject
      Set fso=Server.CreateObject("Scripting.FileSystemObject")
      application("FileName")="c:\UserCount.txt"
      'If the file exists, get the value; if not, create it
      If fso.FileExists(application("FileName")) then
            Set File=fso.OpenTextFile(application("FileName"))
            lCurrentUserCount=File.ReadLine
      Else
            Set File=fso.CreateTextFile(application("FileName"))
            File.WriteLine "1"
            lCurrentUserCount=0
      End If
      File.Close
      application("UserCount")=lCurrentUserCount
      application("DBconn")="Provider=SQLOLEDB;User ID=sa;Initial
Catalog=northwind;Data Source=laptop;PASSWORD=;"
End Sub

Sub Session_OnStart
      'Increment the UserCount
      application.Lock
```

```
application("UserCount")=application("UserCount")+1
session("UserNumber")=application("UserCount")
application.UnLock

'Save the number of visitors every 10 users
If application("UserCount") mod 10=0 Then
    Dim fso
    Dim File
    Set fso=Server.CreateObject("Scripting.FileSystemObject")
    Set File=fso.CreateTextFile(application("FileName"))
    File.WriteLine(application("UserCount"))
    End If
End Sub

</SCRIPT>
```

Let's start by examining the various pieces of this code. First, the Application_OnStart routine fires when the application first starts. The first few lines of code simply create some variables, and then instantiate the FileSystemObject. The application variable FileName holds the name of a text file you use to track the total number of users over time. Feel free to change the path and filename.

The program then looks to see if the file in application("FileName") already exists. The first time you run this, it won't be there, so the program will create it, put the number one in it, and save it. If the file already exists, you read out the value in it. You create an application variable, application("UserCount"), to hold a running count of the number of users.

The last part of the Application_OnStart procedure creates an application variable for the database connection string. The string may well need to be modified for your environment, especially when it comes to your Data Source (server name). You might also need to change the User ID and Password parameters to match your environment.

So, after running the Application_OnStart, you have three application variables: application("FileName"), application("UserCount"), and application("DBconn"). These variables are now in memory and available to all users.

The first user fires the Application_OnStart and also fires the Session_OnStart. The first thing the Session_OnStart does is lock the application object, and then increment the application("UserCount") variable by one. The last part of the routine saves the current count of users every tenth visitor. If the machine were to crash, the application("UserCount") would be lost. To avoid losing the count, write out the current user number every tenth user by using the MOD function. The MOD function returns the remainder of the division operation, so if the user count is 30, dividing by 10 won't return a remainder (it is zero). When the remainder is zero, you create the file (just overwriting the old copy) named in application("FileName") and write out the new number. Notice you are writing out the application("UserCount"). In an application with many users, the count could possibly change from when this user incremented it. In this case, though, it doesn't matter because you want the most accurate number possible and, by writing out application("UserCount"), you always have the latest value.

Next, look at Default.asp, which is the start of your application. Your Default.asp should look like this:

```
<%@ Language=VBScript %>
<%
'Retrieve the UserName from the cookie on the user's machine
session("UserName")=Request.Cookies("UserName")
if session("UserName")<>"" then
    'If the UserName is already there, just go to main
        server.Transfer("main.asp")
end if
%>
<HTML>
<HEAD>
</HEAD>
<BODY>

<H1>Welcome to Real App</H1>
<P>Please Create a UserID:</P>
<FORM Name="frmUser" Method="Post" Action="ProcessUser.asp">
UserID: <INPUT Type="text" Name="txtUser"><BR>
```

```
<INPUT Type="submit"><BR>
</FORM>
</BODY>
</HTML>
```

In the opening part of this script, you use the Request.Cookies collection to determine if a UserName exists in a cookie on the client machine. If it does, you now have the user's name in the session("UserName") variable and you can go straight to Main.asp page. If, however, you don't already know the user's name, you show a form that prompts them for a UserName. This is a standard HTML form that calls another ASP, ProcessUser.asp. When the user clicks the submit button, you pass the user name in txtUser using the post method. ProcessUser.asp looks like this:

```
<%@ Language=VBScript %>
<%
'Check to see if the user wants to clear out the cookie
if Request.QueryString("Clear")="True" then
      Response.Cookies("UserName")=""
      Response.Cookies("UserName").expires=Date + 30
      session("UserName")=""
      server.Transfer("default.asp")
else
      if Request.Form("txtUser")<>"" then
            'write out the user name and save the cookie
            Response.Cookies("UserName")=Request.Form("txtUser")
            Response.Cookies("UserName").expires=Date + 30
            session("UserName")=Request.Form("txtUser")
            server.Transfer("main.asp")
      else
            'the user hit submit without filling in a value
            server.Transfer("default.asp")
      end if
end if
%>
```

ProcessUser.asp first checks to see if you want to clear out the cookie. This is more for testing purposes, so you can clear out the cookie to make sure the Default.asp comes up again. In the real world, you have probably seen sites that "remember" you and say things like "Welcome back, Craig," but then have a place to click if you aren't actually Craig. This clears out the cookie and directs you to the login page with a blank UserID.

If you aren't trying to clear the cookie, you drop into the procedure to save the cookie. First, realize that if the person didn't enter a name at all, but simply hit the submit button, you push her right back to Default.asp. It looks like she isn't going anywhere but, in reality, she is making an expensive server round-trip. She goes from her browser to the server, which processes ProcessUser.asp, and then processes Default.asp, which it sends to the browser. (It would be better to handle a blank user name field with some client-side script, but I decided not to clutter up this example.)

If the user did send up a user name, you save it in a cookie as UserName, and then set the expiration date. If you fail to set the expiration date, the cookie is not written to the hard drive, so don't forget to do this. You also assign the value to session("UserName"), and then call Main.asp.

The code for Main.asp looks like this:

```
<%@ Language=VBScript %>
<HTML>
<HEAD>
</HEAD>
<BODY>

<H1>Country Chooser</H1>
<H2>Welcome back, <% =session("UserName") %></H2>
<A href="ProcessUser.asp?Clear=True">Clear Cookie</A><BR>
You are visitor #: <% =session("UserNumber") %><BR>
<HR>
<H2>Enter a country here:</H2>
<FORM Name="frmState" Method="Post" Action="CustList.asp">
    <INPUT Type="text" Name="txtCountry"><BR>
    <INPUT Type="submit" id=submit1 name=submit1>
</FORM>
```

```
<H2>Or choose the country from this list</H2>
<%
dim cn
dim rs
set cn=server.CreateObject("ADODB.Connection")
cn.Open application("DBconn")
sSQL="Select distinct Country from Customers order by Country"
set rs=cn.Execute(sSQL)

do until rs.EOF
     Response.Write("<A href=CustList.asp?txtCountry=" & _
        rs("Country") & ">" & rs("Country") & "</A><BR>")
     rs.movenext
loop
%>

</BODY>
</HTML>
```

The first line of code that does anything special is this one:

```
<H2>Welcome back, <% =session("UserName") %></H2>
```

This line prints the session variable for the user name. This doesn't seem so impressive at first, but after the first time the customer uses the site, it remembers who he is and automatically takes him to this page.

The following line is what gives you the capability to clear the cookie on the user's machine. If you didn't have this link on some page, the user would have to locate the cookie on the hard drive physically and delete it. This way, you call ProcessUser.asp and clear out the cookie.

```
<A href="ProcessUser.asp?Clear=True">Clear Cookie</A><BR>
```

With the next line of code, you print out this user's session("UserNumber"). You have to use the session variable here, instead of the application variable because (you hope) the application variable is always changing. Every person who uses the application increases application("UserCount") by one, so this number should constantly be changing. However, session("UserNumber") doesn't change for this user as long as the Session object is in memory.

Next, you have a simple HTML form that enables the user to type in the name of a country. The data is sent back to the server using the Post method, which means the ASP receiving the call must check the Form collection of the Request object.

In the next part, things get a little interesting. Examine this code snippet:

```
<%
dim cn
dim rs
set cn=server.CreateObject("ADODB.Connection")
cn.Open application("DBconn")
sSQL="Select distinct Country from Customers order by Country"
set rs=cn.Execute(sSQL)

do until rs.EOF
      Response.Write("<A href=CustList.asp?txtCountry=" & _
         rs("Country") & ">" & rs("Country") & "</A><BR>")
      rs.movenext
loop
%>
```

To start, you create an ADO connection object. This uses the Server.CreateObject method and you instantiate an object of type ADODB.Connection. With this ADO Connection object, you call the Open method and pass it the database connection string in application("DBconn"). Make sure the application("DBconn") value is correct in Global.asa! After you open this connection, you have a SQL string in a variable and use the Execute method of the Connection object to run the SQL statement. Because the statement is a select statement, it returns records. The Execute method returns an ADO Recordset object, so you must set a variable to the return value. When this is done, you have a recordset in memory with a list of unique country names from the Customers table, sorted alphabetically.

Next, you run through the records and display them on the page, building an anchor tag for each one as you do. Because you are passing the values on the address line, the page you are calling must read the values using Request.QueryString. Also, don't forget to do a MoveNext inside the loop or you wind up in an infinite loop and have to wait for the script to time out on the server, the default of which is 90 seconds.

NOTE: This isn't the most efficient way to do this, but it is the simplest, and it's used as an example for now. More efficient ways of looping through records are discussed periodically throughout the book.

If you were to view the HTML, the end result of the anchor tags would look like this in the browser:

```
<A href=CustList.asp?txtCountry=Norway>Norway</A>
```

You can see Main.asp has a form that calls CustList.asp, and the anchor tags you build also call CustList.asp. Main.asp provides two ways for you to call the same form. This means CustList.asp must be able to find values using either Request.Form or Request.QueryString. Remember, with the Request object, you needn't specify the collection. Instead, you can call Request and the key name, and the Request object finds the value by scanning through the collections. Your CustList.asp should look like this:

```
<%@ Language=VBScript %>
<HTML>
<HEAD>
</HEAD>
<BODY>
<H1>Customers for <% =Request("txtCountry") %> </H1>

<TABLE Border="1" Cellspacing="2" Cellpadding="2">
<TR>
    <TH>Company Name</TH>
    <TH>Contact Name</TH>
    <TH>Phone Number</TH>
</TR>
```

```
<%
dim cn
dim rs
set cn=server.CreateObject("ADODB.Connection")
cn.Open application("DBconn")
sSQL="select CompanyName, ContactName, Phone from Customers " & _
      "where Country='" & Request("txtCountry") & "'"
set rs=cn.Execute(sSQL)
do until rs.EOF
      %>
      <TR>
        <TD><% =rs("CompanyName") %></TD>
        <TD><% =rs("ContactName") %></TD>
        <TD><% =rs("Phone") %></TD>
      </TR>
      <%
   rs.movenext
loop
%>
</TABLE>
</BODY>
</HTML>
```

The first thing you do is use the Request object to request the txtCountry key. Both the form and the anchor tags on Main.asp pass their data using the txtCountry key, so you needn't specify the Form or QueryString collections. Take this value and display it for the user.

NOTE: Normally, you would run a check to make sure you had been passed a value and, if not, you would kick the user back to an earlier page. That check is being skipped here.

After starting an HTML table and filling in a header row, you begin filling in the table with values from the database. To do this, you again have to open a connection and execute a SQL statement. Here, though, your SQL statement is not completely hard-coded; instead, your statement gets the value of the country passed in from the previous page. Once again, you loop through the recordset and pull out the fields you want to display.

Now that you have all the necessary files, run your browser and point it to http://localhost/RealApp/default.asp. Figure 4-6 shows you what to expect when Default.asp runs.

Type in a UserID and press the submit button. You should be taken to a page that looks like Figure 4-7. It has a box for you to type a Country name and a list of the countries, as links, below.

After clicking a country, in this case, Finland, the CustList.asp page presents the customers for that country in a table, as seen in Figure 4-8.

Figure 4-6. The Default.asp screen waiting for a user name

Now, you can test the cookie by closing the browser (all open copies) and reopening the browser and returning to http://localhost/RealApp/default.asp. You should be taken immediately to Main.asp, which "remembers" your name, which it retrieved from the cookie. The visitor number should have incremented by one; however, because you have a new session object, Session_OnStart was run, which incremented application("UserCount").

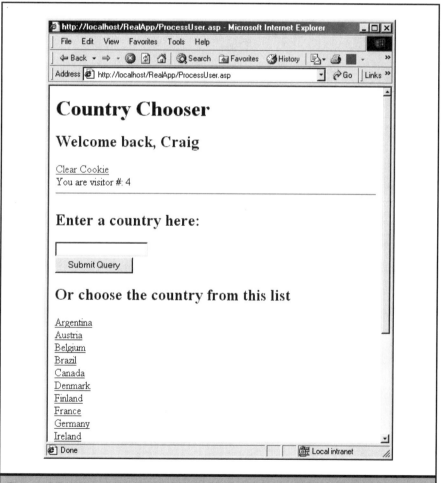

Figure 4-7.   The end result of Main.asp. Notice the address line still says ProcessUser.asp. This is a side-effect of how the Server.Transfer works

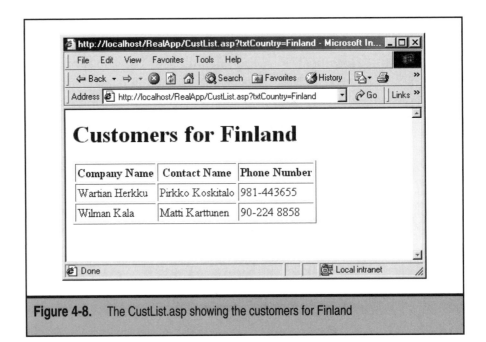

Figure 4-8. The CustList.asp showing the customers for Finland

SUMMARY

Creating a Web application involves a lot more than just HTML. Here, you are using the built-in objects given to you by IIS to interact with your environment. You can write out information to client browsers, read information being passed by the client browsers, and have built-in objects to handle state management for you.

In addition, you have the ability to extend your applications greatly through the use of calling COM components. These components, such as ADO, give you the ability to do complex processing in your Web applications. Leveraging both ADO and COM components enables you to build scalable, high-performance Web applications.

PART II

Server-Side Database Access

CHAPTER 5

Introducing ADO: Making the Connection

ActiveX Data Objects (ADO) is a Microsoft technology built to enable access to data. ADO represents a simple, easy-to-use way for a developer to connect to nearly any data source. Despite its simplicity, ADO is powerful and has nuances that need to be understood to write scalable, robust Web applications.

In this chapter, you use ADO from within your ASPs. This isn't normally the way you would build an application; instead, you would put the ADO into COM components and make calls from your ASP to the components. The ADO code is the same whether it's in an ASP or a COM component, however, so you work with the ADO code inside your ASPs until Chapter 13, when you begin to focus on n-tier Web applications.

INTRODUCTION TO ADO

Just what is ADO? The short answer is ADO is one of several methods Microsoft gives you to access data. ADO is the only focus of this book because Microsoft has stated it is *the* direction for future development. ADO is a simple, flat set of objects wrapped up in a COM component. Understanding what ADO is about, why it exists, where it came from, and where it is going is helpful.

A Brief History of Microsoft's Data Access

In late 1991 or early 1992, Microsoft released Microsoft Access as its desktop database for Windows. Access incorporated the JET database engine. *JET* is Microsoft's desktop database engine, just like SQL Server is Microsoft's server database engine. Nothing was really wrong with JET, but Microsoft knew many people had data residing in back-end systems, such as SQL Server, Oracle, DB2, and others. So, with the release of JET, Microsoft also introduced a data access layer, called *Open Database Connectivity (ODBC)*. ODBC is quite old in terms of Microsoft's technology.

The idea behind ODBC was to allow transparent access from the desktop to mid-range and mainframe databases. By transparent, I mean it would look to the user as if the data were residing locally in the JET database. The remote tables would look just like local tables, and the user could even perform joins between local and remote tables. Remote tables from heterogeneous back-end databases could be linked into one JET database, so a table in SQL Server and a table in Oracle could be joined in one query inside the JET database.

When Microsoft created the JET engine, it added an object layer on top of it called *Data Access Objects* (*DAO*). DAO was a simple way for a programmer to work with tables, queries (think of views), and the data itself. With DAO, a developer could open a connection to a database, access or create tables, and perform SQL statements against the tables, whether they were truly JET tables or were actually just linked in via ODBC. DAO was a boon for the productivity of developers writing desktop database applications, but it had one drawback: what if all the data were in the back-end database? There was nothing illegal about having a JET database that only contained linked tables from some back-end source. DAO took memory, however, and it loaded the entire JET engine into memory. If all the data was in the back-end database, this memory use was wasted. Worse, JET included a query processor, and it would process all the SQL statements flowing through it. These back-end databases also included query processors, so the statements were being processed twice, which slowed the process. While the JET engine seems small by today's standards (it took up about 1MB), these were the days of 4MB or 8MB machines using 16-bit operating systems. As you can imagine, for fast applications using a minimal amount of memory, using DAO to access only back-end data was slow and costly.

An alternative existed to using DAO: you could program directly against the ODBC layer. However, ODBC was not object-based. ODBC relied on a series of API calls. When it came to accessing back-end data, this ODBC-only code was much faster than using DAO, but it was much more of a challenge. With the ODBC API, the developer had to do all the steps, many of which were handled internally by DAO. The developer had to manage memory, pointers, and cursors, among other things. While it might only take five lines of code to open a database connection and update a table in DAO, it might take you 30 lines to do the same thing with the ODBC API. Any API calling is notoriously unfriendly when it comes to handling errors, and the ODBC API was no exception.

At this point, developers were stuck with two choices: they could use the easy-to-use, but slow, DAO, or they could use the fast, but hard-to-program, ODBC API.

Microsoft heard the cries of developers and responded with a new object model in Visual Basic 4.0: *Remote Data Objects* (*RDO*). RDO was an object model built on top of ODBC. It offered the ease-of-use of DAO, while also giving nearly ODBC API speeds. RDO could even be used to access JET tables; it just had to fire up the JET engine first. This is no different, of course, from saying that to access SQL Server tables, SQL Server had to be up and running. The RDO data model was similar to the DAO object model, except many of the names had changed. This made upgrading from DAO to RDO a challenge, but for applications with only back-end data, it was a worthwhile investment simply for the speed increase achieved.

Here Windows developers sat, with two object models (DAO and RDO) both using ODBC to access server data. Everything seemed fine, but Microsoft wasn't sure this was the best approach for the future. You see, ODBC assumed a relational database as the back-end. While some ODBC drivers had been written for data sources such as flat files or Excel spreadsheets, the core of ODBC wanted to see databases, tables within those databases, and fields within those tables. Both DAO and RDO were more than happy to open a connection to a database and automatically fill up a collection listing all the tables in that database. If you examined a table in either object model, it already knew the fields in each table. DAO and RDO could prefill all this information because they assumed a relational database as the data source.

Microsoft knew, of course, that not all data was actually stored in relational databases. Many systems use a flat file structure or hierarchical data structures. Some people stored data in spreadsheets. Important company data was in e-mail systems, such as Exchange. Microsoft decided a technology was needed that didn't assume a relational data source, but one that could be used to access any data source, regardless of the format.

About the time Microsoft was deciding to produce a way to access any data source with one piece of technology, a debate was raging in the industry. The debate centered on Universal Data Storage versus

Universal Data Access. Some database vendors favored the *Universal Data Storage* approach, where data of any type was stored in their relational product. This meant all e-mail systems, multimedia files, and other data should be stored in their database. This provided one consistent place to store all the data, and a known way to retrieve it.

Microsoft took the *Universal Data Access* approach, which basically said, "You keep the data where it is, and we'll give you one way to access it all." The cornerstone of this philosophy was OLE DB. *OLE DB* is sometimes called *OLE for Databases* or *Object Linking and Embedding for Databases,* but Microsoft long ago said OLE no longer stands for Object Linking and Embedding, claiming it only stands for OLE. Whichever definition you prefer, the fact remains OLE DB was an attempt to create one technology that would allow equal access to relational and nonrelational data alike.

OLE DB, like ODBC, is a low-level API. When Microsoft released OLE DB, however, it already had an object model on top of it: ADO. This meant developers already had a simple, COM-based object model with which to access OLE DB immediately. ADO represented a departure from Microsoft's previous database access object models (DAO and RDO) in two important respects: first, the object model was very small, and second, the object model wasn't the standard hierarchical structure seen with most other Microsoft object models. Figure 5-1 shows a visual representation of the various object models and how they fit in with their underlying technologies.

To think of Microsoft's approach to hierarchical object models, let's consider Excel. If your task, as a developer, was programmatically to put a number in a cell, you couldn't simply create a cell in memory and stick a number in it. The cell resides on a worksheet. Still, you can't just create a worksheet; a worksheet is part of a workbook. Workbooks only exist inside the Excel application. So, as a developer, you would have to create an Excel object. Once that is done, you use methods in the Excel object to create a workbook. From the workbook, you access a particular worksheet, and, finally, a cell on that worksheet. Once you have navigated from Excel to a workbook to a worksheet to a cell, you can put a value in the cell. This is an example of the rigid hierarchy in most Microsoft products.

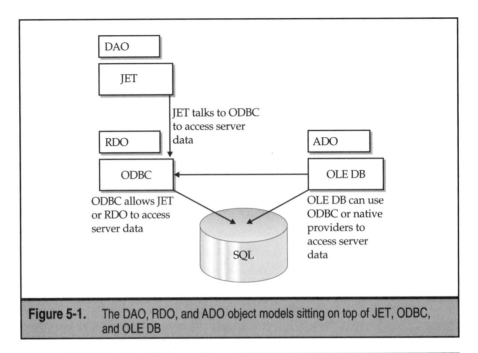

Figure 5-1. The DAO, RDO, and ADO object models sitting on top of JET, ODBC, and OLE DB

NOTE: This isn't the actual Excel object model, but it clearly describes the concept of a hierarchy in the object model.

ADO, on the other hand, doesn't have this rigid hierarchical structure. In fact, its structure is flat, as each main object can be independently created. The ADO object model, and the benefits of its flat structure, is examined throughout this chapter.

A Quick ADO Example

You have already used ADO from an ASP. Still, let's create your project for this chapter and begin by creating a simple page with some simple data access. You modify this page, and the project, throughout the chapter as you build your knowledge of ADO.

For now, create a new project in Visual InterDev and call it ADOTest. In ADOTest, add a database connection string to an application variable in Global.asa. Your Global.asa should look like this:

```
<SCRIPT LANGUAGE=VBScript RUNAT=Server>
Sub Application_OnStart()
```

```
        application("DBconn")="Provider=SQLOLEDB;
        Integrated Security=SSPI;Initial Catalog=Northwind;
        Data Source=laptop;"
End Sub
</SCRIPT>
```

NOTE: At this point in the book, I got my hands on SQL Server 2000 Beta 2. When I installed it, I went with Integrated Security. Therefore, the connection string looks different from what I have used so far. Continue to use the type of connection string needed in your environment.

Next, create an ASP called Customer.asp. The code for Customer.asp should look like this:

```
<%@ Language=VBScript %>
<HTML>
<HEAD>
</HEAD>
<BODY>

<%
dim cn
dim rs

set cn=server.CreateObject("ADODB.connection")
cn.Open(application("DBConn"))
sSQL="select CustomerID, CompanyName, " & _
        "ContactName, Country from Customers"
set rs=cn.Execute(sSQL)
%>

<TABLE Border="1" Cellspacing="2" Cellpadding="2">
    <TR>
        <TH>Customer ID</TH>
        <TH>Company Name</TH>
        <TH>Contact Name</TH>
        <TH>Country</TH>
    </TR>
<%
```

```
do until rs.EOF
    Response.Write("<TR>")
    Response.Write("<TD>" & rs("CustomerID") & "</TD>")
    Response.Write("<TD>" & rs("CompanyName") & "</TD>")
    Response.Write("<TD>" & rs("ContactName") & "</TD>")
    Response.Write("<TD>" & rs("Country") & "</TD>")
    Response.Write("</TR>")
    rs.MoveNext
loop
%>
</BODY>
</HTML>
```

When you execute Customer.asp, you should see a customer listing similar to Figure 5-2. There isn't anything here you haven't

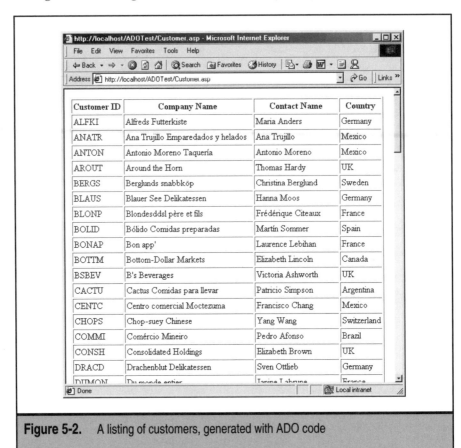

Figure 5-2.   A listing of customers, generated with ADO code

done before, however, you use this page as the basis for your exploration of the ADO object model and how you can work with it.

USING THE ADO OBJECT MODEL

As mentioned previously, the ADO object model is small and flat. Figure 5-3 illustrates how small the ADO object model is. You deal with three main objects on a regular basis: the Connection, the Command, and Recordset objects. Each of these objects is examined in more detail in this chapter.

ADO Constants

You can use a number of constants to specify particular values in ADO. For example, when it's time to specify the type of cursor you want, you have four choices: Forward-only, Keyset, Dynamic, and Static. For ASP programmers, Microsoft has created two include files that contain the ADO constants and their associated numbers. One file is for VBScript and the other for JavaScript.

To include the file in your page, you can simply put in this line of code:

```
<!-- #Include File="adovbs.inc" -->
```

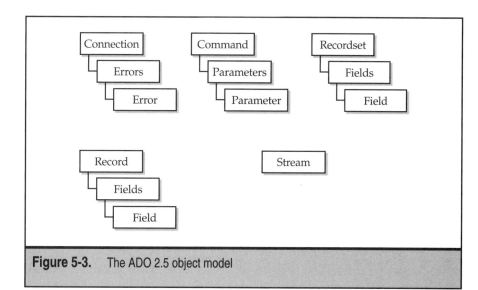

Figure 5-3. The ADO 2.5 object model

The adovbs.inc file needs to be in the same directory as the ASP in this example, of course. Otherwise, you would have to specify the path as well. The JavaScript version is called adojavas.inc.

You can use the constants in another way: add a reference to the ADO type library. Visual Basic developers are familiar with adding references in VB programs. ASP enables you to do the same thing with a metadata tag. Don't worry that it's a file called msado15.dll; this is the latest version of ADO. Microsoft simply builds type libraries that mimic previous versions, so code written against older versions doesn't break. The code looks like this:

```
<!-- Metadata Type="typelib"
    File="c:\Program Files\Common Files\System\ado\msado15.dll" -->
```

You see later how to use these constants. Often these constants are used to speed performance, but they are optional. Other times, they are required to achieve certain objectives within your program.

The Connection Object

Not surprisingly, the Connection object opens connections to your data stores, regardless of the actual format. In this book, I stick to relational data because SQL Server is being used as the back-end database. The Connection object can be used not only to connect to the database, but also to control transactions and actually execute SQL statements. The Connection object also has an Errors collection within it, which can hold one or more Error objects.

Understanding How to Connect

The first thing you normally do with the ADO Connection object is to establish a connection to the data source. From the previous discussion, you know two underlying technologies enable you to do this: ODBC and OLE DB. ODBC has been around for about nine years, so chances are you will run into it often. ODBC can store connections to a database in a file called a Data Source Name (DSN). The idea behind a DSN is that it can provide a layer of indirection between an application and the back-end database. You can set up a DSN to point to, say, a JET database. The application has only the DSN name coded inside it. Later, if you move your database to SQL Server, you simply delete the old DSN and create a new one with the same name, but point it to your SQL Server database. The application continues to run unchanged, provided your SQL was written as standard SQL and not as a JET-specific dialect.

As helpful as ODBC DSNs are, some problems occur with them. First and foremost, they are based on ODBC, which Microsoft has stated is definitely not the future direction. Second, the DSN must be created on every machine on which the application will run. The DSN must be named exactly the same thing on each machine. A client once spent days troubleshooting an in-house application that seemed to run fine on the developer's machine, but nowhere else. The answer was as simple as needing to create an ODBC DSN on each client machine that was running the application.

If ODBC is no longer the preferred technology, why spend time on it here? For two reasons: 1) some data sources don't have native OLE DB drivers (called providers) yet, and 2) many applications are already built using ODBC. Therefore, the likelihood of you running into ODBC DSNs is high. In fact, when OLE DB was first released, the only OLE DB provider was for ODBC! For a year or so, all developers using ADO were still calling ODBC under the covers. Unfortunately, many developers still do this.

To create an ODBC DSN in Windows 2000, click the Start Button, and then choose Programs | Administrative Tools | Data Sources (ODBC). Once there, you see a dialog box as shown in Figure 5-4. This enables you to create a new DSN.

Before you get started, however, notice a number of tabs are along the top of the dialog box. The first says User DSN. If you create the DSN here, only the user who created it can see it. Realize that in a Web environment, IIS doesn't see User DSNs, so you want to create your DSNs using either the System DSN or File DSN tabs. The code to call a File DSN is a little different from calling a System DSN, so I stick with System DSNs in this book. The only real difference is the file DSN is stored as plain text, while the System DSN is stored in binary format.

Click the System DSN tab. Next, click the Add button. A screen similar to Figure 5-5 is shown. This screen lists all the drivers available. In this screen shot, I have drivers for Oracle, FoxPro, text files, and SQL Server. Because this book is about SQL Server, I click SQL Server, and then click Finish.

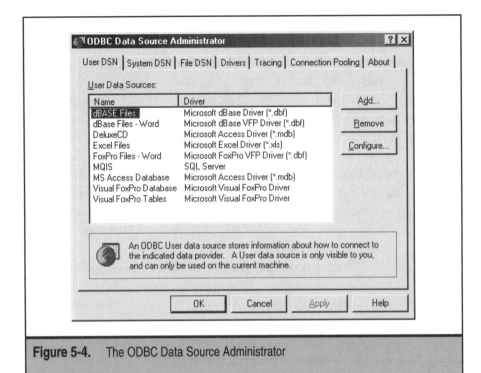

Figure 5-4. The ODBC Data Source Administrator

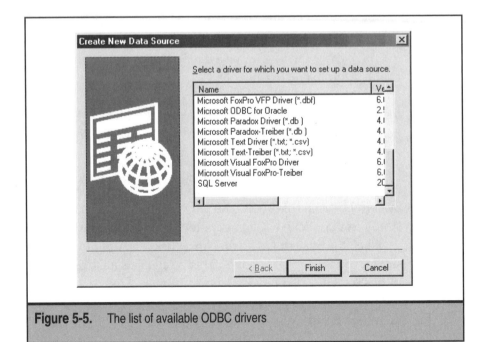

Figure 5-5. The list of available ODBC drivers

Now, let's move on to the first step of a wizard designed to aid in the creation of new ODBC DSNs. Three fields are shown in Figure 5-6: a Name, a Description, and a Server. The name is critical: it must be unique on the machine and it's what will be used in code later. The description is optional. The Server is required, and is the name of the server hosting SQL Server. You should fill out the name field with Northwind, and the server field with the name of your server. If you prefer, you can use "(local)" (without the double quotes) as the name of your server if you are performing this operation on the database server machine.

After clicking Next, the second page appears. Realize this screen is what you see when setting up a SQL Server DSN. Different databases have different requirements, so these screens may look different, depending on the type of your back-end database. In this

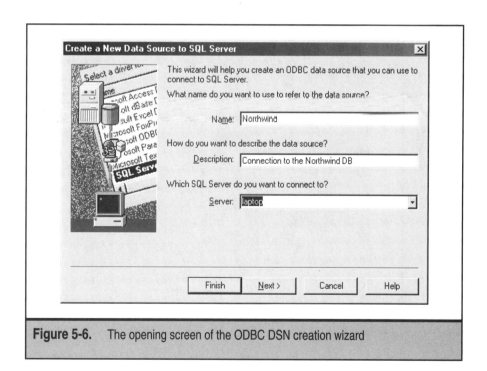

Figure 5-6.   The opening screen of the ODBC DSN creation wizard

case, Figure 5-7 shows a screen asking what type of authentication you want to use. Depending on your situation, choose either NT authentication or SQL Server authentication, and enter the appropriate Login ID and Password.

After pressing Next, the third screen comes up, as seen in Figure 5-8. The top box is important. It asks you which default database to use. By default, this is pointing to the master database. Make sure you change this to the database you really want to use with this connection! I have seen countless people struggle with a failed connection only to discover they are pointing to master and not the database they expected!

The fourth and final screen of the wizard, shown in Figure 5-9, is where you could change some of the options to affect performance or resource use. Because ODBC won't be the focus of your data access in this book, leave these as the defaults and click Finish. You are

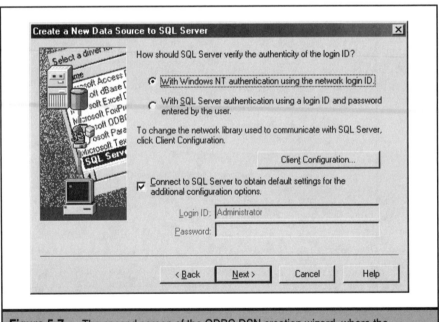

Figure 5-7. The second screen of the ODBC DSN creation wizard, where the authentication questions are asked

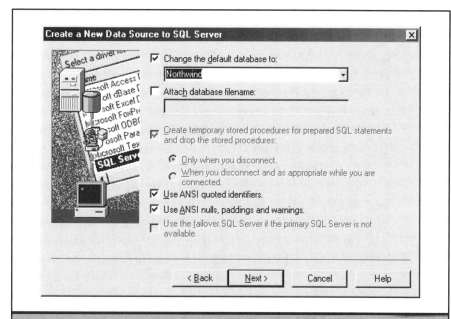

Figure 5-8. The third screen of the wizard is where you set the database you want to use

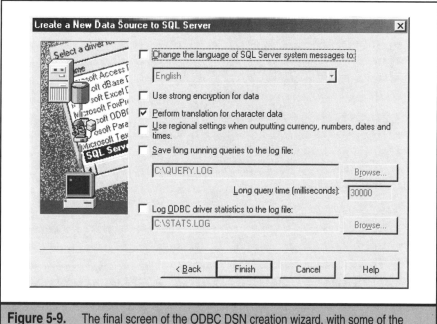

Figure 5-9. The final screen of the ODBC DSN creation wizard, with some of the ODBC tuning parameters

now shown a summary screen, pictured in Figure 5-10. This screen confirms the choices you made in the wizard and enables you to test the connection. Feel free to test the connection and when you finish, click OK to close the wizard. You are now returned to the ODBC Data Source Administrator and you see the DSN you just created.

Why would someone want to create a DSN if it involves so many steps? Realize what a DSN is—a file that holds the connection information. If you want to connect to Northwind from an application, you needn't know what type of database engine it is, or what the server name is, to connect to it. In fact, if the database moves from one server to another, you simply update the DSN without changing a line of code in the program. The database could even change from one engine or platform to another without affecting the program, as long as you deleted this DSN and created a new DSN with the same name.

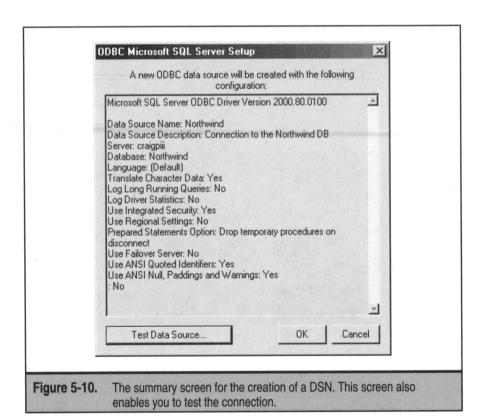

Figure 5-10. The summary screen for the creation of a DSN. This screen also enables you to test the connection.

Look how simple your ADO code can be now. You could replace the large connection string in the application("DBconn") variable with the DSN name. Your new line in Global.asa would look like this:

```
application("DBconn")="DSN=Northwind"
```

This looks much simpler than your previous connection string, and you might be tempted to use this method. I caution you against using this for two reasons. First, it uses ODBC, and your goal is to use OLE DB. Even though you are coding with ADO, OLE DB is calling the OLE DB provider for ODBC, so you are using ODBC for the actual access. Second, if this Web application is moved to another server, the person doing the move must be aware that a DSN needs to be created on the new server and its name must be Northwind, and that person must also know the security, server, and default database settings. This isn't a monumental task, but it can lead to broken applications when it isn't carefully followed.

One technique around the DSN issue was to create a DSN-less connection. A DSN-less connection didn't store the name of the DSN; instead it was a string that stored all the information that would be in a DSN. Using the SQL Server ODBC driver, your string would look something like this:

```
application("DBconn")="DRIVER={SQL Server};UID=Administrator;" & _
    "Trusted_Connection=Yes;Database=Northwind;Server=Laptop"
```

As you can see, all the necessary information that would normally be stored in the DSN was included. No DSN is referenced; instead, you tell ODBC which driver to load (the one for SQL Server), the name of the server, the name of the database, and some authentication information. Every possible keyword here wasn't included for the sake of brevity, but you get the idea.

When it comes time to use OLE DB, you have a few choices. OLE DB doesn't have DSNs, but it has something similar: a *Universal Data Link* (*UDL*). Like ODBC DSNs, a UDL is a file that holds connection information. Unlike DSNs, UDLs hold their information about which OLE DB providers to use, which is in contrast to DSNs storing the ODBC driver to use. Both UDLs and DSNs store the database and server information, as well as information about the authentication to use. On NT4, you could create a UDL by right-clicking the desktop and choosing to create a New Microsoft Data Link. This option is unavailable in Windows 2000, but you can still create a UDL. Create a UDL by right-clicking the desktop (or in a folder) and creating a new text document. Rename the text document to Northwind.udl, as seen in Figure 5-11. Double-clicking the UDL opens the Data Link Properties dialog box. The box starts on the second tab, but click the Provider tab to start. The provider tab shows a list of the available OLE DB providers, as shown in Figure 5-12. Notice the default provider is actually the Microsoft OLE DB Provider for ODBC Drivers. Click the Microsoft OLE DB Provider for SQL Server, and then click Next.

NOTE:　Don't put anything in the text file! Make sure the text file is empty when you create it and rename it to Northwind.udl. If anything is in it, this process won't work.

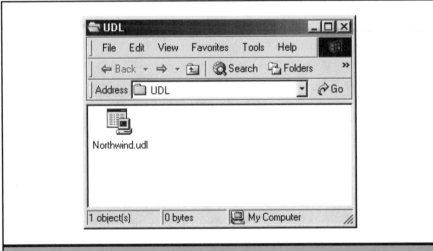

Figure 5-11.　A text file renamed to Northwind.udl

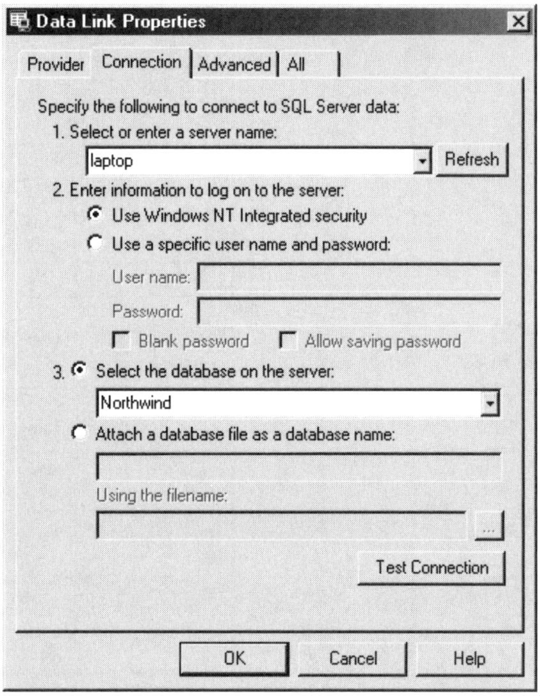

Figure 5-12.   The Provider tab of the Data Link Properties dialog box.

After clicking Next, you are sent to the Connection tab. This is where you started, but if you hadn't gone to the Provider tab, you would be defining an OLE DB to ODBC connection. We would rather use just OLE DB, so choose the native OLE DB provider for SQL Server. The Connection tab is similar to what you filled out for your ODBC connection. In this case, you have already named the UDL file, so you simply have to enter the server, authentication information, and database name. You can see the choices made in Figure 5-13, so fill in your choices to match, making sure you provide the appropriate server name and user name/password combination if you are using SQL Server authentication. At this point, you can

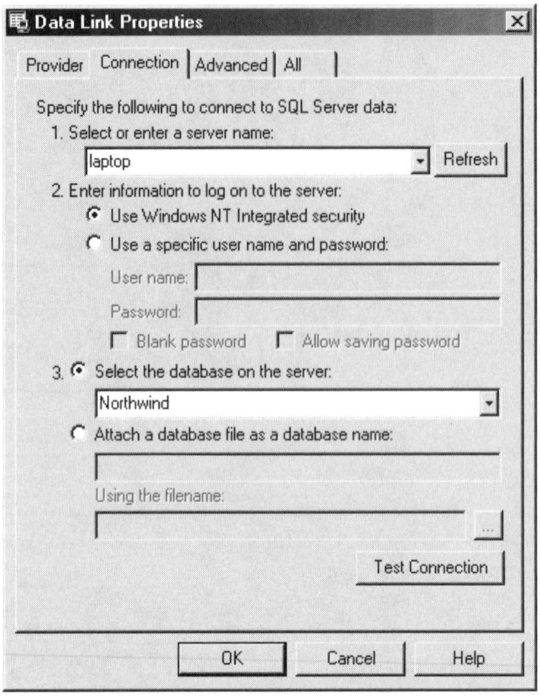

Figure 5-13. The Data Link Properties Connection tab filled out with the appropriate information

click the Test Connection button to make sure the information is correct. Two other tabs are there: Advanced and All. Depending on your database, the Advanced tab may enable you to change many options, few options, or no options. Finally, the All tab shows all the information to be stored in this UDL and enables you to change it. You needn't make any changes at this point, so just click OK.

Your UDL is now created. This is a lot like a File DSN; you have reference to the UDL name in your application. However, you usually don't want to hard code in a filename for the UDL because this UDL must then be created on every machine, much like a DSN. The alternative is simply to embed the connection string in the database, as you did with DSN-less connections. The nice thing about the UDL is you can open it in Notepad to see what the string looks like. Figure 5-14 shows

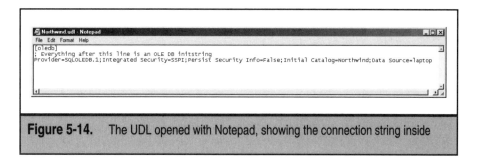

Figure 5-14. The UDL opened with Notepad, showing the connection string inside

the UDL opened in Notepad. I have stretched Notepad out, so you can see the whole string without any line wrapping. At this point, you could just copy and paste this string into your application. This is what you have been doing all along: using an OLE DB connection string in an application variable defined in Global.asa.

Understanding Where to Connect

If the previous discussion on how to connect didn't keep you glued to your seat, this discussion will. Every time I teach a class in how to create data-driven Web applications, I am asked: "Where should we make our database connection?" You see, you can open the database connection in three places: in the Application object, in the Session object, and in each ASP. So, where should you open the connection? The short answer is, of course, "It depends." Here's a hint for the future: the answer to 99 percent of all IT questions is "It depends." Let's look at the advantages and disadvantages of each of the three possible places to open the connection.

Application Object Connections First, you could open the connection in the Application object. To do this, you would have to modify the Application_OnStart event handler in Global.asa to contain code similar to this:

```
DBconn="Provider=SQLOLEDB;Integrated Security=SSPI;" & _
    "Initial Catalog=Northwind;Data Source=laptop;"
set application("conn")=server.CreateObject("ADODB.connection")
application("conn").open(DBconn)
```

Next, you would have code in each page that looked something like this:

```
sSQL="select CustomerID, CompanyName, " & _
    "ContactName, Country from Customers"
set rs=application("conn").Execute(sSQL)
```

In each ASP, it is using the application-level connection you created when the application started.

What are the benefits of making the database connection in the application object? First, you keep the connection open all the time. This means you don't pay the price of having to connect to the database every time you need data, so you should see a speed benefit over making page-level connections. Second, no matter how many users of an application you may have, you know exactly how many connections you will have: one. Because only one Application object exists per application, making the connection in the Application object limits your number of connections for this Application object to one.

If those benefits sound good, consider the drawbacks of making the connection in the Application object: the connection is always open and only one connection exists. Before you think some strange typo is in this book, you are correct that the benefits and drawbacks are the same. First, the connection is always open. This means, even if no one is using the application, you have an open connection to SQL Server. Database connections consume resources on both the client and server machines, so a constantly open connection is usually undesirable.

The other drawback is you only have one connection. This is good for limiting resource use, but what if you have 10,000 simultaneous users? They are all using the same connection! This is similar to trying to squeeze too much ketchup through that little hole in the top of that plastic bottle. If you squeeze too hard, it eventually pops off the entire lid. If you try to squeeze too many people through the one application-level connection, you will begin to experience degraded performance because the single database connection becomes a bottleneck.

Session Object Connections Now that you have seen the advantages and disadvantages of building application-level connections, let's examine building the connections in the Session object. The code is similar to what you saw for the application-level connection. This time, the code is placed in the Session_OnStart event procedure in the Global.asa. Assume you have still defined your database connection string in the Application object. After all, if it's the same for each user, you might as well define it once. Your code in Session_OnStart would look something like this:

```
set session("conn")=server.CreateObject("ADODB.connection")
session("conn").open(application("DBconn"))
```

Next, you would modify the code in each page to look similar to this:

```
sSQL="select CustomerID, CompanyName, " & _
    "ContactName, Country from Customers"
set rs=session("conn").Execute(sSQL)
```

Let's examine the benefits of making the database connection in the Session object. First, a database connection is once again open as long as the session is active. This means for each page that needs a connection, the connection is already established and you needn't take the time to connect to the database. The second major advantage is each user has her own connection to the database. This completely avoids the bottleneck possible with connections made in the Application object.

The first disadvantage to making session-level database connections is obvious: the number of open connections can be frighteningly high. If you have 10,000 simultaneous users and you're using an application connection, you have one connection. If you're using session connections, you have 10,000 connections to your database. This represents a load on both the server and the client. Can the server handle 10,000 simultaneous database connections? Do you have enough licenses for it? How thrilled is your DBA going to be with that many connections?

The second disadvantage is sometimes harder to guess (students who correctly guess it in my classes usually receive extra brownie points). Let's look at the page you built back at the beginning of the chapter. Open a connection to the database, and then retrieve a recordset showing some fields from the Customers table. You display the fields for all the records in a table for the user to see. Understand what is happening on the server: when the user requests the ASP, it begins processing, which includes performing the database query. By the time the page is rendered in the client browser, the page is out of memory on the server. This means no need exists for a connection to the database by the time the page is done being rendered in the client browser.

Let's take a simplified scenario. Assume a page takes one second to process on the server. The user then looks at it for 59 seconds. This means the connection to the database is only needed $1/60^{th}$ of the time. If you are making session-level connections, most of the time the connection is open is wasted. You need the connection only a small percentage of the time. If you assume the connection is only needed $1/60^{th}$ of the time and you have 10,000 Session objects in memory, only about 167 will be actively using the database at any given time. This is a lot of wasted overhead. Also, while Session objects do time out, if you leave them in memory for ten minutes of inactivity, the last ten minutes of a session-level database connection are completely wasted. The client has disconnected, but the connection remains open, consuming resources, until the session times out.

Making the Connection in Each ASP   Finally, here's the part about making the connection on each page. This is the method you have been using for every example in the book so far. The code snippet for the connection is in each page, like this:

```
set cn=server.CreateObject("ADODB.connection")
cn.Open(application("DBConn"))
sSQL="select CustomerID, CompanyName, " & _
    "ContactName, Country from Customers"
set rs=cn.Execute(sSQL)
```

In this example, you create the connection object on each ASP, and then run the query. The advantage of this approach is you only have a live connection to the database while the page is being processed. In the earlier example, this would mean the connection is only alive for one second per minute. This would mean that even with 10,000 simultaneous users, you would only have about 167 live database connections at a time. This enables you to reduce the overhead significantly on both the Web server and the database server.

The main disadvantage of this approach is probably obvious at this point: speed. Establishing a database connection takes time; there's no way around that. Usually, your request has to go across a network link. SQL Server must verify your user credentials. Finally, the message comes back to the client indicating a success or failure on login. This speed hit is why some people do not like to use page-level database connections.

Microsoft realized this was a potential disadvantage of making the connection at the page level and built a solution to try to lessen some of the impact using database connection pooling. For ODBC, this is called *ODBC Connection Pooling.* For OLE DB, it is called both *OLE DB Resource Pooling* and *OLE DB Session pooling.* I use "connection pooling" as a generic term because the good news is that you, as a developer, needn't do anything to take advantage of this; it is given to you automatically. In Windows 2000, you can look at the ODBC connection pooling options by launching the ODBC Data Source Administrator and clicking the Connection Pooling tab. Scroll down in the list to SQL Server and double-click it. You see a window pop up similar to Figure 5-15. This shows the SQL Server ODBC driver is pooled for 60 seconds.

NOTE: By default, ODBC connection pooling isn't on in Windows NT. Installing MTS turns it on automatically, however, and IIS 4.0 and higher require MTS. In other words, people may tell you to turn on MTS, but chances are it's on already. Check Microsoft's Web site for the proper registry entries to enable or disable ODBC connection pooling.

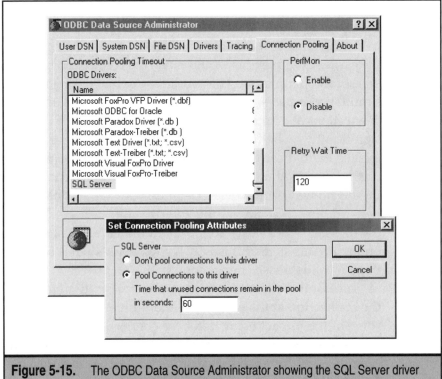

Figure 5-15. The ODBC Data Source Administrator showing the SQL Server driver will be pooled for 60 seconds

For OLE DB, session pooling is on automatically. To turn it off, you have to make some registry changes, which is beyond the scope of this book. This information can be found online at Microsoft's site in the article "Pooling in the Microsoft Data Access Components."

So, just what is connection pooling (again, using the term generically for both ODBC and OLE DB)? The concept is simple: keep the connection open even if no one is using it. The purpose is equally simple: to speed connections to the database. That initial connection is an expensive operation, so if an unused connection already exists, you can grab that and save much of the time normally required to connect to the database. Both ODBC and OLE DB can keep connections alive for a certain period of time and give them to another user as requested. If one user requests a particular database connection, then, when the ASP is done processing, the connection falls back into a pool. If someone comes along within 60 seconds, ODBC or OLE DB gives him the pooled connection instead of creating a new one. If none are in the pool or none are free, a new connection is then created and opened.

All this leads back to the question about page-level connections. The main drawback of establishing connections on each page is they are slower than using session or application connections, unless many people are squeezing through an application connection. Connection pooling, however, eliminates much of the time disadvantage.

So, Where Do I Connect?   If you're still wondering where to connect, you should now realize no absolute answer can be given. Instead, you have to weigh the pros and cons of each situation. The following table sets out the pros and cons, as well as some recommendations:

Connection Location	Pros	Cons	Recommendations
Application	1. Only one connection exists for the entire application, so resource use is minimized. 2. The connection is always alive, so the time required to connect is only paid when the application first starts.	1. Because only one connection exists, many users could be fighting for that one pipe to the database. This could limit scalability quickly. 2. The connection is always alive, consuming resources even when it's not needed.	Application connections may be tempting, but remember, they can quickly limit the scalability of the application. Performance can degrade dramatically as the number of users increases. Because of this, application connections are rarely used.

Connection Location	Pros	Cons	Recommendations
Session	1. One connection exists for each session, or user, of the application. This eliminates the potential bottleneck found in application connections. 2. The connection is open during the entire session, so the time required to connect is only paid once by each session.	1. Because each session has an open connection, there could be thousands, or even millions, of connections to the database at one time. This could negatively impact the performance of the Web and database servers. 2. The connections are held open during the entire session, even though they are only needed a small percentage of the time.	Session connections are faster than page connections and don't have the possible bottleneck of application connections. Because of their higher resource use, however, they should typically be used only when the number of simultaneous users will be relatively small.
Page	1. The connection is made as late as possible, is kept open only when needed, and is then closed. This helps limit overhead and reduces the number of simultaneous connections.	1. Having to connect on each page slows down the process. Connection pooling helps, but this is still a slower approach than application or session connections.	While this is the slowest approach, it is the most scalable. At some point, in fact, it would be faster than session connections as the overhead of many session connections would actually start to bog down the server. This is, by far, the most common approach.

Recall that I mentioned at the beginning of the chapter that you don't normally put your database code in your ASP files. Instead, you usually create COM components and put the database access in the components. All these arguments are the same, however: where do you create the COM components that perform the database access? You have the same three choices: you can instantiate the components in the Application object, in the Session object, or in each ASP. These issues are examined in Chapter 13.

Executing Statements

Even though the topic of opening a database connection has been covered in great detail, there is more to what the Connection object can do. Namely, it can execute statements. Most of the time this means SQL statements, although ADO can be used for other types of data. The Execute method allows the Connection object to issue SQL statements of any kind. In the example at the beginning of this chapter, a SQL select statement was created, and then the statement using Connection.Execute was run. You could also execute insert, update, and delete statements, as well as execute DDL statements such as CREATE TABLE, ALTER TABLE, and CREATE INDEX. The Execute method can even be used to call stored procedures if you like.

A number of SQL statements don't return any records. Inserts, updates, and deletes don't return records, but a select statement usually returns records. The Execute method can pass on a select statement, but it cannot hold any records that come back from it. Examine the following snippet:

```
<%
'This statement will not return records
sSQL="Delete from Foo where FooID=3"
cn.Execute sSQL

'This statement will return records
sSQL="Select FooID, FooName from Foo"
set rs=cn.Execute(sSQL)
%>
```

The first statement has a simple delete and no records are returned. Notice the statement is issued by calling the Execute method. Because there will be no return from the query, you needn't have a variable on the left-hand side to catch the return value.

In the second statement, you issue a select, so you (probably) will have records coming back. The Execute method actually returns an ADO Recordset object, so you must have a variable on the left-hand site to catch the results. In fact, because it is an object, you have to use the "set" keyword. In this case, the rs variable will now be of type ADO Recordset, and you can then call all the properties and methods of the Recordset object. As is discussed later, this may or may not return the optimal type of recordset for your needs.

Finding the Number of Records Affected

In the previous code snippet, you started with a SQL delete statement. How many records did this delete statement just remove from the Foo table? There is a way to find out: using the second parameter of the Execute method. The first parameter is the CommandText. The second parameter, however, is the RecordsAffected parameter. This parameter is passed by reference, so OLE DB can set its value. After running the Execute method, you can examine the variable passed to the RecordsAffected parameter to see how many records were deleted. The code would look like this:

```
<%
dim lRecs
sSQL="Delete from Foo where FooID=3"
cn.Execute sSQL, lRecs
Response.Write "Number of records deleted: " & lRecs
%>
```

This parameter can obviously be used with both delete and update statements. With a select statement, the RecordsAffected is returned as a –1. Obtaining the number of records returned in a recordset is discussed in the next chapter.

Checking Errors

You have now seen how the Connection object can be used not only to connect to the database, but also to execute SQL statements. The Connection object can do one more thing for you: it stores a collection of Error objects. As you know, a single SQL statement can result in multiple error or warning messages from SQL Server. The Errors collection of the Connection object stores these errors in individual Error objects, and you can examine these Error objects to see what has happened when you issue your SQL statement. Return to the ADOTest application in VI for a moment and create a new ASP called Errors.asp. Make the code look like this:

```
<%@ Language=VBScript %>
<HTML>
<HEAD>

</HEAD>
<BODY>
<%
dim cn, sSQL, vErr, sErrMsg
On Error Resume Next
set cn=server.CreateObject("ADODB.Connection")
cn.Open(application("DBconn"))
sSQL="Delete from Foo"
cn.Execute sSQL
If cn.Errors.Count>0 then
    for each vErr in cn.Errors
        sErrMsg="Error number: " & vErr.Number & "<br>"
        sErrMsg=sErrMsg & "Description: " & vErr.Description & "<br>"
        sErrMsg=sErrMsg & "Source: " & vErr.Source  & "<br>"
        sErrMsg=sErrMsg & "SQL State: " & vErr.SQLState & "<br>"
        sErrMsg=sErrMsg & "Native Error: " & vErr.NativeError & "<br><br>"
        Response.Write sErrMsg
    next
end if
%>
</BODY>
</HTML>
```

Save and execute this page. You should wind up with a page similar to that in Figure 5-16. This screen shows you only one error was returned and this error is that no table named Foo exists. Because some statements can return more than one error or warning message, however, you have a For Each block in your VBScript to run through the entire Errors collection and look at all the Error objects. For each object, it prints a number of properties pertaining to that error. This block of code also has an On Error Resume Next statement.

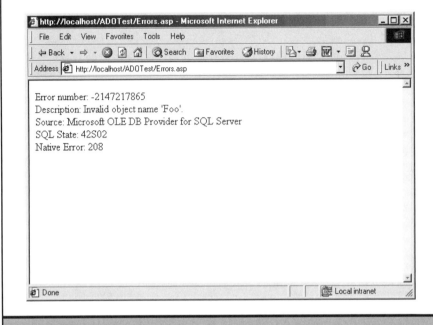

Figure 5-16.   The error message from the Error object in the Errors collection in the ADO Connection object

Setting Properties

You can do things a little differently with the Connection object. That is, you can set properties instead of passing parameters into the methods. For example, examine the following block of code:

```
<%
'These statements...
cn.ConnectionString=application("DBconn")
cn.Open

'...are equivalent to this one
cn.Open application("DBconn")
%>
```

In the first part, the connection string is set as a property of the Connection object, and then the Open method can be called without passing in the connection string. In the second example, the connection string is passed in as a parameter to the Open method. In this example, you may not save much, but as you examine the Command and Recordset objects later, setting parameters becomes more important.

Other properties have not yet been examined. For example, a ConnectionTimeout property determines how long ADO should attempt to connect to the database before giving up (the default is 15 seconds).

Transactions

The Connection object can also handle transactions for you. Quite simply, a transaction is an all-or-nothing approach to making changes. The classic example is moving money from savings to checking. If you are moving money, you need to delete the money from the savings account and add it to the checking account. Two distinct steps exist to this one logic transaction. If you complete just one step and then encounter a problem, your data would be in an inconsistent state: your savings would be minus money that never made it to checking or your checking account would have money in it that was never deducted from savings. The idea of a transaction is for both pieces to work or for neither piece to work.

The ADO connection object controls transaction through the BeginTrans, CommitTrans, and RollbackTrans methods. Examine the following code snippet:

```
<%
On Error Resume Next
set cn=Server.CreateObject("ADODB.Connection")
cn.Open application("DBconn")

cn.BeginTrans
cn.Execute "Update OrderDetails set Quantity=5 where OrderID=3 and ProductID=2"
cn.Execute "Update OrderDetails set Quantity='a' where OrderID=3 and ProductID=7"
if err.number<>0 then
   cn.RollbackTrans
else
   cn.CommitTrans
end if
```

In this example, you must turn on error-handling again with the On Error Resume Next statement. The first SQL statement is fine; you are updating a quantity to five. The second one, however, fails because you are trying to set a quantity to a string value. This causes an error to occur. Notice, however, you are in a transaction, thanks to the cn.BeginTrans statement. This means, even though the first SQL statement was fine, the value has not yet been updated in the database. After both statements run, you check to see if an error number is in the Err object (which is built into VBScript). If the error number is not zero, you call RollbackTrans, which reverses any statements that succeeded, such as the first SQL statement. If both statements had succeeded, you would have called cn.CommitTrans, and both records would be updated at once.

Better Living Through Constants

Remember earlier in the chapter when you looked at some code you could add to your ASPs so you could use some of the ADO constants? Now is the time to examine what some of those constants might be, and why they would be useful.

Two properties on the Connection object haven't been examined yet: Mode and IsolationLevel. Neither is critical for what you are doing, but both can give you added power. The *Mode property* indicates whether you have the ability to modify data in the Connection object, while *IsolationLevel* indicates the level of isolation for transactions started by the Connection object. Let's examine the following piece of code:

```
<%
dim cn
dim cmd
dim rs

set cn=server.CreateObject("ADODB.connection")
set cmd=server.CreateObject("ADODB.command")
cn.Mode=12
cn.IsolationLevel=256
cn.Open(application("DBConn"))
%>
```

NOTE: These are not recommended settings!

What does this code mean? What is a Mode of 12 and an IsolationLevel of 256? For those of us who programmed back in the early days of Visual Basic, we got used to these magic numbers. Microsoft now provides constants for most of these. Let's rewrite the code using the constants.

```
<!-- #Include File="adovbs.inc" -->
<%
dim cn
dim cmd
dim rs

set cn=server.CreateObject("ADODB.connection")
set cmd=server.CreateObject("ADODB.command")
cn.Mode=adModeShareExclusive
cn.IsolationLevel=adXactReadUncommitted
cn.Open(application("DBConn"))
%>
```

Granted, it's possible that you might not know exactly what "adModeShareExclusive" means, but if I tell you it prevents others from opening a connection, you can see what the word "exclusive" in it really means. Similarly, the "ReadUncommitted" in the IsolationLevel should let you know that with this setting, you can view uncommitted changes (although only in other transactions).

This code snippet assumes you have moved the file adovbs.inc into the same directory as the ASP itself. You can add the adovbs.inc file into your project if you want. If you chose the other method mentioned earlier—of adding the metadata tag with a reference to msado15.dll—you must include the path to the file or have it copied into the same directory as the ASP.

The Open method of the Connection object has four optional parameters. Only one of those is used here: the connection string.

The second and third options are a username and password, which aren't used because those are included in the connection string or connect via integrated security. The fourth parameter, however, is just called Options, and can be used to connect either synchronously (the default) or asynchronously. Because of the interpreted nature of ASP, asynchronous connections don't often make sense. However, asynchronous connections might make sense in standard Win32 applications, such as those written in Visual Basic or Visual C++.

The Execute method can also make use of constants. As you have seen, the Execute method takes a CommandText parameter, as well as a RecordsAffected parameter. A third parameter exists, which is optional, called Options. This is a catch-all parameter that tells the OLE DB provider how to evaluate the CommandText. The default is adCmdUnknown, which means OLE DB can figure out what it is. Other possible values include adCmdText, which tells OLE DB the command is either a command or a stored procedure name. If this sounds silly, realize you could pass a table name as the CommandText and set an option of adCmdTable, and you would get back a recordset of all the columns in that table. For example, these two blocks produce identical results:

```
<%
'These two statements...
sSQL="Select * from Customers"
set rs=cn.Execute(sSQL,,adCmdText)

'will return the same values as these two
sSQL="Customers"
set rs=cn.Execute(sSQL,,adCmdTable)
...
```

Other values can be passed as well, but you get the idea. Now, if OLE DB will figure out what you mean (the default is adCmdUnknown, remember) why do you specify it? Speed. Telling the engine what kind of command it is keeps the engine from having to figure it out, which saves time and speeds the query or command.

SUMMARY

A lot of information is in this chapter, and only one of the ADO objects was covered: the Connection object. You have seen how to make the connection to the database, *where* you should make the connection, and why. The next step is learning how to execute commands, call stored procedures, and work with recordsets. Chapter 6 deals with the Command and Recordset objects. Chapter 7 covers ADO MD, a different, and substantially more complex, object model for dealing with multidimensional data structures. Chapter 8 explains how to use English Query over the Web. Chapter 9 then examines some advanced features of ADO and also looks at XML.

CHAPTER 6

ADO: Commands and Recordsets

A great deal of time has been spent examining ADO. Most of this time was spent with the Connection object, which you saw could connect you to the database and execute SQL statements. The Connection object could return records, as long as a Recordset object was around to hold the records. If the Connection object can do all this, why do you need anything else? As you see, the Command object is often optional, but it is important for dealing with stored procedures. The Recordset object not only can hold records, but it can also let you modify records. Both the Command and Recordset objects have options that enable you to increase the performance of your Web applications significantly.

THE COMMAND OBJECT

Now that you have learned a bit about the Connection object, it's time to examine the second major object: the Command object. The purpose of the *Command object* is to execute commands. If this sounds like something you've been doing since Chapter 3, you're correct. However, the Command object has a number of special capabilities, many of which are for working with stored procedures. Are stored procedures a good thing? In almost every case, yes. Stored procedures can increase performance. If you currently do a lot with stored procedures, go to the head of the class. If, like many Web developers, you code all your SQL statements in the ASP, as you have done so far, learn about the power of stored procedures and use them to increase speed and achieve some measure of reusability.

Executing Statements

To begin, you can use a Command object to do just what you have been doing: executing SQL statements built into the ASP. In the ADOTest project from the previous chapter, create a new ASP called CommandObj.asp with the following code:

```
<%@ Language=VBScript %>
<HTML>
```

```
<HEAD>
</HEAD>
<BODY>
<!-- #include file="adovbs.inc" -->
<%
dim cn
dim cmd
dim rs

set cn=server.CreateObject("ADODB.connection")
set cmd=server.CreateObject("ADODB.command")
cn.Open(application("DBConn"))
sSQL="select CustomerID, CompanyName, " & _
      "ContactName, Country from Customers"
set cmd.ActiveConnection=cn
cmd.CommandText=sSQL
set rs=cmd.Execute
%>

<TABLE Border="1" Cellspacing="2" Cellpadding="2">
   <TR>
      <TH>Customer ID</TH>
      <TH>Company Name</TH>
      <TH>Contact Name</TH>
      <TH>Country</TH>
   </TR>
      <%
      do until rs.EOF
         Response.Write("<TR>")
         Response.Write("<TD>" & rs("CustomerID") & "</TD>")
         Response.Write("<TD>" & rs("CompanyName") & "</TD>")
         Response.Write("<TD>" & rs("ContactName") & "</TD>")
         Response.Write("<TD>" & rs("Country") & "</TD>")
         Response.Write("</TR>")
         rs.MoveNext
      loop
      %>
```

```
</TABLE>
</BODY>
</HTML>
```

This starts out much the same way as the example in the previous chapter using only the Connection object, but now you have an extra object. Obviously, you create a Command object, but you then set its ActiveConnection property to the Connection object. Next, you set its CommandText property to the SQL statement you created. At this point, the Command object has what it needs: it has the connection information and the statement to execute. Finally, you call the Execute method and, because this is a select statement, you return a Recordset object into the variable rs.

Connecting Without a Connection Object

Remember, you have seen that the ADO object model is very flat. What this means in part is that most of the ADO objects are independently creatable. You can create a Command object independent of a Connection object. Of course, if you don't create the Connection object, how will the Command object know how to connect to the database? The Command object can actually take a connection string as the value for its ActiveConnection property. For example, you could use the following statement:

```
cmd.ActiveConnection=application("DBconn")
```

Using this statement would completely eliminate the need to create a Connection object explicitly. The connection string in the application variable DBconn contains the server name, database name, and security credentials needed.

In reality, a Connection object is still created. However, you don't have a variable name with which to reference this Connection object and, therefore, you have no way to access it. In this example, you may not need to reference it, but this implies you cannot reference the Connection object's Errors collection. If you choose not to create a Connection object, you lose the ability to receive multiple error messages from the database because you do not have the Errors collection available.

In addition, if you are going to create multiple Command objects tied to the same database on the same server, you should create only one Connection object and set all the Command objects' ActiveConnection properties to that one Connection object. If you use the "no Connection object" method shown previously, each Command object would open its own connection to the database. Explicitly creating the Connection object would give you the control to ensure only one connection exists to the database and would give you access to the Errors collection.

Options when Executing Commands

Just as the Connection object could accept options to help optimize it, the Command object can accept many of the same arguments. For example, your code might look something like this:

```
sSQL="Update Customers set..."
cmd.CommandText=sSQL
cmd.Execute lRecs,,adCmdText + adExecuteNoRecords
```

In this example, you have an update statement, so no records are returned. You do, however, want to know how many records are affected by the update, so pass in a variable called lRecs, just as you did in Chapter 5 when you worked with the Connection object. Then skip the next parameter, which can be parameters you're passing into a stored procedure. The last argument contains your constants for optimization. Your command is not a stored procedure or table name, so tell ADO it is only a text string with a SQL statement or a stored procedure name in it, using the adCmdText constant. You also want to let ADO know you aren't returning any records, so it doesn't need to create the Recordset object. You do this by specifying the adExecuteNoRecords constant.

Working with Stored Procedures

Perhaps the main reason people use the Command object is to work with stored procedures. Calling stored procedures from the Connection object is possible by simply executing a SQL statement that calls a stored procedure. For example, create a new ASP called StoredProc.asp and type in the following code. A few comments were added to highlight the lines you will modify throughout this discussion.

```
<%@ Language=VBScript %>
<HTML>
<HEAD>
</HEAD>
<BODY>
<!-- #include file="adovbs.inc" -->
<%
dim cn
dim cmd
dim rs
set cn=server.CreateObject("ADODB.connection")
set cmd=server.CreateObject("ADODB.command")
cn.Open(application("DBConn"))
'********** These are the lines we will change
sSQL="exec CustOrderHist ANTON"
set rs=cn.Execute (sSQL,,adCmdText)
'*******************************************
%>

<TABLE Border="1" Cellspacing="2" Cellpadding="2">
   <TR>
      <TH>Product Name</TH>
      <TH>Total</TH>
   </TR>
   <%
   do until rs.EOF
      Response.Write("<TR>")
      Response.Write("<TD>" & rs("ProductName") & "</TD>")
      Response.Write("<TD>" & rs("Total") & "</TD>")
      Response.Write("</TR>")
      rs.MoveNext
   loop
   %>
```

```
</TABLE>
</BODY>
</HTML>
```

After running this ASP, you should wind up with a page similar to that shown in Figure 6-1. The stored procedure—called CustOrderHist—accepts one parameter, a customer ID. The procedure then calculates the number of each item this particular customer has ordered and returns the item and total.

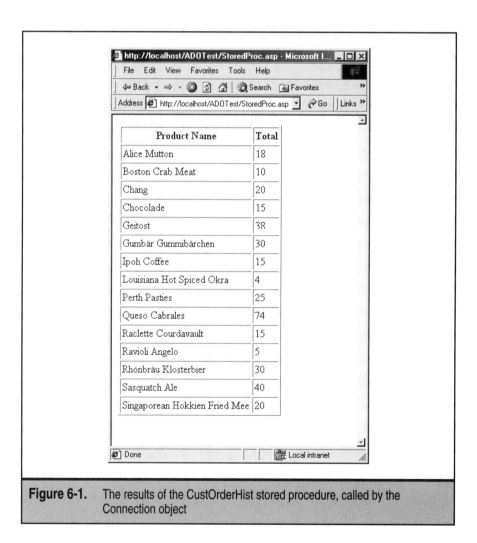

Product Name	Total
Alice Mutton	18
Boston Crab Meat	10
Chang	20
Chocolade	15
Geitost	38
Gumbär Gummibärchen	30
Ipoh Coffee	15
Louisiana Hot Spiced Okra	4
Perth Pasties	25
Queso Cabrales	74
Raclette Courdavault	15
Ravioli Angelo	5
Rhönbräu Klosterbier	30
Sasquatch Ale	40
Singaporean Hokkien Fried Mee	20

Figure 6-1.   The results of the CustOrderHist stored procedure, called by the Connection object

All this is well and good, but you want to use the Command object. You could just change a few lines of code and make it look like this:

```
'********** These are the lines we will change
sSQL="exec CustOrderHist ANTON"
set cmd.ActiveConnection=cn
cmd.CommandText=sSQL
set rs=cmd.Execute (,,adCmdText)
'***********************************************
```

Now, you have switched to using the Command object, and if you save and run this code, it should look just like Figure 6-1, which means it is identical to what you saw when using the Connection object.

The real strength of using the Command objects comes through when you start to use the Parameters collection, which is made up of Parameter objects. The purpose of *a Parameter object* is to represent a parameter or argument in the called stored procedure or parameterized query. In the previous example, the CustOrderHist stored procedure takes one parameter, a Customer ID. You pass this argument in on the command line through a SQL statement. Notice in the previous example, however, you still have it set as adCmdText, so you're telling ADO you are passing in a command string. You can tell ADO what you're calling a stored procedure, but to do this, you need a way to set the parameters. That is what the Parameters collection, with its Parameter objects, is all about. If you modify the previous code, you can make it look like this:

```
'********** These are the lines we will change
sSQL="CustOrderHist"
set cmd.ActiveConnection=cn
cmd.CommandText=sSQL
dim pCust
set pCust=cmd.CreateParameter("CustomerID",adVarChar,adParamInput,5)
cmd.Parameters.Append pCust
pCust.value="ANTON"
set rs=cmd.Execute (,,adCmdStoredProc)
'***********************************************
```

The results, once again, are identical to what you had in Figure 6-1. The differences in the code, however, are numerous. First, your SQL statement is only the name of the stored procedure now, without the "exec" keyword or the parameter value.

The next big difference is the creation of a variable, and then assigning that variable to a Parameter object. You create the Parameter object by calling a method of the Command object called CreateParameter. The CreateParameter method creates a Parameter object and assigns it certain values. In this case, the Parameter object is named "CustomerID." This name doesn't have to correspond to the actual parameter name in the stored procedure, although most people make them match for easier tracking. Second, you specify the data type of the parameter, using one of the ADO constants. You then specify the direction, meaning you tell ADO whether this is an input, output, input/output, return, or unknown type of parameter. Finally, you specify the size of the parameter as five characters.

At this point, you have created a Parameter object. However, the Parameter object, like the Connection, Command, and Recordset objects, can act as a free agent. The Parameter object is not currently owned by anyone; it is independent of the Command object, even though you used the Command object to create it. To tie this Parameter object to the Command object, you must append it to the Command object's Parameters collection, which you do using the Parameters collection's Append method. This adds a reference to the Parameter object into the Parameters collection. You can still directly access the Parameter object, which you do in the next line by setting the actual value you want to pass to the stored procedure.

Finally, you run the stored procedure by calling the Execute method and specifying you are calling a stored procedure by using the adCmdStoredProc constant. Executing this statement calls the stored procedure and sends along the parameters you have specified.

In this example, you set all the options on the line of the CreateParameter method. An alternative method to this would be to set properties of the Parameter object after it was created. For example, the previous code could look like this:

```
'********** These are the lines we will change
sSQL="CustOrderHist"
```

```
set cmd.ActiveConnection=cn
cmd.CommandText=sSQL
dim pCust
set pCust=cmd.CreateParameter("CustID")
pCust.Type=adChar
pCust.Direction=adParamInput
pCUst.Size=5
cmd.Parameters.Append pCust
pCust.value="ANTON"
set rs=cmd.Execute (,,adCmdStoredProc)
'***********************************************
```

In this example, you have simply set the various values after the object is created, instead of passing them in the method call to the CreateParameter method. In addition, notice in all these examples so far, you are setting the size of the parameter. This is required for any parameter type that is a variable length, which includes strings of all kinds. You must set the size before adding the Parameter object into the Parameters collection.

NOTE: Pay special attention to the size of parameters before you add them to the collection. Both variable- and fixed-length strings require you to set the size. If you don't do this, you get all sorts of interesting errors.

In addition, you must set the type of the parameter before it's added to the collection. This means you must specify adChar, adDate, adInteger, and so on before the parameter can be appended to the Parameters collection.

Calling Stored Procedures with Multiple Input Parameters

Calling a stored procedure with more than one parameter is fairly simple. You just have to create multiple Parameter objects and append them to the Parameters collection. For example, create a new page called EmpSalesByCountry.asp and enter the following code:

```
<%@ Language=VBScript %>
<% option explicit %>
<HTML>
<HEAD>
</HEAD>
<BODY>
<!-- #include file="adovbs.inc" -->
<%
dim cn
dim cmd
dim rs
dim sSQL
dim pBeginDate
dim pEndDate

set cn=server.CreateObject("ADODB.connection")
set cmd=server.CreateObject("ADODB.command")
cn.Open(application("DBConn"))
sSQL="[Employee Sales by Country]"
set cmd.ActiveConnection=cn
cmd.CommandText=sSQL



set pBeginDate=cmd.CreateParameter("Beginning_Date",adDate,adParamInput)
set pEndDate=cmd.CreateParameter("Ending_Date",adDate,adParamInput)
pBeginDate.Value="1/1/1998"
pEndDate.Value="12/31/1998"
cmd.Parameters.Append pBeginDate
cmd.Parameters.Append pEndDate
set rs=cmd.Execute (,,adCmdStoredProc)
%>
```

```
<TABLE Border="1" Cellspacing="2" Cellpadding="2">
    <TR>
        <TH>Country</TH>
        <TH>Salesperson</TH>
        <TH>Order No.</TH>
        <TH>Total</TH>
        <TH>Ship Date</TH>
    </TR>
    <%
    do until rs.EOF
        Response.Write("<TR>")
        Response.Write("<TD>" & rs("Country") & "</TD>")
        Response.Write("<TD>" & rs("FirstName") & _
            " " & rs("LastName") & "</TD>")
        Response.Write("<TD>" & rs("OrderID") & "</TD>")
        Response.Write("<TD>" & rs("SaleAmount") & "</TD>")
        Response.Write("<TD>" & rs("ShippedDate") & "</TD>")
        Response.Write("</TR>")
        rs.MoveNext
    loop
    %>
</TABLE>
</BODY>
</HTML>
```

The Employee Sales by Country stored procedure accepts two parameters as arguments: a beginning date and an ending date. Notice you just created two Parameter objects and, after setting the values, appended them to the Parameters collection. The only caution here is to make sure you add the parameters into the collection in the order in which they appear in the stored procedure. The name of the Parameter object you create doesn't make it automatically map to any particular parameter in the stored procedure, so take care you append them to the collection in the correct order. Figure 6-2 shows the results of this ASP.

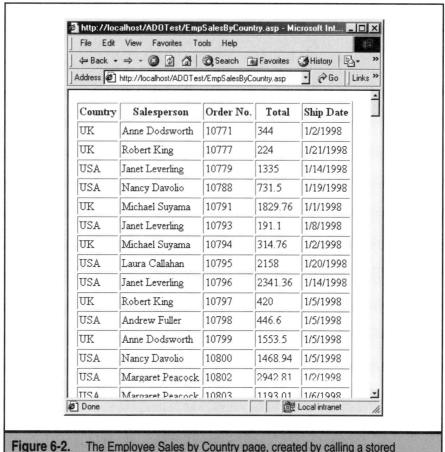

Figure 6-2.   The Employee Sales by Country page, created by calling a stored procedure with multiple input parameters

Working with Output Parameters

Some stored procedures have output parameters. Output parameters are actually an efficient way to return data and are used to retrieve both "extra" information and individual records. To work with output parameters, start with a simple stored procedure that enables you to add a new region to the database.

One thing to understand about the Region table in the Northwind database is that the RegionID field is not an identity column. If you want, feel free to modify the table to make the RegionID field an identity column. If you do this, just make sure you modify the code for the stored procedure to use the Region table.

If you don't want to alter the tables in the Northwind database, use the following script to create a new table called NewRegion. NewRegion is identical to Region except the RegionID field is an identity column. The Transact-SQL to create the table is

```
if exists (select * from dbo.sysobjects where
    id = object_id(N'NewRegion') and
    OBJECTPROPERTY(id, N'IsUserTable') = 1)
drop table NewRegion
GO


CREATE TABLE NewRegion (
      RegionID int IDENTITY (1, 1) NOT NULL ,
      RegionDescription nchar (50) NOT NULL
) ON [PRIMARY]
GO
```

The previous T-SQL should be run in Query Analyzer and not typed into an ASP. This is standard T-SQL for creating a table in SQL Server and, therefore, is outside what you want to do in InterDev (for now, at least).

Now that you have created a table with an identity column, it's time to create a stored procedure that enables you to insert a new region. An insert statement doesn't return any records, but what if your program needs to know the RegionID of the newly added region? Inserting a new record and wanting to know the ID of the new record is a common request, so your stored procedure passes back the identity of the newly created record using an output parameter. The code for the stored procedure is

```
CREATE PROCEDURE AddRegion
@RegionDesc nchar(50),
@NewRegionID int OUTPUT
AS
```

```
INSERT INTO NewRegion (RegionDescription)
VALUES (@RegionDesc)

set @NewRegionID=@@IDENTITY
GO
```

This Transact-SQL has created a stored procedure called AddRegion. It accepts a parameter from you for the region description, and then inserts a new record. The RegionID is assigned automatically because the RegionID field is an identity column. After the insert occurs, the stored procedure assigns the newly created identity value to the output parameter @NewRegionID.

The goal now is to capture the value of the output parameter in your calling program. This is done by creating a new Parameter object and setting its direction to adParamOutput. Create a new ASP called OutputParam.asp with the following code:

```
<%@ Language=VBScript %>
<% option explicit %>
<HTML>
<HEAD>
</HEAD>
<BODY>
<!-- #include file="adovbs.inc" -->
<%
dim cn
dim cmd
dim rs
dim pRegionDescription
dim pNewRegionID
dim lRecs
set cn=server.CreateObject("ADODB.connection")
set cmd=server.CreateObject("ADODB.command")
cn.Open(application("DBConn"))
set cmd.ActiveConnection=cn
cmd.CommandText="AddRegion"
cmd.CommandType=adCmdStoredProc
```

```
set pRegionDescription= _
    cmd.CreateParameter("RegionDesc",adChar,adParamInput,50)
set pNewRegionID= _
    cmd.CreateParameter("NewRegionID",adNumeric,adParamOutput)
pNewRegionID.Precision=4
pRegionDescription.Value="Xanadu"
cmd.Parameters.Append pRegionDescription
cmd.Parameters.Append pNewRegionID
cmd.Execute lRecs,,adExecuteNoRecords

Response.write cmd.Parameters("NewRegionID").Value
%>
</BODY>
</HTML>
```

Upon execution of this ASP, you get back a number in IE showing the identity of the new record. If you get it right the first time, the number will simply be 1. If you keep hitting the refresh button, the number climbs by one each time, as new records are added to the table.

To make this work, you had to create two Parameter objects: one for the input parameter and one for the output parameter. After setting the necessary properties of the Parameter objects and adding them to the Parameters collection, you executed the Command object. On execution, the values of the output parameters are returned to any Parameter objects you defined as having a direction of adParamOutput. In this case, you had only one, NewRegionID. To retrieve the value out of the Parameter object, you simply ask for the "NewRegionID" parameter in the Parameters collection and pull out the Value property. In reality, Value is the default property, so specifying Value is optional, but recommended.

Dealing with Return Codes

A stored procedure can return an integer as a return value that can indicate success or some form of failure in the stored procedure. Handling return codes is fairly straightforward: it's just another direction of a Parameter object. You create a Parameter object and set its direction to adParamReturnValue. For example, here's a simple example of a stored procedure. I've actually left out what the stored procedure does and assumed a "success" or "failure" value is being passed back:

```
CREATE PROCEDURE AddRegion2
AS
-- Some processing task...


IF @@ERROR<>0
BEGIN
    RETURN(1)
END
ELSE
BEGIN
    RETURN(0)
END
GO
```

The procedure includes a simplified error-handling routine that returns a 0 back to the client on successful completion of the task—or a 1 on a failure of the task. You can check for this return value using the following code. Again, this code is scaled down to the bare minimum to show you how to retrieve the return value.

```
<%
dim pReturnCode
dim lRecs
set cn=server.CreateObject("ADODB.connection")
set cmd=server.CreateObject("ADODB.command")
cn.Open(application("DBConn"))
set cmd.ActiveConnection=cn
cmd.CommandText="AddRegion2"
cmd.CommandType=adCmdStoredProc
set pReturnCode= _
    cmd.CreateParameter("ReturnCode",adInteger,adParamReturnValue)
cmd.Parameters.Append pReturnCode
cmd.Execute lRecs,,adExecuteNoRecords
If cmd.Parameters("ReturnCode").Value=0 Then
    'success code...
```

```
Else
    'failure code...
End If
%>
```

In this VBScript snippet, you simply create a parameter and set its type to adInteger and its direction to adParamReturnValue. To retrieve the value, ask for the value of the parameter from the Parameters collection, just as you did for an output parameter.

NOTE: In this example, the name of the return parameter, ReturnValue, is only a name. This is not a magic keyword.

Returning a Record with Output Parameters or a Recordset

One thing you can do with output parameters is to return multiple fields of a single record. For example, someone may pass you a ProductID, and then you return the product name, category name, supplier name, and unit price. You could return these fields using a recordset, which would be the common way to do it. However, you could return the fields using output parameters from a stored procedure. The advantage of using output parameters is that there is no need for building a Recordset object, which is both faster and requires less overhead on the client. Let's build the following two stored procedures to look at the difference:

```
CREATE PROCEDURE ProductInfo
@ProductID int
AS
SELECT p.ProductName,
       c.CategoryName,
       s.CompanyName,
       p.UnitPrice
FROM Products p INNER JOIN Suppliers s ON p.SupplierID = s.SupplierID
     INNER JOIN Categories c ON p.CategoryID = c.CategoryID
WHERE p.ProductID=@ProductID
GO
```

This stored procedure, ProductInfo, simply returns a resultset to the client (in this case, an ASP), which is then stored in an ADO Recordset object.

```
CREATE PROCEDURE ProductInfo2
@ProductID int,
@ProductName nvarchar(40) OUTPUT,
@CompanyName nvarchar(40) OUTPUT,
@CategoryName nvarchar(15) OUTPUT,
@UnitPrice money OUTPUT
AS
SELECT @ProductName=p.ProductName,
       @CategoryName=c.CategoryName,
       @CompanyName=s.CompanyName,
       @UnitPrice=p.UnitPrice
FROM Products p INNER JOIN Suppliers s ON p.SupplierID = s.SupplierID
     INNER JOIN Categories c ON p.CategoryID = c.CategoryID
WHERE p.ProductID=@ProductID
GO
```

The second stored procedure, ProductInfo2, returns the fields using output parameters, so no ADO Recordset object needs to be created on the client.

The client code to call these two stored procedures is different, of course. Building an ASP to make only one call to each stored procedure won't give you a noticeable difference. I've built a couple of not-quite-scientific pages that loop for 30 seconds, however, making calls to the stored procedures and keeping a running count while doing so. At the end of the 30 seconds, the total number of calls made are displayed, as well as the fields that were returned.

The first ASP, which I named CallSP.asp, calls the ProductInfo stored procedure. In other words, the stored procedure returns a resultset, or cursor, for each call, which you have to store in an ADO Recordset object. The code is

```
<%@ Language=VBScript %>
<% option explicit %>
<HTML>
<HEAD>
```

```
</HEAD>
<BODY>
<!-- #include file="adovbs.inc" -->
<%
dim cn
dim cmd
dim rs
dim pProductID

set cn=server.CreateObject("ADODB.connection")
set cmd=server.CreateObject("ADODB.command")
set pProductID= _
    cmd.CreateParameter("ProductID",adInteger,adParamInput)
cn.Open(application("DBConn"))
set cmd.ActiveConnection=cn
cmd.CommandText="ProductInfo"
cmd.Parameters.Append pProductID
pProductID.Value=1
dim StartTime
starttime=Time
dim lCount
lCount=0
do while DateDiff("s",StartTime,time)<30
    lCount=lCount+1
    set rs=cmd.Execute (,,adCmdStoredProc)
loop
response.write lCount
%>

<TABLE Border="1" Cellspacing="2" Cellpadding="2">
   <TR>
       <TH>Product Name</TH>
       <TH>Category Name</TH>
       <TH>Company Name</TH>
       <TH>Total</TH>
   </TR>
       <%
```

```
        do until rs.EOF
            Response.Write("<TR>")
            Response.Write("<TD>" & rs("ProductName") & "</TD>")
            Response.Write("<TD>" & rs("CategoryName") & "</TD>")
            Response.Write("<TD>" & rs("CompanyName") & "</TD>")
            Response.Write("<TD>" & rs("UnitPrice") & "</TD>")
            Response.Write("</TR>")
            rs.MoveNext
        loop
        %>
</TABLE>
</BODY>
</HTML>
```

The second ASP, creatively named CallSP2.asp, calls the ProductInfo2 stored procedure, which only returns data via output parameters. The page does the same processing as the previous one, looping for 30 seconds and repeatedly calling the stored procedure. At the end, it prints out the number of times through the loop, as well as the fields, which are held in the Value property of the Parameter objects. The code for CallSP2.asp is

```
<%@ Language=VBScript %>
<% option explicit %>
<HTML>
<HEAD>
</HEAD>
<BODY>
<!-- #include file="adovbs.inc" -->
<%
dim cn
dim cmd
dim rs
dim pProductID
dim pProductName, pCompanyName, pCategoryName, pUnitPrice

set cn=server.CreateObject("ADODB.connection")
set cmd=server.CreateObject("ADODB.command")
```

```
set pProductID= _
   cmd.CreateParameter("ProductID",adInteger,adParamInput)
set pProductName= _
   cmd.CreateParameter("ProductName",adVarChar,adParamOutput,40)
set pCompanyName= _
   cmd.CreateParameter("CompanyName",adVarChar,adParamOutput,40)
set pCategoryName= _
   cmd.CreateParameter("CategoryName",adVarChar,adParamOutput,15)
set pUnitPrice= _
   cmd.CreateParameter("UnitPrice",adCurrency,adParamOutput)
cn.Open(application("DBConn"))
set cmd.ActiveConnection=cn
cmd.CommandText="ProductInfo2"
cmd.Parameters.Append pProductID
cmd.Parameters.Append pProductName
cmd.Parameters.Append pCompanyName
cmd.Parameters.Append pCategoryName
cmd.Parameters.Append pUnitPrice
pProductID.Value=1
dim StartTime
starttime=Time
dim lCount
lCount=0
do while DateDiff("s",StartTime,time)<30
      lCount=lCount+1
      cmd.Execute ,,adCmdStoredProc + adExecuteNoRecords
loop
response.write lCount
%>


<TABLE Border="1" Cellspacing="2" Cellpadding="2">
   <TR>
      <TH>Product Name</TH>
      <TH>Category Name</TH>
      <TH>Company Name</TH>
      <TH>Total</TH>
   </TR>
```

```
<%
Response.Write("<TR>")
Response.Write("<TD>" & cmd.Parameters("ProductName").Value  & "</TD>")
Response.Write("<TD>" & cmd.Parameters("CategoryName").Value & "</TD>")
Response.Write("<TD>" & cmd.Parameters("CompanyName").Value & "</TD>")
Response.Write("<TD>" & cmd.Parameters("UnitPrice").Value & "</TD>")
Response.Write("</TR>")
%>
</TABLE>
</BODY>
</HTML>
```

Both CallSP.asp and CallSP2.asp produce results similar to Figure 6-3. Note, the number above the table represents the number of times the stored procedure was called in 30 seconds. Your number will be different, but the number in CallSP2.asp should be higher than the number in CallSP.asp.

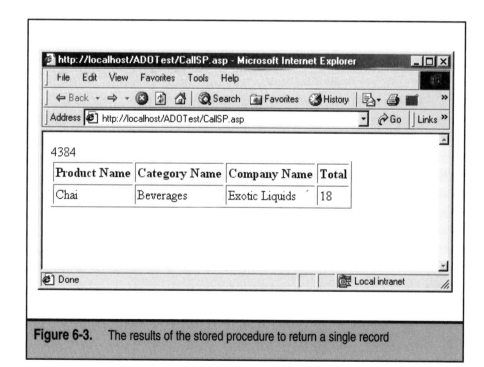

Figure 6-3.   The results of the stored procedure to return a single record

The results aren't perfect and, if you click the refresh button, you can see the actual number can fluctuate. In fact, the number can fluctuate wildly if you perform other tasks on your machine, such as starting a new application. Still, repeatedly running the page without any other processor-intensive tasks running in the background usually gives you numbers within a 10 percent range.

Just how much faster is it to return output parameters instead of returning a recordset? In my tests, the CallSP.asp averaged 4,780 calls in 30 seconds, while CallSP2.asp averaged 16,823 calls per 30 seconds! This is an increase of 252 percent, which is a significant number. As you can see, this is a great technique for enhancing performance when retrieving single records.

THE RECORDSET OBJECT

The third, and final, top-level object you examine for now is the ADO Recordset object. You have already used the Recordset object a lot; both the Connection and Command objects return Recordset objects when their source statements return records. The Recordset object is powerful and it can perform many of the functions you have seen previously. Not only can it execute statements that return records, it can also connect you to the database. The important thing to remember about the Recordset object is it is the only object that can actually hold records in memory.

Opening Recordsets

You can modify your earlier CommandObj.asp to use only a Recordset object by making the code look like this:

```
<%@ Language=VBScript %>
<HTML>
<HEAD>
</HEAD>
<BODY>
<!-- #include file="adovbs.inc" -->
<%
```

```
dim rs
set rs=server.CreateObject("ADODB.Recordset")
sSQL="select CustomerID, CompanyName, " & _
    "ContactName, Country from Customers"
rs.Open sSQL,application("DBConn")
%>

<TABLE Border="1" Cellspacing="2" Cellpadding="2">
    <TR>
        <TH>Customer ID</TH>
        <TH>Company Name</TH>
        <TH>Contact Name</TH>
        <TH>Country</TH>
    </TR>
    <%
    do until rs.EOF
        Response.Write("<TR>")
        Response.Write("<TD>" & rs("CustomerID") & "</TD>")
        Response.Write("<TD>" & rs("CompanyName") & "</TD>")
        Response.Write("<TD>" & rs("ContactName") & "</TD>")
        Response.Write("<TD>" & rs("Country") & "</TD>")
        Response.Write("</TR>")
        rs.MoveNext
    loop
    %>
</TABLE>
</BODY>
</HTML>
```

In this example, the only object explicitly created is the Recordset object. You use the Open method to perform the equivalent of a Connection.Open and a Connection.Execute (or Command.Execute). The Recordset object makes the connection to the database using the connection string (or a valid Connection object), and then executes the statement. The records are returned and then held in memory in the Recordset object.

In this example, you don't have an explicit ADO Connection object so, once again, you don't have access to the ADO Errors collection. To use a Connection object, you can modify the code to look like this:

```
<%
dim cn
dim rs

set cn=server.CreateObject("ADODB.connection")
set rs=server.CreateObject("ADODB.Recordset")
cn.Open application("DBConn")
sSQL="select CustomerID, CompanyName, " & _
    "ContactName, Country from Customers"
rs.Open sSQL,cn
%>
```

In this example, you now have a valid Connection object and, therefore, could access the Errors collection if needed.

The Recordset.Open can be used to call stored procedures simply by making the SQL statement "exec <stored procedure name>". Notice that using only the Recordset object would prevent you from receiving the values of return codes or output parameters from a stored procedure; you need a Command object for that.

Navigating Recordsets

What a recordset physically looks like in memory isn't important; what it looks like logically is important. The easiest way to imagine a recordset in memory is to picture a spreadsheet. If you imagine each record taking up one row, with the columns being the fields of the record, you have a pretty good idea of what a recordset looks like.

When you have a recordset in memory, only one current record exists at a time. This means if you ask for a particular field, such as the SupplierName, you get the supplier only for the current record. If you move to the next record, you get the SupplierName field for that record. All records look alike, however, so all records have a SupplierName field (although, depending on your database, the value in SupplierName for any particular record could be null).

When you open a recordset, you are on the first record by default. This means you can immediately start looking at field values. To move to the next record, you simply use the MoveNext method of the Recordset object. This moves your data pointer from one record to the next one. When you initially return a recordset, you don't know how many records are in it. There is a RecordCount property, but it is negative one (-1) when you first open the recordset with most OLE DB providers. How to get the real RecordCount is discussed in a moment.

If the *MoveNext* method moves you down one record in the recordset, *MovePrevious* moves you up one record in the recordset. MoveNext works with any cursor type (see the next section) while MovePrevious only works some of the time. Still, it is the way to walk backwards through a recordset.

If moving one record at a time seems tedious, you can use two other methods: MoveFirst and MoveLast. *MoveFirst* simply moves you to the first record in the recordset. *MoveLast* moves you to the last record in the recordset. If this sounds simple, it is. But, I can hear you saying, "Look, Craig, you just told us we don't know how many records just came back, so how can MoveLast move us to the last record of the database?"

Good question. Think back to the spreadsheet sitting there in memory holding your records. Right after the last record is a marker called *EOF,* which stands for *End of File.* The EOF marker says there aren't any more records. The EOF is *not* a record, but you can be sitting on it as your current "record" which can cause you some trouble if you aren't careful.

Imagine you've been using the MoveNext method and you're sitting on what is actually the last record. You don't know it's the last record, so you issue another MoveNext. Now, you're sitting on the EOF marker. You better check to see if you're on the EOF marker, because if you try to retrieve a field value, you'll get an error. For example, asking for rs("SupplierName") is valid for any field, but it's not valid for the EOF. So, after each MoveNext, you should check to see if you're on the EOF. Do this by checking the EOF property of the Recordset object. The code looks like this:

```
If rs.EOF Then
```

This statement is also equivalent to:

```
If rs.EOF=True Then
```

Both of these will determine if you have reached the EOF marker. You have gotten around this so far by simply looping until the recordset's EOF property is true.

Just as an EOF marker exists, there is a BOF, or Beginning of File, marker at the beginning of the recordset. Remember, you start on the first record, not the BOF. One easy way to determine if a recordset returned any records is to check the BOF status right after opening the recordset. For example, this code opens the recordset, and then checks to see if records were returned:

```
...
set rs=cn.Open(sSQL)
if rs.BOF then
    Response.Write ("No records found")
else
    'do stuff
end if
```

An alternative approach is to check both the BOF and EOF properties. If both are true, then you have an empty recordset. In the previous example, checking both would be unnecessary, but many people still do check both because it's much clearer to any developer who comes along later that, if you are checking for both EOF and BOF to be true at the same time, you are checking for an empty recordset.

If you happen to be on the EOF and issue a MoveNext, you get an error. Similarly, if you're on the BOF and issue a MovePrevious, you get an error. The MoveLast is safe because it runs through the records until it finds the EOF, and then it does the equivalent of a MovePrevious to wind up on the last real record. The MoveFirst is similar, looking for the BOF, and then doing the equivalent of a MoveNext to wind up at the first record. Figure 6-4 shows what the recordset looks like, logically, in memory. The fields are shown as a grid, or a spreadsheet. Above the records is a BOF marker, and after the records is an EOF marker. Moving beyond the BOF or EOF results in an error.

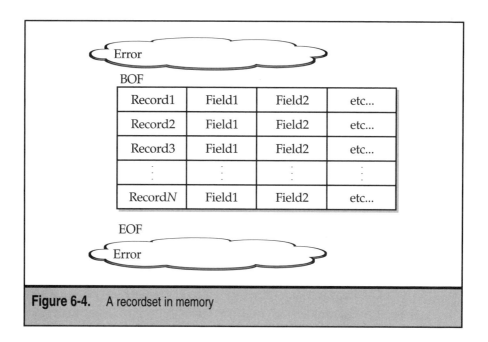

Figure 6-4. A recordset in memory

Once you hit the EOF, which means all the records have been accessed, the RecordCount property is accurate. The RecordCount is only accurate after all the records have been accessed, which is why it's negative one when you first open the recordset. Some people do an immediate MoveLast, and then a MoveFirst to get an accurate record count, but this process can be slow with large recordsets, and it assumes a fully scrollable cursor, which is typically not efficient, especially for Web applications. Unsure of what a fully scrollable cursor is? Read on.

Cursor Types

The Open method of the Recordset object can take five arguments. The first two arguments are simple: they are the source (or command) and the active connection (be it a connection object or a connection string). The last three parameters can affect performance and overhead. The third argument represents the cursor type. Four cursor types are available: forward-only, static, keyset, and dynamic.

The default cursor type is forward-only. The *forward-only* cursor is sometimes called a *firehose* cursor because it works like a firehose; the data comes down to the client in a stream that can only be read by performing a MoveNext. Of the various forms of cursors, forward-only can be the most efficient. The forward-only cursor can only be stepped through by moving forward one record at a time. In other words, you cannot jump to the first or last record, or move to the previous record. The data in a forward-only cursor can be updateable, but only the current record can be updated.

> **NOTE:** Even though this cursor type is called a forward-scrolling cursor, Microsoft says it is actually cursorless; in other words, it doesn't create a cursor in SQL Server.

The forward-only cursor is unable to see changes made to the underlying data once you open the cursor. If another user adds or deletes a record while you are looping through the recordset, or if a record in your recordset is modified while you run through it, you won't see those changes. Changes aren't seen because a copy of the data is captured, but presented to the user as only a single record at a time. You can see this behavior by opening a forward-only cursor and using the SQL Enterprise Manager to delete a record that hasn't yet been accessed by the cursor. The cursor still sees the record, relying on the copy that was made when the cursor was first opened.

The *static* cursor is similar to the forward-only cursor in that it makes a copy of all the data at once. The static cursor, however, is fully scrollable, which means you can jump to the first or last record, or move forward or backward one record at a time. Because the data is a copy, the cursor won't be aware of additions, deletions, or changes to the underlying data. Static cursors can be important too because they enable you to pull down all the data and, if you choose, to disconnect from the database. Therefore, you can work with the records locally and not have a live connection. This is called a disconnected recordset, which is covered in Chapter 9. You also see that saving a static cursor and allowing others to access it is possible, completely obviating the need to connect to the database.

The *keyset* cursor is a fully scrollable cursor that simply builds a cursor containing a list of the keys for the records to be accessed, but it does *not* grab all the values for the fields for each record. Instead, as the cursor moves from one record to another, that record is accessed from the underlying database to make sure the data returned is the most current. This means the cursor is aware of updates made to the data but, because the cursor builds a list of keys, you don't see additions and deletions. If you are scrolling through the list of keys and a particular record has been deleted, you receive a trappable error telling you the record has been deleted.

NOTE: We say the cursor goes back to the database for each record. By default, this is true, but you can modify the CacheSize property of the recordset so you actually retrieve more than one record at once. Increasing the cache size can lead to better performance by reducing round-trips to the database server.

The last cursor type is the dynamic cursor. The *dynamic* cursor is fully scrollable and, like the keyset cursor, can see changes to the underlying data. Unlike keyset cursors, the dynamic cursor can also see additions and deletions on the fly. You can imagine the cursor constantly monitoring the situation to make sure it has the latest information. You can also imagine the dynamic cursor requires the most overhead.

Which cursor should you use? Like the question of where to make the database connection, it depends. Most of the time, with Web applications, you are making a single pass through the data because you are displaying the data in a table or list box or some similar list. Most of the time with Web applications, therefore, forward-only cursors make the most sense. They are the friendliest cursors as far as resources, which is good both for keeping overhead to a minimum and maximizing speed. If having the most current data is critical to you, a keyset or dynamic cursor will have to do. Static cursors can present some interesting possibilities, which are examined in more detail in Chapter 9 when disconnected recordsets are discussed.

Cursor Locations

Cursors can reside in one of two locations: on the client or on the server. When client-side cursors are discussed, however, realize the client here is the Web server running the ASP—this doesn't mean sending the cursor (or recordset) down to the client running IE. Sending data down to the browser is discussed in Chapter 12.

For now, you need to consider what happens when you place the cursor on the client or the server. The default is to use a server-side cursor, which means the cursor set is created on the database server in some temporary storage area, such as tempdb. In some cases, server-side cursors can give you improved performance: I once worked with a client who had a query that could return recordsets ranging from one to two million records in size. At first, the client was using a client-side static cursor. When the query returned two million records, the entire contents of the recordset had to be copied across the network down to the client, where he then printed the first 100 records. The time required to copy the entire recordset to the client—approximately 15 seconds to bring down the cursor—turned out to be a killer. This was a full 15 seconds the user sat waiting for any kind of response. In an attempt to speed the query, we moved to using a server-side cursor. The response time dropped from 15 seconds to 2 seconds! This isn't a guarantee that you'll see such speed improvements, but using server-side cursors can speed your application in most cases.

NOTE: Server-side cursors attempt to use the vendor's cursor engine. Not all vendors support all the features discussed, such as the four different cursor types. Microsoft provides the Microsoft Cursor Service for OLE DB, which tries to simulate all the cursor functionality across various back-end databases. Because this book focuses on SQL Server, differences in other database cursor engines aren't discussed.

If server-side cursors can speed the application, why wouldn't you always use them? The main reason, of course, is because of the additional resources required on the server. If you maintain a large number of cursors on the database server, you can consume vast amounts of temporary storage and, eventually, overburden the server. Now, understand that server-side cursors are the default, and throughout this book so far, all we have used are server-side cursors.

The cursor location can be set for the Recordset or Connection object. The setting must be made before the recordset is opened. Changing the value after the recordset is opened won't have any effect on the current recordset.

Client-side cursors only allow one type of cursor: static. This means the lightweight forward-scrolling cursor and the powerful, more "real-time" keyset and dynamic cursors, must be kept on the server. This means static cursors should be used with care. They make a copy of all the data, which means you don't have to make round-trips back to the database server, but it means all the fields for all the records must be moved to the Web server. Large recordsets using a static cursor can take a considerable amount of time to bring to the client and, again, the client here is your ASP running in IIS, not the browser sitting down on the client machine. Bringing down recordsets asynchronously is possible, but this usually doesn't make sense for Web applications because you can't return an HTML stream to the client until the data is back. Despite this limitation, using static cursors can be a performance booster in the right cases, as you see in Chapter 9.

Lock Types

Just as four types of cursor types can greatly affect performance, you must concern yourself with four types of locks. You haven't yet inserted, updated, or deleted records with the Recordset object. To use this functionality, you need to open a recordset that is updateable and, by default, recordsets are read-only. This is good, by the way, because read-only recordsets require the least overhead. The default lock type, adLockReadOnly, is what you have used so far. If you want to try another type of lock, make sure you set the lock type before opening the recordset. You can do this by setting the LockType property of the Recordset object or by specifying the lock type as a parameter in the Open statement.

If you want to update records using the Recordset object, which is examined in the next section, you must open the recordset with a lock type other than adLockReadOnly. The first such lock type examined is optimistic locking, which is referenced by adLockOptimistic. *Optimistic locking* implies the record is not locked until the update is actually attempted. In a real-world environment, this means two people could be editing the same record at the same time. Both users would be on the same record, making changes. When the first user is done, he presses the submit button and the record is updated. The second user then finishes and presses the submit button, but her changes would overwrite some of the ones the first user just applied. Optimistic locking is called optimistic because you don't believe this will happen. In systems with a small number of updates, optimistic locking usually works fine. As you can imagine, optimistic locking keeps the locks around a very small amount of time.

In contrast to optimistic locking, *pessimistic locking* can be used by specifying the constant adLockPessimistic. This lock type avoids the previously mentioned problem by placing a lock on the record as soon as the first user starts to edit the record. In other words, the lock is placed on the record early, so the second user couldn't even start to edit it until the first user releases his lock by either updating the record or canceling his changes. If the second user attempted to make a change to the record, she would receive a message that the record was locked. As you can see, pessimistic locking holds locks on the database much longer, which may be necessary in situations where many updates are made to the records. SQL Server developers are taught to minimize locks whenever possible. Locks use resources and they limit access to the records. Pessimistic locks, therefore, are rarely used.

The last type of locking is *batch optimistic locking,* specified by adLockBatchOptimistic. Batch optimistic locking isn't supported by all databases and, with SQL Server, it is supported only when using keyset or static cursors. Normally, when you update a record with ADO, you are only updating the current record. With batch optimistic locking, you can make a number of changes, and then apply them all at once. No locks are put on the database until all the record updates are attempted. The database then applies row, page, or table locks to the table, depending on its own analysis of the most efficient method.

Be aware of these two facts when you use batch optimistic updates:

▼   This is not a transaction. If you have changed three records and two are successful but one fails, you get an error. You must check the Errors collection to determine which updates failed and why.

▲ The order of the updates is not necessarily the same order in which you made the changes. In other words, if one record is dependent on another, you cannot guarantee the updates will be made in the correct order.

Updating Records

It should come as no surprise that retrieving records isn't enough. You also need a way to update the records. Two main approaches exist to update records: using the recordset with an updateable lock type/cursor type combination or executing statements using the Connection or Command objects. Using the Connection or Command object to execute SQL statements or stored procedures can have a dramatically positive effect on scalability and resources. Using the Recordset object to make changes is usually easier.

Modifying Records using the Recordset Object

Modifying records using the Recordset object requires that you open a cursor with a lock type of something other than adLockReadOnly. By opening the recordset with an updateable lock, you allow inserts, updates, and deletions to be made to the records as you scroll through them. With optimistic or pessimistic locking, you can change the current record. With batch optimistic, you can make a number of changes and submit them all at once. Updating records with the Recordset object is fairly simple, as the following code shows. Start by creating a new ASP called ModifySuppliers.asp. Enter the following code:

NOTE: You are about to begin making changes to the data in the Northwind database. If you prefer to keep Northwind "pure," feel free to make a copy of the database and make these changes to the copy. Just make sure to update the database connection string in the Global.asa file to point to the new database you create.

```
<%@ Language=VBScript %>
<HTML>
<HEAD>
```

```
</HEAD>
<BODY>
<!-- #include file="adovbs.inc" -->
<%
dim cn
dim rs
dim sSQL

set cn=server.CreateObject("ADODB.Connection")
set rs=server.CreateObject("ADODB.Recordset")
cn.Open application("DBconn")
 '****** these are the lines of code that will change
sSQL="select * from Suppliers"
rs.Open sSQL,cn,adOpenKeyset,adLockOptimistic,adCmdText
rs.AddNew
    rs("CompanyName")="Westie Enterprises"
    rs("ContactName")="Torrey Spinoza"
    rs("ContactTitle")="Top Dog"
rs.Update
rs.Close
sSQL="select * from Suppliers order by SupplierID desc"
rs.Open sSQL,cn
Response.Write "Company: " & rs("CompanyName") & "<br>"
Response.Write "Contact: " & rs("ContactName") & "<br>"
Response.Write "Title: " & rs("ContactTitle")
'****** here end the lines of code that will change
%>
</BODY>
</HTML>
```

This ASP shows you how to add a record to the Suppliers table. You only fill in the first three fields of the record for simplicity. To get to the point where you could add records, you simply open a recordset by using the Open method, but set the cursor type to keyset and the lock type to optimistic. This gives you an updateable, fully scrollable cursor. You then call the AddNew method of the Recordset object. The AddNew method sets a property of the Recordset object called EditMode to adEditAdd. This means you are now adding a new record, but the changes are cached on the client until you call the Update method of the Recordset object. When you call the Update method, the record is sent to the database and the insert is made.

After adding the new record, you simply query the Suppliers table, retrieving the records in reverse order. The first record is the one you just added, so you print the three fields of the record you just added, in case you don't believe the insert was made.

Now, let's modify this record. Add a value to a field that is currently null and you can change one of the fields you just added. For brevity, just list the code between the comments. Change ModifySuppliers.asp to look like this:

```
'****** these are the lines of code that will change
sSQL="select * from Suppliers order by SupplierID desc"
rs.Open sSQL,cn,adOpenKeyset,adLockOptimistic,adCmdText
rs("ContactTitle")="CEO"
rs("Region")="West Highlands"
rs.Update
rs.Close
sSQL="select * from Suppliers order by SupplierID desc"
rs.Open sSQL,cn
Response.Write "Company: " & rs("CompanyName") & "<br>"
Response.Write "Contact: " & rs("ContactName") & "<br>"
Response.Write "Title: " & rs("ContactTitle") & "<br>"
Response.Write "Region: " & rs("Region")
'****** here end the lines of code that will change
```

You have now retrieved a recordset with the records in descending order by SupplierID, so your new record is first. Then just start making changes. You could have explicitly changed the EditMode to adEditInProgress, but this happens automatically when you pick a field and set it to a new value. After changing the values of two fields, call the Update method and the new values are sent to the database where updates are made into the database. Once again, you retrieve the records and show the fields for your record, to prove the changes have been made.

Finally, let's get rid of this new record. Modify the ASP to delete the record. Be careful; I'm only going to delete the last record in the database. If you try to call this page multiple times, you could delete records that came with the Northwind database or you could receive a foreign key violation. To delete this record, make the code look like this:

```
'****** these are the lines of code that will change
sSQL="select * from Suppliers order by SupplierID desc"
rs.Open sSQL,cn,adOpenKeyset,adLockOptimistic,adCmdText
rs.Delete
rs.Close
sSQL="select * from Suppliers order by SupplierID desc"
rs.Open sSQL,cn
Response.Write "Company: " & rs("CompanyName") & "<br>"
Response.Write "Contact: " & rs("ContactName") & "<br>"
Response.Write "Title: " & rs("ContactTitle") & "<br>"
'****** here end the lines of code that will change
```

This code simply opens a recordset and then calls the Delete method. This deletes the current record. You are deleting the first one here, which, of course, is the last one you added. If you added more than one, you can keep refreshing the page until you see a "real" record. Don't delete beyond that if you want to preserve the original data.

Modifying Records Without a Recordset Object

Using a Recordset object's methods to add, update, and delete records is simple, however, it isn't always recommended. Why? Quite simply, opening a recordset for editing purposes requires a lot more overhead than opening a forward-scrolling, read-only recordset. To enable editing on a recordset, you must open a cursor with some sort of lock type other than read-only. This requires resources on the server and client. With pessimistic locking, you keep locks around for a long time (in computer time) and potentially interfere with the work of other users.

To minimize locks and resources, most people use the Execute method of either the Connection or Command objects to run SQL statements or stored procedures. Insert, update, and delete statements don't return records, so the Execute method is preferred over creating a recordset just to make the change. If you need to retrieve records first, you should use a forward-scrolling, read-only recordset to minimize overhead. Then, you make your changes with the Execute method to minimize overhead and reduce lock time to a bare minimum.

In your ModifySuppliers.asp, you could have added your first record into the database using a SQL statement built into the page or by calling a stored procedure. Because stored procedures were already covered in this chapter, you won't create one for this purpose. Instead, let's embed the SQL into the page with the understanding that you'd probably want to build a stored procedure to handle this in the future.

Take the ModifySuppliers.asp page and make the following changes:

```
'****** these are the lines of code that will change
sSQL="Insert into Suppliers " & _
    "(CompanyName,ContactName,ContactTitle) " & _
    "values ('Westie Enterprises', " & _
    "'Torrey Spinoza', 'Top Dog')"
cn.Execute sSQL,,adExecuteNoRecords
sSQL="select * from Suppliers order by SupplierID desc"
rs.Open sSQL,cn
Response.Write "Company: " & rs("CompanyName") & "<br>"
Response.Write "Contact: " & rs("ContactName") & "<br>"
Response.Write "Title: " & rs("ContactTitle")
'****** here ends the lines of code that will change
```

Again, this would be more efficient if you made the embedded SQL statement a stored procedure, but you can see here how you can manipulate data without having to use a recordset with an updateable cursor. This is a far more efficient approach to use as far as resource use on SQL Server. In fact, this is the preferred method to achieve better scalability and performance.

Handling Apostrophes in the Data   If this method is so wonderful, what could be a potential problem? In this example, you have only hard-coded in the values to insert, but often these values would be getting passed to you from an HTML form. Your code would look something like this:

```
SSQL="Insert into Suppliers (CompanyName,ContactName,ContactTitle) " & _
    "values ('" & request.form("txtCompanyName") & "','" & _
    request.form("txtContactName") & "','" & _
    request.form("txtContactTitle") & "')"
```

Now, what if the company name had been "Luck o' the Irish" and the contact name had been "Pat O'Neal"? The actual string that would be built would look something like this:

```
Insert into Suppliers (CompanyName,ContactName,ContactTitle)
    values ('Luck o' the Irish','Pat O'Neal','CEO')
```

As you can see, a problem exists. The apostrophes in the words close the single quotes, so this statement wouldn't be properly parsed by SQL Server. For this statement, SQL Server would return an "Incorrect syntax near 'the Irish'" and the insert would fail.

The solution to this problem isn't earth-shattering: you simply have to add a second apostrophe right after the first one. This does mean you must write a routine that scrubs all the incoming data and, when it finds an apostrophe in a string, it adds a second one. In other words, you want your end result to look like this:

```
Insert into Suppliers (CompanyName,ContactName,ContactTitle)
    values ('Luck o'' the Irish','Pat O''Neal','CEO')
```

This statement will now be processed properly, and the record will be inserted.

What would such a scrubbing routine look like? This is a simple example of a VBScript routine to parse an incoming string and return a modified string, where all apostrophes become double apostrophes.

```
Function EncodeString(psIn)
    Dim sFirstPart
```

```
    Dim sSecondPart
    For x=1 to Len(psIn)
       If Mid(psIn,x,1)="'" Then
          If Mid(psIn,x+1,1)<>"'" Then
             sFirstPart=Mid(psIn,1,x)
             sSecondPart=Mid(psIn,x+1,Len(psIn))
             psIn=sFirstPart & "'" & sSecondPart
             x=x+1
          End If
       End If
    Next
    EncodeString=psIn
End Function
```

This routine accepts a string as a parameter. It walks through the string one character at a time, looking for an apostrophe. If an apostrophe is found, it appends another one right after. It then skips an extra character to avoid an infinite loop, where it would just keep adding an apostrophe after the one you just added. If the Len, Mid, and InStr functions aren't familiar to you, learn them. You need to do a lot of string manipulation as you add or update records in a database.

If this process of having to modify strings sounds like a pain, it is to some degree. After all, if you just opened a recordset, you could have a line of code like the following one, and there would be no need to modify the string:

```
rs("ContactName")="Pat O'Neal"
```

This works just fine. When you call the Update method, ADO can figure out what you want and made the insert or update. It gets down to ease-of-programming versus scalability and performance. Having an updateable recordset is much easier, but less resource-friendly. Using the Execute method to issue SQL commands or call stored procedures requires a little more work, but it is much more friendly in terms of minimizing resources.

A Better Way to Display Recordsets

Here it is, Chapter 6, and recordsets have been displayed for most of the book. Truthfully, you haven't been retrieving your data in the most efficient way. Let's look at what's been done and how to improve it. Look at the following code snippet:

```
<%
rs.Open "Select * from Suppliers",cn
Do Until rs.EOF
    Response.Write "Company Name: " & rs("CompanyName") & "<br>"
    Response.Write "Company Name: " & rs("ContactName") & "<br>"
    Response.Write "Company Name: " & rs("ContactTitle")
Loop
```

Using this code, you're making a round-trip to the database for each record if you have left the CacheSize parameter at the default of one. Depending on the size of the table (and the number of fields because I was lazy and just did a "select *"), this could require many, many round-trips to the server to get all the fields you need for all the records.

ADO gives you a method to help speed this along: GetRows. *GetRows* is a method of the Recordset object that retrieves all the data at once. In other words, you only have to make one trip to the server to get all the fields for all the records that match your query. The data is brought back and put into a two-dimensional array. Create a new page called GetRows.asp and enter the following code:

```
<%@ Language=VBScript %>
<HTML>
<HEAD>
<META NAME="GENERATOR" Content="Microsoft Visual Studio 6.0">
</HEAD>
<BODY>
<!-- #include file="adovbs.inc" -->
<%
dim cn
dim rs
```

```
dim sSQL
dim myData

set cn=server.CreateObject("ADODB.Connection")
set rs=server.CreateObject("ADODB.Recordset")
cn.Open application("DBconn")
sSQL="Select * from Suppliers"
rs.Open sSQL,cn,adOpenForwardOnly,adLockReadOnly,adCmdText
myData=rs.GetRows
rs.Close
cn.Close
lColumns=ubound(myData,1)
lRows=ubound(myData,2)
%>
<TABLE Border="1" Cellpadding="2" Cellspacing="2">
    <% For x=0 to lRows %>
    <TR>
        <% For y=0 to lColumns %>
        <TD><% =myData(y,x) %></TD>
        <% Next %>
    </TR>
    <% Next %>
</TABLE>
</BODY>
</HTML>
```

In this ASP, you open a recordset like you have in the past, but then you call GetRows. This immediately retrieves all the data for you. You can then close the connection and the recordset before continuing, following the old programmer's adage of opening resources as late as possible and releasing them as early as possible. In this case, you now have all the data in a two-dimensional array, so you can close your connection to SQL Server.

Once you have the data, you use the Ubound function of VBScript to determine how many values are in each dimension. You use this to determine the number of rows and columns. Then, you start looping through the array. You move to the first record and loop through all the fields. You then move to the second record and loop through all the fields again. You are doing all of this with no round-trips to SQL Server and, in fact, with no open connection. This method is often the fastest way to display data for what you do with Web applications: make a single pass through the data for the purposes of displaying it. You can see the resulting page in Figure 6-5.

Figure 6-5.   Data from the Suppliers table, displayed after being retrieved with the Recordset object's GetRows method

SUMMARY

Many topics were covered in this chapter. On the surface, this should be an easy chapter because it discusses the Command and Recordset objects. In reality, the powerful features that can make your Web applications much more efficient are beginning to be tapped. The advantages of using stored procedures were discussed, and you've seen an example of how output parameters can be used effectively. The Recordset object and how the various lock types and cursor types can affect your application were also covered.

Remember a few things as you move forward. First, use the constants to give ADO some help. The constants can figure out if your statement is a command string, a stored procedure, or a table name, but why make it figure it out? If you tell it, you'll gain some efficiencies. Tell ADO when your statement won't be returning any records. Obviously, don't do what your author often does and issue a "select *" when you only want a few of the fields.

Avoid opening recordsets with any kind of locking other than adLockReadOnly, if you can. Opening cursor-less recordsets (those with forward-scrolling, read-only parameters) is the most efficient way to work with recordsets. Inserts, updates, and deletes can be accomplished using the Execute method of the Connection of Command object.

If anything was obvious in this chapter, it should be that stored procedures can have a huge speed advantage over embedded SQL statements. Even if you don't use output parameters, the fact that stored procedures are compiled on the server, with an execution plan already figured out, makes them much faster than passing a SQL string. In addition, stored procedures give all developers a common way to access data.

Finally, don't be upset because all your database code is in an ASP. This isn't the most efficient way to go about designing for scalability and performance, but nothing you have learned is wasted. In fact, almost all your code so far is directly transferable into the COM components you build in Chapters 13 and 14.

CHAPTER 7

Accessing SQL Server 2000 Data Warehouses over the Web

When Microsoft released SQL Server 7, it included data warehousing tools for the first time. These tools were designed to allow even small companies to develop large, enterprise-wide data warehouses, using a mix of relational and multidimensional technologies. The tools included with SQL Server 7 were good and, when you consider that many of Microsoft's competitors were selling similar tools for tens, or even hundreds, of thousands of dollars, the tools Microsoft included free were nothing short of spectacular. With SQL Server 2000, the tools have been made even more powerful.

Data warehousing is a subject that can be covered in a book by itself and, in fact, has been covered by Osborne in *SQL Server 7 Data Warehousing*. The purpose of this chapter isn't to cover data warehousing itself, although it has a quick introduction into that topic. Most of the chapter is spent programmatically accessing the structure of cubes and the data in cubes through SQL Server Analysis Services (called OLAP Services in SQL Server 7) and displaying it for Web users. If you thought ADO was fun, wait until you see ADO MD!

A QUICK LOOK AT DATA WAREHOUSING

Exactly what is data warehousing? Data warehousing means a lot of different things to different people but, in general, it means a system designed for analysis or decision support, instead of transactions. Most of you are familiar with the concept of normalization and its role in *online transaction processing* (*OLTP*) systems. OLTP is all about performing inserts, updates, and deletes as quickly as possible. Therefore, you don't store any redundant data or any data that could be derived from other data, such as order totals. You break data out into separate tables and join those tables using keys to avoid having to repeat data. In your OLTP system, you store individual transactions and expect the system to be in a fairly constant state of flux.

Data warehousing is the other side of the coin. Sometimes called OLAP (online analytical processing), warehousing is all about storing aggregated data. For example, how many sprockets did you sell yesterday? How many did you sell last week? What about sales last week versus the prior week? Or last week versus the same week last year?

None of these questions is impossible to answer with an OLTP system, but normalization actually slows down data retrieval; in other words, the SQL select statement. If you optimize for inserts, updates, and deletes, you must perform a great number of joins when you want to retrieve data, and joins slow down queries. To speed retrieval queries, OLAP systems denormalize data. Redundant data is introduced with the sole purpose of gaining speed when it comes time to answer questions. In addition, you can store aggregations in your warehouse so numbers like the total sprockets sold yesterday, last week, last month, and last year are already calculated, and you can retrieve them without SQL Server having to sum up a large number of records.

Before moving on, I should point out something that may confuse you. Most people use the term "OLAP" to imply a structure—built-in relational tables—that is denormalized for the purposes of speed. This structure is called a *Star* or *Snowflake schema*, depending on how it was built. This star or snowflake schema may or may not include aggregate numbers in it. *Warehousing*, on the other hand, is often used to imply you are building multidimensional structures, called *cubes*, which are different from standard relational tables. This chapter discusses cubes. If you only had a star or snowflake schema, you would use standard SQL statements and ADO to retrieve it. Microsoft gave you a great cube builder with SQL Server, and you'll use that because of its added power. Once you use a cube, however, you have to use a different approach to get the data back out.

How You View Data

Normally, when you want to analyze data, you phrase a request similar to this: "I want to see how many sprockets I sold by day." The report that comes back shows the total number of sprockets sold by day. Let's assume the report shows the data for the last ten days. Using this, you could determine how many were sold yesterday versus the previous day, or how many were sold yesterday versus the same day of the week from the previous week.

Most companies break up the world into regions, regions into territories, and so forth, for the purposes of tracking sales. You might then further refine your question by making a statement like this: "I want to see how many sprockets were sold by month by region. I want to compare same month sales this year to last year." Now you want monthly totals for this year and last year grouped by region.

Most companies have more than one product, so your question might actually be: "I want to see monthly sales by product by region." Now, you have monthly numbers for sprockets, monthly numbers for widgets, and so on. What if you wanted to compare sales quarterly instead of monthly? You could use the monthly report and pull out your calculator or you could produce another report.

NOTE: I'm using "report" here as a fairly generic term. Obviously, you'd rather not destroy a forest to answer each request. Most of your reports will actually be online using some sort of front-end tool, such as Microsoft Excel or ProClarity from Knosys (http://www.knosysinc.com). With the Web, you usually don't have such powerful front-end tools, so you have to use your raw programming capability (and a lot of caffeine) to get the job done.

You're starting to see the requests are similar. You describe *what* you want to see, and then *how* you want to see it. What you want to see are things like sales—called *measures*. For the sake of this brief introduction, measures are almost always numeric and additive. In other words, you add a series of individual transactions to find out how many sprockets you sold. Daily totals sum nicely into weekly totals, and so on. Your measures may need to be better defined: when you asked for sales, were you talking about the number of units sold or the dollar value of units sold? Those are two different measures, but they can be asked for in exactly the same way. In other words, you probably want to track both those measures inside your warehouse.

How you want to see your data, the *by* part of the questions, represents what is called the *dimensions*. In the last statement, three dimensions were mentioned: time, geography, and product. It wasn't called time, actually asking for monthly sales, but it is the time dimension, nonetheless. Similarly, the region is part of the geography dimension. More on measures and dimensions in a moment.

Let's look at how your data is viewed logically. Figure 7-1 shows a cube. The horizontal axis represents the time dimension; monthly data is represented by this cube at the moment. Along the vertical axis, the geography dimension is represented, in this case showing

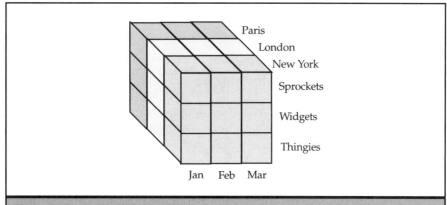

Figure 7-1.   A multidimensional cube represents how data is actually perceived. Here, a cube holds sales information by product by time by geography

various cities. The z-axis represents the different products being tracked. You have a three-dimensional cube in this case, but a real data warehousing cube could contain a large number of dimensions. While those of you familiar with linear algebra know about working with *n*-dimensional space, drawing a cube over three dimensions poses real problems in a book, so I stick to three-dimensional cubes for most of this explanation.

If you look at the cube, you can see how you would use it to answer questions. The intersection of the dimensions is called a *cell*. However, this is where things truly depart from relational tables: a cell can have more than one value in it. If you think about a relational table, you go to a particular record, and on the record, you go to a particular field, and you are in a cell. Exactly one value is in that cell (even if the value is null). With a cube, however, when you get to the intersection of the product, time, and geography dimensions, there is one cell, but it can contain multiple values (measures). If you think about it logically, this makes sense. You might want to see the number of units sold, or the dollar volume sold, or the profit on the sales. These three values are called measures and are what you find in the cells inside a cube. Figure 7-2 shows one cell exploding from the cube. If you want to examine sales of sprockets in New York in February, you would wind up with the cell shown. Inside this cell, however, are multiple measures that can be examined.

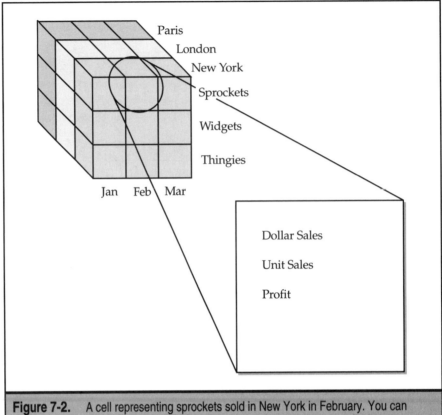

Figure 7-2. A cell representing sprockets sold in New York in February. You can see multiple values, or measures, can actually be in a cell when you are dealing with multidimensional, or cubed, data

Understanding one thing about dimensions is important: dimensions usually have a built-in hierarchical structure. For example, the time dimension is usually built to start at the year, and then down to the quarter, months, and, finally, individual days. Similarly, the geography dimension is often a hierarchical structure. You may start with the entire world, and then break the world down into countries, states (or provinces), and, finally, cities. Figure 7-3 represents how these two hierarchies might appear. Such dimensions are called *dimensional hierarchies*, and they are common in data warehousing. The various steps within the hierarchy are called *levels*, and the possible values at each level are called *members*. For example, the Geography dimension has a City level. In the City level, three members are New York, London, and Paris.

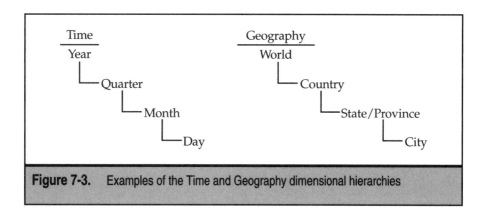

Figure 7-3.   Examples of the Time and Geography dimensional hierarchies

If a dimension has a hierarchical structure, what exactly does the cube look like? You can imagine a series of cubes, one each at the various levels of the hierarchies. In reality, this is more like cubes within cubes. This is a difficult concept to draw or explain, but not a particularly difficult one to grasp. Just realize that if you are at the State level of the Geography dimension, certain measures exist for each state. If you drill down to the individual cities within a state, you have the same measures for each city. The fact that the measures at all levels of the hierarchy may already be calculated is what gives you the huge speed benefit you see with data warehousing.

Why go through all of this? Because, as you will see, many dimensions can exist for a cube, hierarchies within the dimensions, and more than one value in a cell, which makes displaying cube data quite a challenge. First, let's examine how to view the information with Microsoft's Cube Browser before you begin looking at the data over the Web.

Viewing Cube Data with Microsoft's Cube Browser

Microsoft provides the Cube Browser with Analysis Services that lets you view the data in the cube. The Cube Browser isn't really an end-user tool; instead, it's more for you to browse the cubes and make sure you have the structure down that you expected.

Open the Analysis Services Manager by clicking the Start button, and then clicking Programs, Microsoft SQL Server, Analysis Services, Analysis Manager. Along the left-hand side, the Analysis Services Manager shows you the servers available and the databases on those servers. In the case of Figure 7-4, you can see I have only one server

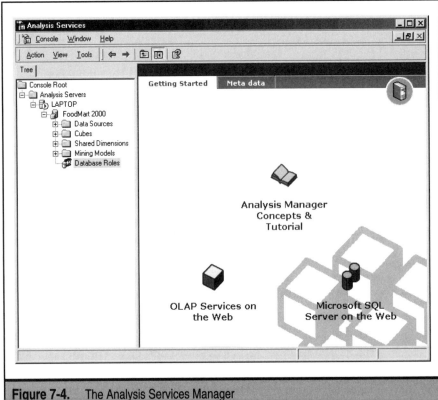

Figure 7-4.   The Analysis Services Manager

listed (LAPTOP) and only one database listed (FoodMart 2000). If
you expand the Cubes folder, you find a listing of all the cubes
available on that server.

Expand the cubes folder and you see the Sales cube. Right-click
the Sales cube and choose Browse Data. The Cube Browser opens
and enables you to begin working with the cube's data. As you can
see in Figure 7-5, the Cube Browser has a series of fields along the
top, as well as a display area in the bottom two-thirds of the screen.
When the browser first opens, you see all the measures in the grid,
with the Customers dimension in the rows. Because only the USA
has data, double-click USA and the browser expands USA down one
level in a standard drilldown operation. As you can see in Figure 7-6,
you are now viewing CA, OR, and WA as the members of the level
State Province.

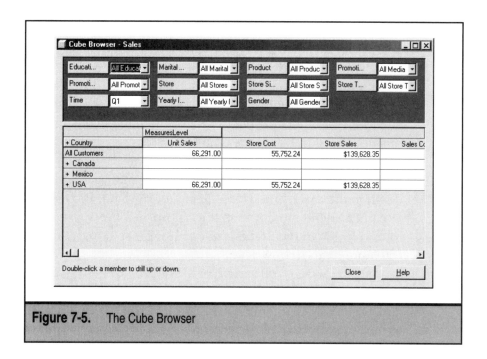

Figure 7-5.   The Cube Browser

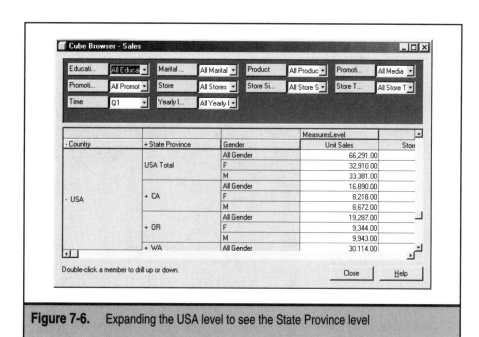

Figure 7-6.   Expanding the USA level to see the State Province level

Right now, the equivalent of two dimensions are shown: measures (which can act like a dimension) and Customers. Along the top are all the other available dimensions. They can still act as filters, even if you don't bring them down to the grid. For example, drop down the arrow in the Time dimension, expand the 1997 value, and choose only the Q1 member. This filters the data so now you only see the measures for the first quarter of 1997, not the whole year.

Perhaps more interesting is how you can drag other dimensions down to either the rows or columns. For instance, if you drag Gender down to the rows, and drop it just after the State Province column, you get a layout similar to that in Figure 7-7. Now, you can see that for California in the first quarter of 1997, men bought approximately 450 more items than women.

As you can see, you can pivot the data by dragging-and-dropping dimensions from the top or moving dimensions from rows to columns and vice versa. You can filter data by limiting values in the check boxes in the upper portion of the window.

As previously stated, the cube browser that comes with SQL Server isn't really for end users. If you expand the dimensions out far enough, you might see only headers and not be able to see any measures! The

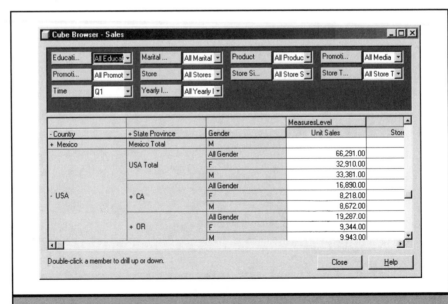

Figure 7-7.   The Gender dimension added to the rows

headings don't scroll, so if you push the measures off the screen, you have to collapse some dimensions to get them to reappear. Browsing the cubes in other ways is possible. Microsoft Excel has a Pivot Table that connects to Analysis Services. And as I've also mentioned, ProClarity from Knosys is an excellent tool for working with multidimensional data.

ACCESSING CUBED DATA WITH ADO MD

Remember the discussion about OLE DB? In Chapter 5, you learned OLE DB was designed to access data in its native format—in other words, whether that data was in a relational format. OLE DB, however, is designed to return data in a tabular format and is not quite up to the unique task of multidimensional, or cubed, data. To handle multidimensional data, Microsoft created OLE DB for OLAP. This version of OLE DB is built for accessing and processing multidimensional data.

Just as Microsoft put ADO on top of OLE DB, they put *ADO MD* (*ActiveX Data Objects Multidimensional*) on top of OLE DB for OLAP. ADO MD is similar to ADO in several respects: it connects to a data source, it executes statements against this back-end data source, and it returns results that can be read and displayed. Unlike ADO, the data source is a cube presented through Analysis Services, the command statements are *MDX* (*Multidimensional Expressions*) instead of SQL, and the results of our queries are called cellsets instead of recordsets. Obviously, the *cellsets* are in a multidimensional format instead of the standard rows and columns of a recordset.

The last two chapters discussed three main ADO objects (the Connection, Command, and Recordset objects) and two other objects (the Parameter and Error objects). ADO is a simple, flat object model. ADO MD, on the other hand, is a hierarchical, fairly complex object model. If going back to a rigid hierarchical structure sounds like a step backward, realize that a major component of cubes is a hierarchical structure within the dimensions, so walking up and down these dimensions through an object hierarchy can make a lot of sense. Figure 7-8 shows the ADO MD object model.

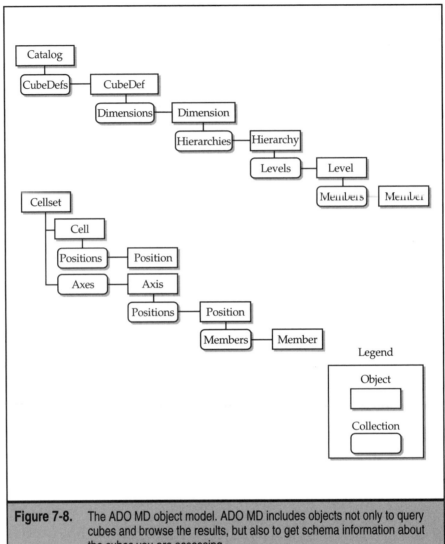

Figure 7-8.   The ADO MD object model. ADO MD includes objects not only to query cubes and browse the results, but also to get schema information about the cubes you are accessing

Looking at a Cube's Structure: The Catalog Object

ADO MD includes a Catalog object used to view the structure of a cube. With ADO, you don't normally have a way to browse the structure of the database because you cannot be certain your data source is a relational database with tables and fields. In other words, when you connect to a data source, you don't have a Tables collection automatically filled in with the names of all the tables.

Microsoft does provide an object model to do this: *ActiveX Data Objects Extensions* (*ADOX*), which includes schema information. However, with ADO MD, you have the objects both to provide schema, or metadata, information and to enable you to query cubes and browse the results.

The Catalog object is similar to the Connection object you learned about with ADO; it is what makes the connection to the warehousing product you're using. In this case, of course, you're connecting Analysis Services in SQL Server 2000. To connect, you simply set the ActiveConnection property of the Catalog object to a valid connection string. The connection string looks almost identical to the connection string you have been using, with some minor differences. The connection string is examined soon.

Once you established the connection to the catalog, one or more cubes might be in that Analysis Services database. On connecting, each cube in the database is assigned to a CubeDef object. All the CubeDef objects are added to the Catalog's CubeDefs collection. You can iterate through this CubeDefs collection to get a list of available cubes.

To see how you can begin using this schema information, create a new Web application called ADOMDtest. In this application, use the following code for the Global.asa:

```
<SCRIPT LANGUAGE=VBScript RUNAT=Server>
Sub Application_OnStart()
    application("OLAPconn")="Provider=MSOLAP.2;Integrated
Security=SSPI;Data Source=laptop;Initial Catalog=FoodMart 2000"
End Sub
</SCRIPT>
```

If you are using mixed security, your connection string looks more like this:

```
Application("OLAPconn")Provider=MSOLAP.2;Password="";User ID=sa;Data
Source=laptop;Initial Catalog=FoodMart 2000;
```

As you can see, the connection string is different from what has been used in the past. The provider is MSOLAP.2, with the ".2" representing the version number. The initial catalog is only the name of the database in Analysis Services. Also, don't forget to change the name of the Data Source to match your server's name.

Next, create a page called SchemaInfo.asp and enter the following code:

```
<%@ Language=VBScript %>
<HTML>
<BODY>
<%
dim cat
set cat=server.CreateObject("ADOMD.Catalog")
cat.ActiveConnection=application("OLAPconn")
Response.Write cat.Name
%>
</BODY>
</HTML>
```

If this seems overly simple, it is. In fact, this page simply returns the name of the catalog in Analysis Services: in this case, FoodMart 2000. This is the name of the database, or catalog, you have connected to with the Catalog object. Remember, this catalog object has a CubeDefs collection, which is automatically filled in when you connect to the catalog. You can loop through this CubeDefs collection and get the names of all the cubes in this catalog by modifying SchemaInfo.asp to look like this:

```
<%@ Language=VBScript %>
<HTML>
<BODY>
<%
dim cat
set cat=server.CreateObject("ADOMD.Catalog")
cat.ActiveConnection=application("OLAPconn")
Response.Write cat.Name & "<br>"
For Each cube in cat.CubeDefs
    Response.write cube.Name & "<br>"
Next
%>
</BODY>
</HTML>
```

After opening the connection to the Catalog, you simply iterate through the CubeDefs collection. For each CubeDef object, you print the Name property. Your page should look similar to that shown in Figure 7-9. Don't worry that it isn't in a pretty format at the moment; you can clean that up in a minute.

Just as every Catalog has a CubeDefs collection holding a CubeDef object for each cube, each CubeDef object has a Dimensions collection. As you can probably guess, the Dimensions collection holds a set of Dimension objects. There is one object for each dimension in a cube. Our example earlier only had three dimensions, but some of these cubes have a dozen dimensions, or more. To iterate through the dimensions for each cube, you can modify SchemaInfo.asp to look like this:

```
<%@ Language=VBScript %>
<HTML>
<BODY>

<%
dim cat
dim cube
dim dm
set cat=server.CreateObject("ADOMD.Catalog")
cat.ActiveConnection=application("OLAPconn")
Response.Write "<H1>" & cat.Name & "</H1>"
%>
<TABLE Cellpadding="2" Cellspacing="2">
   <TR>
      <TH>Cube Name</TH>
      <TH>Dimensions</TH>
   </TR>
   <%
    For Each cube in cat.CubeDefs
         Response.Write "<tr><td colspan=2>" & cube.Name & "</td></tr>"
         For Each dm in cube.Dimensions
            Response.Write "<tr><td width=50> </td><td>" & _
               dm.Name & "</td></tr>"
```

```
            Next
        Next
        %>
</TABLE>
</BODY>
</HTML>
```

WARNING: At this point, I ran into a security problem with Roles on the cubes (even though I was logged in as the Administrator.) The error I got back, however, was "Unknown Error." If you receive errors here, go into the Analysis Services Manager, right-click Database Roles, Manage Roles, and then click the ellipses button in the field for Cubes & Mining Models. Make sure the role "All Users" has permissions on every cube. On my system, "All Users" didn't have access to two cubes, causing this ASP to fail.

In this code, you loop through the CubeDefs collection, and for each CubeDef object you loop through its Dimensions collection and print the name of each dimension. Your screen should look similar to

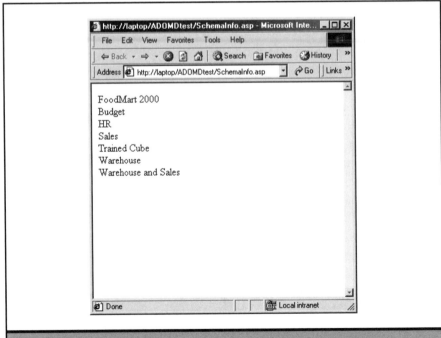

Figure 7-9. The name of the Catalog and all the CubeDef objects in that catalog

Figure 7-10. You have two cubes showing: the Budget and HR cubes. The Budget cube has five dimensions showing, although one is called "measures." These are actually the measures you retrieve later, so the cube actually only has four dimensions you can use for navigation.

By using the For Each loop, the variable "cube" becomes a pointer to the next object in the list. The actual name of the object is unimportant, as is the number of objects. This code just loops through every object in the collection, looking at one at a time.

Once you are working with the Dimension object, you have access to a Hierarchies collection, which holds a series of Hierarchy objects. Most Dimension objects only have one Hierarchy object, but the same dimension can have multiple hierarchies. For example, think about the time dimension for a moment: many companies have a fiscal calendar in addition to the regular calendar. Fiscal months

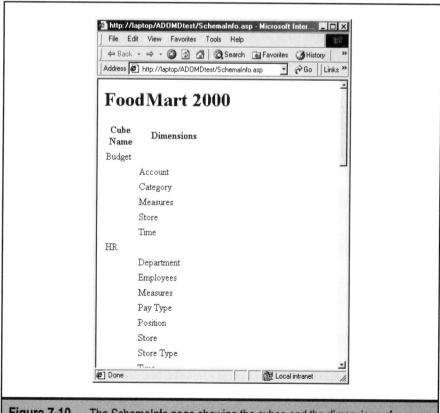

Figure 7-10. The SchemaInfo page showing the cubes and the dimensions of the cubes

don't necessarily begin and end with the calendar months. Therefore, you might want to build two hierarchical structures within the time dimension: one for the regular calendar and one for the fiscal calendar.

You can examine the hierarchies within the dimensions by modifying SchemaInfo.asp to include a loop through the Hierarchies collection of each Dimension object.

```
<%@ Language=VBScript %>
<HTML>
<BODY>
<%
dim cat
dim cube
dim dm
dim hr
set cat=server.CreateObject("ADOMD.Catalog")
cat.ActiveConnection=application("OLAPconn")
Response.Write "<H1>" & cat.Name & "</H1>"
%>
<TABLE Cellpadding="2" Cellspacing="2">
    <TR>
        <TH>Cube Name</TH>
        <TH>Dimensions</TH>
        <TH>Hierarchies</TH>
    </TR>
    <%
    For Each cube in cat.CubeDefs
            Response.Write "<tr><td colspan=2>" & cube.Name & "</td></tr>"
            For Each dm in cube.Dimensions
                Response.Write "<tr><td width=50> </td><td>" & _
                    dm.Name & "</td></tr>"
                For Each hr in dm.Hierarchies
                    Response.Write "<tr><td width=50> </td>" & _
                        <td width=50> </td><td>" & _
                        hr.UniqueName & "</td></tr>"
                Next
            Next
    Next
    %>
```

```
</TABLE>
</BODY>
</HTML>
```

As you can see in Figure 7-11, each dimension in your cubes only has one hierarchy. For the hierarchies, the UniqueName property was chosen because the Name property for each hierarchy was blank (the default). Both Dimension and Hierarchy objects have UniqueName properties.

No doubt, you're starting to get the point. Inside each Hierarchy object is a Levels collection that holds a series of Level objects. The level of a hierarchy is easy to understand: in the Geography dimension mentioned earlier, were the World, Country, State, and City levels. Each Level object can have a Members collection, where

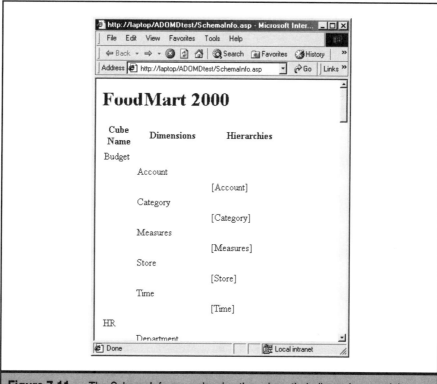

Figure 7-11.   The SchemaInfo page showing the cubes, their dimensions, and the hierarchies of the dimensions

each Member object represents a member within the level. For example, from the earlier City level, were the members New York, London, and Tokyo.

Expanding the SchemaInfo.asp to show all the members for all the levels of each cube is possible, but it takes a long time to build and might time out on some machines. Therefore, I am modifying SchemaInfo.asp to focus on only the Sales cube. Modify SchemaInfo.asp to look like this:

```
<%@ Language=VBScript %>
<HTML>
<BODY>

<%
dim cat
dim cube
dim dm
dim hr
dim lvl
dim mbr
set cat=server.CreateObject("ADOMD.Catalog")
cat.ActiveConnection=application("OLAPconn")
Response.Write "<H1>" & cat.Name & "</H1>"
%>
<TABLE Cellpadding="2" Cellspacing="2">
    <TR>
        <TH>Cube Name</TH>
        <TH>Dimensions</TH>
        <TH>Hierarchies</TH>
        <TH>Levels</TH>
        <TH>Members</TH>
    </TR>
    <%
    set cube=cat.CubeDefs("Sales")
    Response.Write "<tr><td colspan=2>" & cube.Name & "</td></tr>"
    For Each dm in cube.Dimensions
        Response.Write "<tr><td width=50> </td><td>" & _
            dm.Name & "</td></tr>"
```

```
    For Each hr in dm.Hierarchies
        Response.Write "<tr><td width=50> </td>" & _
            "<td width=50> </td><td>" & hr.UniqueName & _
            "</td></tr>"
        For Each lvl in hr.Levels
            Response.Write "<tr><td width=50> </td>" & _
                "<td width=50> </td><td width=50>" & _
                 </td><td>" & lvl.Name & "</td></tr>"
            For Each mbr in lvl.Members
                Response.Write "<tr><td width=50> " & _
                "</td><td width=50> </td><td width=50>" & _
                " </td><td width=50> </td><td>" & _
            mbr.Name & "</td></tr>"
            Next
        Next
    Next
Next
    %>
</TABLE>
</BODY>
</HTML>
```

Even with limiting this to only the Sales cube, the page can take a while to load. As you see in Figure 7-12, you're looking at the Customers dimension, the [Customers] hierarchy, the (All), Country, and State Province levels, and the members within those levels. If you scroll down to the City or Name levels, you can see how many members are in the cube for those levels.

What is the point of this exercise? Obviously, this isn't something clients would want to see. Clients want the data and they could care less about the structure of the cube, as long as they can use it to answer their questions. Instead, the previous pages were shown for two reasons:

▼ Understanding the ADO MD object model is helpful.

▲ Knowing how cubes work—with dimensions, hierarchies, levels, and members—is important to understand how to phrase your queries.

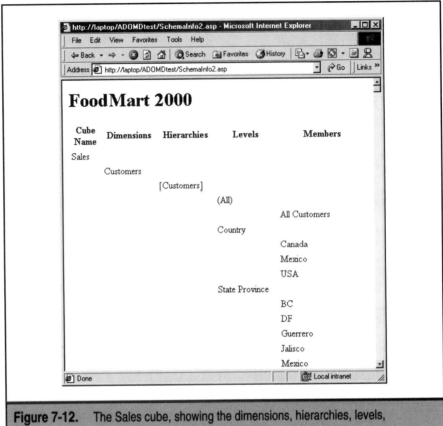

Figure 7-12. The Sales cube, showing the dimensions, hierarchies, levels, and members

Viewing the Results of a Query

Viewing the structure of a cube is not something you do that often over the Web, although viewing the data from a cube is something some people might want to do over the Web. Using a standard Web interface, which is done here, can be quite limiting for viewing cubed data. More often, it makes more sense to use a rich client, such as ProClarity or Excel. In fact, slicing off part of a cube, sending that chunk down to a client as a file, and letting them browse it with a richer tool is possible. Also possible is to embed an ActiveX control in a Web page for cube browsing, but client-side data access is discussed in Chapter 12.

When you want to query a database, you use SQL. When you want to query a cube through Microsoft's Analysis Services, you use *Multidimensional Expressions* (*MDX*). MDX is a query language, much like SQL, but it's a different structure. This book doesn't go into any real detail on MDX. Learning MDX requires patience, gallons of your favorite caffeinated beverage, and throwing away some of what you know about SQL. I should point out that MDX is a Microsoft language, but its goal is to develop a language that can be used to access data in any data warehousing product.

The challenge of working with cube data is twofold: MDX makes retrieving the data a challenge, and the format in which it is returned makes processing and displaying the data a challenge. With the ADO Recordset object, there's a nice, tabular structure with rows and columns. With ADO MD, queries return Cellset objects, which store data in a multidimensional format. If you don't know what multidimensional data looks like, just think of arrays of arrays of arrays. As the Cellset object and its associated collections are examined, you see how you can loop through the Cellset to display data for users.

Opening a Cellset

Follow these three steps to return a Cellset object:

1. Connect to the database using a Catalog object.

2. Set the Cellset's Source property to a valid MDX query.

3. Retrieve the data using the Open method of the Cellset object.

You just spent a lot of time working with the Catalog object and its collections. To work with a Cellset, you could use the following line of code:

```
Set cst=server.CreateObject("ADOMD.Cellset")
```

Now that you have a Cellset object in memory, you can create an MDX statement and assign it to the Source property. After that, you simply call the Open method:

```
sMDX="Select {[Store].[Store Country].USA.children} on columns, " & _
       "{[Product].[Product Family].members} on rows From sales " & _
       "Where ([1997], [Unit Sales])"
cst.Source=sMDX
cst.Open
```

This is a simple MDX statement. In it, you specify the dimensions you're interested in (Store and Product) and whether these should appear on columns or rows. The dimensions appear in a Select clause, so this looks similar to regular SQL so far. You then have a From clause that tells you the name of the cube in which you're interested. Again, this is similar to SQL. In the Where clause, you have two items listed: the year 1997, and the measure Unit Sales. Here, you use 1997 to limit your values in the time dimension. Unit Sales, however, is the measure you want to see. This is the value that appears at the intersection of the Store and Product dimensions. In other words, this Cellset has the Unit Sales by Product Family by Country, for the total year 1997. Now, if you are somewhat confused because the "what" you are really after—the measure—shows up in the Where clause, welcome to MDX. You aren't in Kansas anymore.

Getting this Cellset back is the easy part. Now it's time to display the data. Create a new ASP called Cellset.asp and add the following code:

```
<%@ Language=VBScript %>
<HTML>
<BODY>
<%
dim cat
dim cst
dim sMDX
dim x,y
set cat=server.CreateObject("ADOMD.Catalog")
set cst=server.CreateObject("ADOMD.Cellset")
cat.ActiveConnection=application("OLAPconn")
Response.Write "<H1>" & cat.Name & "</H1>"
sMDX="Select {[Store].[Store Country].USA.children} on columns, " & _
        "{[Product].[Product Family].members} on rows From sales " & _
        "Where ([1997], [Unit Sales])"
set cst.ActiveConnection=cat.ActiveConnection
cst.Source=sMDX
cst.Open
%>
<TABLE Border="1" Cellpadding="2" Cellspacing="2">
    <%
    Response.Write("<TR><TD> </TD>")
    For x=0 to cst.Axes(0).Positions.Count-1
            Response.Write "<TD>" & cst.Axes(0).Positions(x).Members(0).Caption & "</TD>"
    Next
```

```
      Response.Write "</TR>"
    For y=0 to cst.Axes(1).Positions.Count-1
        Response.Write "<TR>"
        Response.Write "<TD>" & _
            cst.Axes(1).Positions(y).Members(0).Caption & "</TD>"
        For x=0 to cst.Axes(0).Positions.Count-1
            Response.Write "<TD>" & cst(x,y).FormattedValue & "</TD>"
        Next
        Response.Write "</TR>"
    Next
  %>
</TABLE>
</BODY>
</HTML>
```

First, look at Figure 7-13 to see the end result of this ASP. Now, let's examine how this code produces the page. I've already discussed the MDX query a little but, now, look at what I'm asking for: In the Store dimension, I'm asking for the children of USA in the Store Country level. In other words, I want to go the Store Country level.

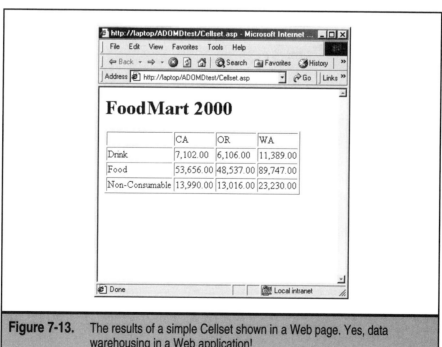

Figure 7-13.   The results of a simple Cellset shown in a Web page. Yes, data warehousing in a Web application!

You know USA is one of the members of that level and I want the children of the USA. In the hierarchy, the children of USA are the members of the level below Store Country, or in this case CA, OR, and WA. I could have specified those three values but, this way, I get all the children at a certain level, so I don't have to know the specific members at a particular level.

With the Product dimension, you only want all the members of the Product Family level. This happens to be the top of the hierarchy, so there aren't that many values. In fact, only three members exist: Drink, Food, and Non-Consumable.

The trick here is walking through the various collections in the proper order and pulling out the Unit Sales measure correctly. To begin, let's walk through the Cellset's Axes collection, looking at the first Axis (number zero). The first Axis represents the values put on the columns in the MDX query. Count how many positions are in this first Axis object, and then loop through the Positions collection. For each Position object, you print out the Caption property of the first Member object. This first Axis, your columns, becomes your column headings. Don't forget you're adding a blank cell at the beginning of the first row so you can place the row headings in their proper place later.

```
For x=0 to cst.Axes(0).Positions.Count-1
    Response.Write "<TD>" & _
        cst.Axes(0).Positions(x).Members(0).Caption & "</TD>"
Next
```

After you run through the first Axis, you drop to the second Axis. This Axis represents the items you placed on the rows in your MDX query; in this case, the Product Family. Normally, you loop through only this Axis, and then go back and grab the measures. Because you're building a table in HTML and not accessing an ActiveX grid, however, you need to create the row, and then add the row headings and the measures at the same time. You loop through the second Axis much like you did the first but, after printing out each row header, you then perform a second loop to pull out the measures.

```
For y=0 to cst.Axes(1).Positions.Count-1
    Response.Write "<TR>"
    Response.Write "<TD>" & _
        cst.Axes(1).Positions(y).Members(0).Caption & "</TD>"
```

```
    For x=0 to cst.Axes(0).Positions.Count-1
        Response.Write "<TD>" & cst(x,y).FormattedValue & "</TD>"
    Next
    Response.Write "</TR>"
Next
```

As you run through the second Axis, you also retrieve the actual
measures. You do this by simply specifying the array indexes of the
Cellset object. The Cellset object actually contains an Item property
that can return a Cell object given the coordinates of the cell. The x
coordinate represents the columns, and the y coordinate represents
the rows. Because you're building an HTML table, you're already on
the second row when you start displaying the second Axis. Therefore,
you stay on that row, but loop through all the column, or x, values.
This lines up the values under the columns you displayed earlier.

Adding Drilldown Capabilities

You can expand the example a bit by allowing at least one level
of drilldown. You can modify Cellset.asp to provide links for the
Product Family members, so clicking one expands that category
down to the next level. You can make Cellset.asp a reentrant page,
which means it's a form that calls itself. You build links that call back
to Cellset.asp. If Cellset.asp doesn't see a value coming in a query
string, it shows what you've been viewing. If a product comes in a
query string variable called product, however, you use a different
MDX query that goes to the next lower level and shows you that
data. The code for that page looks like this:

```
<%@ Language=VBScript %>
<HTML>
<BODY>
<%
dim cat
dim cst
dim sMDX
dim x,y
set cat=server.CreateObject("ADOMD.Catalog")
set cst=server.CreateObject("ADOMD.Cellset")
cat.ActiveConnection=application("OLAPconn")
```

```
Response.Write "<H1>" & cat.Name & "</H1>"
If Request.QueryString("product")="" Then
    sMDX="Select {[Store].[Store Country].USA.children} on columns, " & _
        "{[Product].[Product Family].members} on rows From sales " & _
        "Where ([1997], [Unit Sales])"
Else
    sMDX="Select {[Store].[Store Country].USA.children} on columns, " & _
        "{[Product].[Product Family]." & Request.QueryString("product") & _
        ".children} on rows From sales " & _
        "Where ([1997], [Unit Sales])"
End If
set cst.ActiveConnection=cat.ActiveConnection
cst.Source=sMDX
cst.Open
%>
<TABLE Border="1" Cellspacing="2" Cellpadding="2">
    <%
    Response.Write("<TR><TD> </TD>")
    For x=0 to cst.Axes(0).Positions.Count-1
            Response.Write "<TD>" & _
                cst.Axes(0).Positions(x).Members(0).Caption & "</TD>"
    Next
    Response.Write "</TR>"
    For y=0 to cst.Axes(1).Positions.Count-1
        Response.Write "<TR>"
        Response.Write "<TD><a href=cellset.asp?product=" & _
            cst.Axes(1).Positions(y).Members(0).Caption & ">" & _
            cst.Axes(1).Positions(y).Members(0).Caption & "</a></TD>"
        For x=0 to cst.Axes(0).Positions.Count-1
            Response.Write "<TD>" & cst(x,y).FormattedValue & "</TD>"
        Next
        Response.Write "</TR>"
    Next
    %>
</TABLE>
</BODY>
</HTML>
```

With this page, check the Request object to see if a product variable came in the QueryString collection. If it did, you assume a valid product ID and build a new MDX statement that uses the value in the product variable and chooses its children. Notice in this example, when I build the page with the breakdown of the product department (the level below product family), I don't bother turning off the links. If you try to drill down from this page, you won't get anywhere. After running the new Cellset.asp, if you click the Food link, you see a screen like that in Figure 7-14.

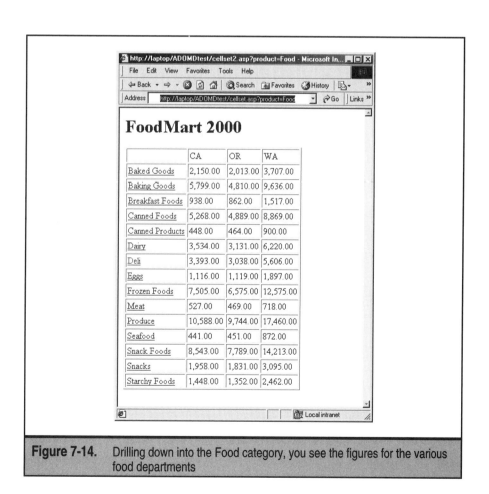

Figure 7-14.   Drilling down into the Food category, you see the figures for the various food departments

Viewing Multiple Measures

So far, you have only chosen one measure. What if you want to see more than one? Theoretically, a Cell object can contain multiple measures, but that doesn't help show them on a Web page. In reality, the way to do this is fairly simple: treat measures like any other dimension. Remember when you were listing the dimensions of your cubes and measures were showing up? Well, when you have multiple measures, you can treat them just like a dimension and display them on the row or column headers. In the following ASP, I showed two measures: Store Sales Net and Unit Sales. I added the measures to the column, or first, Axis. This means, for each state, you can see two measures below it. Look at Figure 7-15 to see what the end result looks like. Modify Cellset.asp to use the following code:

```
<%@ Language=VBScript %>
<HTML>
<BODY>
<%
dim cat
dim cst
dim sMDX
dim x,y
set cat=server.CreateObject("ADOMD.Catalog")
set cst=server.CreateObject("ADOMD.Cellset")
cat.ActiveConnection=application("OLAPconn")
Response.Write "<H1>" & cat.Name & "</H1>"
sMDX="Select Crossjoin({[Store].[Store Country].USA.children}," & _
    "{[Measures].[Store Sales Net],[Measures].[Unit Sales]}) on columns, " & _
    "{[Product].[Product Family].members} on rows From sales " & _
    "Where ([1997])"
set cst.ActiveConnection=cat.ActiveConnection
cst.Source=sMDX
cst.Open
%>
<TABLE Border="1" Cellspacing="2" Cellpadding="2">
```

```
<%
Response.Write("<TR><TD> </TD>")
For x=0 to cst.Axes(0).Positions.Count-1
   Response.Write "<TD>" & _
       cst.Axes(0).Positions(x).Members(0).Caption & "</TD>"
Next
Response.Write "</TR>"

Response.Write("<TR><TD> </TD>")
For x=0 to cst.Axes(0).Positions.Count-1
   Response.Write "<TD>" & _
       cst.Axes(0).Positions(x).Members(1).Caption & "</TD>"
Next
Response.Write "</TR>"
For y=0 to cst.Axes(1).Positions.Count-1
   Response.Write "<TR>"
   Response.Write "<TD>" & _
       cst.Axes(1).Positions(y).Members(0).Caption & "</TD>"
   For x=0 to cst.Axes(0).Positions.Count-1
      Response.Write "<TD>" & cst(x,y).FormattedValue & "</TD>"
   Next
   Response.Write "</TR>"
Next
%>
</TABLE>
</BODY>
</HTML>
```

The only major difference here, other than adding another loop, is that to get the second dimension on the columns, you must move to the second Member object in the Members collection. You needn't build nested loops because when you have a second dimension, the first, or outer, dimension has values repeated for each member in the inner dimension. Look at Figure 7-15 and you see that CA, OR, and WA are all listed twice, once for each measure.

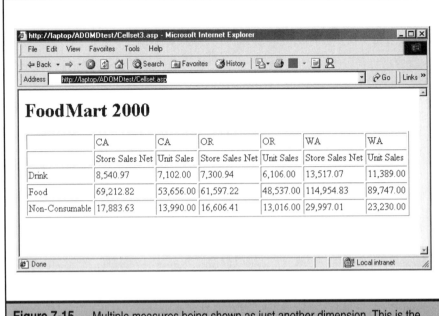

Figure 7-15.   Multiple measures being shown as just another dimension. This is the same approach you would use to show more than two dimensions

SUMMARY

This chapter has shown you how to use the ADO MD object model to perform some data warehousing functions from the Web. The pages here have been simple, but you can see how you can return results and even drill down on data residing in Analysis Services cubes on the server, especially in the last sections.

Analysis Services is a complex and rich tool, that can be used to build high-speed decision support/business intelligence systems. Being able to access this data is always a challenge and being able to view the data over the Web is a huge step in providing decision makers with the necessary information anytime, anywhere.

CHAPTER 8

Using English Query over the Web

English Query is another tool, like the data warehousing tools, that first shipped with SQL Server 7. The goal was to provide a natural language engine for people to query the database. Your customers shouldn't have to learn SQL to ask questions of the database; their expertise lies in marketing, manufacturing, finance, or some other area. If they wanted to be developers, they would be in IT. To make life simpler for your customers and to keep the IT group from becoming nothing more than glorified report writers, Microsoft decided to include a product to enable end users to enter regular English questions and receive the results. Now, with SQL Server 2000, English Query has been enhanced and can be used against relational data, as well as cubed data in Analysis Services.

UNDERSTANDING ENGLISH QUERY

Today, English Query understands one language: English. Microsoft says support may exist for other languages in the future but, for today, English is the only supported language. In fact, you should realize English Query supports *American* English. English Query ships with a large dictionary of words and, of course, you can add words as you work with it.

What English Query Does

English Query, at its heart, is an engine to take an English statement and generate either SQL or MDX. English Query does the translation for you; you then take the output of the engine and execute it against the database.

While English Query understands a lot of English words already, it doesn't understand your database structure by nature. The new version in SQL Server 2000 can read your database schema and make some guesses, but you still have to set up a number of rules about your schema manually.

With English Query, you create what is called a "model." This *model* contains the terms that map to your database; for example, you might set up the model so the words "product," item," and "food" all point to the underlying Products table in the Northwind database. Just as important, you define the relationships between items. For example, you tell the model that customers buy products. You also tell the model that "purchase" is a synonym for "buy."

After setting up the model, you compile the model into a binary file. This *binary* file is then what the English Query engine accesses, which means it must be distributed to the server where you will run English Query.

After you build and compile the model, you add code to your application that calls the English Query engine, which accesses the model you created. You pass the English Query engine an English question and it reads the model. It uses the model you created to translate the English question into a valid SQL or MDX query, depending on the type of model you create. This process can be seen in Figure 8-1.

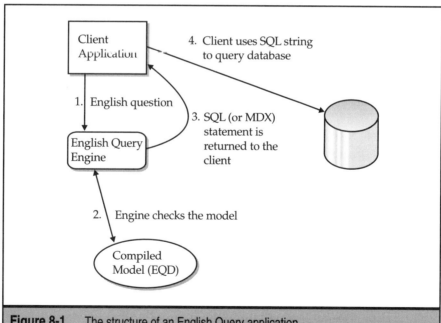

Figure 8-1. The structure of an English Query application

CREATING AN ENGLISH QUERY PROJECT

With SQL Server 2000, English Query is now integrated with Visual Studio. This means you use the familiar Visual Studio environment to create, test, and then compile the model.

To start an English Query project, you can do one of two things: you can create it through Visual InterDev or you can create it from the menus by starting with the Start button, choosing Programs, Microsoft SQL Server, English Query, and then choosing Microsoft English Query.

If you choose to start the project using Visual InterDev, you simply start Visual InterDev. On the New Project dialog box, notice that on the left-hand side of the dialog box, there's a folder for English Query Projects. If you choose this folder, the right-hand side shows options for a SQL Project Wizard, an OLAP Project Wizard, and an Empty Project, as you can see in Figure 8-2. Select SQL Project Wizard and name the project NWind, then click the Open button.

NOTE: To have these projects show up in Visual Studio, you must already have English Query installed when you install SQL Server.

After clicking the Open button, you are prompted to select an OLE DB provider. Choose Microsoft OLE DB Provider for SQL Server and click the Next button. On the second screen of the Data Link Properties dialog box, you need to enter the server name, the user name and password, and, finally, the database. Make sure you select the Northwind database. Now, you can click the OK button.

Next, you see the New Database Tables and Views dialog box, shown in Figure 8-3. This dialog box asks you which tables you want included in the model. Feel free to include all the tables from the Northwind database. In Figure 8-3, three tables were left out because they aren't normally part of the Northwind database. Including them wouldn't have hurt, but they were left out because you probably don't have them in your Northwind database. After selecting the tables and views, click the OK button.

The next screen of the wizard, shown in Figure 8-4, asks you which tables you want to include in your model. It calls each table or

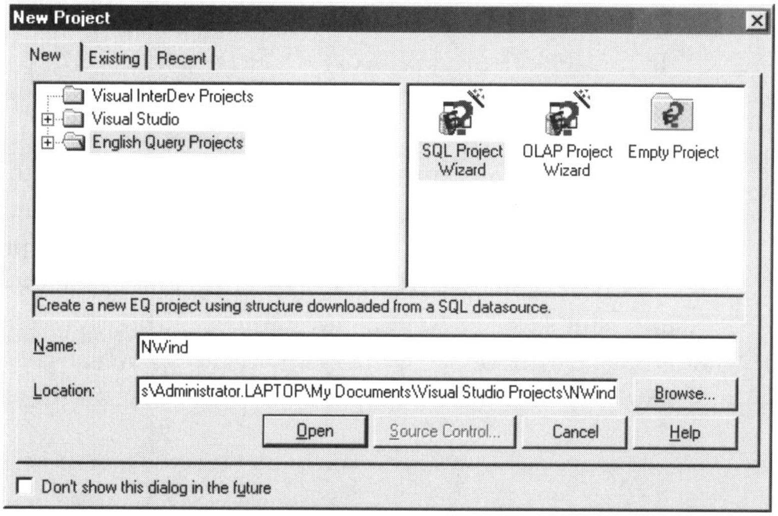

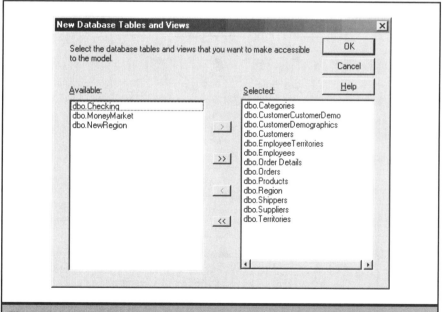

Figure 8-2.   The New Project dialog box in Visual InterDev shows the choices for creating a new English Query application

Figure 8-3.   The New Database Tables and Views dialog box, asking you which tables and views you want to add to your English Query model

view an entity, which is the term used in English Query to designate a primary object (such as a person, place, or thing).

If you click the red plus (+) sign to expand one of the entities, you can see the relationships the English Query has already figured out for you. The table name usually represents a major entity. The fields in the tables usually represent minor entities, similar to properties. Notice in Figure 8-4 that English Query has already decided the entity "customer" has several relationships, which happen to match the fields in the table. By default, English Query creates such relationships as "customers have cities," but it gives you the alternative form of "customers are in cities," which makes more sense. For now, don't worry too much about changing all these

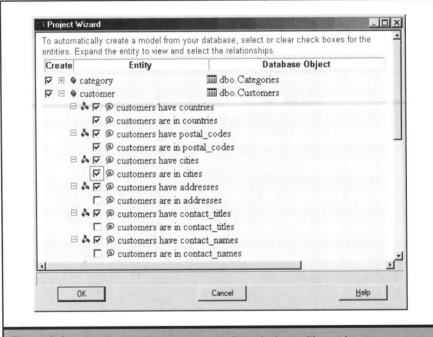

Figure 8-4.   The Project Wizard, automatically assigning entities and some relationships for the English Query model

options. In this case, add the following three rules by expanding the customer node and selecting the lines.

▼   Customers are in countries

■   Customers are in postal_codes

▲   Customers are in cities

If you click the red "a" symbol next to one of the relationships, it opens the relationship dialog box. You examine this in more detail later but, for now, understand this is how you create new relationships and modify existing ones.

Once you finish looking at this screen, click the OK button. You are now taken into the Microsoft Development Environment, which is what you have been using with VI since the beginning. Figure 8-5 shows

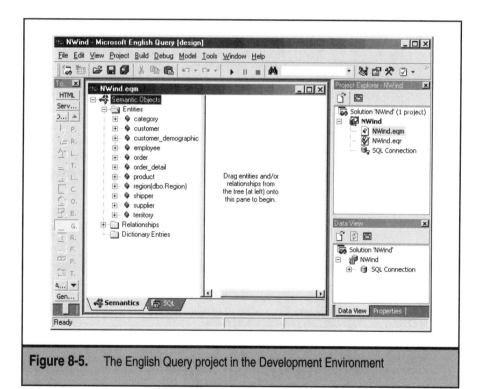

Figure 8-5.   The English Query project in the Development Environment

what the environment looks like with the new project. The main window shows the NWind.eqm, which is a graphical representation of the English Query model. In the Project Explorer window, you can see the model file along with NWind.eqr, which is used for regressions. *Regressions* are an automated way to feed in a series of questions to see if the engine can handle them. Finally, there's a graphical representation of the database connection. The rest of the windows, such as the Data View and Toolbox, are the same as you are used to seeing.

Testing the Application for the First Time

Now that you've created a project, go ahead and test it. To test your project, click the Debug menu and choose start. This opens the Model Test window, shown in Figure 8-6, which is simply a small application that enables you to test your English questions. The Model Test

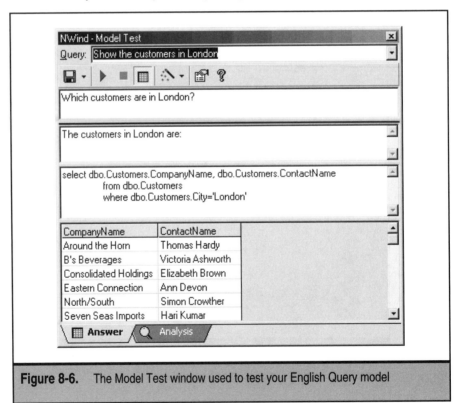

Figure 8-6. The Model Test window used to test your English Query model

converts the English statement into SQL (or later, MDX) and even executes the resulting SQL Statement and shows you the results.

In the Model Test window, click the button on the toolbar that enables you to view results. This opens a results pane and shows the results of the statement by running the SQL against the database. In the Query textbox, type the following English statement and press the ENTER key:

```
Show the customers in London
```

If you look at Figure 8-6, you'll notice several things. First, after you type the statement and execute it, English Query restates what you typed in the way it understands your question. In this case, the restatement is "Which customers are in London?" which is, indeed, what you are asking. The next pane shows the "answer" to the restated question, in this case displaying "The customers in London are:"

The next pane shows what the English Query engine is really doing: it is taking your English Question and converting it to SQL. The resulting SQL statement is

```
select dbo.Customers.CompanyName, dbo.Customers.ContactName
    from dbo.Customers
    where dbo.Customers.City='London'
```

Finally, in the bottom pane, you see the actual results of the SQL statement—you see the CompanyName and ContactName fields for all the customers that have a City field of London.

How did English Query figure this out? Remember that when looking at the relationships the wizard had created, it knew customers had, or were in, cities? Therefore, when you asked for customers in London, it had to figure out if London was a city, postal code, or country.

Now, try the next statement:

```
What clients are in London?
```

Notice this statement translates into the same statement as the previous question. How did English Query know clients and customers are the same thing? English Query makes guesses about certain words and assigns them certain synonyms. You can modify these synonyms, as you see later.

Now, try this sentence:

```
What suppliers are in London?
```

This might sound like a valid request, but English Query doesn't understand it. If you remember the customer entity, you had to add the relationship to tell English Query customers are in cities. You didn't make this same change to the supplier entity, so it doesn't understand your question. You can rephrase your statement, however, so English Query does understand it. Try this phrase:

```
What suppliers have cities of London?
```

This produces the SQL you would expect. It translates to:

```
select dbo.Suppliers.CompanyName, dbo.Suppliers.ContactName
    from dbo.Suppliers
    where dbo.Suppliers.City='London'
```

Now, try one more statement. Type the following query and see what happens:

```
Which customers buy Chai?
```

This is another statement that would appear reasonable ("Chai" is the name of a product), but English Query doesn't know how to handle it. While English Query creates a number of relationships using the wizard, it generally only creates relationships based on an individual entity. In other words, English Query doesn't know how two entities are related, so it doesn't know customers buy products. To handle these multi-entity relationships, you must manually modify the model and create the relationships.

Modifying the Model

You can modify the English Query model you've created in numerous ways. Remember, in the previous section, you tried to ask which suppliers were in London, but the engine was unable to respond? This is because the relationship to tell the engine that suppliers are in cities hasn't been set up. You can add this relationship in multiple ways, but you start with a simple way.

In the model window shown in Figure 8-5, the left-hand pane has a node for the entities, as well as a node for relationships and dictionary entries. Expand the Relationships node and look at all the relationships created by the wizard. Scroll down until you find the relationship that says "suppliers_have_cities." This is the relationship set up for you by the wizard and it allows the statement "What suppliers have cities of London" to work. This is a rather strange way to ask the question, however, so you probably want to add the relationship that suppliers are in cities. To do this, double-click the "suppliers_have_cities" relationship.

Double-clicking the relationship opens the Relationship dialog box, shown in Figure 8-7. This box enables you to add more relationships to the model. In this case, you see two entities are

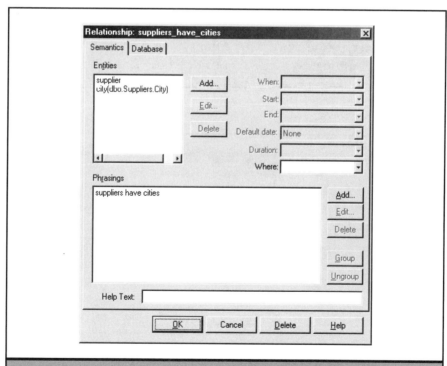

Figure 8-7.   The Relationship dialog box enables you to add relationships to your English Query model

in the Entities box: supplier and city. You might notice the city entity is followed by "(dbo.Suppliers.City)." This happens when more than one field is named "City" in various tables; English Query has to know from which table you are pulling the City field.

You don't need any more entities, but you do need to add a phrasing. In the Phrasing box, you can see the current relationship: "suppliers have cities." Press the Add button next to the Phrasing box. This opens the Select Phrasing dialog box, shown in Figure 8-8. This box enables you to choose what kind of phrasing you want to add. In this case, you want to add that suppliers are in cities, which is a prepositional phrase. If you aren't sure exactly what the different phrases will give you, clicking one shows you several examples. For now, choose Preposition Phrasing and click OK.

Next up is the Preposition Phrasing dialog box. This is where you actually create the new relationship. As you can see in Figure 8-9, this particular phrase consists of a subject, a preposition, and an object. The Subject box probably already has the word "suppliers" in it; if not, select suppliers from the drop-down list box. In the Prepositions box, type the word "in." After typing the word "in," you can press the button next to the Preposition box. This button has ellipses (...) on it. If you press this button, it drops down a list similar to what you

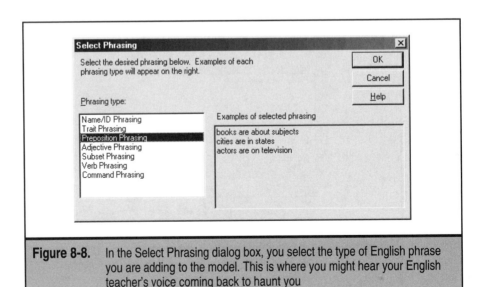

Figure 8-8. In the Select Phrasing dialog box, you select the type of English phrase you are adding to the model. This is where you might hear your English teacher's voice coming back to haunt you

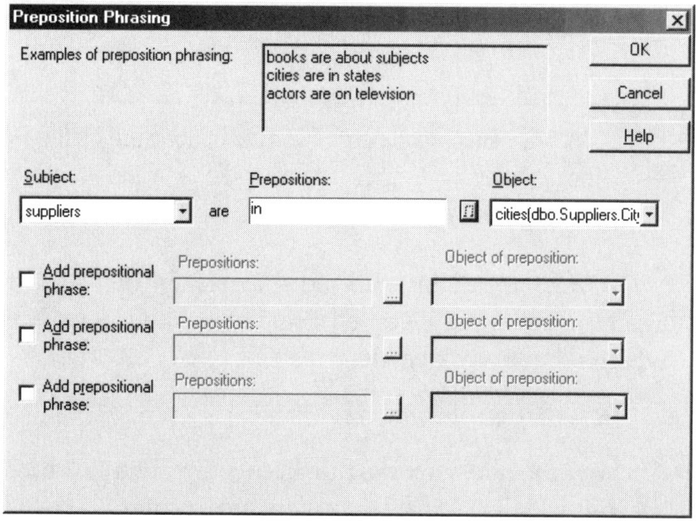

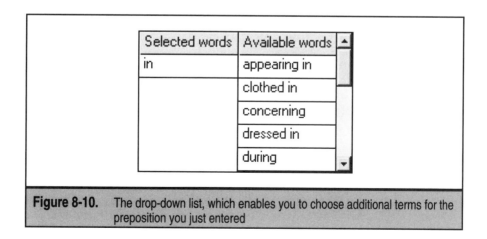

Figure 8-9.   The Preposition Phrasing dialog box

see in Figure 8-10. This list enables you to assign additional terms to your prepositional phrase. If you scroll through the list, you might see the word "within." Saying "suppliers are within cities" might make sense, so if you choose, you can click the word "within" and it is then added to the prepositional phrase. Finally, in the Object box,

Selected words	Available words
in	appearing in
	clothed in
	concerning
	dressed in
	during

Figure 8-10.   The drop-down list, which enables you to choose additional terms for the preposition you just entered

pick "cities," click the OK button, and then click the OK button again on the Relationship dialog box.

NOTE: Be careful here. Two Add buttons are on the Relationship dialog box: one by the Entities list box and one by the Phrasings list box. Make sure you choose the appropriate one.

Now that you have added this new phrase, test the application again by choosing Debug | Start from the menu. Reenter this query, which didn't work earlier:

```
What suppliers are in London?
```

Now the query works fine because you have added the relationship that tells English Query suppliers are in cities.

Relating Multiple Entities

The earlier question "Which customers buy Chai" couldn't be answered because the current model doesn't relate customers and products in any way. To correct this, you need to add a relationship to the model that tells it customers to buy or purchase products.

To add the relationship, look at the model in the Development Environment. Right-click on the Relationships node and choose Add Relationship. This opens the New Relationship dialog box, which is the same as the Relationship dialog box shown in Figure 8-7. Click the Add button by the Entities list box and choose both the customer and product entities. Next, click the Add button next to the Phrasings list box.

This opens the Select Phrasing dialog box you saw back in Figure 8-8. This time, you want to choose the Verb Phrasing choice. After you click the OK button, you see the Verb Phrasing dialog box, shown in Figure 8-11. Under the Sentence Type list, choose Subject Verb Object. In the Subject box, choose "customers". In the Verb box, type "buy". Click the button with the ellipses and choose the word "purchase". In the Direct Object drop-down box, choose "products" and then click the OK button.

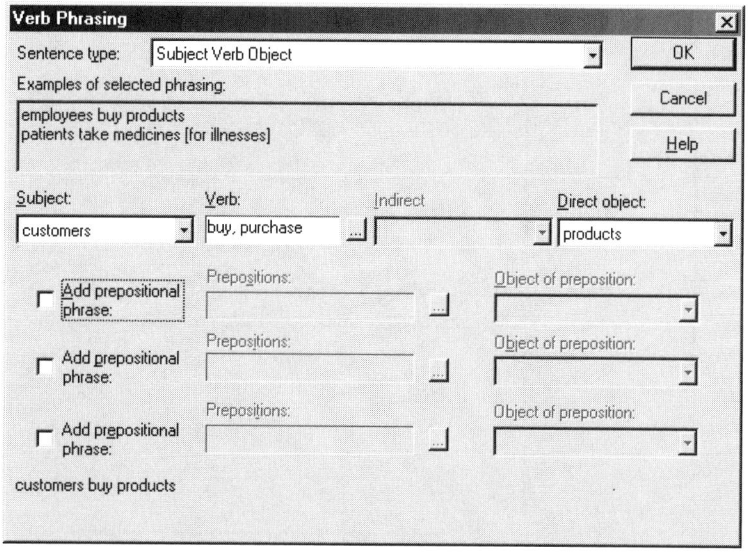

Figure 8-11. The Verb Phrasing dialog box, being used to tie customers and products together

When done, the New Relationship dialog box should look like what you see in Figure 8-12. Click the OK button to close the dialog box. Now, test the application again by selecting Start from the Debug menu. Now, enter this question:

```
Which customers buy Chai?
```

With the addition of your new rule, this statement works fine. You have successfully mapped the relationship between customers and products. You can see this simple English statement generates the following SQL statement:

```
select distinct dbo.Customers.CompanyName, dbo.Customers.ContactName
    from dbo.Products, dbo."Order Details", dbo.Orders, dbo.Customers
    where dbo.Products.ProductName='Chai'
    and dbo."Order Details".OrderID=dbo.Orders.OrderID
    and dbo.Products.ProductID=dbo."Order Details".ProductID
    and dbo.Orders.CustomerID=dbo.Customers.CustomerID
```

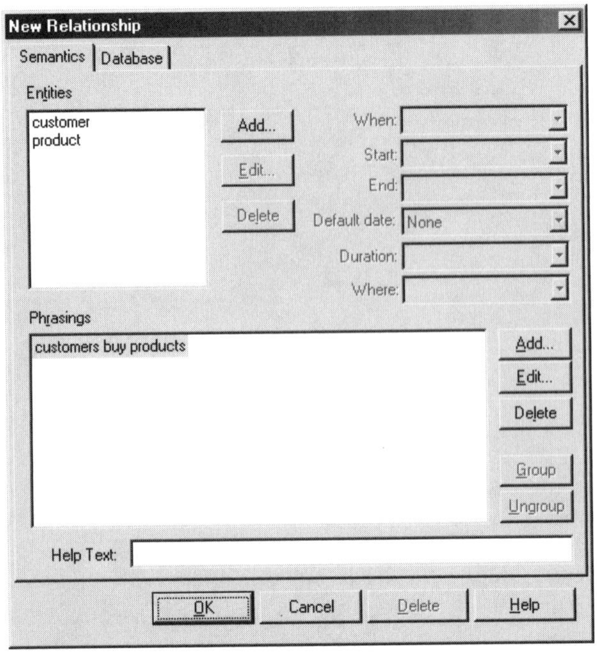

Figure 8-12.   The finished New Relationship dialog box

You can now perform some other queries. For example, you can ask the following questions:

```
How many customers buy Chai?
```

```
Which customers in London buy Chai?
```

You can add relationships in another way: the test tool can guide you through the process. For example, type the following statement:

```
What supplier sells Chai?
```

The model doesn't currently tie suppliers and products together, so the test application reports it cannot answer this question. You know you need to add a relationship that ties suppliers and products with the verb "sells." However, in the test tool, you can click the Suggest Relationships button. Doing so opens the dialog box you see in Figure 8-13. This box walks you through the process of adding

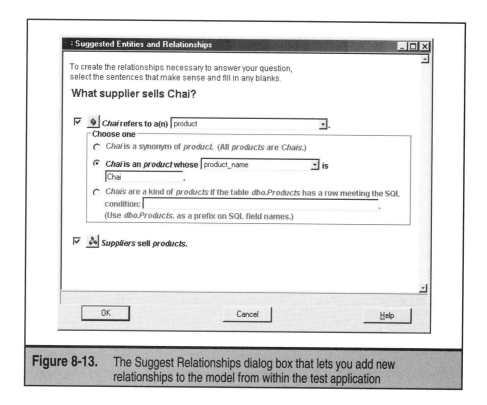

Figure 8-13. The Suggest Relationships dialog box that lets you add new relationships to the model from within the test application

a relationship. The first thing it asks you is to what Chai refers. Drop the list down and choose Product. Then, tell the dialog box that Chai is a product whose product_name is Chai. Finally, make sure the dialog box shows the new statement "Suppliers sell products."

After clicking the OK button, rerun the English statement. The engine can now answer the question because the relationship "suppliers sell products" has been added.

Compiling the Application

Now that you've created the model, it's time to compile it. Compiling the model is necessary both to distribute the model and to have it used by the English Query engine in another application. To compile the application, simply click the Build menu and choose Build. This compiles the model into a .EQD file. This used to be the acronym for "English Query Domain," but the name doesn't seem to have been carried into SQL Server 2000.

This compiled file is what the English Query engine uses. It contains the entity and relationships definitions you set up throughout the chapter. Now you point to this file when you build your application. After compiling the file, it should be in the directory where you created the application. By default, the application will be in C:\Documents and Settings\Administrator\ My Documents\Visual Studio Projects\NWind.

USING ENGLISH QUERY FROM A WEB APPLICATION

To use English Query you need to call the English Query engine from an ASP. The engine is a COM component, so using English Query should be fairly simple. Indeed, instantiating the objects is simple, but the object model itself is far more complex than you might expect.

What English Query is doing is taking your English statement, and then generating a SQL command (or, as you see later, an MDX command). So, you pass English Query the English sentence you want to have it parse and you can expect to receive a SQL string. Think about what can go wrong, though: what if the engine cannot create a valid SQL statement from your question? You saw this in the previous section when you tried to ask the question "Which customers buy Chai?" At first, English Query couldn't respond because you hadn't yet added the rule that told the engine customers to buy products.

To handle such situations, the English Query engine needs to respond with either a SQL or MDX string, or a response that it couldn't process the statement. Different objects are created for these different situations, so you must check to see what kind of object was created to make sure you are handling the return value in the appropriate way.

To start coding with the English Query engine, the first thing you have to do is instantiate what English Query calls a "Session." The *Session object*, which represents your current session or connection to the English Query engine, is similar to an ADO Connection object. The code to instantiate the Session object looks like this:

```
Dim eqEng
Set eqEng=Server.CreateObject("Mseq.Session")
```

NOTE: Don't confuse an English Query Session object with an IIS Session object. The English Query Session object is similar to the ADO Connection object because it represents the connection you have to the English Query engine. The English Query Session object has nothing to do with the IIS Session object or any other part of IIS.

After creating the English Query Session object, you use the InitDomain method to connect to the model you compiled earlier. You need to include the path to this file so, for ease-of-use, I moved this file to the root of my C: drive. The code to connect to the compiled model, which used to be called a domain, is

```
eqEng.InitDomain("c:\NWind.eqd")
```

At this point, you've created an English Query session in memory and you have connected to the model file you created earlier. This file contains all the entities and relationships you created earlier, and will be used by the English Query engine to parse your English statements into SQL.

Next comes the process of parsing the English statement. The English Query Session object has a method called ParseRequest that passes a string to the English Query engine. The ParseRequest method returns a Response object—this is where things can get strange. Three kinds of Response objects exist: a CommandResponse, an ErrorResponse, and a UserClarifyResponse. A *CommandResponse* assumes some normal statement was returned, although there can be different kinds of returned statements. The *ErrorResponse* says EnglishQuery couldn't parse the input string. The *UserClarifyResponse* needs additional input from the user before it can finish processing. To parse an English string, the code looks like this:

```
Set eqResponse=eqEng.ParseRequest("Which customers live in London?")
```

You start with a simple example that contains the normal amount of error-handling developers like to put in (which is, of course, none). Create a new project in Visual InterDev and name it EQtest. Now, add an ASP and name it EQ.asp. For now, assume no errors will be returned. Enter the following code in EQ.asp:

```
<%@ Language=VBScript %>
<HTML>
<BODY>
<Form Name="frmEQ" Action="EQ.asp" Method="Get">
Enter Query: <Input Name="txtEQ" Size="40"><BR>
<Input Type="Submit"><BR><BR>
<%
If Request.QueryString("txtEQ")<>"" Then
     dim eqEng
     dim eqResponse
     dim eqQueryCmd
     set eqEng=server.CreateObject("Mseq.Session")
     eqEng.InitDomain("c:\NWind.eqd")
     set eqResponse=eqEng.ParseRequest _
         (Request.QueryString("txtEQ"))
     set eqQueryCmd=eqResponse.Commands(0)
     Response.Write "<HR><H2>SQL restatement:</H2>"
     Response.Write eqQueryCmd.SQL
End If
%>
</Form>
</BODY>
</HTML>
```

This ASP creates a simple HTML form that accepts your English statement. Once you enter your statement and click the Submit Query button, the English Query engine is instantiated, it is connected to the domain, and the English statement is passed in to be parsed. Once you have the return value in the form of an English Query Response object, look at the Response object's Commands collection and pull out the first Command object. This is *not* an ADO Command object, but an English Query Command object. This object has a property called SQL, which shows you the resulting SQL generated by the English Query statement.

NOTE: Before executing this ASP, you might need to change some permissions. The problem is the DLLs that make English Query work are in a directory to which the default IIS user, IUSR_<servername>, doesn't have access. You can go in and manually set up the permissions or take the easy way out: in your development environment, temporarily add IUSR_<servername> into the Administrators group.

Execute this page and, in the Enter Query field, type the string "Which customers are in London?" and press the Submit Query button. The page that comes back should be similar to what you see in Figure 8-14. The English statement has been converted to SQL by the English Query engine.

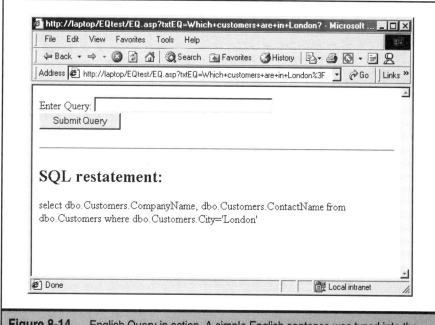

Figure 8-14. English Query in action. A simple English sentence was typed into the text box, and the English Query engine responded with a SQL statement

An alternative to the SQL property is the QueryText property. Both properties hold the SQL string returned from English Query. Now you have the SQL string back. This is the main point of English Query: take an English question and convert it to SQL or MDX. Now you have to display the results yourself. You do this using standard ADO. Modify the EQ.asp so it contains the following code:

```
<%@ Language=VBScript %>
<HTML>
<BODY>
<Form Name="frmEQ" Action="EQ.asp" Method="Get">
Enter Query: <Input Name="txtEQ" Size="40"><BR>
<Input Type="Submit"><BR><BR>
<%
If Request.QueryString("txtEQ")<>"" Then
    dim eqEng
    dim eqResponse
    dim eqQueryCmd
    set eqEng=server.CreateObject("Mseq.Session")
    eqEng.InitDomain("c:\NWind.eqd")
    set eqResponse=eqEng.ParseRequest _
        (Request.QueryString("txtEQ"))
    set eqQueryCmd=eqResponse.Commands(0)
    Response.Write "<HR><H2>SQL restatement:</H2>"
    Response.Write eqQueryCmd.SQL

    Response.Write "<HR>"
    dim cn
    dim rs
    dim myData
    set cn=Server.CreateObject("ADODB.Connection")
    cn.Open "Provider=SQLOLEDB;Password=;User ID=sa;" & _
        "Initial Catalog=Northwind;Data Source=laptop"
    set rs=cn.Execute(eqQueryCmd.SQL)
```

```
        myData=rs.GetRows
        rs.Close
    cn.Close
    lColumns=ubound(myData,1)
    lRows=ubound(myData,2)
%>
<TABLE Border="1" Cellpadding="2" Cellspacing="2">
    <% For x=0 to lRows %>
    <TR>
        <% For y=0 to lColumns %>
        <TD><% =myData(y,x) %></TD>
        <% Next %>
    </TR>
    <% Next %>
</TABLE>
<%
End If
%>
</Form>
</BODY>
</HTML>
```

With this modified ASP, you are still having English Query process your English statement and return a SQL command. Now, however, you are passing that SQL command into a standard ADO Command object's Execute method and building a table of the results. This is what you have been doing for most of the book so far, so this should look familiar to you. The results of this new page can be seen in Figure 8-15. Not only does English Query turn your English statement into SQL, but you now call the database using ADO and execute the SQL statement. Don't hesitate to try another statement, such as "Which customers buy Chai?" Realize, though, that if you put in something the page doesn't understand, no error handling occurs at this point.

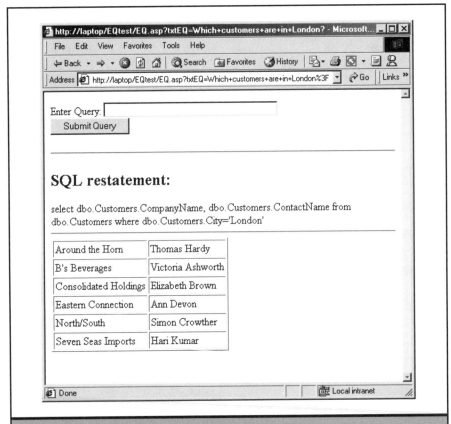

Figure 8-15. The English Query page taking shape, returning a SQL string and then executing it against the database

Adding Some Error Handling

At this point, your EQ.asp chokes if you ask a question it doesn't understand. For example, it understands the question "Which suppliers sell Chai?", but it doesn't understand the question "Which vendors sell Chai?" This lack of understanding is simply because English Query doesn't understand the word "vendor." While this is easy enough to add, how do you handle such events in the ASP?

Remember, when you call the ParseRequst method, it returns a Response object. Multiple types of responses can come back, however. One of these is a UserClarifyResponse, which is what has been passed back with the statement "Which vendors sell Chai?" Therefore, you can't assume you'll get back a valid SQL statement;

instead, you must check to see exactly what kind of Response object was returned, and then handle it appropriately.

Without going into all the details, finding out what type of Response object was returned is fairly simply. You simply look at the Type property of the Response object which tells you what type of Response object was returned. To handle the error that was returned, you can modify the code to check the type of Response object that was returned and display the appropriate result. In this case, the question "Which vendors sell Chai?" returns a request for clarification. Because English Query doesn't understand the word "vendors," it gives you a list of possible alternatives. Modify the EQ.asp to contain this code:

```
<%@ Language=VBScript %>
<HTML>
<BODY>
<Form Name="frmEQ" Action="EQ.asp" Method="Get">
Enter Query: <Input Name="txtEQ" Size="40"><BR>
<Input Type="Submit"><BR><BR>
<%
If Request.QueryString("txtEQ")<>"" Then
    dim eqEng
    dim eqResponse
    dim eqQueryCmd

    const nlResponseCommand=0
    const nlResponseError=2
    const nlResponseUserClarify=3

    set eqEng=server.CreateObject("Mseq.Session")
    eqEng.InitDomain("c:\NWind.eqd")
    set eqResponse=eqEng.ParseRequest _
       (Request.QueryString("txtEQ"))
    Select Case eqResponse.Type
       Case nlResponseCommand
          set eqQueryCmd=eqResponse.Commands(0)
          Response.Write "<HR><H2>SQL restatement:</H2>"
          Response.Write eqQueryCmd.SQL
          Response.Write "<HR>"
```

```
        dim cn
        dim rs
        dim myData
        set cn=Server.CreateObject("ADODB.Connection")
        cn.Open "Provider=SQLOLEDB;Password=;User ID=sa;" & _
            "Initial Catalog=Northwind;Data Source=laptop"
        set rs=cn.Execute(eqQueryCmd.SQL)
        myData=rs.GetRows
        rs.Close
        cn.Close
        lColumns=ubound(myData,1)
        lRows=ubound(myData,2)
        %>
        <TABLE Border="1" Cellpadding="2" Cellspacing="2">
            <% For x=0 to lRows %>
            <TR>
                <% For y=0 to lColumns %>
                <TD><% =myData(y,x) %></TD>
                <% Next %>
            </TR>
            <% Next %>
        </TABLE>
    <%
    Case nlResponseUserClarify
        Response.Write eqResponse.UserInputs(0).Caption & "<BR>"
        sChoices=eqResponse.UserInputs(0).Items
        for i=0 to ubound(sChoices)
            Response.Write sChoices(i) & "<BR>"
        next
    Case nlResponseError
        Response.Write "Error message:" & "<BR>"
        Response.Write eqResponse.Description
    End Select
End If
%>
</Form>
</BODY>
</HTML>
```

Now, view the page in IE, type "Which vendors sell Chai?", and click the Submit Query button. The Response object that comes back is a UserClarifyResponse, and it contains a list of alternatives to the word "vendors." You can see the results in Figure 8-16. This list shows the English Query dictionary does include the word "venders," which is an alternative spelling.

It should now seem like a simple matter to type "Which venders sell Chai?" and run with it. Go ahead and try it, but now you have another problem: English Query has no idea to what "venders" refers. It knows the word "venders," but doesn't know it should be a synonym for suppliers. An error is returned, as shown in Figure 8-17.

You can present the user with a nice message because you can trap the error. In addition, you can log the original question in a file, so you can go back and modify the model to handle that question in the future.

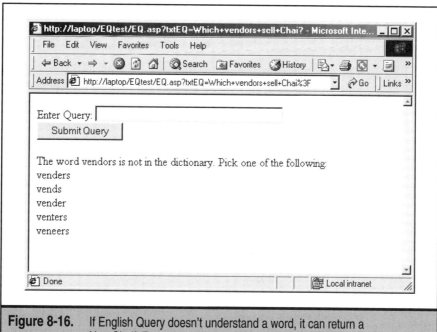

Figure 8-16. If English Query doesn't understand a word, it can return a UserClarifyResponse object, which can list alternatives

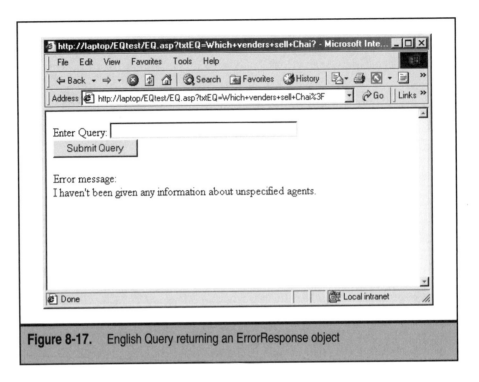

Figure 8-17.   English Query returning an ErrorResponse object

USING ENGLISH QUERY WITH ANALYSIS SERVICES

Just as English Query can be used to access relational tables, SQL
Server 2000 also allows it to access cubes in Analysis Services. In the
previous chapter, you saw how to access cubes using ADO MD. Now
you can create a simple English Query model to access cubes using
simple English statements. English Query generates MDX to query
the multidimensional data.

Start a new project with Visual InterDev but, this time, choose
OLAP Project Wizard, as shown in Figure 8-18. Name the project
EQolap and click the Open button. Figure 8-19 shows the next form,
which asks for the server and database names. Pick the appropriate
server, and then choose the FoodMart 2000 OLAP database.

The next screen, shown in Figure 8-20, asks you to choose one
or more cubes. Choose the Sales cube and then click OK. The next
screen is the one showing the entities and relationships that have
been automatically generated, and is shown in Figure 8-21. This is

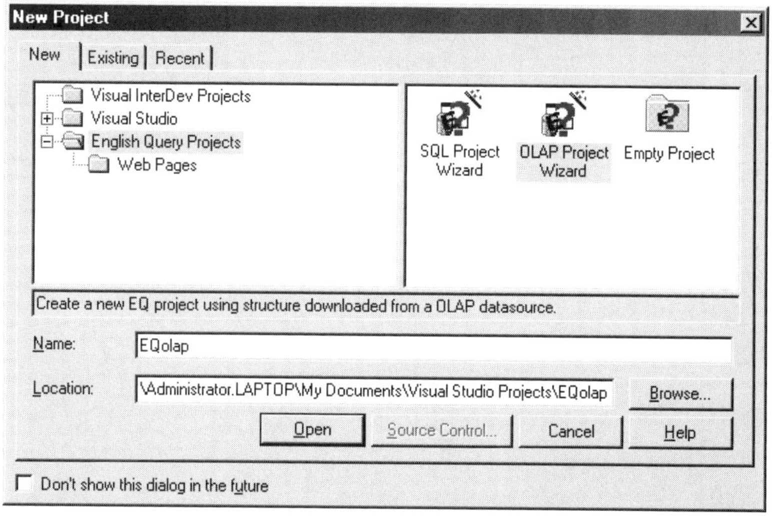

Figure 8-18. Starting an OLAP Project with English Query

similar to the screen you saw earlier, in Figure 8-4. Feel free to browse the entities and relationships created, but leave them unchanged. When you're finished, click the OK button.

You've already seen how English Query works and what it does. Now it's time to jump straight to an example. Go ahead and compile the English Query model by choosing the Build menu, and then Build. Once again, copy the .EQD file to the root of the C: drive.

Figure 8-19. Choosing the appropriate server and OLAP database

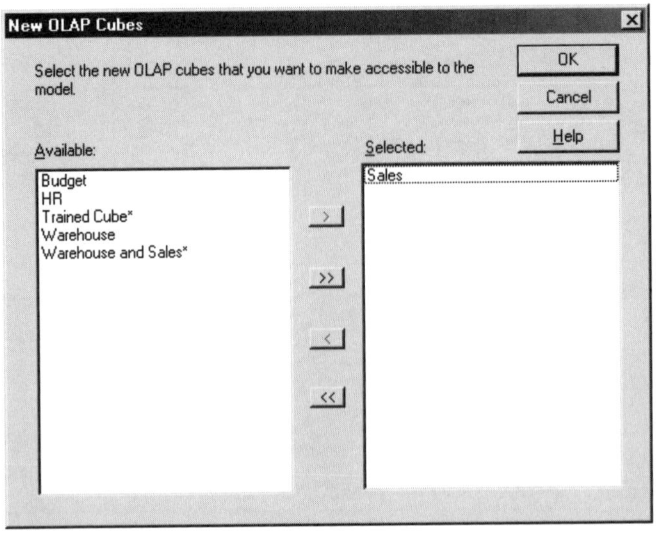

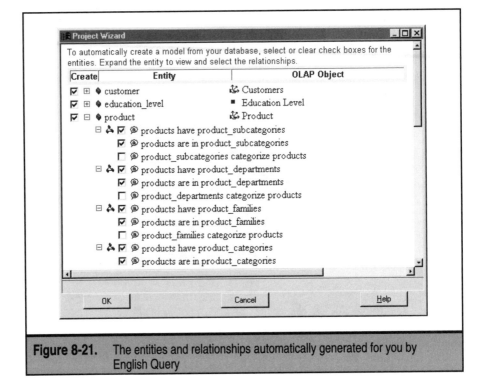

Figure 8-20. The screen asking you to choose the cubes to use in the model

Figure 8-21. The entities and relationships automatically generated for you by English Query

Now, in your EQtest application, create a new ASP named EQolap.asp. Enter the following code:

```
<%@ Language=VBScript %>
<HTML>
<BODY>
<Form Name="frmEQ" Action="EQolap.asp" Method="Get">
Enter Query: <Input Name="txtEQ" Size="40"><BR>
<Input Type="Submit" id=Submit1 name=Submit1><BR><BR>
<%
If Request.QueryString("txtEQ")<>"" Then
    dim eqEng
    dim eqResponse
    dim eqQueryCmd

    const nlResponseCommand=0
    const nlResponseError=2
    const nlResponseUserClarify=3

    set eqEng=server.CreateObject("Mseq.Session")
    eqEng.InitDomain("c:\EQolap.eqd")
    set eqResponse=eqEng.ParseRequest _
        (Request.QueryString("txtEQ"))
    set eqQueryCmd=eqResponse.Commands(0)
    Response.Write "<HR><H2>MDX restatement:</H2>"
    Response.Write eqQueryCmd.SQL
    Response.Write "<HR>"
    dim cat
    dim cst
    dim sMDX
    dim x,y
    set cat=server.CreateObject("ADOMD.Catalog")
    set cst=server.CreateObject("ADOMD.Cellset")
    cat.ActiveConnection="Provider=MSOLAP.2;Password=;" & _
        "Persist Security Info=True;User ID=sa;" & _
        "Data Source=laptop;Initial Catalog=" & _
        "FoodMart 2000;Client Cache Size=25;" & _
        "Auto Synch Period=10000"
    Response.Write "<H1>" & cat.Name & "</H1>"
```

```
sMDX=eqQueryCmd.SQL
set cst.ActiveConnection=cat.ActiveConnection
cst.Source=sMDX
cst.Open
%>
<TABLE Border="1" Cellspacing="2" Cellpadding="2">
<%
Response.Write("<TR><TD> </TD>")
For x=0 to cst.Axes(0).Positions.Count-1
    Response.Write "<TD>" & _
        cst.Axes(0).Positions(x) _
        .Members(0).Caption & "</TD>"
Next
Response.Write "</TR>"
For y=0 to cst.Axes(1).Positions.Count-1
    Response.Write "<TR>"
    Response.Write "<TD>" & cst.Axes(1) _
        .Positions(y).Members(0).Caption & "</TD>"
    For x=0 to cst.Axes(0).Positions.Count-1
        Response.Write "<TD>" & _
            cst(x,y).FormattedValue & "</TD>"
    Next
    Response.Write "</TR>"
  Next
  Response.Write "</TABLE>"
End If
%>
</Form>
</BODY>
</HTML>
```

This page lets you run some simple English statements and generates the MDX. The MDX is then executed against the Analysis Services cube and the resulting data displayed. The queries you can run must be simple because OLAP English Query models generally take more modifications than an English Query model against a relational database. Try the following statement: "Show the stores in WA." This shows the page you see in Figure 8-22.

This example has been brief. You've already seen how to handle errors from English Query, and you've seen how to build and modify the models. Working with Analysis Services isn't much different from working with relational databases, once you have identified your entities and relationships.

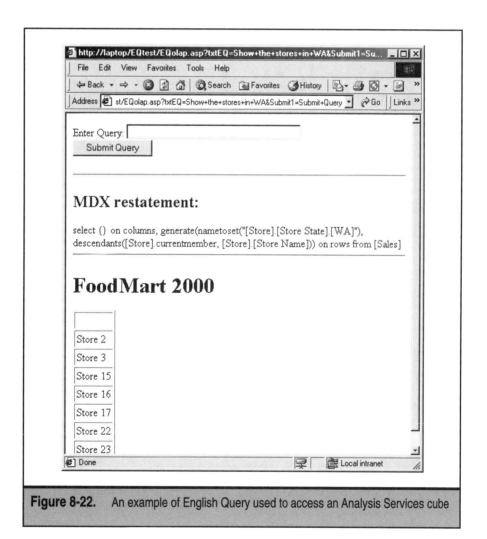

Figure 8-22.   An example of English Query used to access an Analysis Services cube

SUMMARY

English Query is an interesting tool, and it can be fun to work with and demonstrate. English Query holds out the promise of providing a natural language interface into your data, enabling your users to ask standard English questions and to have meaningful data returned.

What are the drawbacks? First, of course, only English is supported. I had the honor of teaching data warehousing to 24 students from around the world, none of whom were from the United States or Canada. When I asked who would be using English Query, the one student from England raised his hand and asked if it would understand "the Queen's English."

Second, you can see that setting up a model takes some time and effort. Allowing natural language access can require a lot of work for an administrator or developer to build the model and test it. In addition, working with the English Query object model can prove interesting.

Finally, perhaps the most frightening thing is the user doesn't know if the question was translated correctly. I've seen rare cases where English Query rephrases a question in such a way that it returns something that appears reasonable to the user but, in fact, the numbers are wrong. It's not creating invalid data, it's just pulling the wrong data to answer the question. The user would have a hard time detecting when this has happened.

Despite these drawbacks, English Query has its place, and some complex models can be built. It's good to know you have yet another tool you can bring to bear as you work on building Web applications.

CHAPTER 9

Advanced
Data Access

As you have already seen, ADO is powerful. You spent two entire chapters looking at the ADO objects and what they can do for you. Then, you spent another chapter on ADO MD and another on English Query. It's time to return to ADO and look at a few more capabilities that make it even more powerful for creating your Web applications. You'll learn about two little-used, but powerful, features: data shaping and disconnected recordsets.

After looking at these two ADO features, you'll examine XML in general. ADO has some powerful XML features, and so does SQL Server 2000. You'll learn about both of these and see how you can use these technologies to extend your applications into the future.

DATA SHAPING

Data shaping provides you with a way to create recordsets that are hierarchical in nature; in other words, a parent-child relationship exists between two or more entities. Building hierarchical recordsets can reduce the size of the overall recordset by removing repeated data, and this can lead to faster download times when sending the records from the database server to the Web server.

A Typical Recordset Made with Joins

A typical recordset made with joins contains the parent and child records in a flat, two-dimensional structure. As an example, assume you want to print off an order from a customer. To print an order, you need the information in the Orders table, such as the order date, the required date, and the ship-to name and address. You also need information from the Order Details table, such as each item ordered, the quantity, and the price. To keep the example simple, let's join only the Orders and Order Details tables in Northwind and examine the output. Enter the following SQL statement in SQL Server's Query Analyzer:

```
Select * from Orders, [Order Details]
   where Orders.OrderID=[Order Details].OrderID
```

The result set of this query contains 19 fields. The OrderID field appears twice, but other than that, you need almost all those fields to print a copy of the order. I realize you would also have to join to the Customers and Products tables and, perhaps, even the Employees table, but for now, let's leave those out to keep this as simple as possible.

The problem with this recordset, which can be represented in Figure 9-1, is the data from the Orders table is repeated for each record in the Order Details table. You only need the information for each order one time, which means you only need the ship-to address once, regardless of how many items the customer ordered. What are your alternatives?

Clearly, you could perform multiple queries. You could query the Orders table, and then return to the Order Details table once for each customer. Logically, your code would look like this:

```
Perform query "Select * from Orders"
Loop through OrderIDs
    For this OrderID, perform query "Select * from [Order Details] " & _
        "where OrderID=" & nOrderID
Go to next OrderID
```

In this pseudocode, you are getting all the records from the Orders table one time, and then making a round-trip to the database and retrieving only the Order Details records on the subsequent trips. This approach has the advantage of not retrieving all the Orders

OrderID	CustomerID	OrderDate	Ship Name	ShipAddress	ProductID	Quantity	UnitPrice
14732	TORR1	10/27/2000	Westie Enterprises	123 Main Street, Suite 24	1R74B	12	$14.00
14732	TORR1	10/27/2000	Westie Enterprises	123 Main Street, Suite 24	1R75A	25	$3.95
14732	TORR1	10/27/2000	Westie Enterprises	123 Main Street, Suite 24	TR14J-FW	144	$0.33
14732	TORR1	10/27/2000	Westie Enterprises	123 Main Street, Suite 24	MLJ19	2	$179.40
14733	HAIL3	10/28/2000	Scottie Industries	519A Oak Street	1R74B	3	$14.00
14733	HAIL3	10/28/2000	Scottie Industries	519A Oak Street	2S22B-T	20	$79.95

Figure 9-1. A recordset created with the standard SQL join syntax

fields for each Order Details record, but it has the disadvantage of making many round-trips to the database, which is typically slower.

Faced with the option of repeating the fields from the Orders table for each record in the Order Details and making one round-trip, or making multiple round-trips and retrieving the Orders and Order Details records separately, most people choose to make only one trip to the database and bring back all the fields using a join.

Hierarchical Recordsets

You do have another alternative: you can use data shaping to create a hierarchical recordset. A *hierarchical recordset* can store data from multiple recordsets and tie these multiple recordsets together. The logical structure, shown in Figure 9-2, shows that the data from the parent table is only retrieved once, regardless of the number of child records. This makes the recordset smaller than a similar one created with a join, which means it downloads to the client faster.

To create a hierarchical recordset, the Shape command is used. The Shape command is powerful and has a great number of options. First, you'll start with a simple example by tying one child table to one parent table. To do this, you start with the Shape command, as you can see in this pseudocode:

```
SHAPE {select statement for parent table}
```

OrderID	CustomerID	OrderDate	Ship Name	ShipAddress	ProductID	Quantity	UnitPrice
14732	TORR1	10/27/2000	Westie Enterprises	123 Main Street, Suite 24	1R74B	12	$14.00
					1R75A	25	$3.95
					TR14J-FW	144	$0.33
					MLJ19	2	$179.40
14733	HAIL3	10/28/2000	Scottie Industries	519A Oak Street	1R74B	3	$14.00
					2S22B-T	20	$79.95

Figure 9-2. A logical view of a hierarchical recordset created with data shaping commands

This statement merely brings back the fields in the parent table. No join to the child table is here; you are pulling back the records from the parent only. The next step in this process is to pull out the records from the child table. To do this, you use the Append clause of the Shape command. The Append clause only adds one or more columns to the recordset. Most often, at least one of these columns is what is called a *chapter column,* which is a column used to relate the child records to the parent record.

The Append clause has a Relate clause that tells you which field in the parent ties to which field in the child. These fields needn't have the same name but, of course, they must have the same data type. The Append clause looks similar to this pseudocode:

```
APPEND ({select statement for child table}
   RELATE {field in parent table TO field in child table})
      AS chapter name
```

The last part of the Append clause is the As clause, which defines a chapter name. In a sense, this chapter name becomes a field in the parent recordset. When you reference this field, you get access to the child records for that parent record. You can access the records in the child table as if each parent record has a field that holds a recordset object of the child records. You do this by setting a new recorder object to the value of the chapter field.

In this example, you want to tie the order header to the order detail records. The order header information is in the Orders table, and the details records are in Order Details. Because a space is in the name of the Order Details table, you must enclose it inside of square brackets, like this: [Order Details]. Your finished query looks like this:

```
SHAPE  {select * from Orders}
APPEND ({select * from [Order Details]}
RELATE OrderID TO OrderID) AS chapOrderDetail
```

In this statement, you first select all the fields from the Orders table. Then, you append on all the fields from the Order Details table, but you relate the two recordsets on the OrderID fields in each table. The As clause says you are relating them on a chapter field named chapOrderDetail. When you walk through the parent recordset, you walk through the fields of the Orders table. An additional field is on the parent recordset that's called chapOrderDetail and, if you access that field, the field acts like a recordset. You get a reference to it as a Recordset object, and then retrieve the fields from it.

Let's look at a concrete example. You've already seen the code you use as the command text. Now, go ahead and create a full ASP that not only runs the previous query, but also displays the data on the page. Create a new VI project and call it AdvData. Then create an ASP named DataShape.asp. Now enter the following code:

```
<%@ Language=VBScript %>
<HTML>
<BODY>
<%
    Dim cn
    Dim rsOrder
    Dim rsOrderDetail
    Set cn = Server.CreateObject("ADODB.Connection")
    Set rsOrder = Server.CreateObject("ADODB.Recordset")
    Set rsOrderDetail = Server.CreateObject("ADODB.Recordset")
    cn.Provider = "MSDataShape"
    cn.Open "Data Provider=SQLOLEDB;Data Source=laptop;" & _
        "Initial Catalog=Northwind;User ID=sa;Password=;"

    rsOrder.Open "SHAPE  {select * from Orders} " & _
        "APPEND ({select * from [Order Details]} " & _
        "RELATE OrderID TO OrderID) AS chapOrderDetail", _
        cn
    Set rsOrderDetail = rsOrder("chapOrderDetail").Value
%>

<%
    Do Until rsOrder.EOF
        Response.Write rsOrder("CustomerID") & " - " & _
            rsOrder("ShipName") & " - " & _
            rsOrder("ShipAddress") & " - " & _
            rsOrder("ShipCountry") & "<TABLE Border=1>"
```

```
        Response.Write "<TR><TH>Product</TH><TH>Price</TH>" & _
            "<TH>Quantity</TH><TH>Discount</TH></TR>"
      Do Until rsOrderDetail.EOF
         Response.Write "<TR><TD>" & _
            rsOrderDetail("ProductID") & "</TD><TD Align=Right>" & _
            FormatCurrency(rsOrderDetail("UnitPrice"))& _
              "</TD><TD>" & _
            rsOrderDetail("Quantity") & "</TD><TD>" & _
            rsOrderDetail("Discount") & "</TD></TR>"
         rsOrderDetail.MoveNext
      Loop
      Response.Write "</TABLE><BR><BR>"
      rsOrder.MoveNext
   Loop
%>
</BODY>
</HTML>
```

If you look at the code, you notice several things are new. First, examine how you connected to the database:

```
cn.Provider = "MSDataShape"
cn.Open "Data Provider=SQLOLEDB;Data Source=laptop;" & _
   "Initial Catalog=Northwind;User ID=sa;Password=;"
```

Data shaping requires the use of two providers. The first is a *service provider,* which in this case is the Data Shaping Service for OLE DB, referenced by MSDataShape. The Data Shaping Service is what provides the data shaping functionality. To use this, assign the Connection object's Provider property to the MSDataShape provider or, in the string, include a "Provider=" clause.

The second provider is known as the *data provider,* and can be almost any OLE DB provider. The data provider is what is used to create the records in the shaped recordset. To specify the data provider, you can include a "Data Provider=" clause in the connection string, as you did in the previous example. Or, you can set it in the Connection object. A Data Provider property of the Connection object doesn't exist but, when you specify the Data Shaping Service as the provider, a dynamic property is added to the Connection object's Properties collection. This enables you to set the property this way, if you choose:

```
cn.Properties("Data Provider")="SQLOLEDB"
```

Or, you can use this syntax:

```
cn.Properties.Item("Data Provider")="SQLOLEDB"
```

In the code, notice you also created two ADO Recordset objects: rsOrder and rsOrderDetail. Of course, you only created one Connection object because both the tables you are calling reside in the same database. The first Recordset object is used to open the entire SQL statement, which includes both the tables. How does this work?

Remember, in effect, you are creating recordsets within a recordset. This first Recordset object points to the overall recordset. Inside each row is a field that contains a recordset. You use the second Recordset object to reference this recordset within each row. Therefore, you open the first recordset with this code:

```
rsOrder.Open "SHAPE  {select * from Orders} " & _
     "APPEND ({select * from [Order Details]} " & _
     "RELATE OrderID TO OrderID) AS chapOrderDetail", _
     cn
```

Now you have rsOrder in memory, and it looks similar to what you have in Figure 9-3. This shows that for each parent row, you have what appears to be a recordset inside the chapter column. You use the second recordset to refer to the value, or recordset, inside

OrderID	CustomerID	OrderDate	Ship Name	ShipAddress	chapOrderDetail		
					ProductID	Quantity	Price
					1R74B	12	$14.00
14732	TORR1	10/27/2000	Westie Enterprises	123 Main Street, Suite 24	1R75A	25	$3.95
					MLJ19	2	$179.40
					ProductID	Quantity	Price
14733	HAIL3	10/28/2000	Scottie Industries	519A Oak Street	1R74B	3	$14.00

Figure 9-3.   A logical look at the Orders and Order Details hierarchical recordset

the chapter column of the parent recordset. Tying the second recordset to the child records in the chapter column is accomplished with this line of code:

```
Set rsOrderDetail = rsOrder("chapOrderDetail").Value
```

The rsOrder and rsOrderDetail don't know anything about each other but, by default, the rsOrderDetail will contain a recordset of child records, and this recordset is the one pointed to by the chapter field in the current record in rsOrder. This means, as you move through the parent recordset, rsOrder, the rsOrderDetail stays in synch. If, for some reason, you want to scroll through the parent recordset without affecting your child recordset, you can turn off this default behavior with the following line of code:

```
rsOrderDetail.Properties("StayInsynch") = False
```

At this point, you have created two Recordset objects, and you have executed the Shape statement to return a hierarchical recordset. The first recordset, rsOrder, holds the parent records, and the second recordset, rsOrderDetail, is used to reference the records inside the chapter column. Now it's only a matter of displaying the data on the screen. You do this with two simple, nested Do Until loops. The outer Do Until loops you through the parent records. For each parent record, you loop through all the child records in the recordset in the chapter column. The pseudocode would read like this:

```
Look at one record in the parent recordset
    Print out the parent fields
    Look at one record in the child recordset
        Print out the child fields
    Move to the next child record
Move to the next parent record
```

The actual code in the page you created looks like this:

```
Do Until rsOrder.EOF
    Response.Write rsOrder("CustomerID") & " - " & _
        rsOrder("ShipName") & " - " & _
        rsOrder("ShipAddress") & " - " & _
        rsOrder("ShipCountry") & "<TABLE Border=1>"
```

```
          Response.Write "<TR><TH>Product</TH><TH>Price</TH>" & _
             "<TH>Quantity</TH><TH>Discount</TH></TR>"
       Do Until rsOrderDetail.EOF
          Response.Write "<TR><TD>" & _
             rsOrderDetail("ProductID") & "</TD><TD Align=Right>" & _
             FormatCurrency(rsOrderDetail("UnitPrice"))& _
                "</TD><TD>" & _
             rsOrderDetail("Quantity") & "</TD><TD>" & _
             rsOrderDetail("Discount") & "</TD></TR>"
          rsOrderDetail.MoveNext
       Loop
       Response.Write "</TABLE><BR><BR>"
       rsOrder.MoveNext
    Loop
```

In this code, the output is fairly simplistic. You show four of the fields in the parent record, and then create an HTML table. You then loop through all the child records for this parent record, printing four of the fields and putting them in cells in a table. When you finish, you close the table, drop down a few lines, and do it all over again.

The page can take a minute to run, as quite a few records must be processed. When done, the page should look similar to that in Figure 9-4. The last record in the Orders table contains quite a few Order Details records, so I scrolled down to the top of the last record in this figure.

A Parent with Two Children

The Shape command has a variety of other features. For example, one parent can actually have multiple children. The Shape syntax for this looks similar to this pseudocode:

```
SHAPE {select statement for parent table}
APPEND ({select statement for first child table}
     RELATE {field in parent table TO field in child table})
     AS chapter name
     ({select statement for second child table}
     RELATE {field in parent table TO field in child table})
     AS chapter name
```

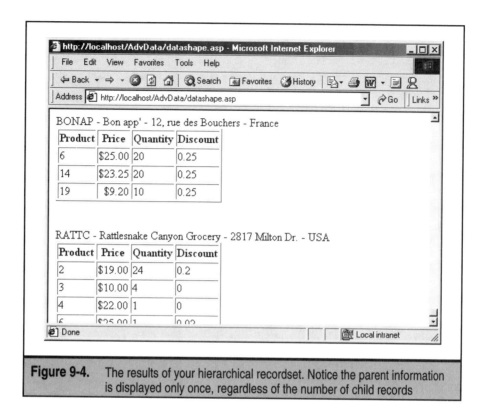

Figure 9-4.   The results of your hierarchical recordset. Notice the parent information is displayed only once, regardless of the number of child records

This yields a recordset in which the parent has two chapter columns. One chapter column points to the first child recordset, and the other chapter column points to the second child recordset. Create a new ASP named TwoKids.asp and enter the following code:

```
<%@ Language=VBScript %>
<HTML>
<BODY>
<%
    Dim cn
    Dim rsOrder
    Dim rsOrderDetail
    Set cn = Server.CreateObject("ADODB.Connection")
    Set rsEmployee = Server.CreateObject("ADODB.Recordset")
    Set rsOrder = Server.CreateObject("ADODB.Recordset")
    Set rsTerritory = Server.CreateObject("ADODB.Recordset")
    cn.Provider = "MSDataShape"
    cn.Properties("Data Provider")="SQLOLEDB"
```

```
    cn.Open "Data Source=laptop;" & _
        "Initial Catalog=Northwind;User ID=sa;Password=;"

    rsEmployee.Open "SHAPE {select EmployeeID, FirstName, LastName " & _
            "from Employees where EmployeeID<4} " & _
            "APPEND ({select OrderID, EmployeeID, ShipName from Orders} " & _
            "RELATE EmployeeID TO EmployeeID) AS chapOrder, " & _
            "({select EmployeeID, TerritoryDescription from " & _
            "EmployeeTerritories et, " & _
            "Territories t where et.TerritoryID=t.TerritoryID} " & _
            "RELATE EmployeeID to EmployeeID) as chapTerritory", _
            cn
    Set rsOrder = rsEmployee("chapOrder").Value
    Set rsTerritory = rsEmployee("chapTerritory").Value
%>


<%
    Do Until rsEmployee.EOF
        Response.Write rsEmployee("FirstName") & " " & _
            rsEmployee("LastName") & "<TABLE Border=1>"
             Response.Write "<TR><TH>Territory</TH></TR>"
        Do Until rsTerritory.EOF
            Response.Write "<TR><TD>" & _
                rsTerritory("TerritoryDescription") & _
                "</TD></TR>"
            rsTerritory.MoveNext
        Loop
        Response.Write "</TABLE>"
        Response.Write "<TABLE Border=1>" & _
            "<TR><TH>OrderID</TH><TH>ShipName</TH></TR>"
         Do Until rsOrder.EOF
            Response.Write "<TR><TD>" &  _
                rsOrder("OrderID") & "</TD><TD>" & _
                rsOrder("ShipName")& _
                   "</TD></TR>"
            rsOrder.MoveNext
        Loop
        Response.Write "</TABLE><BR><BR>"
        rsEmployee.MoveNext
    Loop
%>
</BODY>
</HTML>
```

In this example, the Employees table acts as the parent, and the two children are the Orders and Territories tables. Notice the Territories table actually requires a standard SQL join between Employee Territories and Territories. Nothing is wrong with your parent or the children containing a join.

Figure 9-5 shows what you might see in your browser. It isn't the best formatting job in the world, but you can see that Nancy Davolio covers Wilton and Neward. Below her territories are the orders that have been placed through her.

Was this worth it? Realize that in this example, you not only save bringing down all the parent fields for each child, but you also avoid repeating one child's records for each record in the other child. In

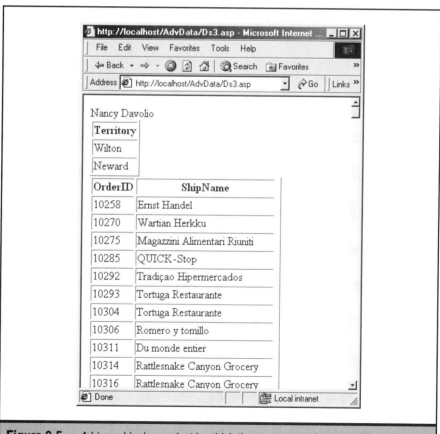

Figure 9-5.   A hierarchical recordset in which the parent contains two children

other words, Figure 9-6 shows what the recordset might have looked like with standard joins, and what you were able to bring down instead. As you can see, you should have accessed significantly fewer total bytes using the shaped recordset.

Grandchildren

Can a child recordset have a child recordset? This is sometimes called a *compound-relation hierarchy*. The pseudocode looks like this:

```
SHAPE {select statement for parent table}
APPEND ((SHAPE {select statement for child table}
   APPEND ({select statement for grandchild table} AS chapter name
       RELATE {field in child table TO field in grandchild table}))
          AS chapter name
       RELATE {field in parent table TO field in child table})
```

To use this, pay careful attention to the parenthesis. There are two AS clauses, and you must make sure you get the names in the correct

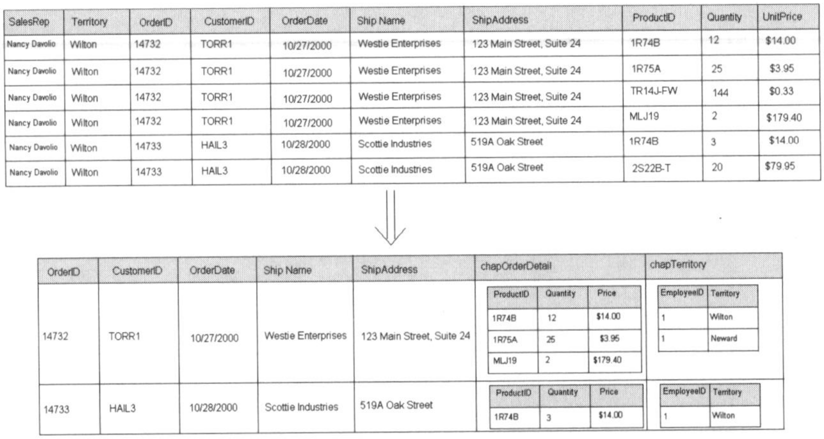

SalesRep	Territory	OrderID	CustomerID	OrderDate	Ship Name	ShipAddress	ProductID	Quantity	UnitPrice
Nancy Davolio	Wilton	14732	TORR1	10/27/2000	Westie Enterprises	123 Main Street, Suite 24	1R74B	12	$14.00
Nancy Davolio	Wilton	14732	TORR1	10/27/2000	Westie Enterprises	123 Main Street, Suite 24	1R75A	25	$3.95
Nancy Davolio	Wilton	14732	TORR1	10/27/2000	Westie Enterprises	123 Main Street, Suite 24	TR14J-FW	144	$0.33
Nancy Davolio	Wilton	14732	TORR1	10/27/2000	Westie Enterprises	123 Main Street, Suite 24	MLJ19	2	$179.40
Nancy Davolio	Wilton	14733	HAIL3	10/28/2000	Scottie Industries	519A Oak Street	1R74B	3	$14.00
Nancy Davolio	Wilton	14733	HAIL3	10/28/2000	Scottie Industries	519A Oak Street	2S22B-T	20	$79.95

<table>
<tr><th>OrderID</th><th>CustomerID</th><th>OrderDate</th><th>Ship Name</th><th>ShipAddress</th><th>chapOrderDetail</th><th>chapTerritory</th></tr>
<tr><td>14732</td><td>TORR1</td><td>10/27/2000</td><td>Westie Enterprises</td><td>123 Main Street, Suite 24</td><td><table><tr><th>ProductID</th><th>Quantity</th><th>Price</th></tr><tr><td>1R74B</td><td>12</td><td>$14.00</td></tr><tr><td>1R75A</td><td>25</td><td>$3.95</td></tr><tr><td>MLJ19</td><td>2</td><td>$179.40</td></tr></table></td><td><table><tr><th>EmployeeID</th><th>Territory</th></tr><tr><td>1</td><td>Wilton</td></tr><tr><td>1</td><td>Neward</td></tr></table></td></tr>
<tr><td>14733</td><td>HAIL3</td><td>10/28/2000</td><td>Scottie Industries</td><td>519A Oak Street</td><td><table><tr><th>ProductID</th><th>Quantity</th><th>Price</th></tr><tr><td>1R74B</td><td>3</td><td>$14.00</td></tr></table></td><td><table><tr><th>EmployeeID</th><th>Territory</th></tr><tr><td>1</td><td>Wilton</td></tr></table></td></tr>
</table>

Figure 9-6. In a hierarchical recordset with two children, you save having to retrieve a significant amount of data

places. If you want to take a customer, and look at the order header and order detail records, the code would look like this:

```
SHAPE   {Select CompanyName from Customers}
APPEND ((SHAPE   {Select * from Orders}
        APPEND ({Select ProductID, Quantity from [Order Details]}
            AS chapOrderDetail
        RELATE OrderID TO OrderID)) AS chapOrder
    RELATE CustomerID TO CustomerID)
```

To see a page with grandchildren recordsets, create a new ASP called Compound.asp and enter the following code:

```
<%@ Language=VBScript %>
<HTML>
<BODY>
<%
    Dim cn
    Dim rsOrder
    Dim rsOrderDetail
    Set cn = Server.CreateObject("ADODB.Connection")
    Set rsCustomer = Server.CreateObject("ADODB.Recordset")
    Set rsOrder = Server.CreateObject("ADODB.Recordset")
    Set rsOrderDetail = Server.CreateObject("ADODB.Recordset")
    cn.Provider = "MSDataShape"
    cn.Properties("Data Provider")="SQLOLEDB"
    cn.Open "Data Source=laptop;" & _
        "Initial Catalog=Northwind;User ID=sa;Password=;"

    rsCustomer.Open "SHAPE {Select CustomerID, CompanyName " & _
    "from Customers} " & _
        "APPEND ((SHAPE   {Select * from Orders} " & _
        "APPEND ({Select OrderID, ProductID, Quantity " & _
        "from [Order Details]} " & _
            "AS chapOrderDetail " & _
          "RELATE OrderID TO OrderID)) AS chapOrder " & _
```

```
            "RELATE CustomerID TO CustomerID)", _
        cn
    Set rsOrder = rsCustomer("chapOrder").Value
    Set rsOrderDetail = rsOrder("chapOrderDetail").Value
%>


<%
    Do Until rsCustomer.EOF
        Response.Write rsCustomer("CompanyName") & _
            "<TABLE Border=1>"
        Do Until rsOrder.EOF
            Response.Write "<TR><TD colspan=2 bgcolor=Silver>" & _
                "Order ID: " &  _
                rsOrder("OrderID") & "</TD></TR>"
            Do Until rsOrderDetail.EOF
                    Response.Write "<TR><TD> Product: " & _
                    rsOrderDetail("ProductID")& _
                    "</TD><TD>Quantity: " & _
                    rsOrderDetail("Quantity") & _
                        "</TD></TR>"
                rsOrderDetail.MoveNext
            Loop
            rsOrder.MoveNext
        Loop
        Response.Write "</TABLE><BR><BR>"
        rsCustomer.MoveNext
    Loop
%>
</BODY>
</HTML>
```

This page produces the output shown in Figure 9-7. The customer is the parent recordset and has a child recordset of orders. Each order, in turn, has a child recordset of order details. You can see this represented in the HTML tables that are produced.

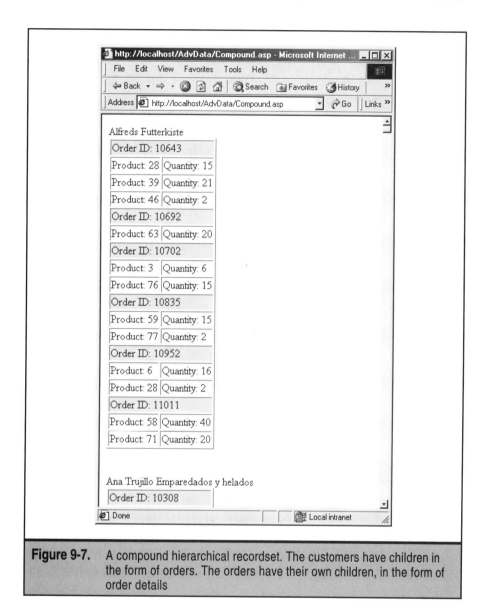

Figure 9-7. A compound hierarchical recordset. The customers have children in the form of orders. The orders have their own children, in the form of order details

Aggregate Hierarchies

In addition to only creating hierarchical recordsets, you can calculate aggregates and store those in the parent recordset. For example, say you want to get all the order header and order detail records in a hierarchical recordset, but you also want the order header record to contain the order total. You could do this by multiplying the quantity times the price for each record in the child, and then storing the total in the parent recordset. The pseudocode for this operation would look like this:

```
SHAPE {select statement for parent table}
APPEND ({select statement for child table, with calculation}
   RELATE {field in parent table TO field in child table})
        AS chapter name
   SUM {child calculation} AS new field name
```

To create a hierarchical recordset with an aggregate value, create a new ASP called OrderTotal.asp and enter the following code:

```
<%@ Language=VBScript %>
<HTML>
<BODY>
<%
    Dim cn
    Dim rsOrder
    Dim rsOrderDetail
    Set cn = Server.CreateObject("ADODB.Connection")
    Set rsOrder = Server.CreateObject("ADODB.Recordset")
    Set rsOrderDetail = Server.CreateObject("ADODB.Recordset")
    cn.Provider = "MSDataShape"
    cn.Open "Data Provider=SQLOLEDB;Data Source=laptop;" & _
        "Initial Catalog=Northwind;User ID=sa;Password=;"

    rsOrder.Open "SHAPE  {select * from Orders} " & _
        "APPEND ({select OrderID, ProductID, " & _
            "UnitPrice * Quantity as Price " & _
            "from [Order Details]} " & _
        "RELATE OrderID TO OrderID) AS chapOrderDetail, " & _
        "SUM(chapOrderDetail.Price) AS Total", _
        cn
    Set rsOrderDetail = rsOrder("chapOrderDetail").Value
%>
```

```
<%
    Do Until rsOrder.EOF
        Response.Write rsOrder("CustomerID") & " - " & _
            rsOrder("ShipName") & " - Total: " & _
            FormatCurrency(rsOrder("Total")) & "<TABLE Border=1>"
            Response.Write "<TR><TH>Product</TH><TH>Price</TH></TR>"
        Do Until rsOrderDetail.EOF
            Response.Write "<TR><TD>" &  _
                rsOrderDetail("ProductID") & "</TD><TD Align=Right>" & _
                FormatCurrency(rsOrderDetail("Price")) & "</TD></TR>"
            rsOrderDetail.MoveNext
        Loop
        Response.Write "</TABLE><BR><BR>"
        rsOrder.MoveNext
    Loop
%>
</BODY>
</HTML>
```

This ASP produces a page such as the one you see in Figure 9-8. In this figure, you can see the total has become a field in the parent recordset by summing up fields in the child recordset. This way, you can capture a grand total and put it at the top or bottom of the detail records.

You can do many other things with hierarchical recordsets, such as adding parameters to them or creating groups, however, this introduction should give you a good idea of what you can do with data shaping. An excellent knowledge base article is available from Microsoft that has examples of how to use the Shape command. (Article number Q189657, at http://support. microsoft.com/ support/kb/articles/Q189/6/57.ASP.)

DISCONNECTED RECORDSETS

Just as hierarchical recordsets can give your applications a speed boost, disconnected recordsets can also be used as a way of achieving increased performance. Disconnected recordsets are just that: they

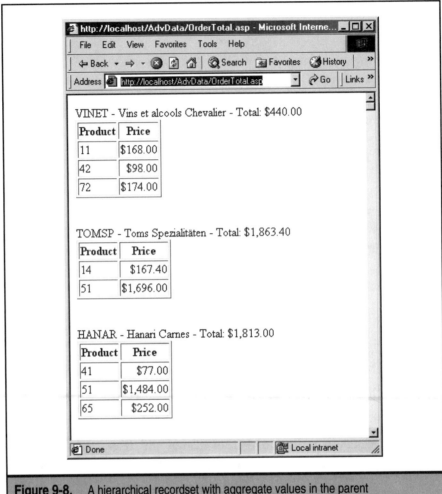

Figure 9-8.   A hierarchical recordset with aggregate values in the parent

are Recordset objects that don't require a connection to a database. The disconnected recordset is most often created by using a static cursor to retrieve all the fields for all the records. A client-side cursor location ensures all the records are in memory on the client machine, and the recordset is then saved to disk.

Once on disk, the recordset can be reopened with the Recordset object's Open method, but no database connection is needed. Instead, you are just opening a local file that is a recordset. You use the same methods to move through it, such as MoveNext and MovePrevious.

You can also sort and filter the disconnected recordset. In fact, you can even modify the records in a disconnected recordset, and later synch it back with the real records in the database.

Most of the time, Microsoft pushes the disconnected recordset as being a tool for a disconnected workforce. For example, if you have a mobile sales force with laptops, you can give them a copy of their records each day in a disconnected recordset. During the day, your mobile sales force can add, update, and delete records. At the end of the day, they reconnect to the server and all their changes are made against the actual tables on the server.

While the use of disconnected recordsets is a boon for disconnected users, it can also be used to increase the speed of a Web application. If you have a table that's accessed frequently and you are using page-level connections, imagine what's happening: you must create a Connection object, which then goes across the network to the database server. There, you are authorized and a notification is returned to the client that the connection was successful. Next, you issue the SQL command, which goes back to the database server, and an action is performed or records are returned. These records must flow across the network back to the Web server.

If you decide to use a disconnected recordset, however, you need only connect to the database and retrieve the records once. You then write those records to the disk on the Web server. From that point on, you access the local file instead of making the expensive trip to the database server.

It is important to remember that this should only be done with tables that aren't updated frequently or for those which you don't need to see the latest data. For example, if you want to see yesterday's sales, you could create a disconnected recordset with yesterday's sales. These shouldn't change during the current day. You could then have a job that created a new disconnected recordset each morning with the previous day's sales.

Notice in the Northwind database, you have four tables that tie an employee to a territory and region: Employees, EmployeeTerritories, Territories, and Region. Figure 9-9 shows the tables and relationships. In this example, assume the territories and regions don't change frequently and the employees covering those territories also don't change often. At least assume the changes won't occur multiple times

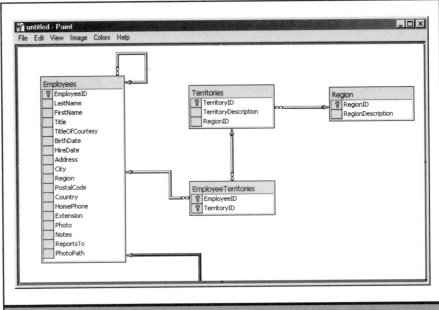

Figure 9-9.   The four tables that show employees and the territories and regions they cover

during the day and you can build a recordset every morning that will be used throughout the day.

To create the recordset, you simply use the Save method of the Recordset object. You can only use the Save method if a recordset is open, which shouldn't come as a major surprise. Two formats exist in which to save the data: as a proprietary, binary format called *Advanced Data TableGram* (*ADTG*) or in *Extensible Markup Language* (*XML*). To specify the type, you must add in the adovbs.inc file, so go ahead and add that to your VI project.

To showcase this functionality, first create an ASP that writes the recordset to disk, creating a persisted recordset. Then, a second ASP opens the persisted, or disconnected, recordset and uses it to display data. Create an ASP and call it PersistRecordset.asp. Enter the following code:

```
<%@ Language=VBScript %>
<HTML>
```

```
<BODY>
<!-- #Include File="adovbs.inc" -->
<%
Dim cn
Dim rsTerritory
Dim sSQL

Set cn = Server.CreateObject("ADODB.Connection")
Set rsTerritory = Server.CreateObject("ADODB.Recordset")

cn.Open "Provider=SQLOLEDB;Data Source=laptop;" & _
    "Initial Catalog=Northwind;User ID=sa;Password=;"
sSQL="Select FirstName, LastName, " & _
    "TerritoryDescription, RegionDescription " & _
    "From Employees e, EmployeeTerritories et, " & _
    "Territories t, Region r " & _
    "Where e.EmployeeID=et.EmployeeID and " & _
    "et.TerritoryID=t.TerritoryID and " & _
    "t.RegionID=r.RegionID " & _
    "Order By LastName"
set rsTerritory=cn.Execute(sSQL)
rsTerritory.Save "c:\Territory.adtg",adPersistADTG
%>
<h1>Done</h1>
</BODY>
</HTML>
```

The query you are using is listed in the following code snippet, to make it easier to read:

```
Select  FirstName, LastName,
        TerritoryDescription, RegionDescription
From    Employees e, EmployeeTerritories et,
        Territories t, Region r
Where   e.EmployeeID=et.EmployeeID and
        et.TerritoryID=t.TerritoryID and
        t.RegionID=r.RegionID
Order By LastName
```

This is a fairly simple join between the four tables shown in Figure 9-9. The only fields you are pulling out are the first and last names of the employees, as well as the territory and region names.

If you look at this ASP, it might strike you this is a prefect place for a hierarchical recordset. It is, indeed, and hierarchical recordsets can be saved using the Recordset object's Save method.

The ASP is simple: you open a connection, execute the previous SQL statement, and then save the recordset to disk. In this case, you are saving it to a file called Territory.adtg in the root of the C: drive but, obviously, you could save it to another location, if you want.

NOTE: If you run this ASP again, you get an error. The Save method doesn't automatically overwrite an existing file. If you want to rerun this ASP, you must delete the file or give it a new name.

Now you have a recordset saved to disk that contains the employees, territories, and regions for which they are responsible. To use this persisted recordset, create a new ASP called EmployeeResponsibility.asp and enter the following code:

```
<%@ Language=VBScript %>
<HTML>
<BODY>
<TABLE Border=1>
<%
Dim rs

Set rs = Server.CreateObject("ADODB.Recordset")
rs.Open "c:\Territory.adtg"
Do Until rs.EOF
    Response.Write "<TR><TD>" & _
        rs("FirstName") & " " & _
        rs("LastName") & "</TD><TD>" & _
        rs("TerritoryDescription") & "</TD><TD>" & _
        rs("RegionDescription") & "</TD></TR>"
    rs.MoveNext
Loop
```

```
%>
</TABLE>
</BODY>
</HTML>
```

This code is simple. The only object you have to create is a Recordset object. No need exists for a Connection object because you needn't make a database connection. Instead, you only have to use the Recordset object's Open method to open the persisted recordset. Once you issue the Open command, the recordset is in memory and can be accessed using the standard navigation methods. The end result of this page is shown in Figure 9-10.

Disconnected recordsets can be filtered and sorted. For example, to filter the data to only one salesperson, set the Filter property of the

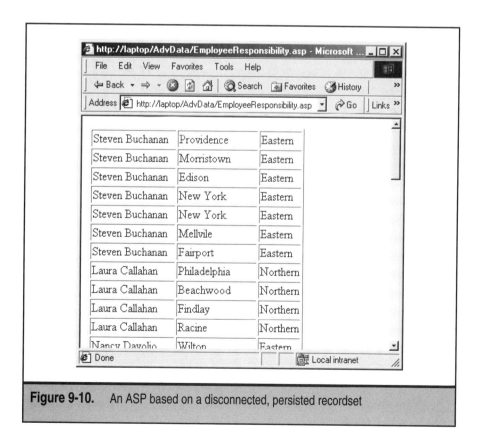

Figure 9-10.   An ASP based on a disconnected, persisted recordset

Recordset object to what would evaluate to a Where clause, but without the word "where." To see only the records for the salesperson with the last name Callahan, make your ASP look like this:

```
<%@ Language=VBScript %>
<HTML>
<BODY>
<TABLE Border=1>
<%
Dim rs

Set rs = Server.CreateObject("ADODB.Recordset")
rs.Open "c:\Territory.adtg"
rs.Filter="LastName='Callahan'"
Do Until rs.EOF
      Response.Write "<TR><TD>" & _"
          rs("FirstName") & " " & _
          rs("LastName") & "</TD><TD>" & _
          rs("TerritoryDescription") & "</TD><TD>" & _
          rs("RegionDescription") & "</TD></TR>"
      rs.MoveNext
Loop
%>
</TABLE>
</BODY>
</HTML>
```

This code does exactly what the last code did, but it only shows the records for Laura Callahan.

You can also save disconnected recordsets in another format: XML. XML is the topic of the next section, so you learn about it in a few moments.

XML

Much has been written about XML, including many books, so trying to cram all the information about XML into one part of one chapter is a tall order. Instead of being an XML primer from the ground up, you see a quick blurb about what XML is, how XML is integrated with SQL Server 2000 and ADO, and how you can use XML in your applications.

What Is XML?

XML stands for Extensible Markup Language (sometimes written eXtensible Markup Language). Like HTML, it is all text, and is made up of tags enclosed in the less-than (<) and greater-than (>) symbols. However, XML has some major differences from HTML. In HTML, if you enter a <TABLE> tag, you know the browser will start the creation of a table with rows and cells. How do you know this? Because the World Wide Web Consortium has defined how the <TABLE> tag should be rendered.

What if, instead, you wanted to describe a table, like the one you might be sitting at right now. In HTML, you can't describe a table in the sense of creating new tags that describe a physical table. XML, however, is all about letting you define your own tags. In fact, XML is really a language that lets you build your own language; a metalanguage, if you will. This language can be used to describe the data it contains. For example, assume you want to pass information about a customer and her orders to someone. Examine the following code:

```
<CUSTOMER>
    <NAME>Alfreds Futterkiste</NAME>
    <CONTACT>Maria Anders</CONTACT>
    <ORDERS>
        <ORDERID>10643</ORDERID>
        <ORDERID>10692</ORDERID>
    </ORDERS>
</CUSTOMER>
```

This may look like HTML, but it's actually XML. No Customer, Orders, and OrderID tags are in HTML. Instead, you use XML to define the data. In a sense, you embed the meaning of the data in the XML stream along with the data.

To show you this is valid XML and Internet Explorer understands it, create a new text file and type in the XML you just saw. Save the file as Cust.xml. Now, double-click the file you created; it opens in IE and appears as shown in Figure 9-11.

If you click the minus (-) signs beside the <CUSTOMER> or <ORDERS> tags, you see IE collapses the data, showing it understands, to some degree, what the tag hierarchy represents.

A few words of caution on XML. First, XML is case-sensitive, something you needn't worry about with HTML. Second, the tags must be closed in the proper order. For example, the following HTML code snippet displays properly:

```
<B><I>This text is bold and italicized</B></I>
```

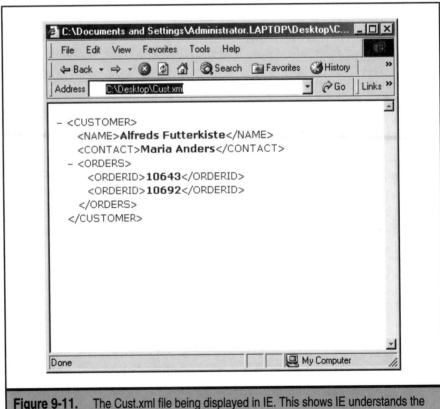

Figure 9-11. The Cust.xml file being displayed in IE. This shows IE understands the hierarchical nature of the data in the XML file

While this HTML text displays properly, it isn't good structured programming. The <I> tag is opened inside the <B> tag, so it should be closed before the <B> is closed. HTML parsers are forgiving and won't care. XML, on the other hand, would have a fit with this sort of sloppy coding. You must close nested tags in the proper order or you'll have problems with XML.

Finally, you might not think Figure 9-11 shows the best formatting of data you've ever seen. In HTML, the tags are all about formatting. In XML, the tags are all about defining the data. To control the display of data, you typically use *XSL* (*Extensible Stylesheet Language*), which is similar to HTML's *cascading style sheets* (*CSS*).

NOTE: At press time, the proposed standard for XSL is actually called *Extensible Stylesheet Language for Transformations* (*XSLT*). XSLT can transform XML into another XML format, into HTML, or into almost any other text-based format.

XML can also include *document type definitions* (*DTDs*) or schemas. A DTD is an optional file that includes the rules of an XML document, such as the elements present and how they relate to each other. This can ensure the data is valid, but DTDs are most often used by two parties to ensure their data is compatible as they pass it back and forth. Both parties agree to conform to the same DTD, so the format is known in advance.

Schemas are the next generation of DTDs and are more flexible. A schema can be made extensible, so elements can be defined with certain data types and presentation rules. A schema can define which elements and subelements are allowed in an XML document, as well as the attributes for those elements and how the elements are related to each other. By creating shared schema, different industries can establish standard ways of presenting data. For example, the insurance industry is currently working on an XML schema as a standard for passing data from one company to another.

SQL Server 2000 and XML

Microsoft is bullish on XML. Many people are already using XML as the de facto standard for transmitting data around on the Web. If you look at a recordset in XML format, it isn't as efficient as a recordset in ADTG format because ADTG compresses numeric data. XML stores everything as text. However, a binary ADTG recordset doesn't have much meaning on non-Microsoft platforms. Just like HTML, XML is a platform-independent standard. XML is all about data, while HTML is all about displaying information.

Because of Microsoft's bullish attitude on XML, it has included XML integration in nearly every product it is developing, and SQL Server 2000 is no exception. For example, you can now directly access SQL Server through a URL, which means you can retrieve data over the Web with only an HTTP connection. This has the advantage of not needing anything more than an HTTP connection to retrieve data.

To enable access to SQL Server through a URL, you must set up a virtual directory and give it the proper access, using the IIS Virtual Directory Management for SQL Server tool. If you click the Start button, and then go to Programs, Microsoft SQL Server, a program is labeled Configure SQL XML Support in IIS. This starts the IIS Virtual Directory Management for SQL Server plug-in in the Microsoft Management Console. Your computer name should appear and expanding it shows two nodes below. Right-click the Default Web Site node and choose New, Virtual Directory. This opens the New Virtual Directory Properties dialog box, as seen in Figure 9-12. On the General tab, name the virtual directory Northwind. This is the name you use to refer to it later. In the local path, you can choose nearly any directory. Choose the directory on the Web server where the AdvData application is running.

On the Security tab, shown in Figure 9-13, enter the information about how you want to log in to the system. If you are using standard SQL Security, enter the user name and password for an account with read access to Northwind database.

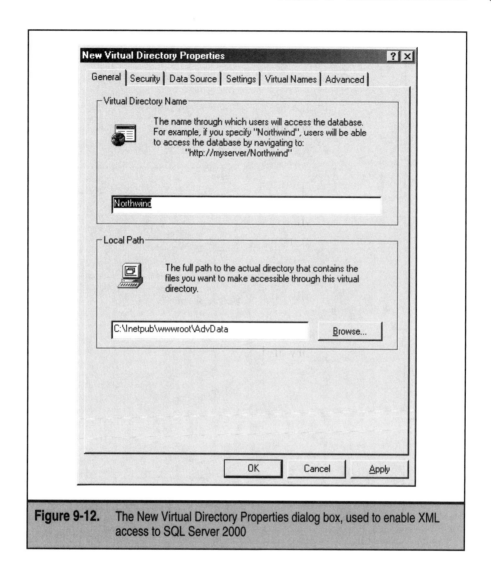

Figure 9-12. The New Virtual Directory Properties dialog box, used to enable XML access to SQL Server 2000

On the Data Source tab, you need to enter the server name and the database to which you are connecting. As you can see in Figure 9-14, you can use (local) as a shortcut to your local server if you are using SQL Server on the same machine on which you are setting up the

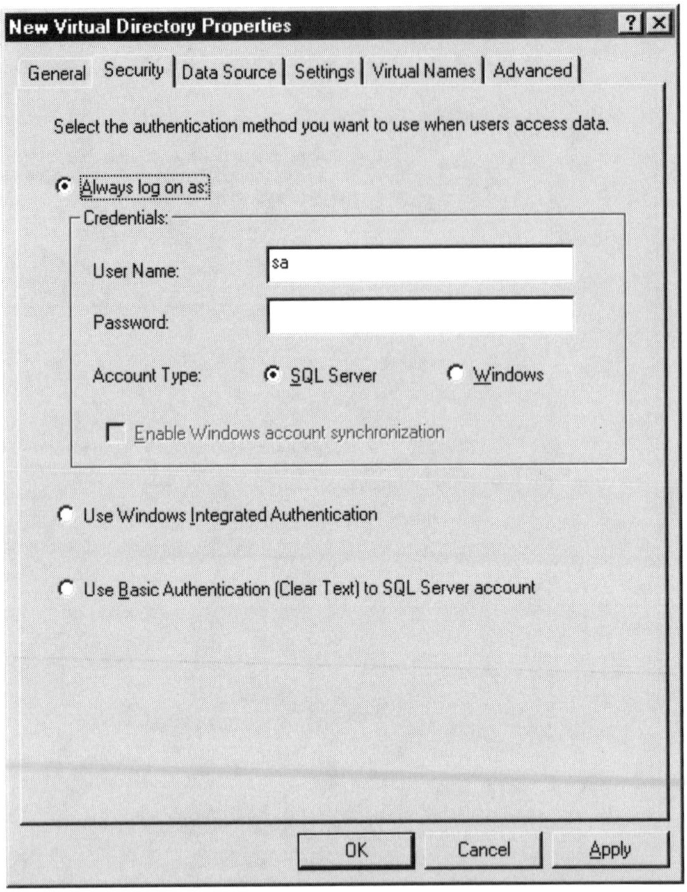

Figure 9-13. The Security tab of the New Virtual Directory Properties dialog box

virtual directory. After entering the server name, choose Northwind as the database name.

Finally, click the Settings tab. By default, only the Allow template queries check box is checked. Go ahead and choose all three check

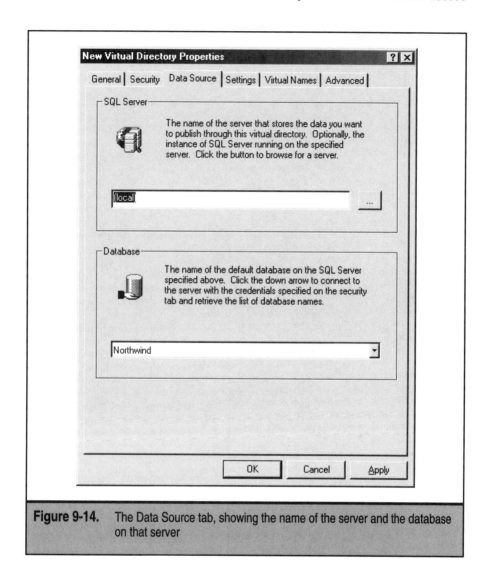

Figure 9-14. The Data Source tab, showing the name of the server and the database on that server

boxes, as shown in Figure 9-15. The first option enables you to run SQL statements through a URL, which is the first thing you should do. After you check all three boxes on this screen, click the OK button to close the dialog box.

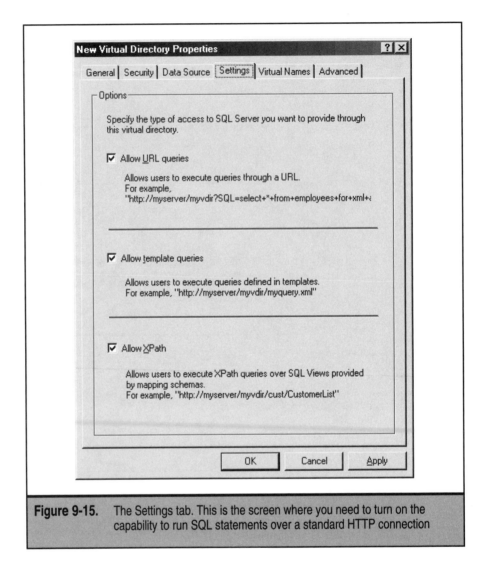

Figure 9-15. The Settings tab. This is the screen where you need to turn on the capability to run SQL statements over a standard HTTP connection

Now that you've set up a virtual directory with XML access, you can access the data over a URL. Open IE and type in a statement with the following syntax:

```
http://server name/virtual directory?SQL=SQL statement
```

In my case, the SQL statement looks like this:

```
http://localhost/Northwind?SQL=select+*+from+Customers+FOR+XML+AUTO
```

Notice something you haven't seen before on the SQL statement: the FOR XML clause. The *FOR XML clause* tells SQL Server to return the results of the query in XML format, instead of a standard recordset. This lets anyone directly access your SQL Server data from anywhere, using only standard HTTP. This means you needn't worry about all those firewall and security issues of opening the database to direct OLE DB access using IP.

This statement returns an XML stream to your browser. IE 5.0 and 5.5 won't display this XML stream exactly. The data that comes down is valid XML, but isn't in the exact format for IE to display it. You could build a program that retrieves the XML data in this format and that program could use the XML stream without any problem. To view the data in the browser, however, you need to try a slightly different approach. You still pull the data over HTTP, but you ask that it come formatted in a different way.

To show the data correctly in the browser, you have to use a template. A *template* consists only of the extra commands needed to make the entire XML stream a valid document, which means it can be displayed by IE. The easiest way to do this is simply to modify the URL you previously entered. This is one long URL with no spaces, so be aware of this as you type it:

```
http://localhost/Northwind?template=<ROOT+xmlns:sql= _
    "urn:schemas-microsoft-com:xml-sql"><sql:query> _
    SELECT+*+FROM+Customers+FOR+XML+AUTO</sql:query></ROOT>
```

Once you type this in and put in the correct server name, you should see something similar to Figure 9-16. By telling SQL Server that you were using a template, it formatted the XML into a document IE could handle. This template is a generic template IE recognizes as a way to display SQL data. Notice the SQL data isn't formatted in a nice table as you have done in most of the other chapters. To

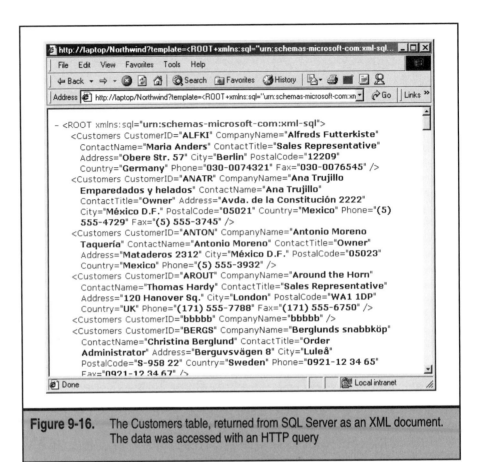

Figure 9-16. The Customers table, returned from SQL Server as an XML document. The data was accessed with an HTTP query

format the SQL data, you would have to create an XSL file that defined how the data should be formatted.

Knowing SQL Server 2000 can directly return a valid XML stream has some benefits. For example, you can directly access from SQL Server over the Web. Is this something you want to do, though? The answer, of course, is "It depends." What's often more useful is to build components (see Chapters 13 and 14) that return XML to the client. You have more control over these components and the XML that is returned. To do this, however, you need to see how the ADO Recordset object works with XML.

ADO and XML

ADO has added some XML features over time. Version 2.5 greatly enhanced its XML capabilities by enabling you to save recordsets in XML format. In addition, you can stream XML using the Stream object. In fact, the Response object is actually a stream, so you can stream XML directly into the Response object.

In the previous section on disconnected (persisted) recordsets, you saved a recordset to disk using the ADTG format. The other format available is XML. Create a new ASP called RecordsetXML.asp and enter the following code:

```
<%@ Language=VBScript %>
<!-- #Include File="adovbs.inc" -->
<%
Dim cn
Dim rsTerritory
Dim sSQL

Set cn = Server.CreateObject("ADODB.Connection")
Set rsTerritory = Server.CreateObject("ADODB.Recordset")

cn.Open "Provider=SQLOLEDB;Data Source=laptop;" & _
    "Initial Catalog=Northwind;User ID=sa;Password=;"
sSQL="Select * from Customers"
set rsTerritory=cn.Execute(sSQL)
rsTerritory.Save Response,adPersistXML
%>
```

If you execute this page, you can see the data dumped into the browser, as shown in Figure 9-17. The data came down in an XML stream because you saved the recordset to an XML data format, as shown in the Save method call. Instead of giving it a filename, however, you sent it to the Response object, which is a type of stream. This simply sends the data directly to the Response object, which is about the same (in this case) of doing a Response.Write.

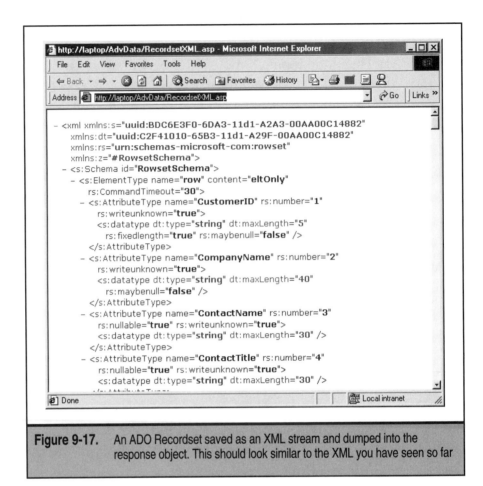

Figure 9-17.   An ADO Recordset saved as an XML stream and dumped into the response object. This should look similar to the XML you have seen so far

If you actually want to format this data, you must create an XSL file, and then modify the ASP slightly. Create a file called Customer.xsl and enter the following code:

```
<?xml version='1.0'?>
<xsl:stylesheet xmlns:xsl="http://www.w3.org/TR/WD-xsl">
  <xsl:template match="/">
    <HTML>
      <BODY>
        <TABLE BORDER="2">
```

```
        <TR>
          <TH>Company Name</TH>
          <TH>Contact Name</TH>
          <TH>Contact Title</TH>
        </TR>
        <xsl:for-each select="*/rs:data/z:row">
          <TR>
            <xsl:for-each select="@CompanyName">
            <TD><xsl:value-of/></TD>
            </xsl:for-each>
            <xsl:for-each select="@ContactName">
            <TD><xsl:value-of/></TD>
            </xsl:for-each>
            <xsl:for-each select="@ContactTitle">
            <TD><xsl:value-of/></TD>
            </xsl:for-each>
          </TR>
        </xsl:for-each>
      </TABLE>
    </BODY>
  </HTML>
  </xsl:template>
</xsl:stylesheet>
```

In this XSL file, you only print the first three fields. As you can see, XSL includes such things as loops (xsl:for-each). XSL is a language unto itself. You could do all the fields, but this is a simplified example. Next, modify your RecordsetXML.asp to look like this:

```
<%@ Language=VBScript %>
<!-- #Include File="adovbs.inc" -->
<?xml version="1.0"?>
<?xml-stylesheet type="text/xsl" href="customer.xsl"?>
<%
Dim cn
Dim rsTerritory
```

```
Dim sSQL
Set cn = Server.CreateObject("ADODB.Connection")
Set rsTerritory = Server.CreateObject("ADODB.Recordset")

cn.Open "Provider=SQLOLEDB;Data Source=laptop;" & _
    "Initial Catalog=Northwind;User ID=sa;Password=;"
sSQL="Select * from Customers"
set rsTerritory=cn.Execute(sSQL)
rsTerritory.Save Response,adPersistXML
%>
```

The only thing you've done is add a reference to the XSL file you just created. If you now run the file, however, you can see the results shown in Figure 9-18. The data is now formatted into the style specified in the XSL file. Just as cascading style sheets were an effort to separate the display from the data in HTML, XML files are the data, and XSL files specify how the data should be displayed in the browser.

XML: So What?

At the end of the day, you might be asking yourself: "What's the big deal?" Remember what XML promises: cross-platform data with flexible formatting. For example, say you want to build an online catalog, selling products from different companies. You could retrieve their data in XML format. Even if the companies used different tag names, you could convert it all (using XSL) into the format needed for your site. That way, companies don't have to change their formats or produce a new output just for you. You can pull data from many sites, but format all the data to look like one coherent site.

You can provide data to others in an XML stream. You can put data in the format others want, or you can let others transform the data using XSL on their end. Microsoft's BizTalk has the capability to let you graphically map someone else's XML data structure to yours, and vice versa, simply by matching up different tag names in the various files. After that, the transformations can happen automatically.

Figure 9-18.   An ADO Recordset saved as an XML stream and dumped into the response object. This time, however, you have formatted the data using XSL

SUMMARY

This chapter focused on several of the advanced features of ADO, as well as an introduction to XML features in SQL Server 2000 and ADO. Shaped, or hierarchical, recordsets can speed access by making the data sets smaller. This means they will move from the data server to the Web server faster. The total number of bytes is smaller because you needn't repeat the parent records for each child record. You can build simple parent-child recordsets, or a parent with multiple children, or a grandparent-parent-child recordset. In addition, you can calculate values from the child and store them in the parent.

Disconnected, or persisted, recordsets can be stored in either ADTG or XML format. You can use disconnected recordsets as a way of accessing data in a recordset format without having to make a trip to the database server. This can significantly increase the speed of accessing the data.

XML is quickly emerging as the standard way to transfer data around the Internet. XML is all text, so it has the platform independence of HTML. XML is all about data and it doesn't contain display information. XSL is how the data can be manipulated and displayed. SQL Server 2000 can directly write XML, and ADO can output XML in to a Stream object, including IIS's Response object.

PART III

Microsoft Data Access Tools and Client-Side Access

CHAPTER 10

The Visual InterDev
Data Tools

When Microsoft released Visual InterDev 6.0, it added a number of elements to support building data-driven Web applications. Microsoft took a rather unusual approach to making data access easy: it added special ActiveX controls, called *Design-Time Controls (DTCs)*, to hide much of the complexity of working with ADO, such as connecting to data sources and looping through and displaying data.

How to build a data-driven set of ASPs is examined in this chapter. You won't actually have to write any code. An object will be named here and there, but no ADO objects will be instantiated and you won't have to write the code to display a recordset in a table, as you have done throughout this book. If this sounds like a panacea, don't get too far ahead of yourself; the DTCs can be great for prototyping, but they often fall short of being ready for production applications. Also, realize that the InterDev tools enables you to work with ADO without writing any code, but no tools exist for working with SQL's Analysis Services. For this, you still have to hand-code the ADO MD.

MAKING THE CONNECTION WITH VISUAL INTERDEV

Let's open VI and create a new project and call this project DTCapp. If you watch the project being created, you might see a number of files being created in the _ScriptLibrary folder. If you didn't see them being copied in, you can simply expand the _ScriptLibrary folder and you will see a number of files. These files actually enable some of the functionality of VI examined in this chapter and the next.

NOTE: During this process, you might sometimes get messages saying the file has been modified outside the source editor and asking if you want to reload it. What this means is that Visual InterDev has actually written some code for you and, therefore, has updated the page. If the page is currently open in the browser, VI asks if you want to refresh the page in the editor window so you can see the changes. Click Yes to see the changes that were made.

Double-click Global.asa and open it in the editor window. When VI first creates the Global.asa, it has nothing but comments in it. So far in this book, you've typed your code into the Global.asa, but now VI is going to write the code for you. Over on the right-hand side of VI, in the Project Explorer window, right-click Global.asa and choose Add Data Connection. You might see a couple of things happen in the Project Explorer window, but the big thing that happens is the Data Link Properties dialog box opens, as shown in Figure 10-1. If this dialog box looks familiar, it should; this is the same dialog box you saw when dealing with OLE DB connections, back in Chapter 5. Choose Microsoft OLE DB Provider for SQL Server and click the Next button.

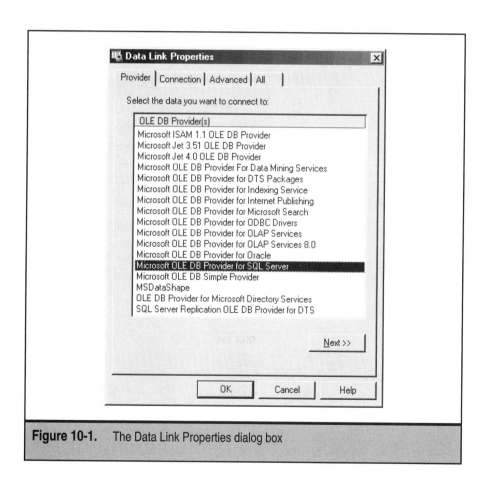

Figure 10-1.   The Data Link Properties dialog box

On the Connection tab, fill out the values to match your environment. Enter the Server name, choose the authentication type, and, if necessary, enter the User Name and Password. Finally, enter the database on the server you want to use. Your form should look similar to that in Figure 10-2. Use Northwind as your database, unless you made a copy of Northwind with a different name earlier so you could modify data without harming the original Northwind. Once you finish, feel free to test the connection, and then click OK to save and close the dialog box.

After you click OK, a new dialog box pops up, as shown in Figure 10-3. This is a dialog box that enables you to set some properties for the connection you are creating. As you see in the figure, I have changed the Connection Name to just "cn" instead of the default of

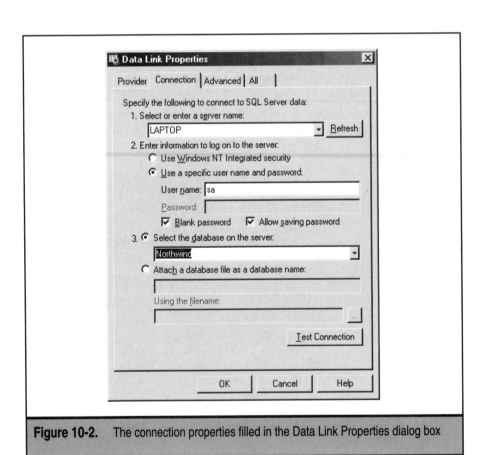

Figure 10-2.   The connection properties filled in the Data Link Properties dialog box

"Connection1". By default, it is using a connection string, which is just like the connection string you have been manually typing into your Global.asa files all along. Go ahead and change the name to "cn," but leave all the other settings as they are and click OK.

If you had Global.asa open, you get a message saying the document has been changed and asking if you want to reload it. Click Yes and something magical happens! Notice real code, not just comments, is now in Global.asa! In fact, if you copy only the piece of Global.asa that was changed, it looks like this:

```
<SCRIPT LANGUAGE=VBScript RUNAT=Server>
Sub Application_OnStart
    '==Visual InterDev Generated - startspan==
    '--Project Data Connection
      Application("cn_ConnectionString") = "Provider=SQLOLEDB.1;
         Persist Security Info=True;User ID=sa;
         Initial Catalog=Northwind;Data Source=LAPTOP;
         Use Procedure for Prepare=1;Auto Translate=True;
         Packet Size=4096;Workstation ID=LAPTOP;
         Use Encryption for Data=False;
         Tag with column collation when possible=False;
         User Id=sa;PASSWORD=;"
      Application("cn_ConnectionTimeout") = 15
      Application("cn_CommandTimeout") = 30
      Application("cn_CursorLocation") = 3
      Application("cn_RuntimeUserName") = "sa"
      Application("cn_RuntimePassword") = ""
    '-- Project Data Environment
      'Set DE = Server.CreateObject("DERuntime.DERuntime")
      'Application("DE") = DE.Load(Server.MapPath("Global.ASA"),
"_private/DataEnvironment/DataEnvironment.asa")
    '==Visual InterDev Generated - endspan==
End Sub
</SCRIPT>
```

VI has created a number of application-level variables for you. The most important one here is the application("cn_ConnectionString"). This is the OLE DB connection string that VI uses throughout the

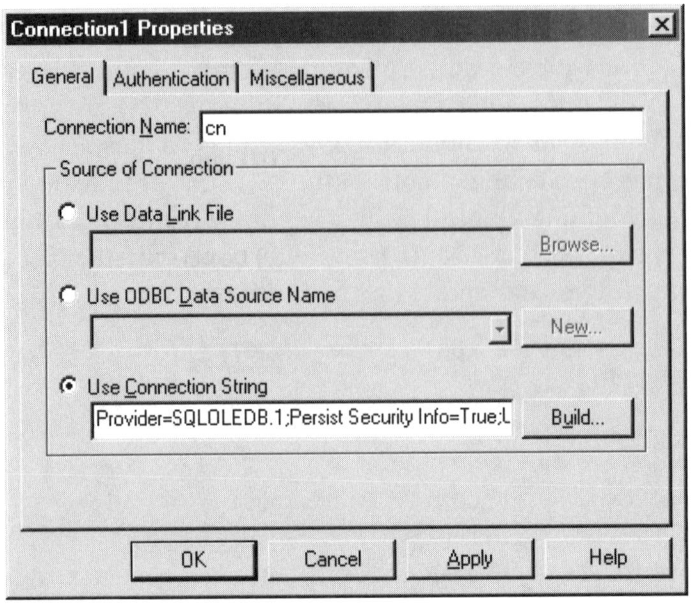

Figure 10-3. The Connection Properties dialog box

project as you work with the data tools. For the first time, though, you didn't have to type in the OLE DB connection string. VI wrote all this code for you. The code even has comments telling you where VI started and ended the code generation.

If you look to the right-hand side of InterDev, as seen in Figure 7-4, two major changes have occurred there. In the top part of the screen, the Project Explorer window now shows a DataEnvironment in two places in your application. Don't worry about the one in the _private folder, but notice one is directly under the Global.asa file. Under this DataEnvironment is the connection you just created, called cn. This is actually a graphical representation of an ADO Connection object. The Data Window is something you haven't seen before and is usually added as a tab in the same window as the Properties window.

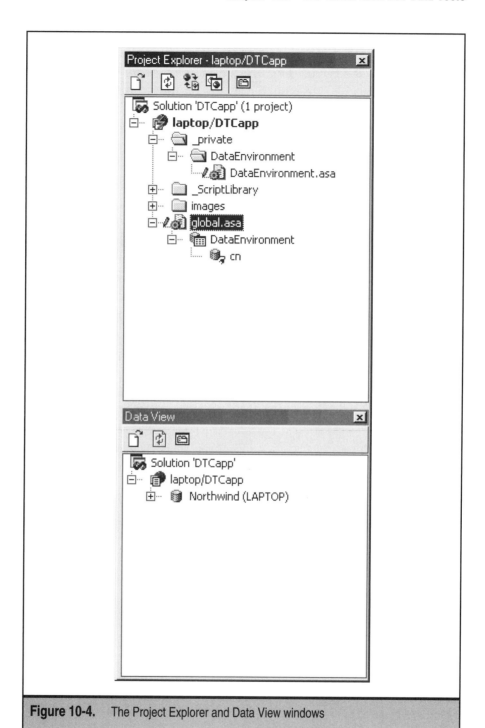

Figure 10-4.   The Project Explorer and Data View windows

Visual InterDev's Data View Tools

Below the Project Explorer window is where the Properties window usually is located, but a new tab has been added. This tab is the Data View window, which is actually a powerful tool for viewing and manipulating data and the actual database structure. Notice, in the Data View, you see a graphical representation of the Northwind database on the server Laptop. If you expand this, you can see items are below Northwind, namely, Database Diagrams, Tables, Views, and Stored Procedures. Figure 10-5 shows the Northwind database expanded to show these choices. If this looks similar to what you get in the SQL Server Enterprise Manager, it is, in some ways, similar.

Next, expand the Tables node and you get a listing of all the tables. Double-click the Customers table and the table opens in a spreadsheet view, as seen in Figure 10-6. Understand something about this: what you see is real data. If you logged into the database with the proper permissions, this is live data that you can edit

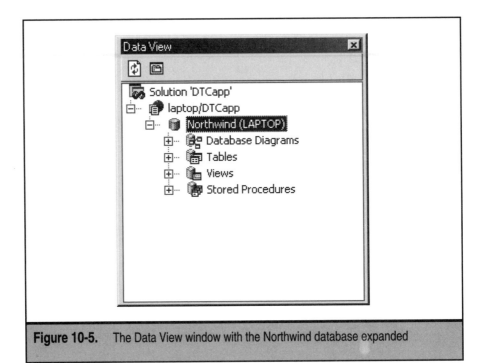

Figure 10-5. The Data View window with the Northwind database expanded

directly through the grid. You can test this by modifying the ContactName field for one of the records. As soon as you move off that record, the change is committed to the database, so be careful because you will be changing the real data in Northwind.

You may see a Query toolbar floating around. You can close this or dock it along the top with the other toolbars. You use it in the next chapter but, for now, you don't really need it.

If you expand one of the tables, you see a list of the fields for that table. If you right-click a table name, you see that you can perform a variety of tasks on the table. The Open command is the same as double-clicking the table; it opens the table in an editable grid. The second choice in the list, though, is Design. If you choose design, you see a window similar to that in Figure 10-7. This grid shows you the design of the table and enables you to modify the structure. For example, the ContactName field is an nvarchar type with a size of 30.

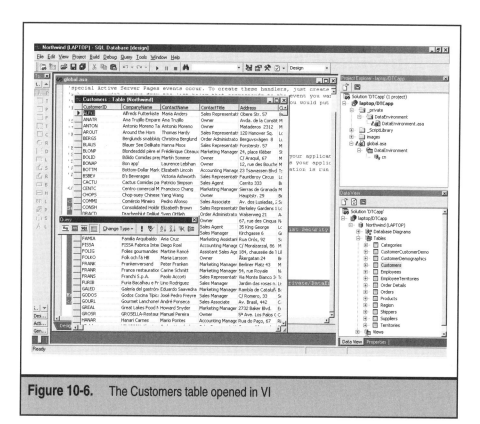

Figure 10-6.   The Customers table opened in VI

If you determine that 30 characters is too small, you can simply modify the field to make it a larger number. When you close the Design view, save the changes and the table structure on the back-end database is updated automatically.

If you go back to the Tables node and right-click it, you see New Table. That's right: you can add new tables to the database. Simply type in the field names, with data types and sizes, set the Null and Identity properties, and save the table. The table is actually created in the database on the server. After creating a new table, you can right-click that table name and choose Delete to remove it from the back-end database.

If the user has permissions, she can modify data in any table, modify the structure of existing tables, add new tables, and delete tables. This is some powerful functionality. In fact, if you look at the

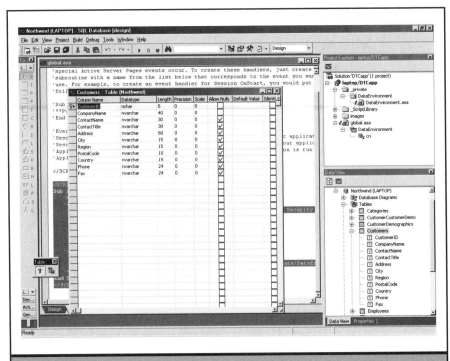

Figure 10-7.   The design of the Customers table. You can actually modify the structure of the tables from within VI

other choices available, the user can also add, modify, and delete stored procedures, views, and database diagrams. This tool is great for developers, but it isn't meant for end users. Realize, of course, you must have a login with the proper permissions to perform all these functions, but the power of the tool shouldn't be underestimated.

Microsoft's goal in providing these tools in VI (and the other Visual Studio 6 products) is for developers to be able to perform most of their database work within the development environment, so you do not have to switch between your development tool and SQL Server's Enterprise Manager continually. The biggest limitation of the tools in Visual Studio is they don't enable you to create new databases. Once you have a database, however, the Visual Studio tools are powerful.

ADDING A COMMAND

A connection from your Web application to the Northwind database has just been established. Just performing this action has

1. Caused Visual InterDev to write some code for you in Global.asa, creating a number of application-level variables

2. Given you access to a powerful set of tools in the Data View window

You still don't have any data to display to the user, so you want to make sure you have some data for the user to see. Let's start by creating a command, which can be done in several ways. For now, go to the Project Explorer window, right-click the Global.asa, and choose Add Data Command. This pops up a Command Properties dialog box like the one seen in Figure 10-8. Set the Command Name field to cm. Leave the Connection set to cn, which is the connection you created earlier. Note, you can have multiple connections, so a command needs to know to which connection it belongs. Finally, under the Source of Data, choose Table in the Data Object field, and then choose dbo.Customers in the Object Name field.

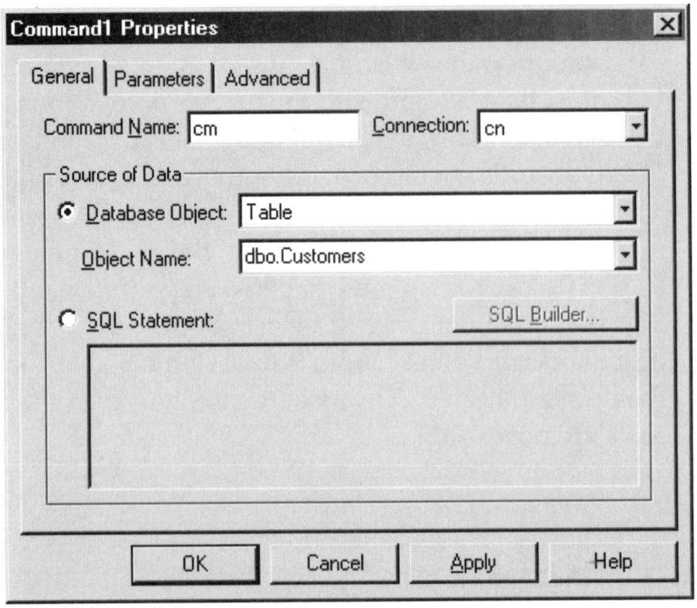

Figure 10-8. The Command Properties dialog box

Don't worry about the other settings for now. Just click the OK button and the dialog box closes and saves your changes. If your Global.asa file was still open, you get a message that it was changed outside the source editor, so go ahead and refresh your view.

The big change is what happens in the Project Explorer window. Notice in Figure 10-9 that the command just added—cm—now appears below the connection, cn. The cm command is expanded to show all the fields it will return. This is a graphical representation of an ADO Command object and is equivalent to setting the CommandText property to "Customers" and telling the Execute method that the CommandText is of type adCmdTable.

The command you just added will run a query for you, but it's only a pretty wrapper thrown around the ADO Command object. As you have learned, the ADO Command object can't hold records in memory. The only ADO object that can do this is the Recordset object. If you right-click the Global.asa, however, you don't see an

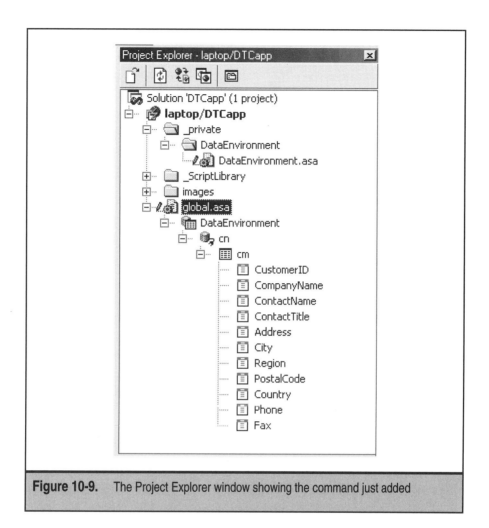

Figure 10-9.   The Project Explorer window showing the command just added

Add Recordset option. Instead, you need to create a Recordset object and point it to the command you just added to your project. If you are tempted to write a little code, don't! Adding a recordset can be handled with a simple drag-and-drop operation.

ADDING DATA TO A PAGE

Add an ASP to your application called Customers.asp. Leave the code exactly as it is; don't change a thing. Now, in the Project

Explorer window, drag the cm command and drop it on the Customers.asp inside the <BODY> and </BODY> tags. When you release the mouse button, you get a message box, as shown in Figure 10-10. Basically, this box is telling you that to do what you are trying to do, you need to enable the Scripting Object Model for this page. Don't worry about what the *Scripting Object Model* (*SOM*) is right now; just click Yes and continue.

When you click Yes to enable the SOM, you see some code added to your page. Again, for now, don't worry about that. This is where something strange happens, however. Here you are, in Source view, and you see this big graphical control sitting in the middle of your source, as you can see in Figure 10-11.

Design-Time Controls

So, just what is this large graphical control in the middle of your source code? This is one of Microsoft's Design-Time Controls. These large graphical controls are called *Design-Time Controls* because they appear to be graphical controls, but they only appear this way at design time. In fact, you can manipulate them like controls, by changing values in drop-down boxes and by setting properties in the Properties window. In fact, you can reference the control just as you would an ActiveX control in a Visual Basic application. But the control is only a control at design time. At run time, the control becomes regular text, as you see in a minute.

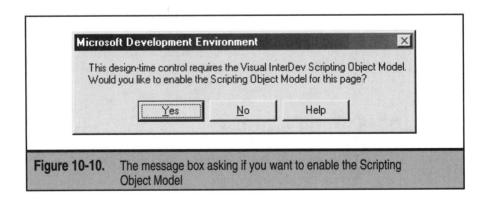

Figure 10-10. The message box asking if you want to enable the Scripting Object Model

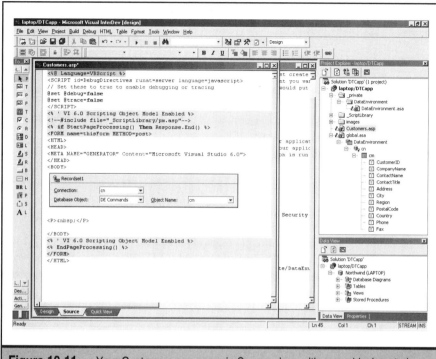

Figure 10-11. Your Customers.asp page, in Source view, with a graphical control sitting in the middle of the page

For now, realize this control represents an ADO Recordset object. In fact, if you look at the top of the control, you can see it's named Recordset1. The control has a drop-down box to show what connection you are using; in this case, cn. The next drop-down box is for the Database Object and currently says DE Commands. *DE* stands for *Data Environment*, and *DE Commands* simply means a command added to the project. The Object Name drop-down box shows the name of the DE Command; in this case, cm. Using the Database Object drop-down box, you could choose a stored procedure, a table, or a view instead. If you changed this drop-down box to Tables, for instance, the Object Name drop-down box would be filled with the table names from the Northwind database.

In this project so far, you have added a data connection and a data command. You dragged the data command over to the page and dropped it, where it created a recordset DTC. Without writing any code, what you have done could basically be represented with the following code:

```
dim cn
dim cm
dim Recordset1
set cn=server.CreateObject("ADODB.Connection")
set cm=server.CreateObject("ADODB.Command")
cn.Open Application("cn_ConnectionString")
set cm.ActiveConnection=cn
cm.CommandText="Customers"
cm.CommandType=adCmdTable
set Recordset1=cm.Execute
```

As you can see, you avoided a great deal of code just by doing a lot of pointing and clicking. What you are doing so far is opening a recordset; you aren't displaying it yet. You can use other DTCs to do that in a moment.

Remember I said the DTC is only a control at design time? In other words, the DTC doesn't appear as anything except text when you actually run the page. You can verify this in two ways. You could save the ASP and then open it with Notepad, but you would only see text, not some big graphical control sitting in the middle. An easier way to see what you want is to right-click the control and choose Show Run-time Text. This expands a large block of text in a gray box. The code in this box is read-only; you can't modify it at this point. You can see what this looks like in Figure 10-12.

This block of text is all that is in the file. In fact, notice that the code is all JScript. The DTCs all generate JScript and no way exists to change this. Still, because you can't edit the DTC code in the page, this isn't a big deal. All the code you write can still be VBScript, with no negative consequences. VI's editor provides a way to make the run-time text look like a graphical control. For example, notice you have the following line of code in the run-time text:

```
function _initRecordset1()
```

The name of your object right now is Recordset1. In the editor, right-click the control and choose properties. The first text box is

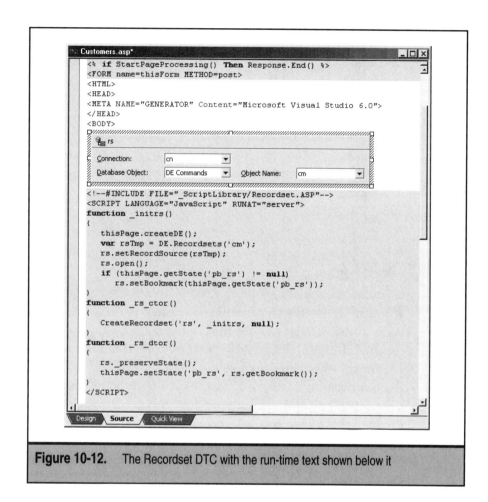

Figure 10-12.   The Recordset DTC with the run-time text shown below it

Name, so change it to rs, and then click the close button. Now save the page and notice the line of run-time text has automatically been changed to:

```
function _initrs()
```

As you can see, you're only changing properties and VI is writing code for you. Basically, one of the main functions of the DTCs is to write code for you. This isn't a bad thing; you still haven't had to type any code, and you've already opened a recordset in memory. Before you move on, feel free to close the run-time text by right-clicking the recordset DTC and choosing Hide Run-time Text.

The Data Environment

Before you display any data on the screen, let's discuss what the Data Environment represents. The data environment is simply your repository for storing all your Web application's connections and commands. It enables you to represent your data objects graphically in the environment, where you can reuse them easily. You can also place them directly on pages to speed your development. The DE is actually an object you can reference through code, acting as a wrapper to ADO. In my opinion, ADO is fairly simple already, but Microsoft's goal with the DE is to make it even easier.

Displaying Data

If you look back at Figure 10-9, you can see the Project Explorer window shows the command you added, named cm. The command is expanded in that picture to show you the fields that will be returned into the recordset when you execute this command. Let's use those fields to display some data on the page. In the Project Explorer window, single-click the CompanyName field. Hold down the control key and also choose the ContactName, ContactTitle, and Phone fields. Once you select these four fields, drag them to the Customers.asp file, and then drop them just below the recordset DTC. When you do this, something magical happens. Your page should look like the one in Figure 10-13.

When you drop the fields on the page, VI builds a table. The table has one row for each field. Two cells are in each row: one for the label and one for the actual field. The fields appear as graphical text boxes; in fact, they are named Textbox1, Textbox2, and so forth. Go ahead and view the page in the browser. You should see a page as shown in Figure 10-14. Notice VI automatically adds labels for each text box. The label is just the name of the field. However, what if you want to display "Company Name" with a space in it, instead of the actual field name of "CompanyName"? You have a couple of options. First, you could change the code in the HTML that VI generated for you, but that's no fun. The alternative is to right-click the CompanyName field in the Project Explorer window and choose Properties. When

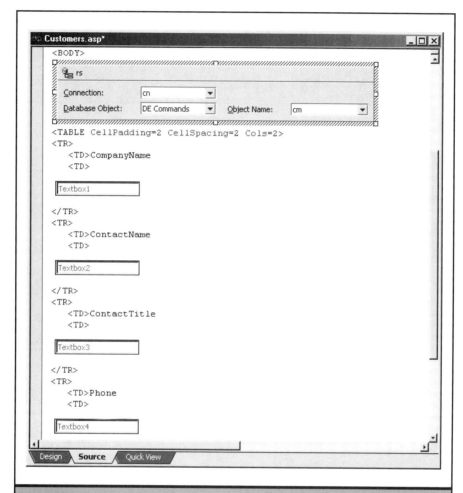

Figure 10-13.   Four of the fields in the recordset have been brought over from the listing in the Project Explorer. VI automatically builds a table and places the fields in the table

the Field Properties dialog box comes up, you see a text box for Caption. Feel free to change this to "Company Name" (without the quotes) or any other value. When you press OK, you won't see any change in how the field is listed in the Project Explorer window. For that matter, you won't see a change in the label in Customers.asp. In the future, though, if you drag-and-drop the field on a page, the label VI generates will be the caption you just set in the properties.

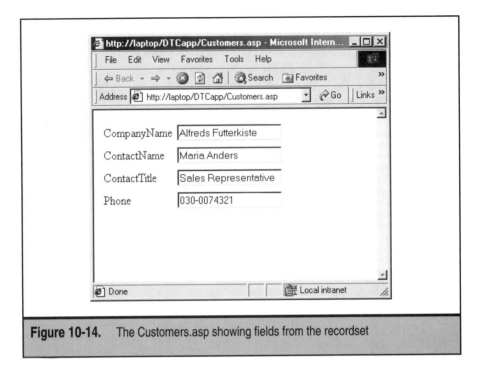

Figure 10-14. The Customers.asp showing fields from the recordset

When you viewed the ASP in VI, you saw four text boxes in the source view. These are only text box design-time controls. The text box DTC can be bound to a field in a recordset. When you drag the fields over from the command object shown in the Project Explorer window, the text box DTCs are automatically bound already; you needn't do anything else.

You already know the DTCs are only controls in the source view in VI; they are just blocks of text in the page. When the page is processed on the server and sent to the client, what happens to the text box DTCs? It looks like they are still in the page once shown in the browser, but DTCs are only controls at design time. If you view the source of the page in the browser, you see the text boxes are only standard HTML <INPUT> tags. For example, the CompanyName is shown with the following code:

```
<TR>
   <TD>CompanyName
   <TD>
   <INPUT type="text" id="Textbox1" name="Textbox1"
      size=20 maxLength=40 value="Alfreds Futterkiste">
</TR>
```

Moving Through the Data

You are now displaying four fields of the first record in the recordset. This is great if you need to call Maria Anders, but what if you need to see other records? Let's go back to the Customers.asp in VI for a moment. The Toolbox is along the left-hand side of VI. If you choose the Toolbox tab, there are a number of horizontal tabs. One of those horizontal tabs is Design-Time Controls. If you choose this tab, you see a number of DTCs, as shown in Figure 10-15.

In the Design-Time Control tab of the Toolbox is a DTC called the RecordsetNavBar. This is a control you will use often, so get used to it. Drag this control over to Customers.asp and drop it on the page after the closing </TABLE> tag, as shown in Figure 10-16.

Adding the RecordsetNavBar to the page is not enough. Whenever you drag a DTC that will be data-bound over from the toolbox, you have to bind the DTC to the recordset. In this case, right-click the DTC and choose Properties. In the RecordsetNavBar Properties dialog box that opens, as shown in Figure 10-17, is a Data section. In the drop-down list box labeled Recordset, choose rs (the only recordset listed) and then click OK. You have now tied the RecordsetNavBar DTC to the Recordset DTC called rs. Now, save the page and view it in IE. As you see in Figure 10-18, the RecordsetNavBar appears in the client browser as a series of buttons. If you view the source, you see these buttons are standard HTML tags that look like this:

```
<INPUT TYPE="Button"...>
```

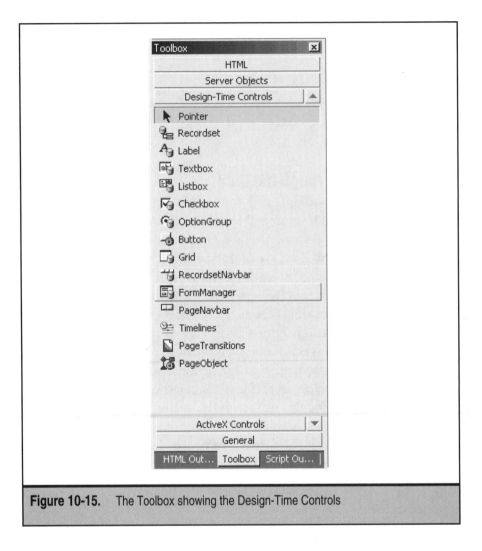

Figure 10-15.   The Toolbox showing the Design-Time Controls

Now, with the navigation buttons showing in the browser, you can scroll forward and backward through the records. You can move to the last record or jump back to the first record using the buttons. As you click to move from one record to another, watch the left-hand panel of the status bar at the bottom of IE; notice the window changes as you move from one record to the next. Realizing what is happening is important: you are making a server round-trip for each record. You aren't storing the data on the client. Instead, a new page is rendered on the server for each record and sent back to the browser. That means this

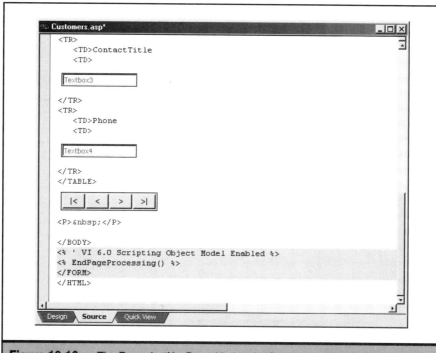

Figure 10-16.   The RecordsetNavBar added to the Customers.asp

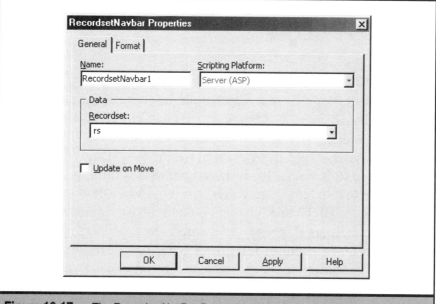

Figure 10-17.   The RecordsetNavBar Properties dialog box

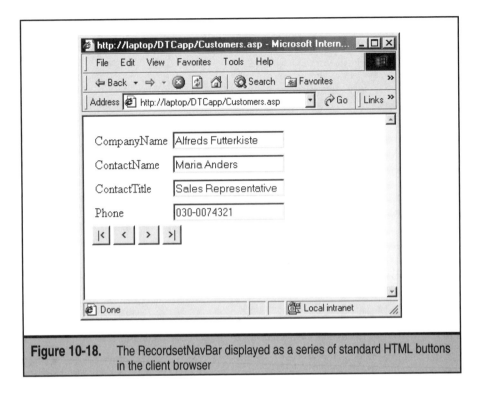

Figure 10-18. The RecordsetNavBar displayed as a series of standard HTML buttons in the client browser

page will work in any browser, not just in IE. To the client, this is just a standard HTML page.

Updating Data

Go back to VI for a moment. Right-click the RecordsetNavBar and choose Properties. As you can see in Figure 10-17, a check box on the General tab is labeled Update on Move. Check this box and click OK. Save the page and view it in the browser. Don't forget to refresh if you didn't close the browser, because nothing will appear to have changed. However, you have now told VI that if you change a value in any of the text boxes, you want it to update when you move to a different record. On the first record, change a field value. For instance, change Maria Anders to Maria Flanders. Now, click the Next button to move to the next record. When you click the Previous button to return to the first record, you should see the new value you just entered. That's right: you have now created a page that allows updates over the Web. And, of course, you still haven't written a single line of code!

This is a fairly substantial feature. If you think about doing this manually, you have to create an ASP that will display a record. When the user clicks the Next button, or any button for that matter, the button actually acts as a submit button and passes the data to the server. A page on the server (possibly the same one used to display the data) must call code to update the data in the database. Then, the next record (assuming the user pressed the Next button) must be rendered and sent back to the client. Having VI do this work for you makes creating an update page simple.

The Listbox DTC

So far, you've used the Recordset, the Textbox, and the RecordsetNavBar DTCs. Other DTCs do exist, however, as you can see in the Toolbox. One control you can use is the Listbox DTC, which enables you to bind to a field in the database. From the toolbox, drag a Listbox DTC to Customers.asp, and then drop it between the Recordset DTC and the opening <TABLE> tag. Then, right-click the Listbox DTC and choose Properties. You see two tabs on the Listbox Properties dialog box and, for now, choose the Lookup tab. Remember, for DTCs you drag over from the Toolbox, you need to bind them to a Recordset DTC. On the Lookup tab, you see where you can set the list source. At the bottom, you can build a static list, but you are interested in pulling the values from a recordset. In the Row source box, choose the name of your recordset; in this case, rs. The Bound column field determines the value that is actually passed up to the server. Recall that with a standard HTML <SELECT> tag, which is how the Listbox DTC will be rendered on the client, you can display a nice description to the user, but actually only pass back an ID value. The Bound column is this ID value, so choose the field CustomerID. In the List field drop-down box, choose the field you want the user to see; in this case, choose CompanyName. Your completed Listbox Properties dialog box should look like Figure 10-19. Click OK to close the dialog box.

Now, if you view the page in the browser, you see a list box at the top of the page that shows all the company names from the Customers

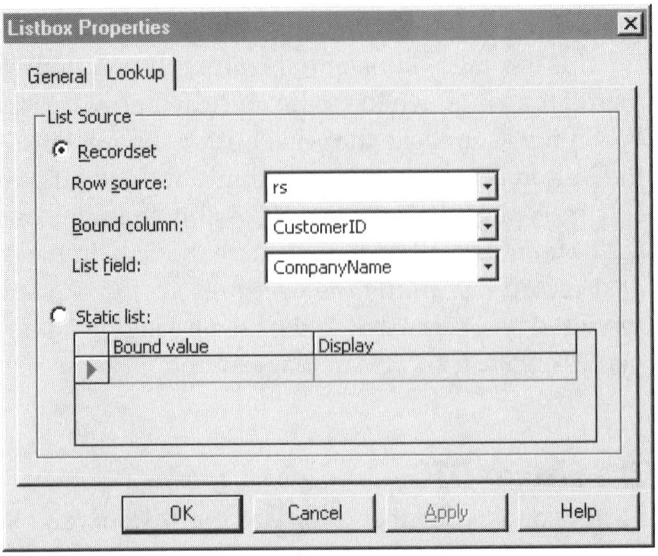

Figure 10-19. The Listbox Properties dialog box showing the list box bound to our recordset

table. Right now, all you can do is drop down the list and view it; choosing a different company doesn't actually do anything. You add some code in the next chapter that works with these controls but, for now, let's just show what they can do. Even without any code, many of the DTCs can be used to create good prototypes.

The Grid DTC

Create a new ASP called PhoneList.asp. Drag the cm command object to the page and drop it after the body tag. It creates a Recordset DTC called Recordset1. Next, from the Toolbox, drag a Grid DTC over and drop it in on the page after the Recordset DTC. Remember, the first thing you need to do when you drag fields over from the Toolbox is to bind them to the recordset, so right-click the grid and choose Properties. The Grid Properties dialog box is displayed. Click the Data tab and in the Recordset drop-down box, choose Recordset1. This binds the grid to the recordset, but you must now bind the fields in the recordset to columns in the grid. If you look in the Available

Fields list, you see all the fields in the recordset and a check box next to each one. Check the CompanyName, ContactName, and Phone fields. Your dialog box should end up looking like Figure 10-20. When you finish, click the OK button. The Grid DTC now shows the fields you have bound to the columns.

Looking at the grid on the page, you can resize the entire grid by moving the handles around the border of the grid. You can also resize columns within the grid by clicking the separator between columns and dragging to resize it. When you finish, save the page and view it in the browser. Your page should look something like Figure 10-21, depending on how wide you made the columns. The

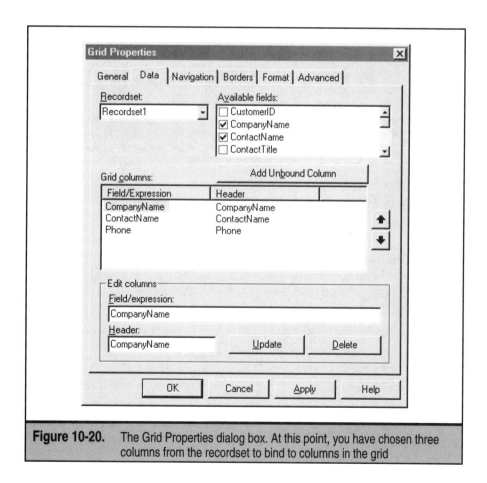

Figure 10-20. The Grid Properties dialog box. At this point, you have chosen three columns from the recordset to bind to columns in the grid

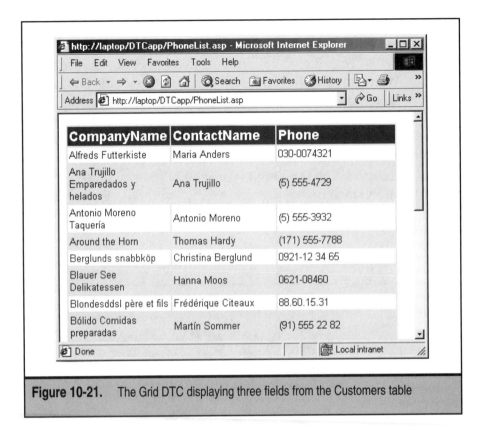

Figure 10-21.   The Grid DTC displaying three fields from the Customers table

color of the header row and the shading on the alternating data rows can be changed through the properties of the grid.

If you scroll to the bottom of the grid, you see a series of navigation buttons. What's this all about? You didn't add a RecordsetNavBar DTC to this page, did you? In fact, not only do you have a series of navigation buttons, but it also says you are viewing Page one of five. If you go back to VI and right-click the grid, and then choose Properties again, you see a tab for Navigation. By default, paging is enabled and set to show 20 records per page. This means, no matter how many records exist, you'll show them in the grid 20 at a time. Further below, you see the options for which navigation buttons to show and what the caption on each should be. This gives you a great deal of control over how the grid is displayed in the client browser. And speaking of the grid being displayed in the client browser, you shouldn't be shocked to discover that the grid is rendered as a standard HTML table.

You might notice the Navigation tab includes an area for Row Navigation. Don't get too excited here; many people think this means they will have an editable grid, but this isn't the case. This simply enables you to move forward or backward one record at a time, and you can have a highlight showing the current record. However, nothing in the grid is editable, so don't expect the Row Navigation options to solve any problems for you.

The Border tab and Format tab enable you to control borders, gridlines, background colors, fonts, and other options. This gives you great flexibility in changing the appearance of the grid without doing any actual programming.

Let's make one change to the grid. Some of you might actually claim this is a line of code and, in a way, it is. Enter it into the grid dialog box, and not into the ASP (you can fudge and still claim you haven't written a line of code). Let's say you want to display the person's name, followed by a comma, and then his title. You could build a SQL query that concatenates these fields together or you could have the grid do it for you. Because your recordset is currently based on only a table and not a SQL statement, do it the easy way and have the grid display your data with the fields concatenated together.

In VI, right-click the grid, choose Properties, and go to the Data tab again. In the Available Fields list box, uncheck the ContactName field. Now, click the button that says Add Unbound Column. This adds a new value in the Grid columns list. Make sure this new field (which may be named Column2) is selected and go down to the Edit columns area. In the Field/expression text box, replace the text with the following line:

```
=[ContactName] + ', ' + [ContactTitle]
```

Then, in the Header column, make the value "Contact". Now—and this is important—make sure you click the Update button. This dialog box has a bad habit of not updating values when you would expect it to, so make sure you always press the Update button. If you want, use the arrows to the right of the Grid columns list to move this field to the second column in the table. If you don't do this, no harm is done. When you finish, the dialog box should look like the one in Figure 10-22. Now, click OK to save the values and close the Grid Properties dialog box.

Back in the grid, you probably want to make the new column, Contact, wider so you can see the name and title. Save the page and view it in the browser. You should see a page similar to that in Figure 10-23.

If you look at the expression you typed, you might notice it uses the plus (+) sign for concatenation. This is because the DTCs are implemented in JScript and, therefore, your expressions must be valid JScript expressions, not VBScript. Most VBScript programmers have trouble getting used to this. Also, notice field names are enclosed in square brackets.

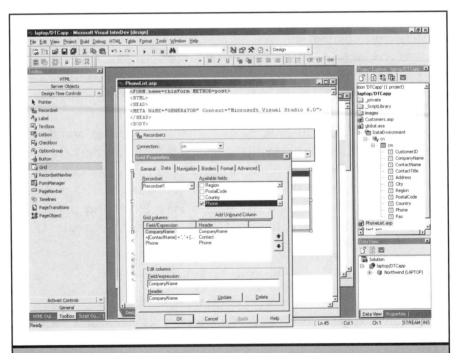

Figure 10-22. The Grid Properties dialog box with an unbound field set to an expression. This expression shows the ContactName, a comma, and then the ContactTitle fields

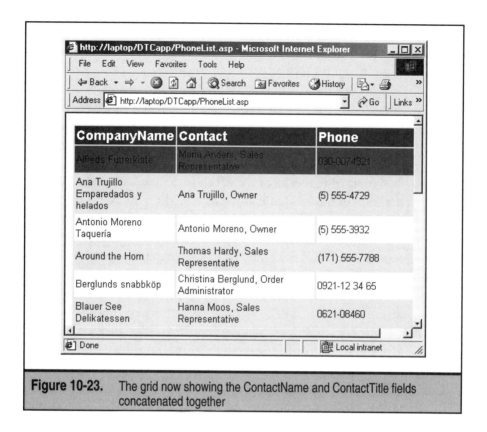

Figure 10-23.   The grid now showing the ContactName and ContactTitle fields concatenated together

Other Design-Time Controls

Other DTCs are available, such as the Checkbox, OptionGroup, and Label, but I won't go into any detail on them here. You are beginning to see how the DTCs work, and you have a feel for what they can do. I continue exploring them in the next chapter.

A Few Words on Design-Time Controls

At the beginning of the chapter, I said the DTCs usually fell short in production applications and were best used for prototyping. Let's discuss why they aren't as powerful as they first appear.

First, Microsoft doesn't seem to be 100 percent behind the DTCs. Support for them has been somewhat spotty; certain service packs of NT or Visual Studio have had, shall we say, unpredictable results on the DTCs. Pages that once worked suddenly stop working, for reasons unknown. This fact alone makes me caution people against using them for a production application.

Second, the code that enables the DTCs to work must be included in each application that uses them. You see all this code in the _ScriptLibrary folder of your project. That's a lot of code and there isn't a good way to have only one copy on a server if you have multiple applications.

Finally, the model of the DTCs is decidedly two tier; in other words, the code in the ASP calls the database directly. No support exists for the DTCs calling middle-tier objects. This is shocking, considering Microsoft pushes three-tier design so heavily. Without support for a three-tier model, the DTCs generally offer slower performance and less scalability than a well-designed n-tier application.

If, after reading these three compelling and fascinating arguments, you decide to use DTCs in a production application, that is your choice. I don't recommend DTCs for production applications but, for some applications with a small number of users, they might be fine. Be aware that the future support of DTCs may be inconsistent as Microsoft pushes people into the new world of Visual Studio 7, which will contain a new paradigm for building Web applications.

SUMMARY

Visual InterDev contains some important tools for working with data. You have the data environment, which enables you to manage multiple connections and commands in your project. You have the Data View window, which allows enormous control when dealing with a database. With the data tools in VI, you can create, modify, and drop tables. You can manipulate data. You can create, modify, and drop stored procedures and triggers. The VI data tools are powerful and useful.

Design-Time Controls enable you to create Web pages quickly that are data-driven. You can display data in text boxes, tables, list boxes, and so forth. You can even update data over the Web, all without programming. Don't forget, though, the DTCs do not scale well when compared to n-tier development.

If you are curious about how you would build more sophisticated pages with the DTCs, read on into the next chapter. So far, you have only had the recordset automatically open and display data. What if you only want customers in a particular country? How do you filter records in a DTC Grid? The next chapter introduces programming against the DTCs to build more functional pages.

CHAPTER 11

Programming the Design-Time Controls

The previous chapter had you create a series of pages using the Visual InterDev Design-Time Controls (DTCs). Using these DTCs, it's easy to create a data-driven ASP without programming. Obviously, this has limitations. For example, you could create a document that created a phone list of your customers. However, what if you only wanted to see the customers in a particular country? You could have embedded this in the query, but how would you have allowed the user to choose different countries?

Trying to answer these questions points out one problem with the DTCs: as good as they are, they can't do it all and, eventually, you have to program against them. Programming against the DTCs isn't difficult, but you need to watch for a few things as you write your code.

WRITING CODE TO MANIPULATE THE DTCS

When it's time to write some code against the DTCs, seeing how this works is fairly straightforward. Even though the DTCs are only blocks of code, you can program against them as if they were actual objects. You reference them like objects, and you manipulate them by referencing their properties and methods.

You start with a simple example of writing some code against a Recordset DTC. Use the same project, DTCapp, from the previous chapter. This already has a connection called "cn" and a command called "cm." Create a new ASP named RsManip.asp. Drag the cm command into the ASP, just after the opening <BODY> tag. Right-click the Recordset DTC created on the page and choose Properties. Name the Recordset "rsCust." Next, drag over a Grid DTC and drop it below the Recordset DTC. Right-click the Grid DTC and choose Properties. On the Data tab, set the Recordset to rsCust. In the available fields, choose the CompanyName, ContactName, ContactTitle, Country, and Phone fields. After clicking the OK button, feel free to resize the grid as needed. The final page should look like Figure 11-1.

Now, if you execute this ASP, you get the grid showing all the customer records, as shown in Figure 11-2. So far, you have

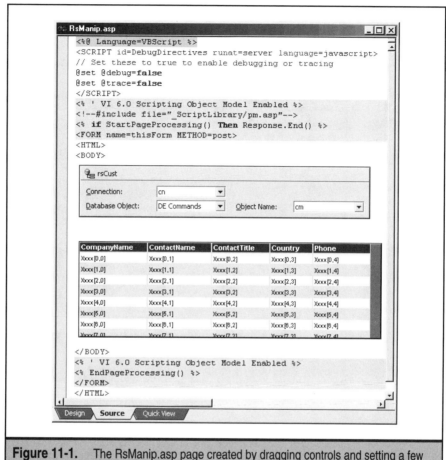

Figure 11-1. The RsManip.asp page created by dragging controls and setting a few properties. So far, still no code

the recordset automatically opening as soon as the page runs. Sometimes you need to turn off this behavior, so you can manipulate the recordset. First, you need to make a change to the recordset. Right-click rsCust and choose Properties. On the General tab, change the Source of Data to SQL Statement and type the following statement:

```
Select * from Customers
```

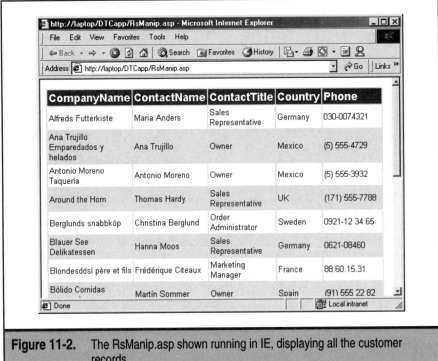

CompanyName	ContactName	ContactTitle	Country	Phone
Alfreds Futterkiste	Maria Anders	Sales Representative	Germany	030-0074321
Ana Trujillo Emparedados y helados	Ana Trujillo	Owner	Mexico	(5) 555-4729
Antonio Moreno Taquería	Antonio Moreno	Owner	Mexico	(5) 555-3932
Around the Horn	Thomas Hardy	Sales Representative	UK	(171) 555-7788
Berglunds snabbköp	Christina Berglund	Order Administrator	Sweden	0921-12 34 65
Blauer See Delikatessen	Hanna Moos	Sales Representative	Germany	0621-08460
Blondesddsl père et fils	Frédérique Citeaux	Marketing Manager	France	88.60.15.31
Bólido Comidas	Martín Sommer	Owner	Spain	(91) 555 22 82

Figure 11-2.   The RsManip.asp shown running in IE, displaying all the customer records

This returns an equivalent recordset to what you had before. Now, click the Implementation tab. As you can see in Figure 11-3, a check box is labeled "Automatically open the Recordset." By default, this is set to true, which means as the page is processed, it automatically performs the query that is the source of the recordset. You must turn off this option if you want to control the recordset through code. Clear this box and then click Close.

At this point, if you run RsManip.asp, it returns a blank page. This is because you never create the recordset in memory, so no records exist to display. To display records, you must add code to RsManip.asp that opens the recordset.

Under the rsCust Recordset DTC, add the following block of code (and make sure it is after the Recordset DTC, but *before* the Grid DTC):

```
<% rsCust.open() %>
```

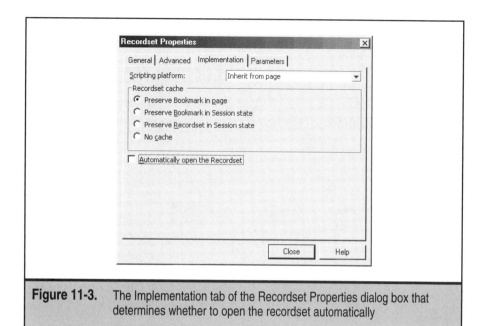

Figure 11-3.   The Implementation tab of the Recordset Properties dialog box that determines whether to open the recordset automatically

Now, this line of code appears simple. In fact, it is simple, but this is one of the areas where you must be extremely careful. The DTCs are written in Java or JavaScript, so even though you're coding in VBScript, the names of properties and methods can be case-sensitive. The *o* in "open" must be lowercase. In addition, many of the methods require you to place the parentheses after the method name.

NOTE: The method names have been case-sensitive for two years, but this seems to have changed recently. I honestly don't know if Windows 2000 or Visual Studio Service Pack 4 changed it. Be aware that it used to matter and, therefore, it still might matter under some circumstances.

Changing the SQL Statement, Method 1

If you're asking yourself, "Utley, why did you have me do this? We're right back where we started, but I had to write a line of code!" Well, that's true, but ask yourself this: What if you only wanted to see the customers from one country? You could modify the SQL statement in the rsCust DTC, but this wouldn't allow the customer to choose the Country from a list. Instead, you want to change the SQL statement programmatically.

Add a new ASP called CountryPicker.asp. This page presents a simple list of three countries from which to choose. Each country simply contains a link to the RsManip.asp, and passes along on the querystring the country the user has chosen. Type in the following code:

```
<%@ Language=VBScript %>
<HTML>
<BODY>
    <a href="RsManip.asp?txtCountry=Germany">
        Germany</a><BR>
    <a href="RsManip.asp?txtCountry=Mexico">
        Mexico</a><BR>
    <a href="RsManip.asp?txtCountry=UK">
        United Kingdom</a>
</BODY>
</HTML>
```

Now, you need to modify the RsManip.asp to respond to the argument selected by the user. In this section, you see one way to do it, which is using the setSQLText method. In the next section, you add a parameter.

In RsManip.asp, change the one line of code you had to this:

```
<%
rsCust.setSQLText("Select * from Customers " & _
    "where Country='" & Request.QueryString("txtCountry") & "'")
rsCust.open()
%>
```

As you can see, you are setting the SQL statement underlying the rsCust Recordset DTC. You are adding a where clause to filter on whichever country the user selects from the CountryPicker.asp. To use the setSQLText method, the recordset must be closed. This recordset is closed because you set the recordset *not* to open automatically. Instead, you change the underlying SQL statement, and then manually open the recordset by using the open method.

You are still able to use the DTCs, but you can see that you can manipulate them through code. Go ahead and run CountryPicker.asp. Click one of the countries, such as Germany, and you see RsManip.asp now shows only the records for Germany.

Changing the SQL Statement, Method 2

The second way to do this is to use parameters. When Visual InterDev was first released, this capability existed, but it was well hidden. Many people now know of this functionality, but it isn't at all intuitive.

First, you need to get into the SQL Builder just a bit. Right-click the rsCust Recordset DTC and choose Properties. Click the SQL Builder button. Sometimes, a dialog box pops up with the title "IDispDataVwProject Properties." If this happens, simply click the OK button. This opens the SQL Builder, a tool that helps you design your queries in a graphical environment. You need to use this tool to work with the parameters you will use in this approach.

As you can see in Figure 11-4, the SQL Builder has four panes. At the top is the Diagram pane that shows the tables and relationships between them. The next pane is the Grid pane. The Grid pane shows the fields you have chosen and any criteria or sorting you've done on those fields. Next is the SQL pane. As you manipulate the Diagram or Grid panes, the SQL pane displays a real-time SQL statement. Finally, at the bottom, is the Results pane. You can execute a statement at any point and examine the records returned in the Results pane to make sure you have what you expect.

Right now, you are using "Select *" to bring back all the fields. You only need five of the fields, and one of the easiest performance-tuning tricks is not to use "Select *" unless you need all the fields. In the Grid pane, select the row with the asterisk in it and press the Delete key to clear it. Then, in the Diagram pane, check the box next to the five fields you want: CompanyName, ContactName, ContactTitle, Country, and Phone. Next, in the Grid pane, put a question mark in the Criteria field for the Country column. You can also put the equals sign in, as shown in Figure 11-4, or you can put in the question mark and SQL Builder will add the equal sign. Your SQL Builder should now look like Figure 11-4.

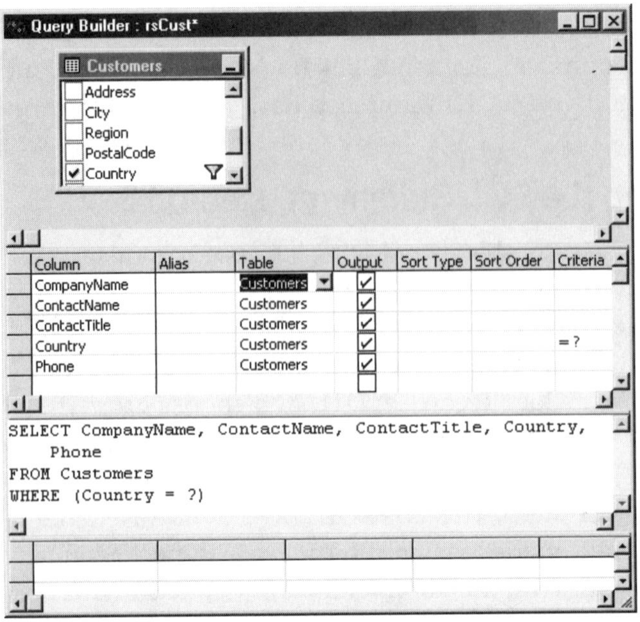

Figure 11-4. The SQL Builder tool in Visual InterDev. You must use this tool to create parameters in your Recordset DTCs

The question mark represents a parameter. You set this parameter at run time in the query. Of course, this requires some extra work but, for now, you simply want to save this query. The SQL Builder, in an odd user-interface quirk, doesn't have an OK or Close button. Instead, you have to press the *X* in the upper right-hand corner to close it. When you click to close the SQL Builder, you're asked if you want to save changes to RsManip.asp. Click the Yes button.

Now, right-click the rsCust DTC again and choose properties. You see the new query in the SQL statement box, with the question mark representing a value that will be passed in shortly. The box should look like what you see in Figure 11-5.

Next, click the Parameters tab. This shows how many parameters are in the current query (just one, in this case) as well as the type (input or output), the data type, and the size. Finally, you can

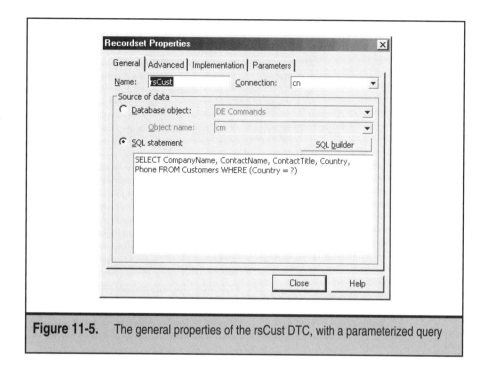

Figure 11-5.   The general properties of the rsCust DTC, with a parameterized query

type in one box, which is labeled Value. You might be tempted to think this is asking for the value of the parameter, but not quite. Instead, you type in a variable name here. This creates a variable in the page hosting this control. In the Value field, type **sCountry** as you see in Figure 11-6.

After clicking the Close button, you're back in RsManip.asp. Modify the code after the rsCust DTC to look like this:

```
<%
sCountry = Request.QueryString("txtCountry")
rsCust.open()
%>
```

If you run CountryPicker.asp again, everything works fine. How does this work? In this case, the variable sCountry gets set to whatever was chosen in CountryPicker.asp. When the recordset is open, the parameter is set to whatever is in the sCountry variable. If you choose Mexico, for example, you should have the page shown in Figure 11-7.

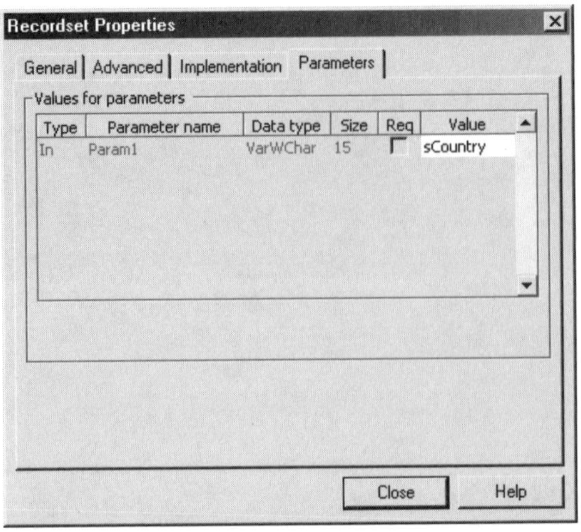

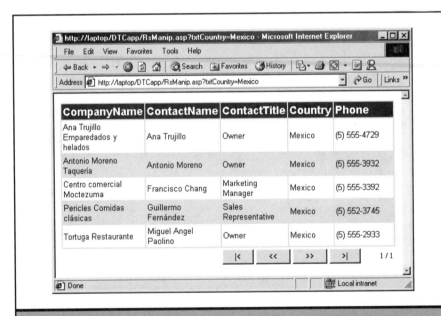

Figure 11-6. The Parameters tab of the rsCust DTC. This is where you enter a variable name that will be used to set the value of the parameter

Figure 11-7. RsManip.asp showing only the customers from Mexico. The query inside the rsCust Recordset DTC has a parameter, which is passed from the CountryPicker.asp

More Fun with the SQL Builder

The SQL Builder can do much more than you just saw. First, right-click the rsCust Recordset DTC and choose Properties. Press the SQL Builder button and look at the SQL Builder. You should have a Query toolbar showing but, if you don't, click View, Toolbars, and then choose Query. This opens the Query toolbar that enables you to open and close the various panes of the SQL Builder, as well as to execute the statement (the results show up in the Results pane), check the SQL syntax, and perform sorting, filtering, and grouping.

Another thing the Query toolbar enables you to do is change the type of the query. So far, you've only been performing select queries. However, it's possible to create insert, update, delete, and make tables queries using the SQL Builder.

First, add another table to the query. Suppose you want to see the orders a customer has placed. To add another table, use the Data View window in the lower right-hand corner of the development environment. Expand the Northwind database, and then the Tables node. Drag the Orders table over to the Design pane and drop it. Immediately, the SQL Builder joins the Customers and Orders tables, and updates the SQL statement in the SQL pane. The join is created because the SQL Builder reads the information from the system tables in SQL Server. The Design pane of the SQL Builder should now appear as it does in Figure 11-8.

Now you can choose fields from either of the two tables in the Design Pane. For example, click the check box next to OrderID in the Orders table. Click the exclamation mark on the Query toolbar to execute the query. It prompts you for a parameter value, and you can enter "UK" without the quotes. This then shows you the results of the query in the results pane, as you see in Figure 11-8.

Suppose you want to do more than select records? Instead, you want to insert, update, or delete records. In the Design pane, click Orders and press the DELETE key. The Orders table is removed from the query. Notice, also, the Results pane is now dimmed. This means the Results pane is showing data that doesn't match the current query; you would have to run the query again to get records that match the current SQL Command.

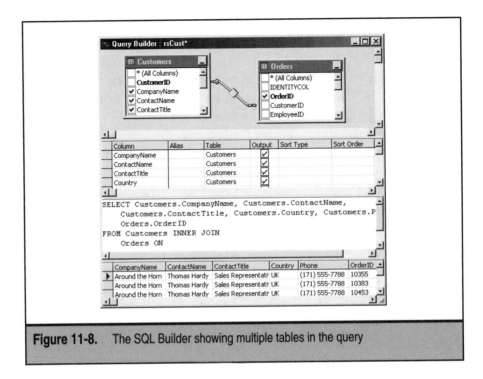

Figure 11-8.   The SQL Builder showing multiple tables in the query

On the Query toolbar, if you drop down the Change Type list, you see Insert. This is to insert records from one table into another (existing) table. The pseudocode of what this will do looks like this:

```
Insert Into Target Table
(Target Fields)
Select Source Fields
From Source Table
```

If you choose Insert Values as the type instead, this is a more traditional Insert statement. The pseudocode looks like this:

```
Insert Into Target Table
(Target Fields)
Values (New Values)
```

If you look at Figure 11-9, you can see one use of this would be to hard-code in a lot of values. Obviously, this isn't all that useful. Instead, you might want to put in a question mark for each field.

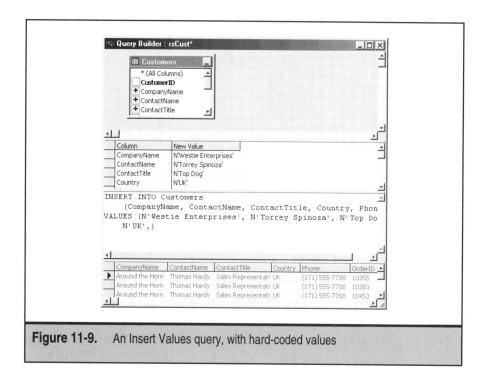

Figure 11-9.   An Insert Values query, with hard-coded values

Select all the fields individually, and then put in a question mark for each field, as shown in Figure 11-10. After doing this, close the SQL Builder and save the changes to RsManip.asp.

NOTE: You wouldn't usually include an ID field because it would be an identity column and automatically be given a value. In Northwind, most fields aren't identity columns, so here you must assign an ID.

In RsManip.asp, right-click the rsCust Recordset DTC and choose Properties. Click the Parameters tab and you can enter the variable names for each parameter. Notice a big problem here, though. As Figure 11-11 shows, the names of the parameters are Param1, Param2, and so forth. You have to know the order in which they appear in the SQL statement. You can try to get some idea of which parameters are which based on the type and size, but this isn't always possible if several fields have the same data type and size, as is the case with Param2 and Param3.

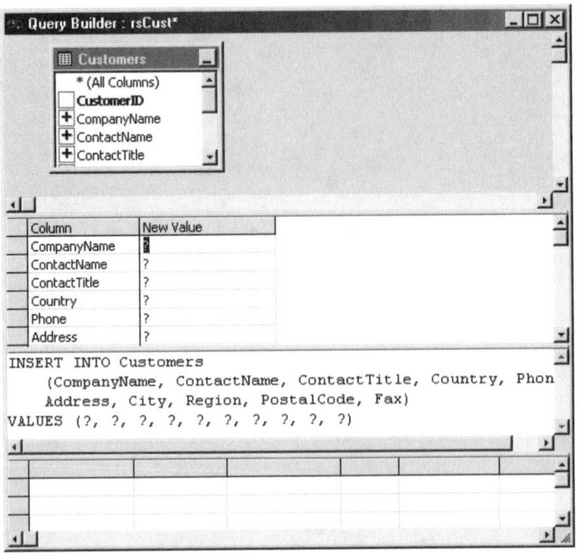

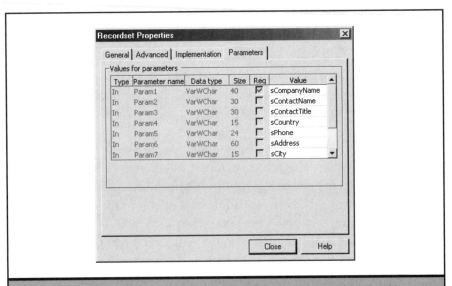

Figure 11-10. An Insert Values query, this time with question marks that act as parameters. You still have to create variables for all the parameters

Figure 11-11. The Parameters tab showing all the parameters created for this insert statement

Check your SQL statement to verify, but you should be able to enter the following variable names in the Value column of the Parameters tab in this order: sCompanyID, sCompanyName, sContactName, sContactTitle, sCountry, sPhone, sAddress, sCity, sRegion, sPostalCode, and sFax. When you finish, click Close.

Now, create a new page named InsertCust.asp. This page enables you to insert new customers using the rsCust Recordset DTC you just updated. Add the following code:

```
<%@ Language=VBScript %>
<HTML>
<BODY>
<FORM Action="RsManip.asp" Method="Post">
    Company ID: <INPUT Name="txtCompanyID"><BR>
    Company Name: <INPUT Name="txtCompanyName"><BR>
    Contact Name: <INPUT Name="txtContactName"><BR>
    Contact Title: <INPUT Name="txtContactTitle"><BR>
    Country: <INPUT Name="txtCountry"><BR>
    Phone: <INPUT Name="txtPhone"><BR>
    Address: <INPUT Name="txtAddress"><BR>
    City: <INPUT Name="txtCity"><BR>
    Region: <INPUT Name="txtRegion"><BR>
    Postal Code: <INPUT Name="txtPostalCode"><BR>
    Fax: <INPUT Name="txtFax"><BR>
    <INPUT Type="Submit">
</FORM>
</BODY>
</HTML>
```

Now, modify the RsManip.asp. First, delete the grid. Second, make your code look like this:

```
<%
sCompanyID = Request.Form("txtCompanyID")
sCompanyName = Request.Form("txtCompanyName")
sContactName = Request.Form("txtContactName")
sContactTitle = Request.Form("txtContactTitle")
sCountry = Request.Form("txtCountry")
sPhone = Request.Form("txtPhone")
sAddress = Request.Form("txtAddress")
```

```
sCity = Request.Form("txtCity")
sRegion = Request.Form("txtRegion")
sPostalCode = Request.Form("txtPostalCode")
sFax = Request.Form("txtFax")
rsCust.open()
%>
```

Now, start InsertCust.asp and fill in some values, remembering the CompanyID has a size of only five characters. When you press the Submit button, the RsManip.asp adds the record to the database. Nothing will be displayed when it is done, but you can go into Query Analyzer to confirm it has been added.

Just as you can insert records, you can also update and delete them using the Recordset DTC and parameters.

Retrieving a Field from a Recordset

Using ADO, it's fairly easy to retrieve a particular field's value from a recordset. Any of these methods can work:

```
rs("FieldName")
rs(index number)
rs.Fields(index number)
rs!FieldName
```

All of these are easy, but pulling a field from a Recordset DTC isn't so easy. To see how to do this, modify RsManip.asp. Delete the current Recordset DTC and the code you've written. Now, drag the cm command over from the Project Explorer window and drop it after the <BODY> tag. Rename the Recordset DTC to rsCust. Next, add the following code just after the rsCust Recordset DTC:

```
<%
Do while not rsCust.EOF
      Response.Write rsCust.fields.getValue("CompanyName") & _
          "<BR>"
      rsCust.moveNext
Loop
%>
```

The EOF property and moveNext methods look familiar, but notice how you have to pull the values out of the recordset. You can't just ask for recordset("FieldName") any longer. Instead, remember you are talking to a Java-based object and you must call its methods. A "fields" property has a getValue method that can return the value of any field. This is the way to access the fields in a Recordset DTC programmatically. Running this ASP can verify that it works as advertised.

MAKING PAGES LOOK EVENT-DRIVEN

Using the design-time controls, you can make pages look event-driven. This is different from Dynamic HTML (DHTML) that can make pages look event-driven. Instead, the DTCs can make pages look event-driven, even though they are simply static HTML. For example, you can use a Listbox DTC that lists the country names. When you choose a new country, a grid could show the customers for that country.

Setting Up the "Event-Driven" Page

Create a new ASP and name it CustByCountry.asp. Now, drag over two Recordset DTCs and place them in the <BODY> section, one right after the other. Right-click the first and name it rsCountry. Make sure its connection is cn, or whatever name you gave the connection in the Data Environment. Now, in the Source of Data, choose SQL Statement and enter the following SQL string:

```
Select Distinct(Country) from Customers
```

This Recordset simply returns a unique list of the countries in which you have customers. Close the property window. Right-click the second Recordset DTC and choose Properties. Name this Recordset rsCustomer and make sure its connection is set to cn. Next, click the SQL Builder button.

In the SQL Builder, drag the Customers table over to the Design pane and choose the following fields: CompanyName, ContactName,

ContactTitle, Phone, and Country. Enter a question mark in the Criteria field of the Country column. Your completed SQL Builder should look like Figure 11-12.

Close the SQL Builder and save the changes. If the rsCustomer Properties dialog box is closed, reopen it. Now, click the Implementation tab and uncheck the "Automatically open the Recordset" check box. Next, click the Parameters tab and enter sCountry in the Value column for the only parameter that shows up. When you're finished, click the Close button.

Next, enter a few blank lines between the two Recordset DTCs if there aren't any. Drag over a Listbox DTC from the Toolbox and place it between the two Recordsets. Right-click the Listbox and choose Properties. Name the Listbox "lstCountry." Now, click the Lookup tab. In the List Source frame, make sure Recordset is chosen. Set the Row Source to rsCountry. This binds the listbox to the rsCountry Recordset DTC you just added. Set both the Bound Column and List Field properties to Country (the only choice you have). Now, click the OK button.

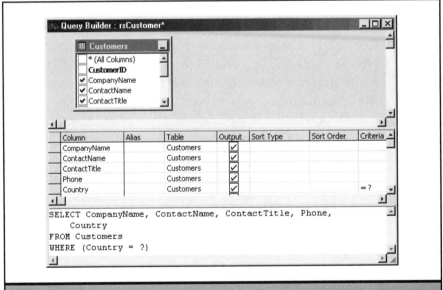

Figure 11-12.   The SQL Builder getting ready to support a customer-chosen country field

You have just tied the Listbox DTC called lstCountry to the Recordset DTC called rsCountry. The list contains a list of the countries in the Customers table.

Now, drag a Grid DTC over and drop it after the second Recordset DTC, the one you named rsCustomer. Right-click the Grid DTC and choose Properties. Click the Data tab and set the Recordset combo box to rsCustomer. In the Available Fields list, choose all five fields. You needn't display the country name, but it can help you validate that your page is working properly. This is all you need to do with the grid's properties, so click the OK button.

If you look down the page, starting just after the <BODY> tag, you should have a Recordset DTC named rsCountry, a Listbox DTC named lstCountry, a Recordset DTC named rsCustomer, and a Grid DTC (the name of the Grid DTC isn't important).

Now, it's time to add some code. After the Listbox DTC, but before the second Recordset DTC (rsCustomer), add the following line of code:

```
<% Dim sCountry %>
```

After the second Recordset DTC, rsCustomer, add the following code:

```
<SCRIPT ID=serverEventHandlersVBS LANGUAGE=vbscript RUNAT=Server>
Sub lstCountry_onchange()
    rsCustomer.close()
    sCountry=lstcountry.getValue()
    rsCustomer.open()
End Sub
</SCRIPT>
```

Confused? Look at Figure 11-13. Your page should be nearly identical to this, with the exception of a label I typed in before the Listbox.

If you are confused by the previous block of code, you can have Visual InterDev insert such code blocks for you, minus the code in the sub, of course. Look at the Toolbox window in Visual InterDev: at the bottom is a tab labeled Script Outline. If this tab isn't in your toolbox, click on View, Other Windows, and then choose Script Outline.

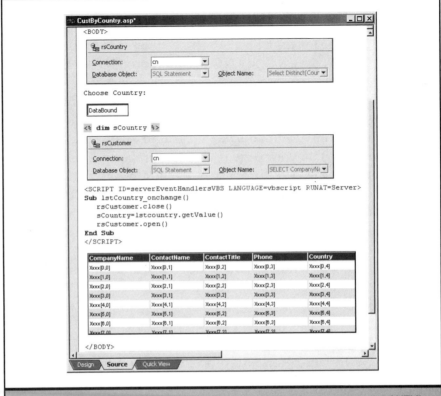

Figure 11-13. The CustByCountry ASP in design view. You now see a mix of HTML, VBScript, and Visual InterDev Design-Time Controls

In the Script Outline, if you expand the Server Objects & Events folder, you see lstCountry in the list. If you expand that, you can see the onChange event listed. onChange is in bold because code already exists for that event. If code didn't already exist for it, you could double-click it and it would create the stub for the routine in the page.

Now that the page is done, save and view it in IE. When the page starts, it only has a listbox show up. Drop down the list and choose a country. The listbox causes the page to refresh, but now the grid appears, showing the customers for that country. As you can see in Figure 11-14, if you choose UK, the seven UK customers are shown.

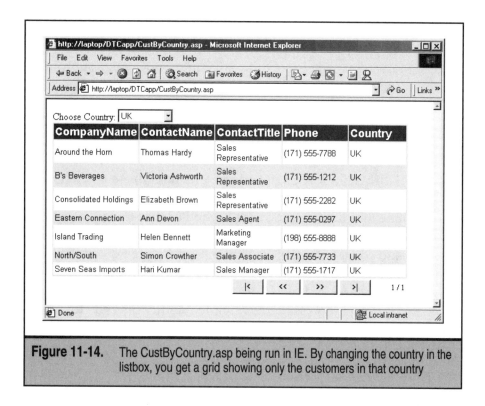

Figure 11-14.   The CustByCountry.asp being run in IE. By changing the country in the listbox, you get a grid showing only the customers in that country

If you look at the code, you notice the Close method is called before the variable is set. The reason is, after the first time the page is run, the Recordset DTC is considered open on the server. Therefore, you must close the Recordset DTC before you change the variable, and then reopen it to get the new value.

Enhancing the "Event-Driven" Page

When CustByCountry.asp first starts, the listbox contains the country Argentina, but the grid doesn't display any records. This is because the onClick event of the listbox hasn't fired, so the grid hasn't been displayed. To get the grid to display something, the onClick event must fire, which means you have to make a choice. Having the listbox start blank would be better, so the user can choose Argentina if she wants, and no country is showing up in the list without also being in the grid.

Adding a blank entry at the beginning of the list appears pretty simple. You have a block of code inside of a <SCRIPT> tag. Right now, that code is only the lstCountry_onChange subroutine. Now, add a new sub by adding the following code:

```
Sub thisPage_onEnter()
    lstCountry.addItem "","",0
End Sub
```

This block of code adds a blank item to the list, in the first position. Run the page, and you see the list now contains a blank line. If you drop down the list and choose Canada, however, when the page refreshes, it doesn't show Canada! In fact, examine the list and scroll to the top. Two blank entries are now at the beginning! Why? Every time you enter the page, a new blank item is added to the list and, obviously, this isn't what you want.

Fixing this problem is simple. Modify the code to look like this:

```
Sub thisPage_onEnter()
    If thisPage.FirstEntered Then
        lstCountry.addItem "","",0
    End If
End Sub
```

If you're confused by what your page should now look like, examine Figure 11-15. This shows where the code goes.

Now, run the page. The first time in, you get a blank line added to the lstCountry Listbox DTC. The blank line is only added the first time you enter the page.

How Events Work

If you stop to think about it, this functionality seems beyond normal HTML. After all, you are making a selection from a listbox, which you've already seen is only a standard HTML <SELECT> box and, by making a choice, you get the records for that country. How does this work?

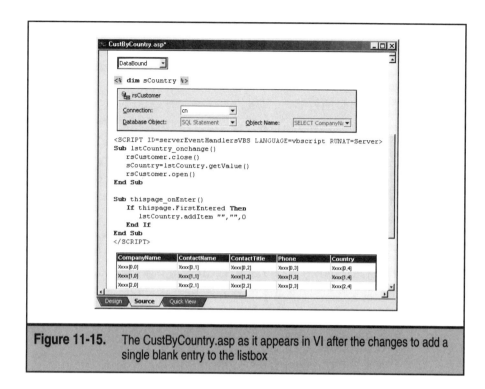

Figure 11-15.   The CustByCountry.asp as it appears in VI after the changes to add a single blank entry to the listbox

If you look at your CustByCountry.asp in VI, you notice a few lines at the top with a gray background. The gray background means the text cannot be edited. The code looks like this:

```
<% ' VI 6.0 Scripting Object Model Enabled %>
<!--#include file="_ScriptLibrary/pm.asp"-->
<% if StartPageProcessing() Then Response.End() %>
<FORM name=thisForm METHOD=post>
```

Scroll down to the bottom of the page and you see three more lines with a gray background. Those lines look like this:

```
<% ' VI 6.0 Scripting Object Model Enabled %>
<% EndPageProcessing() %>
</FORM>
```

Now, look carefully, and you notice a <FORM> tag is in there. This code is part of the Scripting Object Model (SOM) used by Visual InterDev to enable the functionality of the Design-Time Controls. One of the most obvious things the SOM does is to make your entire page an HTML form. Why? This is the only way, using standard HTML, to get data from the client up to the server.

Not only does the SOM turn your entire page into a form, it also includes code that captures events, such as the onClick of the listbox, and uses this to submit the form to the server. This means the page is still only standard HTML and it works in both Internet Explorer and Navigator.

What about the code that let you add a blank line at the beginning of the Listbox DTC, but only ran the first time you entered the page? The SOM makes each page act like an object, named thisPage. When the page is first executed by any user, the FirstEntered property of the thisPage object is set to true. On subsequent runs, this property is set to false. The property is tracked on the server and, therefore, is compatible with either IE or Navigator.

The SOM works by receiving the event in the client browser but, in effect, processing that event up on the server. For example, each page has an onEnter and onExit event. You can write event handlers, as you did a moment ago, to run when one of these events occurs. In addition, events such as the onClick event of the listbox are actually executed on the server.

This "remote execution" of events enables you to build pages that appear event-driven, while still conforming the standard HTML (as long as the browser supports some JavaScript functionality).

SUMMARY

Continuing the work with the DTCs shows how you can actually write some code against them to enable greater functionality. The DTCs are powerful, but the caveats from the previous chapter still apply: they are inherently two-tier, which limits scalability. In addition, the DTCs tend to be slower than writing the code yourself.

On the other hand, the DTCs can be useful for prototyping, as they let you quickly build sample applications that display the power of Web-based applications.

The DTCs are being replaced in the next version of Visual Studio, which was just renamed Visual Studio .NET. DTCs are being replaced with a paradigm where almost all applications will be Web applications, which means they will be a close cousin to the design-time controls. Therefore, their use will continue to be supported in IIS 5.0 and, possibly, in future versions, but the term "Design-Time Control" may fade from use. The concept of what they are and how they work, however, will be seen in versions of Visual Studio for many years to come.

CHAPTER 12

Client-Side Programming and the Future of Visual InterDev

In the previous two chapters, you saw how the Design-Time Controls of Visual InterDev work and what you can do with them. Well, VI can still do more. Some of this undiscovered functionality involves actually pushing some of the processing down to the client, which means a better user experience at the cost of portability. So far, everything you have done can work in both Internet Explorer (IE) and Navigator. Once you start pushing functionality down to the client's desktop, however, you quickly become browser-dependent. If you are strictly building intranet sites and your company has standardized on one browser over another, by all means use all the advanced features you want. On the other hand, if you are going out to the big world Internet, you will usually err on the side of reach versus richness.

After examining some of the ways in which you can push processing down to the client, you get a sneak peak at the future: ASP+. The book editors may well rip out this part of the paragraph, but this is the last chapter of the book to be written. I just got my hands on the first preview release of Visual Studio .NET, and I think covering just what it will do and how it will affect Web development is important. The big news, as you most likely will have heard by the time this book reaches you, is that Visual InterDev, as a product, no longer exists. Instead, you will build your ASP-like pages in either Visual Basic or Visual C++. ASP-like pages can still be built by dragging controls around and dropping them on a page, but several big changes exist: the files are now compiled instead of interpreted, and you will be coding with a "real" language instead of a scripting language.

CLIENT-SIDE PROGRAMMING WITH VISUAL INTERDEV

So far, you've been happily building pages in Visual InterDev, and then running them on the server. However, VI can actually build pages that run on the client as well. By this I mean the page pushes some or all of the processing down to the client to run on their machine. If this sounds like a great thing, it is . . . maybe. You see, some benefits and drawbacks exist to running on the client.

First, running code on the client makes you concerned about which browser the client is using. Microsoft and Netscape don't make browsers that are 100 percent compatible, a fact you probably noticed. As soon as you start using any of the advanced features, you run into problems using one browser or the other. Second, you're concerned about the type of connection the user has to SQL Server. If the application is built to run inside your company, connecting to SQL Server probably isn't much of an issue. If the person is outside your company firewall, however, direct database access from the client machine may be impossible.

Examining VI's DHTML Capabilities

Visual InterDev can build pages that use *Dynamic HTML (DHTML)* to run the DTCs instead of running them on the server using ASP. This is one of the main areas of contention between IE and Navigator: the way they support DHTML is very different, and writing DHTML that works in both browsers is quite challenging. Anyone who has visited more than ten sites with IE 5.5 knows a lot of DHTML out there simply doesn't work with IE.

Dynamic HTML is simply a mix of HTML and a scripting language. In IE, the scripting language can be VBScript or *JavaScript* (also called *JScript* and *ECMAScript*). In Navigator, the language must be JavaScript. DHTML makes the page event-driven: it can respond to mouse-over events, parts of the page can be rewritten without a round-trip to the server, and elements of the page can be hidden and revealed as needed. DHTML is dynamic, meaning you're running code inside the client browser. With what you've done so far, the browser has been acting as nothing more than a dumb terminal, displaying text and accepting user input. With DHTML, the browser actually becomes a container for a real application.

Visual InterDev can create DHTML pages, as long as your client browser is Internet Explorer 4.0 or higher. The advantage is a much faster user experience. The page will now directly bind to the database, so moving from one record to another doesn't require the page to be reprocessed by IIS. This can lead to tremendous speed improvements on the client end. You should realize it also makes managing your database connections nearly impossible, but you probably figured that out already.

Building the DHTML Page

To make VI create a DHTML page for you, you must perform some terribly frightening and difficult tasks. Still, prepare to embark on the journey by opening the VI application you have been using since Chapter 10, DTCapp. Now, create a new ASP and name it DHTMLtest.asp. *Before you do anything else*, right-click a blank part of the page and choose Properties. You should see the box shown in Figure 12-1. Notice you have two radio buttons in the section labeled "DTC scripting platform." The first is for running the Design-Time Controls on the server in the form of ASP, which is the default setting. However, you are going to change this setting to Client (IE 4.0 DHTML), as shown in Figure 12-1. This means the functionality of the DTC will be pushed to the client browser, so it can be executed by IE instead of on the server.

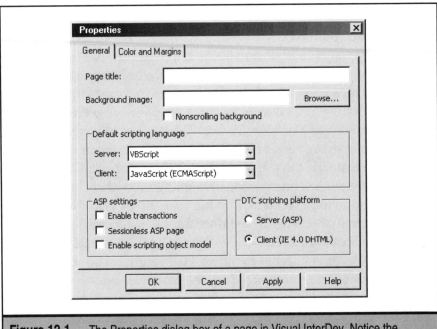

Figure 12-1. The Properties dialog box of a page in Visual InterDev. Notice the Design-Time Controls can run on the server or the client

Once you make this change, click the OK button. You're done! If that didn't seem too treacherous, you are correct. Asking VI to run the DTCs as client-side DHTML is actually simple. Now, all you need to do is build a page like you have in the last two chapters.

NOTE: When Visual InterDev first shipped, it was a great demo to build a page to use server-side DTCs, and then throw this one switch and show it all running as client-side. Somewhere along the Windows 2000, IE 5+, and Visual Studio Service Pack 3 trail something broke, however, and it hasn't been fixed since. You can no longer simply flip this switch and have it work. That's why you must make this change before you add anything to the page.

Start by adding a Recordset DTC by dragging the cm Command over and dropping it just below the <BODY> tag. This prompts you to enable the Scripting Object Model, which you need to do. Now, you have a Recordset DTC on the page, looking as it used to look. Right-click the Recordset DTC, choose Properties, and then rename this DTC rsCustomers.

Next, expand the cm Command in the Project Explorer window so you can see a list of the fields. Select CompanyName, ContactName, and Phone, and then drag them to the page, dropping them under the rsCustomers Recordset DTC. Finally, from the toolbar, drag a RecordsetNavBar DTC and drop it on the page, just after the closing </TABLE> tag. Right-click the RecordsetNavBar DTC and choose Properties. On the General tab, drop down the Recordset list and choose rsCustomers. You have now bound the RecordsetNavBar to the Recordset named rsCustomers. Save the page and then view it in Internet Explorer.

Your page should look like what you see in Figure 12-2. This doesn't look terribly different from the pages you created with the DTC scripting platform still set to use ASP. A slight physical difference exists, however, in that the buttons are one continuous control instead of a series of HTML buttons. You see the code for that shortly.

Another major difference is, as you click the next button, the record changes, but the page doesn't refresh! In fact, if you watch the status bar, you can see it doing exactly nothing. This means no server round-trip is taking place. This page, sitting in your browser, is talking directly to SQL Server.

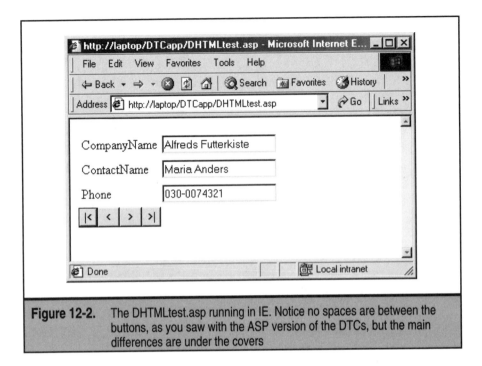

Figure 12-2. The DHTMLtest.asp running in IE. Notice no spaces are between the buttons, as you saw with the ASP version of the DTCs, but the main differences are under the covers

Is this a good thing? It depends, of course. It's decidedly two-tier, in an age of three-tier (or more) applications. You don't have the capability to use things like COM+ Component Services to try to pool database connections. On the other hand, as you click the Next button, the data is retrieved quickly and the flow is smooth. It feels much more like a standard Windows application.

Examining the DHTML Page

In IE, right-click the page and choose View Source. If you just finished the previous chapter, you'll remember that normally, the Scripting Object Model makes the entire page an HTML form, so it can send events (such as clicking the Next button) back to the server to be processed. By targeting client-side execution of the DTCs, there's no need to make the page a form. The events are handled in the browser, so you needn't make a trip back to the server to have the event code run.

In the source code, you might notice these two lines:

```
<SCRIPT LANGUAGE="JavaScript" src="_ScriptLibrary/EventMgr.HTM"></SCRIPT>
<SCRIPT LANGUAGE="JavaScript" src="_ScriptLibrary/Recordset.HTM"></SCRIPT>
```

These are actually pulling down most of the code from the server to run the code on the client. You don't see this code in the page, but you can easily find it on the server. In your DTCapp project, if you look in the _ScriptLibrary folder, you can see files with the names EventMgr.HTM and Recordset.HTM. If you open either one of these, you see a large amount of JavaScript code. This code is actually all DHTML. This is the code run on the client to enable the DHTML page to work.

Just in case you're curious, the answer is Yes, you can update data. All you have to do is what you saw in Chapter 10. In VI, right-click the RecrodsetNavBar DTC, choose Properties, and then turn on the check box labeled "Update on Move." This enables the end user to modify records back in your SQL Server database. Again, you haven't had to write a line of code.

The Remote Data Service (RDS)

To perform direct database access from IE to SQL Server, the DHTML version of the DTCs relies on RDS. Now that you've seen more acronyms in one sentence than should be allowed by law, you should realize the Microsoft Data Access Components contain something called the *Remote Data Service,* or *RDS.* RDS is the new name for the *ADC,* or *Advanced Data Connector.*

RDS is designed to give you access to remote data via OLE DB, whether that data is in a different process on your local machine or on a machine somewhere across the Internet. This means an HTML page can directly bind to a data source on a Web server. You still go through IIS to talk to the database, but the Web page isn't reprocessed. Only the data flows back down to the client. This means that you avoid the time it takes to reprocess the entire page.

In addition, your connection is "live," which means you can modify the data directly, without an ASP on the server having to be run.

RDS works by creating an object on the client, called a DataSpace. This enables the user to specify a server to which to connect and pass SQL statements. A program resides on the server that accepts the SQL statement and makes the call to the database, using standard ADO. This server-side program can be one that comes with RDS by default or a custom one. The sever-side program uses an RDS object called the DataFactory. Finally, in the client application, is an RDS DataControl object that allows data-bound controls to bind to it and it serves up the records returned from the server.

If having a DataControl object in your HTML page looks strange, it is simply because it isn't something you've done before in this book. IE gives you the ability to host ActiveX controls, and the RDS DataControl is an ActiveX control, although it is unusual because it doesn't have a visual interface.

To display the data, you'll usually want more ActiveX controls. In this example, you use the Microsoft DataGrid to display the records. You bind the DataGrid control to the DataControl to display the records automatically.

In Visual InterDev, go to the Toolbox and choose the ActiveX Controls tab. Make sure you aren't on the Design-Time Controls tab, as this can mess up this example! Right-click the Toolbox and choose Customize Toolbox. The Customize Toolbox then appears, as shown in Figure 12-3. Two tabs are in this dialog box. You want to choose the ActiveX Controls tab.

Scroll down the list until you find the Microsoft DataGrid Control, shown in Figure 12-3. Choose this control, and then click the OK button. The DataGrid control now shows up in the ActiveX Controls tab of the Toolbox in VI.

Now, create a new file but, this time, create an HTML file and name it DataConnect.htm. Go into the Source View. Drag the DataGrid control from the Toolbox onto the HTML page, dropping it after the <BODY> tag. Resize it to a more workable size.

Next, you have to type some code (sorry). As you can imagine, this won't be server-side code because you created an HTML file. You must add the code to the page to create the RDS DataControl. Adding the code to the Toolbox would have been nice, so you could

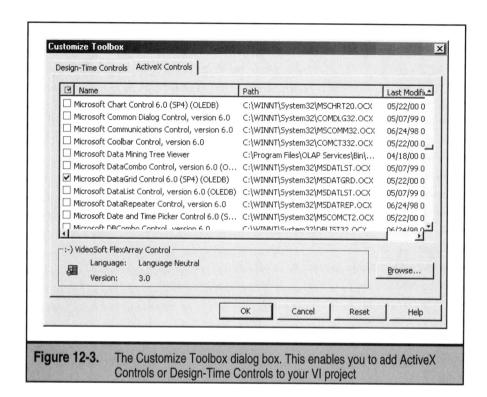

Figure 12-3. The Customize Toolbox dialog box. This enables you to add ActiveX Controls or Design-Time Controls to your VI project

simply drag-and-drop it, but the code doesn't have a visual interface, so you have to add the control the hard way: typing. Type the following code just below the DataGrid:

```
<!-- RDS DataControl -->
<OBJECT id=SControl
     classid=clsid:BD96C556-65A3-11D0-983A-00C04FC29E33
     width=1
     height=1>
   <PARAM NAME="Connect"
     VALUE="Provider=SQLOLEDB;User ID=sa;
     Initial Catalog=Northwind;Data Source=LAPTOP;>
   <PARAM NAME="Server" VALUE="http://laptop">
   <PARAM NAME="ExecuteOptions" VALUE="2">
   <PARAM NAME="FetchOptions" VALUE="3">
   <PARAM NAME="SortDirection" VALUE="-1">
   <PARAM NAME="InternetTimeout" VALUE="300000">
</OBJECT>
```

This is a standard HTML <OBJECT> tag. Standard, at least, for IE! It instantiates, on the client, the object referred to by the CLSID listed in the tag. This CLSID is for the RDS DataControl. Make sure you modify the connection string and server name to get a good connection.

After this block of code, you need to add some script to the page. Type in this block of code:

```
<SCRIPT LANGUAGE="VBScript">
Const adcExecSync = 1

Const adcFetchBackground = 2

Sub Window_OnLoad
    SControl.ExecuteOptions = adcExecSync
    SControl.FetchOptions = adcFetchBackground

    DataGrid1.CAPTION = "Customers"

    SControl.SQL = "Select CompanyName, ContactName, Phone from Customers"
    SControl.Refresh
    set DataGrid1.DataSource=sControl
End Sub
</SCRIPT>
```

This code runs when the page first loads. It sets a caption on the grid (merely a cosmetic touch), and then sets the SQL statement for the RDS DataControl you instantiated with the <OBJECT> tag. The Refresh method gets the data by executing the SQL statement. Then, you bind the DataGrid control to the RDS DataControl and it automatically displays the records.

NOTE: You may get warnings that you are accessing data in another domain. This is fine: go ahead and click Yes. You may get another warning saying the recordset is unsafe. Again, go ahead and click the OK button.

When you finish, you should have something like what appears in Figure 12-4. This isn't the most functional page, but you can see how you can access data from the browser, without the need for any server-side code.

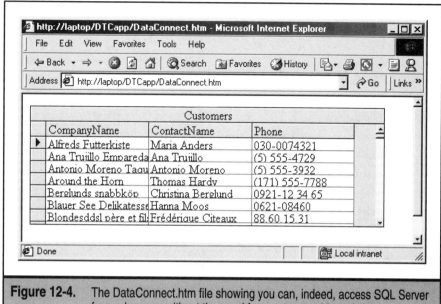

Figure 12-4.   The DataConnect.htm file showing you can, indeed, access SQL Server from a browser without the need for any server-side scripting

THE FUTURE: ASP+

You've now spent two and a half chapters learning all about Visual InterDev, and this just extends what you have been doing from the beginning. You most likely have heard the ancient Chinese saying—part blessing and part curse—that says, "May you live in interesting times." Right now, times are very interesting when it comes to Microsoft's development strategy. Microsoft recently announced its .NET initiative, which is a new infrastructure for applications, especially Web applications. Visual Studio .NET, the next version of Visual Studio, adds a wealth of features to any developer's arsenal. One of the major changes is the evolution of ASP into ASP+.

ASP+ in Brief

Before moving too far along, realize this information is subject to change. Visual Studio .NET isn't even in beta at press time. Instead, Microsoft released a "Preview Edition" at the Professional Developers Conference in Orlando, Florida, during the summer of 2000. At the same time, Microsoft released information about what ASP+ would do and how it would work. Given the early nature of

Visual Studio .NET and ASP+, the material in this section could change dramatically by the time the product is released.

Finally, Compiled Pages!

Perhaps one of the most significant changes in ASP+ is the pages are now compiled. This means you gain performance, but it also means you can use strongly typed languages. No longer must you suffer through using VBScript, where all the variables are of the Variant data type. Now, you can have full Visual Basic at your disposal, with all the error handling, data typing, and object creation of real VB. In addition, you can use Microsoft's new language, C# (pronounced C *Sharp*), which is similar to Visual C++. Third parties have already created a number of other language engines that can plug in to the .NET framework, so you could also use such languages as Perl, Python, and COBOL.

At press time, the pages are compiled on the fly by the .NET framework, which means you don't have to go through a compile process. Working with ASP+ should be as easy as it was to work with ASP; you simply copy the files to a directory and they're ready to go. If you've been building COM+ components to achieve speed alone, then having compiled pages could significantly reduce the amount of work you have to do. As you see in Chapters 13 and 14, however, a number of reasons still exist to build components.

One of the main reasons for the change is speed. You can use a real language, and the ASP+ page can be truly compiled. This should result in a huge speed increase, although the actual performance gain is currently impossible to determine.

You Want Session State *and* Web Farms? No Problem!

One of the drawbacks to using the Session object in ASP is the Session object is tied to a particular machine. This means if you try to use a Web farm for scalability, you have to turn on some sort of client affinity to make sure users return to the same server each time. (For a discussion of Web farms, see Chapter 15.)

Because a Session object only exists on one server, you cannot have multiple servers responding to a particular client if you are using the Session object to maintain state.

With ASP+ and the new .NET framework, however, Session objects can actually be stored out of process, so the session can be accessed from any server. In fact, you can move the session to an entirely different computer to survive such events as an application, or even a server, restart. A performance penalty is expected for moving the Session object to another process or especially a remote machine, but the benefits will be the capability to maintain state across multiple servers, something that can only be faked today.

In addition to storing the state on another machine, it will be possible to store the state in SQL Server, which will provide persistent storage. The details on this are sketchy, but the potential is there to maintain state across client sessions. This is commonly done today, but this would be automated and it would greatly simplify the building of applications that need to store preferences on the server.

Maintaining Session State Without Cookies

Today, the ASP engine uses cookies to pass the SessionID down to the client, and then it reads that value from the client cookie whenever the client sends a new page request. With ASP+, you can have cookieless sessions, which means you can finally support browsers that don't support cookies or have cookies turned off. ASP+ does this by modifying all the links on a page to include all the session information. With each request, therefore, you are passing up all the session information in a query string as part of the URL.

Moving from ASP to ASP+

ASP+ uses a new file extension, .aspx. This tells the ASP+ engine this is a compiled ASP+ file and to treat it as such. IIS supports both ASP and ASP+ running at the same time, so one server can serve up both standard ASP and the new ASP+ applications. These applications don't intermingle; you cannot share state between an ASP and ASP+ application, for example. By allowing them both to run on the same server at the same time, however, you can slowly migrate from ASP to ASP+.

The migration from ASP to ASP+ requires some work. Several differences in ASP+ are worth noting, and three of the most important are the changes to VB itself, the limit of one language per page, and the restriction on how to create functions.

VB Changes   While not technically an ASP+ change, changes to Visual Basic require changes to how you create your pages. Visual Basic no longer supports default properties. So far in this book, you have accessed the field in a recordset using this code:

```
<% =rs("FieldName") %>
```

Now, you must specify the property you want, so the code would look like this:

```
<% =rs("FieldName").Value %>
```

This code works today, so you might want to go ahead and start appending the .Value property onto your database code.

Another VB change is VB now requires you to put parentheses around all your sub and function calls. So, you've been able to get by with this:

```
Response.Write "Hello " & session("UserName")
```

But now, you must type it like this:

```
Response.Write ("Hello " & session("UserName"))
```

One Language per Page   With ASP, you could have one block of VBScript, and then a block of JavaScript. With ASP+, however, you can have only one server-side language per page. This is because the page is compiled, not interpreted; therefore, one compiler needs to process the page. You can still have server-side VBScript and client-side JavaScript, of course, because the compiler doesn't process client-side code. If you need to mix different server-side languages in a page, you can create what is being called a *pagelet*, which is only a miniature ASP+ page that can be linked into another ASP+ page.

Functions Must Be <SCRIPT> Tags   Back in ASP 1.0, you couldn't put a function inside the server-side script tags (<% and %>). Instead, you had to use <SCRIPT> tags to include a function. With ASP 2.0, this was fixed. Now, with ASP+, it's back to the way it used to be. Therefore, this block of code is no longer valid:

```
<%
Sub Foo()
    'code goes here
End Sub
%>
```

Instead, you have to code the functions this way:

```
<SCRIPT Language="VB" RunAt=server>
Sub Foo()
    'code goes here
End Sub
</SCRIPT>
```

Server Controls

You have been introduced to Design-Time Controls and ActiveX Controls. Now get ready for Server Controls. *Server Controls* aren't Design-Time Controls or ActiveX Controls; instead, they are standard HTML form elements that ASP+ lets you treat as controls. Take a look at how you would normally load an HTML <SELECT> box:

```
<SELECT Name="Country">
   <%
   Do Until rsCountry.EOF
      Response.Write "<OPTION>" & rsCountry("Country").Value & _
         "</option>"
   Loop
   %>
</SELECT>
```

This code builds a select box using the standard HTML <SELECT> tag and ASP's Response object. In ASP+, you put the

same HTML <SELECT> box on the page, but add records to it as if
it's an object:

```
<SELECT Name="Country" RunAt=server>
</SELECT>
<%
Do Until rsCountry.EOF
    Country.Add(rs("Country").Value)
Loop
%>
```

As you can see, this code treats the <SELECT> element as a
scriptable object when, in fact, it's a standard HTML element. The
idea here is to separate the execution from the element on the form.

Server Controls also offer another benefit, which is the capability
to handle events. This is similar to the way the SOM handles events
on the client by passing them to the server for processing. ASP+
makes this easier, however. Assume you have a page that can display
a record from a database and you have three buttons: Add, Update,
and Delete. These three buttons could all be HTML Submit buttons
(<INPUT Type="submit">) or they could be standard buttons
(<INPUT Type="button">). Assume the former is the case because
you don't want any client-side code. Your ASP might look something
like this:

```
<FORM Name="frmCust" Method="Post" Action="Me.asp">
    <INPUT Name="txtCompanyName"
        Value="<% =rs("CompanyName").Value %>">
    <INPUT Name="txtContactName"
        Value="<% =rs("ContactName").Value %>">
    <INPUT Type="submit" Value="Add" Name="btnAdd">
    <INPUT Type="submit" Value="Change" Name="btnChange">
    <INPUT Type="submit" Value="Delete" Name="btnDelete">
</FORM>
<%
If Request.Form("btnAdd")<>"" Then
    'Do add code
End If

If Request.Form("btnChange")<>"" Then
```

```
     'Do change code
End If


If Request.Form("btnDelete")<>"" Then
     'Do delete code
End If
%>
```

In this page, you have a reentrant form (it calls the same page). When you click one of the submit buttons, it passes the name of that button to the server, in the form of "btnAdd=btnAdd," so you know which button was pressed. Next, you must set up a series of If statements to determine which button was pressed, and then process the code based on that.

In the ASP+ world, this is much easier. Your ASP+ code would look like this:

```
<FORM Name="frmCust" Method="Post" Action="Me.asp">
   <INPUT Name="txtCompanyName"
      Value="<% =rs("CompanyName").Value %>" runat=server>
   <INPUT Name="txtContactName"
      Value="<% =rs("ContactName").Value %>">
   <asp:button id="Add" OnClick="Add_Click" runat=server />
   <asp:button id="Change" OnClick="Change_Click" runat=server />
   <asp:button id="Delete" OnClick="Delete_Click" runat=server />
</FORM>
<SCRIPT Language="VB" runat=server>
Sub Add_Click
   'Do add code
End Sub


Sub Change_Click
   'Do change code
End Sub


Sub Delete_Click
   'Do delete code
End Sub
</SCRIPT>
```

In some ways, this is similar to what you saw with Visual InterDev's DTCs when they were set to run on the server. The events were fired on the client, but they were sent to the server where the event handler code ran. Here, however, you are using Server Controls, which you can see in the previous code. These controls are rendered as standard HTML controls in the browser, but you can program against them as if they were objects.

Validation

One of the greatest complaints about HTML is no automatic way exists to validate the fields on a form. To perform the field validation, you have to write either client-side code and validate the values locally, or validate the values on the server. Often, you do both: you validate what you can on the client, and then validate the rest on the server.

ASP+ includes a number of server controls that make it easy to validate fields on a form. For example, you can create a RequiredFieldValidator to indicate that a particular field is required. You can create a RangeValidator to make sure the values entered fall within a certain range. For example, look at the following code:

```
<HTML>
<HEAD>
   <SCRIPT Language="VB" runat=server>
      Sub btnValidate_Click()
         If Page.IsValid Then
            'Perform actions
         Else
            lblValidate.Text = "Fill in empty fields"
         End If
      End Sub
   </SCRIPT>
</HEAD>
<BODY>
<FORM runat="server">
   <TABLE Cellpadding=3 Cellspacing=3>
      <TR>
         <TD colspan=3>
            <asp:Label ID="lblValidate"
```

```
                    Text="Fill in the required fields below"
                    runat=server /><br>
              </TD>
         </TR>
         <TR>
              <TD>
                 Your Name:
              </TD>
              <TD>
                 <ASP:TextBox id=txtName runat=server />
              </TD>
              <TD>
                 <asp:RequiredFieldValidator
                    id="NameValidator"
                    ControlToValidate="txtName"
                    Display="Static"
                    Width="100%" runat=server>
                    *
                 </asp:RequiredFieldValidator>
              </TD>
         </TR>
     </TABLE>
     <ASP:Button id=btnValidate text="Validate"
         OnClick="btnValidate_Click" runat=server />
</FORM>
</BODY>
</HTML>
```

If this code looks confusing, don't let it frighten you. The page
starts off with a simple VB function that runs on the server. This is
the routine that is called when the user clicks the Validate button. On
the page itself is a table with two rows and three columns. Actually,
the first row contains only one column, telling the user to fill in all
the required fields. Next is a row with the text "Your Name:", next
a text box for the user's name, and then a RequiredFieldValidator.
It may be difficult to tell exactly what this field is doing without
running it, but what happens is you are marking the txtName field
as required. If the user attempts to validate this form without that
field filled in, the RequiredFieldValidator displays what is between

the opening and closing <asp:RequiredFieldValidator> tags—in this case, only an asterisk.

Realize what this does for you. Without writing any code, you can validate fields in an HTML form! Further, the form retains the values entered into the fields, so the user doesn't have to retype any information. If you have some custom validation you need to do, you can actually identify a field as a CustomValidator and tie it to code on the server. This still requires a server round-trip, but it maintains the values in all the fields if the validation fails, resulting in a much better user experience.

Working with Data

ASP+ also includes new ways of working with data. You create a Dataset object in ASP+ page, which is similar to an ADO Recordset object. ASP+ uses ADO+, but this chapter will not get into ADO+. Once you retrieve records and have them stored in a Dataset, you can actually bind the Dataset to a server control called a *DataGrid*. This is not the DataGrid control you saw earlier in this chapter; instead, it is simply rendered as an HTML table.

To perform SQL access from your ASP+ page, you need to import some namespaces to have the classes you need available. After that, some simple code is all that's required to instantiate the Dataset and bind it to the DataGrid.

```
<%@ Import Namespace="System.Data" %>
<%@ Import Namespace="System.Data.SQL" %>


<HTML>
<SCRIPT Language="VB" runat=server>
    Sub Page_Load()
        SQLConnection cn = new
            SQLConnection("server=laptop;uid=sa;pwd=;database=northwind")
        SQLDataSetCommand cm = new
            SQLDataSetCommand("select * from Customers", cn)
        DataSet ds = new DataSet()
        cm.FillDataSet(ds, "Customers")
        dgCust.DataSource=ds.Tables["Customers"].DefaultView
        dgCust.DataBind()
    End Sub
```

```
</SCRIPT>
<BODY>
   <ASP:DataGrid id="dgCust" runat=server Width="700"
      ShowFooter="false" CellPadding=3 CellSpacing=0
      MaintainState="false"/>
</BODY>
</HTML>
```

This should seem fairly simple. There's no looping through the recordset, intertwining ASP and HTML, as you've seen in the past. In fact, one of the goals of ASP+ is to separate the coding logic from the HTML. You can see this has largely been accomplished.

Debugging

Who needs debugging? Eventually, everyone makes mistakes, and debugging becomes part of building applications. ASP+ has much better debugging tools than those found in ASP and Visual InterDev 6.0. The idea of debugging in ASP+ is this: because the ASP+ pages are compiled, you can debug the ASP+ page and jump right into the components it's calling, even if those are COM+ components you have written yourself. No longer should you have to build test applications to test your components before tying them to a Web page.

You have all the features you got used to in VI, such as breakpoints, single-stepping through the code, and the capability to change variables. In addition, the debugger has a trace feature, similar to the debug window in Visual Basic. This is similar because you can write messages to it using the Trace.Write syntax. This is different because it shows you all the Request object information in a nicely formatted table, so you can see all the Request variables and their values. Trace.Write is nice because, unlike putting in a lot of Response.Write statements to debug the page, you needn't worry about forgetting to take out the Trace.Write statements. If you leave them in, they are simply null when the program is compiled.

ASP+ Summary

As you can see, ASP+ offers great promise when it comes to the future of building Web applications with Microsoft technology. Visual InterDev as a product may be going away, but you can see the concept of programming against controls on the server, but only displaying HTML form elements on the client, is alive and well.

Microsoft's goal with Visual Studio .NET is to assume that many, or even most, applications will be targeted to the Web. To that end, Visual Basic and Visual C++ include Web application projects. These look similar to what you saw in Visual InterDev; they enable you to create HTML pages by dragging-and-dropping and setting properties. However, they will be generating ASP+ code for you, as well as HTML, and these new pages will be the basis for your ASP+ application.

A FIRST LOOK AT VISUAL STUDIO .NET

At press time, Visual Studio .NET hadn't yet been released. By the time this book hits your desk, it may well be in beta and could look significantly different from what you see here. Regardless, these next few pages can give you an idea of what to expect in the new version of Visual Studio and how you can use it to build Web applications.

As you can see in Figure 12-5, when you start a new project, one environment now hosts Visual Basic, Visual C++, and Visual FoxPro.

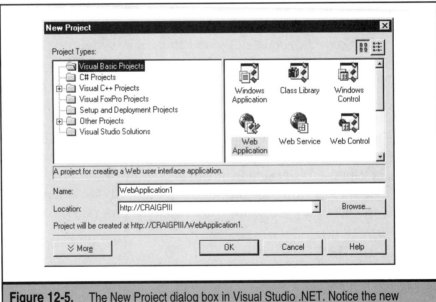

Figure 12-5.   The New Project dialog box in Visual Studio .NET. Notice the new project types for Visual Basic. Other new project types also exist, such as the capability to create Windows 2000 services

Looking at Visual Basic, you can see many types of applications are available, including a Web Application project type. Clicking the OK button on this screen takes you into Visual Studio .NET.

Figure 12-6 shows the actual development environment. This looks similar to what you have seen with Visual InterDev but, remember, this is a Visual Basic project. In the main working area, notice you're working with a file called WebForm1.aspx. This is an ASP+ page. If you look at the window that's now called the Solution Explorer (previously this window was called the Project Explorer), you can see that below the WebForm1.aspx file is a filed named WebForm1.vb. This file can actually store all your VB code, so it can be separated from your ASP+ page. One of Microsoft's goal with Visual Studio .NET is to separate the interface code from the logic code.

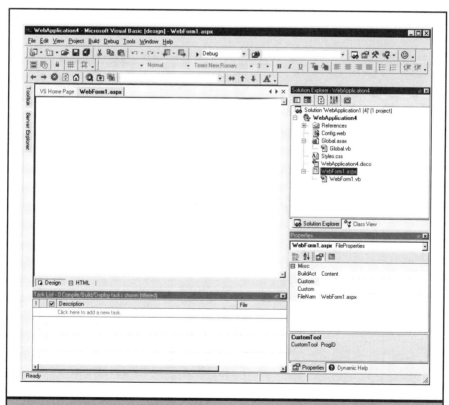

Figure 12-6.   The Visual Studio .NET development environment

If you look closely, you might notice two sideways buttons— labeled "Server Explorer" and "Toolbox"— are located along the left-hand side of the development environment. The toolbox is almost identical to what you have seen in Visual InterDev in that it contains the controls you can use on your pages. The Server Explorer enables you to see not only your data connections, but also the services available on particular servers. For example, Figure 12-7 shows the server named "craigpiii" has Microsoft Message Queue, Crystal Reports Services, and SQL Databases, to name a few. This also enables you to see the available resources on other servers.

In Figure 12-8, a number of steps have been carried out, but they have all been drag-and drop-operations, so there isn't much to show in the interim. First, the Data tab of the toolbox was chosen and an ADODataSetCommand was dragged onto the page. Unlike what you're used to seeing in Visual InterDev, these controls get dropped

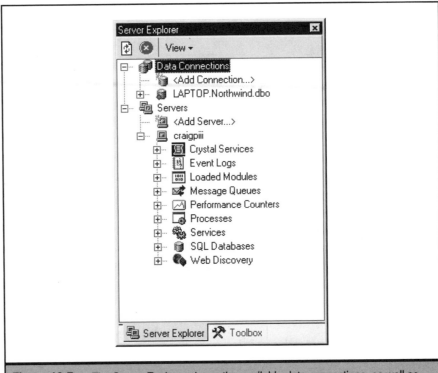

Figure 12-7. The Server Explorer shows the available data connections, as well as the resources available on various servers

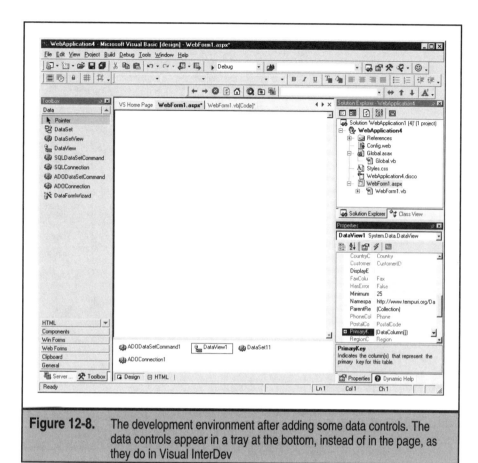

Figure 12-8.   The development environment after adding some data controls. The data controls appear in a tray at the bottom, instead of in the page, as they do in Visual InterDev

to the bottom of the page in a tray. After dragging the control, a wizard starts that enables you to choose a connection, and then a source for the control, such as a SQL string. After finishing the wizard, an ADOConnection is added to the tray automatically. Next, you set the GenerateDataSet property of the page to True, and then drag over a DataView object. You set the DataView object's Table property to one of the tables available in your ADODataSetCommand, and you are done. Controls, such as the DataGrid, can be bound to this DataView object.

Next, a DataGrid control is dragged over and dropped on the page. The DataGrid control's DataSource property is set to the DataView control. This creates a grid bound to a data source. Sound familiar? Look at Figure 12-9, however, and you can see a number of differences. First, only the grid shows in the page; the page isn't

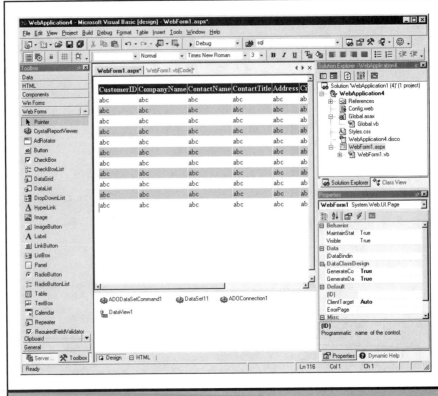

Figure 12-9. The page with the DataGrid control added and bound to the DataView control

cluttered with a Recordset DTC or a RecordsetNavBar DTC. Second, you may notice at the bottom only two views exist for this page: Design and HTML. Because ASP+ is compiled, Microsoft didn't even add a simple Web browser in the editor.

If you switch to the HTML view, however, you see the biggest change. In HTML view, you see the following code:

```
<%@ Page Language="vb" Codebehind="WebForm1.vb"
    Inherits="WebApplication4.WebForm1"%>
<HTML><HEAD>
    <meta name="GENERATOR" content="Microsoft Visual Studio 7.0">
    <meta name="CODE_LANGUAGE" content="Visual Basic 7.0"></HEAD>
  <body>
```

```
    <form id="WebForm1" method="post" runat="server">
<asp:DataGrid id=DataGrid1 runat="SERVER"
  CellSpacing="0" BackColor="Silver" ForeColor="Black"
  ConfigurableProperties="System.Configuration.Design.ComponentSettings"
  DataSource="<%# DataView1%>">

  <property name=AlternatingItemStyle>
    <asp:tableitemstyle BackColor="Gainsboro" >
    </asp:tableitemstyle>
  </property>

  <property name=FooterStyle>
    <asp:tableitemstyle ForeColor="White" BackColor="Silver" >
    </asp:tableitemstyle>
  </property>

  <property name=ItemStyle>
    <asp:tableitemstyle BackColor="White" >
    </asp:tableitemstyle>
  </property>

  <property name=HeaderStyle>
    <asp:tableitemstyle Font-Bold="True" ForeColor="White" BackColor="Navy" >
</asp:tableitemstyle>
  </property>
</asp:DataGrid>
</form>
</body>
</html>
```

Notice how clean the code is. Basically, all you see is the code for the DataGrid. Where is the code for the DataView and other data controls? This code has been pulled into the VB code listing. If you look at the VB code, it looks similar to what you see in Figure 12-10. Too much code exists to print it all on this page.

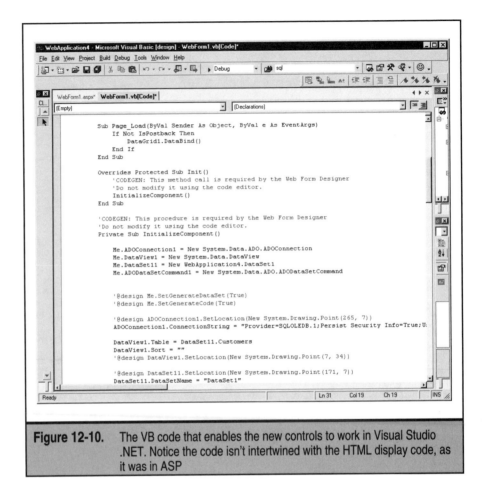

Figure 12-10.   The VB code that enables the new controls to work in Visual Studio .NET. Notice the code isn't intertwined with the HTML display code, as it was in ASP

This page now shows the data for the DataView control in the DataGrid. Naturally, on the client, all this will be straight HTML.

SUMMARY

After spending two chapters on the Design-Time Controls in Visual InterDev, this chapter first examined how the DTCs could be used to build Web pages that ran on the client. VI makes this task relatively simple because the Scripting Object Model enables you to create an application the same way, regardless of the target platform.

Creating applications targeted to the client provides a richer, more pleasing user interface, but it severely restricts the reach of your application. Most client-side enhancements are specific to a particular browser, and this is true of VI's DHTML code; it only runs inside of Internet Explorer.

After looking at much of what VI had to offer, it was time to examine the future: ASP+. ASP+ promises to relieve many of the headaches Web developers have had for several years. ASP+ allows session state to be maintained on Web farms. ASP+ also makes performing HTML form validation and building tables based on data easy, without having to code all the rows and cells yourself. In addition, because ASP+ files are compiled, they can provide a huge speed boost to your applications. And because you can now code with the full version of Visual Basic or the new C# language, you have access to real error-handling and strongly typed variables. Debugging and deployment are also both greatly improved.

Because ASP+ is still some time off in the distance, you know changes will occur. This chapter didn't have you run any of the ASP+ pages because the time frame for a general beta of Visual Studio .NET is still up in the air. By the time this book reaches you, you may have a beta copy of Visual Studio .NET and you can play around with these examples. If not, they should provide you with a partial understanding of the capabilities coming in the near future.

PART IV

Building N-Tier Web Applications

CHAPTER 13

Building N-Tier Applications with ASP and COM Components

Throughout this book, right up until this chapter, you have been simply writing your data access code in your Active Server Pages. This works fine, but it isn't typically the way production Web applications are developed. Instead, most Web applications move a majority of the processing into COM (or COM+) components. The benefits of doing this include better scalability, reusability, and speed.

The ADO code you've used so far to access SQL Server is unchanged because you are now building components in Visual Basic (VB), Visual C++, or other languages. The same rules apply when it comes to opening recordsets with keyset, static, dynamic, or forward-scrolling cursors. The benefits of stored procedures are still evident. The whole issue of when to connect to the database, covered in Chapter 5, still holds, only now we are asking the question of when to instantiate the COM component that connects to the database. The issues are basically the same as those already covered, only *where* the code resides is different, and you can derive additional benefits from the move to n-tier applications.

UNDERSTANDING N-TIER APPLICATIONS

Understanding how n-tier, or three-tier, applications came into being, and why, is important. N-tier applications have many benefits over standard client/server, or two-tier, applications. Those benefits include increased reusability, encapsulation, and improved scalability. Some challenges occur because n-tier applications can be more challenging to design and code. Like most good things, some additional work up-front can lead to a better application in its final form.

Two-Tier Systems

Let's back up a moment and forget the Web. Instead, let's examine the original days of client/server applications. When the first client/server applications were developed, they simply relied on having a rich client that did all the work and a shared repository of data sitting on a centralized, back-end server. The client application contained two important pieces of the application: the user interface and the business rules. The server contained the data and the database engine, and was often just called the "back-end." So, you had the client tier and the server, or data, tier. Let's ignore the data tier for now because it's roughly the same for both two-tier and n-tier systems. Figure 13-1 shows what a two-tier application might look like.

The *user interface* (*UI*) is easy to understand. If the user sees something on the screen and can interact with it, it's part of the user interface. For VB applications, the UI includes all the forms, dialog boxes, and message boxes the user encounters. For Web applications, the UI consists of the HTML or ASP forms the user sees. With ASP, however, realize the UI is only the HTML that makes it down to the client browser. I'm not talking about the server-side code in the ASP unless it generates UI elements.

The business rules are more interesting. Let's assume you have a large company and you have several systems that can add a new customer into the corporate database. This is not unusual; many companies have an order center, an accounting group, and a customer service group, all with the capability to add customers, and often with different systems. In such an environment, ensuring that all the systems are following the same rules can be difficult.

To add a customer to the corporate database, what does it take? Obviously, you want information like the customer name, a contact name and number, an address, and other pieces of information. But

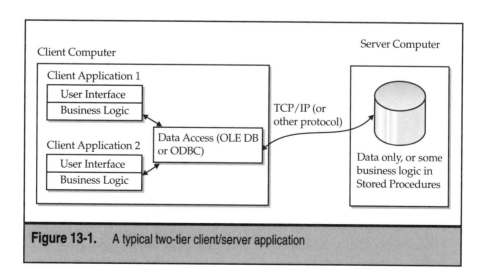

Figure 13-1.   A typical two-tier client/server application

what if you also want to check to see if you already have this customer in the database before she is added? What if you want to notify the sales representative in that area that a new customer has come onboard? What if your company policy is to generate a letter welcoming this customer to your company? These are all part of the overall rules of adding a customer to the database.

In pseudocode, adding a customer might look something like this:

```
Function AddCustomer() as Boolean
    Get all the values from the form
    Check to see if the customer already exists
        use name matching algorithm
        use address matching algorithm
    If customer is not in database
        add customer record
        e-mail salesperson in that area
        generate letter to customer
    Notify user that customer has been added
End Function
```

This is an example of what might happen on the business side when it comes to adding a customer. Much more detail needs to be added; for example, when you go to notify the salesperson, you assume you already know the area in which this customer is located, the salesperson for that area, the e-mail address of that salesperson, and a way to connect to the e-mail server.

In two-tier client/server applications, these business rules exist in the client application. You write a VB or VC++ application and include the code to add a customer that will be called when a button is clicked. So far, this seems fairly simple. But remember, in this example, customer service, accounting, and order entry can all add customers using different systems. This code must be replicated in all three systems. And, if this is a typical company, those three systems were written in three different languages by completely different groups of programmers.

Let's assume the rules change slightly. The sales representatives say they don't like getting e-mail but, in fact, would rather be paged with the information so they can make a call right away, instead of having to wait until the next day. This is because they are on the road during the day and not checking their e-mail. In the previous example, you would have to go in and modify the code to find the appropriate salesperson, look up his pager number, and send a message to some pager gateway. This may or may not be a major change, but you must make sure you do it in all three applications, test the changes, recompile the applications, and redistribute those new programs to the client machines.

The Problems with Two-Tier Systems

The problems with this scenario are probably obvious. First, one business rule change requires you to modify three different programs, perhaps in three different languages. Second, you must redistribute the application to every desktop that uses it. If you have remote offices that need the application, distribution can become quite a challenge. In fact, distributing applications is one of the major challenges with two-tier systems. Even though Web applications don't have the same distribution issues, if you code your Web applications using a two-tier approach, you have the same functionality repeated across several applications. Your business logic exists inside several ASPs, which means you don't have reusable components to help speed your application creation.

Other problems occur with two-tier applications as well. If you are going to develop a VB client application, you are assuming the client machine is an Intel-based computer running some version of Windows. While Windows-based machines are the common denominator, many new platforms are coming online. For example, people are now beginning to use phones and *personal digital assistants (PDAs)* to browse the Web, and they want to be able to run the same applications on these clients as they do on full-featured computers.

With two-tier systems, you are often concerned about the amount of RAM and disk space on the client machines. Because the application actually runs on the client, you must be aware of the capabilities on the client machine.

Two-tier systems didn't encourage reusability of code. The only reusability you have in two-tier systems is to copy and paste code, sometimes called *clipboard inheritance.* The only thing shared in a two-tier application is the data in the back-end database. Moving some processing to the back-end in the form of stored procedures is possible, but many of the business rules remain coupled with the front-end application.

N-Tier Systems

Given the problems with two-tier systems, learning that many developers wanted a better way to produce client/server applications probably isn't a great surprise. When Microsoft introduced VB 4.0, it introduced the class module, which enabled developers to create reusable components. These components could then be called from a central location, meaning a number of applications could reuse the same set of centralized components.

In effect, you're taking the two-tier application and creating a middle tier by separating the business logic from the user interface. The UI still needs to be run on the client in one form or another, but your business logic can be centralized for easier maintenance and to remove the distribution headaches you faced with two-tier applications. The back-end, or data tier, is basically unchanged. Throughout this book, you've seen some advantages exist to using stored procedures, but this is true regardless of a two-tier or three-tier architecture. Figure 13-2 shows the logical structure of a three-tier application.

As you discover in a moment, creating three-tier applications for the Web makes a lot of sense. In fact, it typically gives you better performance and scalability if you do it correctly. In this chapter, you lay the foundation for your scalability gains and, in Chapter 14, you take advantage of the Component Services in Windows 2000 to achieve better scalability and to handle your transactions.

Introduction to Components

Continuing with the earlier example, you have three applications that must be able to add new customers to your corporate database. If you stop there, you see you have the concept of a customer. What is a customer? From a programming standpoint, a customer is an entity with a name, address, contact, and so on. These are the properties, or

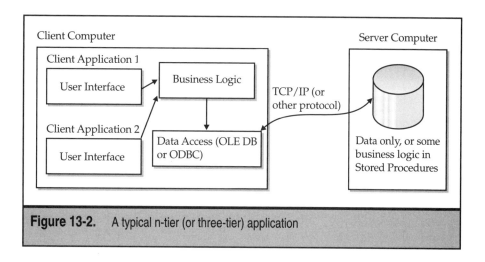

Figure 13-2.   A typical n-tier (or three-tier) application

attributes, of a customer. If you want a Customer object, these will be properties of the Customer object. Properties are usually considered as the physical attributes of an object: an address, a phone number, a name, and so forth.

A customer can also do things. A customer can be added to the database. A customer can be updated or removed. A customer can be billed. These actions are what we call *methods.* Methods are the actions, or capabilities, of the object. Figure 13-3 shows what the Customer component might look like from a logical standpoint.

NOTE: I used the terms object and component almost interchangeably in the previous paragraphs. Technically, classes are written, in this case, a Customer class. One or more classes are complied into a component, usually in the form of a DLL. When a program needs to create, or instantiate, an object, it creates an object out of the appropriate class. In this example, we would say a program has an object of type customer.

VB 4 and above enable you to create components that can be reused by any client who can talk to COM components. One of the great things about COM is it is language-independent. I'm not talking about English, Spanish, and German here; I'm talking about VB, Visual C++, Delphi, and other programming languages. A component can be written in VB, and then called from a C++

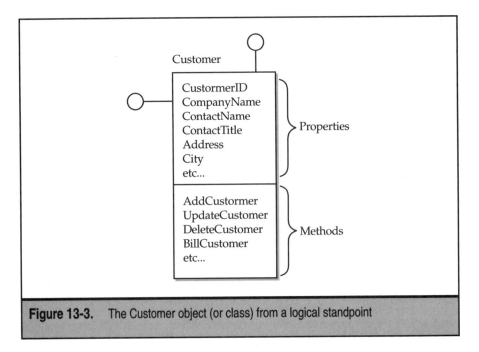

Figure 13-3.   The Customer object (or class) from a logical standpoint

application, or vice versa. All COM components have the same standard way of communicating, so the language used to create the component or the client is unimportant.

With the customer, you could create a Customer class, which I call cCustomer. The cCustomer class has properties of Name, Address, City, Region, PostalCode, ContactName, ContactNumber, and so forth. It has methods for Add, Update, and Delete. To create the Customer class, you must build a component in VB with a class called cCustomer. Before creating the class, however, you need to understand some things about COM and components.

UNDERSTANDING AND BUILDING COMPONENTS

Before you actually build your component with the cCustomer class, a number of things about components should be discussed. Where will the component be physically located? Where will it run? What are some of the performance considerations of the decisions you make? Making the right decisions during the design process is critical to the success of your n-tier application.

Understanding COM

The first step to understanding components is to learn how they work. I won't go into a full discussion of the underlying workings, but I will discuss a little about why components came to be and how they work. Then I examine some of the decisions you should make before you build your components and how those decisions can affect performance.

A Brief History of COM

One of the goals of Windows has always been to be able to reuse code, which enables you to provide common functionality across programs. Remember, one of the promises of Windows is to reduce training by having all applications work in basically the same ways: there can be one common print dialog box, and a common color picker, and a common help system. Not all applications use these standard dialog boxes, but the idea has been there for a long time.

To get reusability early on, you had *Dynamic Link Libraries (DLLs)*. These were not the same as COM DLLs, which is what you will build in this chapter. The original DLLs, still very much in use, were simply libraries of functions. They had no object-oriented features. If you looked inside a standard DLL, you saw a list of functions, along with the arguments for each function and its return value. Using standard DLLs wasn't the most efficient use of resources. If you needed only one function from a DLL, you had to load the entire DLL into memory. What's worse, Windows didn't know when you were done with it, so the DLL stayed loaded in memory from the time it was first called until Windows was shut down.

What was even worse with DLLs was the application that used them needed to know where they were physically located. Most applications tried to call the DLL and hoped it was in the path somewhere. Other applications would place a copy of the DLL in the same directory as the application itself and call that copy. The problem was you ended up with 50 copies of the same DLL all over your machine, and many of them were different versions.

Speaking of different versions, many vendors would simply update their DLLs and not worry about backwards compatibility.

Anyone who did programming in the pre-COM days can remember how a client could install a new application and break the application you wrote, because the new application installed a newer (or sometimes older) version of a DLL you were using, and the function you had been calling had either changed or been removed. This was the genesis of the term "DLL Hell."

The basic idea behind DLLs, that of providing a nice set of reusable functions, was a good one, but the original implementation was less than stellar. Microsoft knew it needed a better approach. It tried a few different approaches. Remember DDE?

DDE was a mechanism to allow one program to talk to another. It was slow and unreliable. So, Microsoft developed *OLE,* which originally stood for *Object Linking and Embedding.* The first time I saw OLE in action was when I embedded an Excel spreadsheet in a Word document. I doubled-clicked the spreadsheet and, five minutes later, Excel opened with the spreadsheet in it. The original implementation of OLE was based on DDE, and it was slow.

Microsoft later released OLE 2, where *OLE* just stood for *OLE.* This version was based on what was to become COM, and gave us things like in-place editing. Now, if I clicked that Excel spreadsheet, I stayed in Word, but the menus and toolbars changed to those of Excel. This was a big step forward, but we weren't all the way there.

Finally, Microsoft implemented COM. The ideas behind COM were powerful: you should be able to create reusable components so any client application can use them. These clients shouldn't care which language the components were written in or where the component is physically located. In addition, these components should remove themselves from memory when they were no longer needed. The COM DLL was born.

What Is COM and How Does It Work?

If you ask ten people what COM is, you get ten different answers. Let's look at some of what COM does and how it does it, and you can decide for yourself.

Location, Location, Location   One of the big features of COM is *location transparency,* which means you don't care where the component physically resides, you just want to be able to call it. You see, the component may be in the same directory as the client program, in a different directory on the same machine, or it may be on a different machine half-way around the world; regardless, the client should be able to use the component without having to find it first. How does this work? The registry is the key.

NOTE: Microsoft used to say COM enabled you to talk across processes on the same machine and *DCOM*, or *Distributed COM*, enabled you to talk across processes on different machines. The term DCOM has lost some favor at Microsoft, because COM, by its very nature, is distributed. Therefore, you may hear DCOM mentioned, but Microsoft doesn't use the term often anymore.

The *registry* is a set of files on your computer that maintains all the hardware and software information about that computer. One of the things the registry maintains is a list of all the COM components it knows about and where they are physically located. When your program asks for a component, COM takes over behind the scenes and looks up, in the registry, where the component is physically located. COM then goes out and instantiates an object in memory of the class you wanted from that component (where it instantiates the actual object varies, as you see in a moment). COM then returns to your application a pointer to the newly created component, and your client application is happy and goes about its business of calling the properties and methods of the class. The program behind the scenes doing this work is the *Service Control Manager*, or *SCM* (pronounced *scum*). Figure 13-4 shows how the SCM works to give you access to your components.

In Process vs. Out of Process COM components can actually run in two places in relation to our program: they can run in-process or out-of-process. *In-process* (*In Proc*) components run in the same process space as your application. In other words, they share memory with your applications. The good news about In Proc components is they are fast relative to out-of-process components. In Proc components are fast because they are in the same process as the client program, which means there's no need for marshalling, which will be explained in a

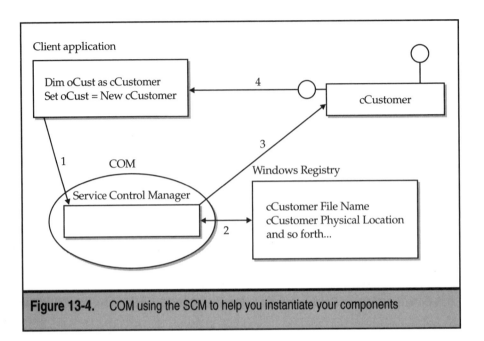

Figure 13-4.   COM using the SCM to help you instantiate your components

moment. One drawback to In Proc components can be that each application that needs a component gets its own copy. This means you might have multiple instances of the component in memory at once, and it means multiple clients cannot share data in the same component. This is usually not needed, however, so this limitation is typically not a major issue.

Out-of-process components actually run in their own memory space, separate from the client using them. In practice, Microsoft tells you this is safer: if the component crashes, it won't bring down the client application. An In Proc component that crashes will also crash the client application because they are in the same process space. In reality, even with out-of-process components, if the component crashes, the client application now has a pointer to some memory address that's no longer the entry point for the component, so the client programs also often crash at this point. Still, if you're taking a Microsoft certification exam, the correct answer is "Out of Process components are safer . . . out-of-process components are safer. . . ."

Out-of-process components are slower. There isn't any argument on this point. One of the features of Windows is it is completely crash-proof, right? Well, no operating system is completely crash-proof but, Windows, like many operating systems, goes for process isolation. By this I mean each program runs in its own separate memory space. If one process crashes, it isn't supposed to bring down any other processes, which means it doesn't crash the OS. To ensure process isolation, talking across process boundaries is intentionally difficult. Microsoft doesn't want you flying across process boundaries on a whim, so it makes you use its underlying plumbing: COM.

COM enables you to talk across process boundaries. In fact, with COM components, COM makes it transparent. Whether your component is In Proc or out-of-process, the client calls it exactly the same way and, most of the time, the component is coded the same way. This is handy because you can write the component and call it without worrying about whether you're going across process boundaries. The slower speed of the out-of-process component is the only difference you would see. Figure 13-5 shows this in action.

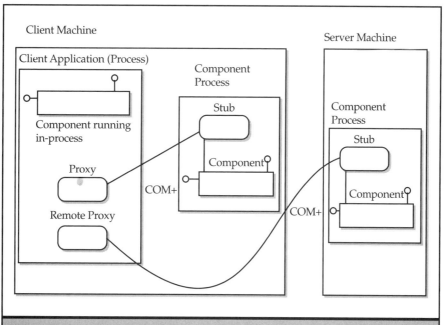

Figure 13-5.   Components running in-process, out-of-process on the same machine, and out-of-process on a remote machine

Marshalling   Imagine getting ready to go on a trip. You pull out all your clothes, pack them in a suitcase, and then travel to your destination. Once there, you unpack and put the clothes in the closet and drawers. You do your work or take your vacation or do whatever caused you to travel. When done, you pack all your things back in the suitcase, travel home, and unpack everything again.

Crossing process boundaries requires the exact same process, only it's called *marshalling.* When you want to make a call across process boundaries, COM has to package up your call and any parameters. COM then passes this packaged, or marshalled, call to the component running in another process. There, the package is unpackaged, the property or method is executed, and the results are readied for return. To return the results, COM again has to package the results, transport them to the client process, unpackage them, and give them to the client application. You can see COM is doing a lot of work for you. And, if you were wondering, In Proc components don't have to do any marshalling because no data is crossing process boundaries. This is why, in relative terms, In Proc components are much faster than out-of-process components.

One of the nice things about out-of-process components is neither the client nor the component know it is running out-of-process to each other. In fact, COM hides this fact from both the client and the component. COM creates a proxy in the client application that looks, to the client, like the actual component. In the component's process space, COM creates a stub that looks, to the component, like the calling application. Therefore, the client and component both go on about their business, blissfully ignorant that they are running in separate processes. Figure 13-5 shows how In Proc, out-of-process, and remote out-of-process (components on another machine) would look.

Other COM Coolness   As you can see, COM is doing a lot for you. COM locates the components (by looking up the information in the registry) and it handles calls across process boundaries if needed. COM also gives you *language independence* by making all the calls use the same basic mechanism. Now you needn't worry about communicating from a calling application written in VB to a component written in VC++. In addition, COM eliminates the previous problem with DLLs staying in memory forever. Each COM component keeps track of how many clients are using it at any time and COM willingly takes itself out of memory when no one is using it anymore. This helps recover memory and return it to the system so it can be used for other applications.

COM has more to it than this. Once you start building components, you'll work with the registry a bit to see what is being added, and where, because using Component Services (formerly Microsoft Transaction Server) can change what you see in the registry. Fortunately, true to COM's heritage, you needn't code your applications differently. The client won't know whether the component is under the control of Component Services.

I'M SOLD ALREADY! LET'S BUILD A COMPONENT

It's time to build a component, and you do this using VB. You could build COM components in a variety of other languages, such as Visual C++, FoxPro, PowerBuilder, Delphi, and others, but VB is the most common language for building components. VB hides much of its complexity, while it still gives you a tremendous amount of flexibility and power.

Beginning to Build the NWindWeb Component

I've been talking a lot about a customer class/object/component, but I want to be clear now about what's next : You are going to build a component, called NWindWeb, that will contain one or more classes to be used by your Web site. The first class you build is going to be called cCustomer and this will be a class that represents the properties and methods of a customer in your application.

Start VB 6 by going to the Start button, and then choosing Programs, Microsoft Visual Studio 6.0, and then Microsoft VB6.0. When VB starts, you are presented with the screen as seen in Figure 13-6, asking you what type of project you want to create. You can create various types of applications with VB. The tongue-in-cheek rule of thumb is, if the project type isn't in the top row, you probably don't need it.

The first choice is for a Standard EXE, which is a standard Windows application. You aren't writing standard Windows applications; instead, you're writing reusable components to be used

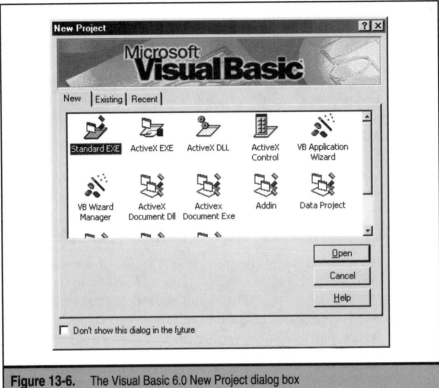

Figure 13-6. The Visual Basic 6.0 New Project dialog box

by other applications. These components have had a variety of names: ActiveX Servers, ActiveX Components, Code Components, COM Components, and so on. Here, the components are called ActiveX EXE and ActiveX DLL. The difference between an ActiveX DLL and an ActiveX EXE is the *ActiveX DLL* runs in-process, while the *ActiveX EXE* runs out-of-process. For now, choose ActiveX DLL, and then click Open. Once you open the project, you can see VB loaded up with one class (called Class1) inside the project called Project1. Figure 13-7 shows what VB should look like when you start an ActiveX DLL project.

First, in the Project window, click once on the Class1 module, and then, in the Properties window, change the Name property to cCustomer. This is a name you refer to later in code. Now, notice some of the other properties. One property is called Instancing, and it is set to Multiuse. In an In Proc component, this means one copy

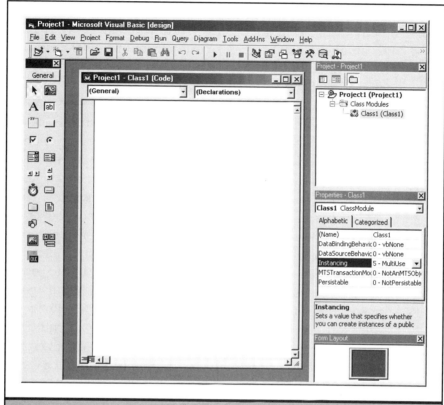

Figure 13-7.   Visual Basic 6.0 with a new ActiveX DLL project type. Notice how similar it is to Visual InterDev: a toolbox on the left, Project and Properties windows on the right, and the main working area in the middle

of the component loaded into memory can serve up multiple objects. If you want to create two customer objects in your program, the operating system only loads the component one time, and that one copy of the component serves up both copies of the Customer object. This makes sense because you couldn't load the same component into the same memory space multiple times. With out-of-process components, however, you could set the component so each component can only serve up one copy of a program. This isn't done often and because you won't be dealing with out-of-process components, this discussion ends here.

VB also has an MTSTransactionMode property. These are discussed more in the next chapter, but understand VB 6 came out well before Windows 2000. *Microsoft Transaction Server* (*MTS*) was, in some ways, a partial preview of COM+ for NT 4, and it came with the NT 4.0 Option Pack. The functionality of MTS is now in Component Services and is part of Windows 2000 itself. Therefore, Windows 2000 doesn't have a product called MTS, but it does have all the functionality, and then some.

In the Project window, click once on the Project name (Project1) and change the Name property in the Properties window to NWindWeb. NWindWeb is now the name of the component you are building. Inside the component is a class called cCustomer. You don't have any objects yet, and you won't write any objects. You only write classes and compile them into components. The client is the one to create, or instantiate, objects from your classes.

The easy way to think of a class is to think of a blueprint. When you want to build a house, an architect draws the blueprints. You cannot live in the blueprints; instead, a builder has to come along and build the house based on those blueprints. The builder could build many houses from that blueprint. Each house could have a different color roof, different doors and windows, and even different brick on the outside. However, the structure of the house is the same. This is exactly how you work with classes. You could build a Customer object of type cCustomer for each customer you have in the database. Each Customer object has the same properties (a Name, Address, and so on), but the values of the properties from one object to the next can be different.

Adding Properties

For now, let's start building a simple component. The first thing you want to do is create the properties. With VB, you can create properties in two ways: the fast way and the right way. Let's start with the fast way. You could, inside the class module code window, enter a line of code like this to create a CompanyName property:

```
Public CompanyName As String
```

Done! You've created a property in one line of code. I can hear you now, saying, "No matter what this guy tells me, that's the way I'm doing it. It's so simple. ..." Well, it is simple, but this approach has two disadvantages:

▼   You cannot make a property read-only.

▲   You cannot perform any validation checking when someone
sets a value.

Making a property read-only is simple using the right method,
which is discussed in a moment. The other disadvantage is pretty
major. Imagine, for a second, that this property was something like
a credit limit. When you try to set someone's credit limit, you could
run a routine that goes out and checks his credit rating. Depending
on his credit rating, you might decide not to grant him the requested
credit limit. This type of checking cannot be done when you create a
property simply using a Public variable in VB.

Let's examine the right way to create properties, which is using
Property Get and Property Let statements, along with a private
module-level variable. Examine the following code:

```
Dim msCompanyName As String


Public Property Get CompanyName() As String
    CompanyName = msCompanyName
End Property


Public Property Let CompanyName(psCompanyName As String)
    msCompanyName = psCompanyName
End Property
```

Now, you have two paired property methods. The Property Get
method enables the user to retrieve the current value. The Property
Let method enables the user to set the value. Examine the following
code snippet, but don't add it anywhere:

```
Customer.CompanyName="Westie Enterprises"
```

Here, the customer is trying to set the property CompanyName to
the value "Westie Enterprises". This calls the Property Let method,
and passes the string "Westie Enterprises" into the parameter
psCompanyName. This value is then assigned to the module-level
variable called msCompanyName. As long as this object stays in
memory, the value of msCompanyName is "Westie Enterprises." If
you ask the value of CompanyName, it calls the Property Get and

returns the value of whatever is in msCompanyName. Calling the CompanyName property from a client ASP would look like this:

```
<% Response.Write Company.CompanyName %>
```

While this is more code, it eliminates the two earlier problems. If you want to have a read-only property, you simply don't create a Property Let procedure. If you want to validate the value being passed in, you simply write the code inside the Property Let statement. For example, a CreditLimit routine might look something like this:

```
Public Property Let CreditLimit (plCreditLimit as Long)
    Dim iCreditRating
    iCreditRating=GetCreditRating(msCustomerID)
    Select Case iCreditRating
        Case >700
            msCreditLimit=psCreditLimit
        Case >400
            msCreditLimit=500
        Case Else
            msCreditLimit=0
    End Select
End Property
```

This is an over-simplified example, but you can see you get a credit rating for this customer. If the credit rating is 700 or higher, you give them what they want. If the credit rating is over 400, but less than 700, you give them a $500 limit. If it is 400 or less, you give them nothing.

In your cCustomer class, you add one property to match each field in the Northwind Customers table. The strange thing about the Customers table is all the fields are of character (or variable character) data types, including the CustomerID. Therefore, don't think all the properties always have to be strings. They are all strings in this case simply to match the field types in the table.

Adding Methods

In addition to creating the properties, you add three methods: AddCustomer, UpdateCustomer, and RemoveCustomer. In a component, a method is simply a standard VB sub or function. You see examples of these in a moment when you add your code. In your properties and methods, I forego such niceties as real error handling and any validation checks to keep the example as simple as possible. Even so, there's a significant amount of code in this example.

Adding the Code

Before you add any code, you must add a reference to the ADO component. A reference is a way to let VB know you're going to be using some of the classes in the component. At that point, VB goes and reads in some information about the classes in the component, so it knows the names of the properties and methods of the classes. To add a reference, on the menu, click Project and then click References. VB goes out and reads the registry to find all the components installed on this machine. Once the list comes up, scroll down until you find the latest version of the Microsoft ActiveX Data Objects, in this case 2.6. Place a check beside this library, as shown in Figure 13-8.

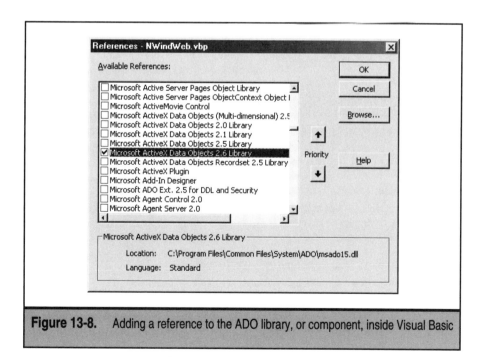

Figure 13-8.   Adding a reference to the ADO library, or component, inside Visual Basic

Finally, you're ready to add the code to your cCustomer class module. Here's the code to enter, and don't forget to modify the database connection string to match your needs:

```
Option Explicit

Dim msCustomerID As String
Dim msCompanyName As String
Dim msContactName As String
Dim msContactTitle As String
Dim msAddress As String
Dim msCity As String
Dim msRegion As String
Dim msPostalCode As String
Dim msCountry As String
Dim msPhone As String
Dim msFax As String

Const sDBconn = "Provider=SQLOLEDB.1;User ID=sa;" & _
    Initial Catalog=Northwind;Data Source=LAPTOP"

Public Property Get CustomerID() As String
    CustomerID = msCustomerID
End Property

Public Property Let CustomerID(psCustomerID As String)
    msCustomerID = psCustomerID
End Property

Public Property Get CompanyName() As String
    CompanyName = msCompanyName
End Property

Public Property Let CompanyName(psCompanyName As String)
    msCompanyName = psCompanyName
End Property
```

```
Public Property Get ContactName() As String
    ContactName = msContactName
End Property


Public Property Let ContactName(psContactName As String)
    msContactName = psContactName
End Property


Public Property Get ContactTitle() As String
    ContactTitle = msContactTitle
End Property


Public Property Let ContactTitle(psContactTitle As String)
    msContactTitle = psContactTitle
End Property


Public Property Get Address() As String
    Address = msAddress
End Property


Public Property Let Address(psAddress As String)
    msAddress = psAddress
End Property


Public Property Get City() As String
    City = msCity
End Property


Public Property Let City(psCity As String)
    msCity = psCity
End Property


Public Property Get Region() As String
    Region = msRegion
End Property
```

```
Public Property Let Region(psRegion As String)
    msRegion = psRegion
End Property


Public Property Get PostalCode() As String
    PostalCode = msPostalCode
End Property


Public Property Let PostalCode(psPostalCode As String)
    msPostalCode = psPostalCode
End Property


Public Property Get Country() As String
    Country = msCountry
End Property


Public Property Let Country(psCountry As String)
    msCountry = psCountry
End Property


Public Property Get Phone() As String
    Phone = msPhone
End Property


Public Property Let Phone(psPhone As String)
    msPhone = psPhone
End Property


Public Property Get Fax() As String
    Fax = msFax
End Property


Public Property Let Fax(psFax As String)
    msFax = psFax
End Property


Public Function AddCustomer() As Boolean
    On Error GoTo AddError
```

```
      Dim cn As ADODB.Connection
      Set cn = New ADODB.Connection
      Dim sSQL As String

      cn.Open sDBconn
      sSQL = "Insert Into Customers Values ('" & msCustomerID & "','" & _
          msCompanyName & "','" & msContactName & "','" & _
          msContactTitle & "','" & msAddress & "','" & msCity & "','" & _
          msRegion & "','" & msPostalCode & "','" & msCountry & "','" & _
          msPhone & "','" & msFax & "')"
      cn.Execute sSQL
      AddCustomer = True
      Exit Function
AddError:
      AddCustomer = False
End Function

Public Function DeleteCustomer(psCustomerID As String) As Boolean
      On Error GoTo DeleteError
      Dim cn As ADODB.Connection
      Set cn = New ADODB.Connection
      Dim sSQL As String

      cn.Open sDBconn
      sSQL = "Delete from Customers where CustomerID='" & _
          psCustomerID & "'"
      cn.Execute sSQL
      DeleteCustomer = True
      Exit Function
DeleteError:
      DeleteCustomer = False
End Function

Public Function UpdateCustomer(psCustomerID As String) As Boolean
      On Error GoTo UpdateError
      Dim cn As ADODB.Connection
      Set cn = New ADODB.Connection
      Dim sSQL As String
```

```
      cn.Open sDBconn
      sSQL = "Update Customers Set CustomerID='" & msCustomerID & "'," & _
          "CompanyName='" & msCompanyName & "', ContactName='" & _
          msContactName & "',ContactTitle='" & msContactTitle & "'," & _
          "Address='" & msAddress & "',City='" & msCity & "'," & _
          "Region='" & msRegion & "',PostalCode='" & msPostalCode & "'," & _
          "Country='" & msCountry & "',Phone='" & msPhone & "'," & _
          "Fax='" & msFax & "' where CustomerID='" & psCustomerID & "'"
      cn.Execute sSQL
      UpdateCustomer = True
      Exit Function
UpdateError:
      UpdateCustomer = False
End Function
```

This class is fairly straightforward. First, you create a property to match each field in the Customers table. Next, you create three methods: AddCustomer, DeleteCustomer, and UpdateCustomer. The properties don't contain any sort of validation code, but they could. The AddCustomer method simply takes the values of the properties and adds the record to the Customers table. The DeleteCustomer accepts a CustomerID and deletes that record from the table. Note, this will fail if the record you try to delete has children records in other tables (unless you turned on cascading deletes). Finally, the UpdateCustomer updates all the fields for the CustomerID that's passed in. In this example, you are actually allowing the client to update the CustomerID itself if they want. To do this, the client must pass in the "original" CustomerID along with the new value.

NOTE: This class is the "old way" to write components. Nothing is wrong with it. I've done it this way to show the concepts in the simplest manner. In the next chapter, I make changes to this class to make it faster and more scalable.

Compiling the Component

Now that you have created the first class, let's go ahead and compile this component. To do this with VB, click File and then NWindWeb.dll. The physical folder you choose as the destination for the DLL isn't important because COM reads the registry and finds out where it is anyway. Choose any directory, click the OK button, and VB compiles the DLL for you. This process happens so quickly you might not even realize VB is done. Despite the speed with which VB compiles the component, however, several magical things happen.

When VB compiles a component, it generates some numbers for you. I won't go into great detail here about what those numbers are, but they have to do with how COM handles components. Remember the discussion on DLL Hell, where I discussed having multiple copies of the same DLL on the computer? Well, you can still have multiple copies of a COM DLL on a computer, but only one version is listed in the registry at a time. Therefore, all applications use the same version of the component. When you compile your component, it is assigned a few unique numbers that live with it forever. Under the covers, COM is actually using these unique numbers. Again, while all this is fascinating, it's well beyond the scope of this book. Still, you should have at least one developer who understands class IDs, type library IDs, and all the other fun things about COM.

NOTE: With Windows 2000 and COM+, it's now possible to have applications that don't use the copy of the component listed in the registry, instead of looking at one in their local directory. Nothing is done with those in this book, but be aware they do exist. They are called *Private DLLs,* and more information can be found on Microsoft's site if you search for (no kidding) DLL Hell. All this brings up the point: Would you want to use Private DLLs? Microsoft claims it is a solution to DLL Hell; I remain unconvinced. To me, it gets back to many copies of the same DLL, with slightly different versions, spread all over the computer.

Registering the Component

Not only does VB generate these numbers for you, it adds all the necessary information to the registry on your machine. In other words, VB compiles and registers the component in one step. If you click the Start button, choose Run, type Regedit, and click OK, you can verify the information is, indeed, in the registry.

The most interesting information is actually listed by one of the unique numbers generated when the DLL was compiled. This number, known as the *class ID* (*CLSID*), is different on each machine, so I can't give you the magic number. Instead, in Regedit, click Edit and then Find. Search for NWindWeb and you should wind up with a key that looks similar to that in Figure 13-9. This shows your component has been added to the registry on this machine. If you click the InProcServer32 folder, you can see the physical location of your DLL, and now you know how COM figures it.

So far, so good. Assume, though, you are working on the development machine and need to move this DLL to the production server. You can do this in two ways. First, you could go into VB and use the Package and Deployment Wizard to build a Setup.exe program to install and register this component on the server. Second, you could copy the DLL to the server … sort of. You can copy the file, but could the server use it? The answer, of course, is "No." Why not? Because the registry on the server doesn't know anything about this

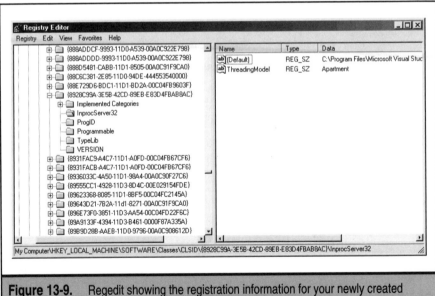

Figure 13-9.   Regedit showing the registration information for your newly created component, NWindWeb.dll

file! Just because you copy the file on to the hard drive doesn't mean the registry knows it's there. Instead, you must add the information to the registry.

Fortunately, there's a tool that can add the necessary information to the registry for you—Regsvr32.exe. Be careful: most people are tempted to type Regsrv32.exe, but the file is actually called Regsvr32.exe. Regsvr32 simply takes the information from a DLL (or other COM component) and adds it to the registry. The syntax is as simple as this, provided you are in the directory holding NWindWeb.dll:

```
Regsvr32.exe NWindWeb.dll
```

Regsvr32 reads the information out of NWindWeb.dll and adds it to the registry on that machine. Until the component is registered, the client applications won't be able to use it.

USING THE COMPONENT IN A WEB APPLICATION

Now that you have the component created and registered, it's time to use it from a Web application. Using the component from a Web application is simpler than you might think, mainly because you've been doing it for some time. You've been using ADO from your Web application from almost the beginning, and ADO is just a COM component with several classes in it. ADO has classes called Connection, Command, and Recordset, for example. You've been calling the classes and instantiating objects from them. Your code here works just the same, except now you can call your own component.

Back in the component, when you wanted to use ADO, you added a reference to ADO inside of VB. While you can do some of those things with Visual InterDev, you can't create the objects the same way. Back in your VB component, you created the object using code like this:

```
Dim cn as ADODB.Connection
Set cn = New ADODB.Connection
```

You can't do this in ASP because VBScript is a weakly typed language. You cannot DIM a variable as any particular type, so your ADO code has always looked like this:

```
Dim cn
Set cn = Server.CreateObject("ADODB.Connection")
```

Now that you have your own component, you can instantiate objects from it the same way:

```
Dim objCustomer
Set objCustomer = Server.CreateObject("NWindWeb.cCustomer")
```

In this case, you're creating an object, objCustomer, of type cCustomer. The string "NWindWeb.cCustomer" is called a *program ID*, or *ProgID* for short. The ProgID is a human-readable name for the class you created. The CLSID is what COM uses in the background and, by using the previous approach, the first thing COM does is look up the CLSID for this ProgID.

Once you run the previous code, an object called objCustomer will exist in memory. objCustomer will have the properties and methods you created in the class. If you want multiple customer objects in memory at once, you could easily do that with code similar to this:

```
Dim objNewCustomer
Dim objOldCustomer
Set objNewCustomer = Server.CreateObject("NWindWeb.cCustomer")
Set objOldCustomer = Server.CreateObject("NWindWeb.cCustomer")
```

You now have two customer objects in memory: objNewCustomer and objOldCustomer. These two objects are actually two instances of the same component. Their structure is identical, like two houses built from the same blueprint. The properties of each can be set to different values, however, just as those two houses with identical structures could be painted two different colors.

Creating the Web Page

To use this component, you create a simple reentrant ASP. By reentrant, I mean the page calls itself when the form is submitted. The idea of this page is to start with a form with blank fields. You fill out those fields, click an Add button, and the new customer is added to the database. You can then change some of the fields and, sure enough, the values are changed in the database. Finally, you can hit the delete button and remove your new record.

The actual process of adding, updating, and deleting records is handled by your COM component. Specifically, you create an object, set the properties, and then call the appropriate method. The component then uses ADO to talk to your database and make the appropriate insert, update, or delete.

Before you move forward, please be aware you aren't doing any error checking here in the ASP or, for all intents and purposes, in the component. You won't be able to enter a name like O'Neal or any other text with an apostrophe in it, because you haven't included any scrubbing routines. I'm also not doing any checking on the value of the CustomerID you enter, so it's possible for you to try to enter a CustomerID that already exists in the Customers table. Obviously, the insert would fail, and you would be notified that it had failed, but you wouldn't be told why it failed.

Using Visual InterDev, create a new project called Components. In this project, create a new ASP called CustomerMaint.asp and enter the following code:

```
<%@ Language=VBScript %>
<HTML>
<HEAD>
</HEAD>
<BODY>
<%
Dim objCustomer
Set objCustomer=Server.CreateObject("NWindWeb.cCustomer")

If Request.Form("txtCustomerID")<>"" Then
    Select Case Request.Form("cmdSubmit")
      Case "Add"
        objCustomer.CustomerID=Request.Form("txtCustomerID")
        objCustomer.CompanyName=Request.Form("txtCompanyName")
        objCustomer.ContactName=Request.Form("txtContactName")
        objCustomer.ContactTitle=Request.Form("txtContactTitle")
        objCustomer.Address=Request.Form("txtAddress")
        objCustomer.City=Request.Form("txtCity")
        objCustomer.Region=Request.Form("txtRegion")
        objCustomer.PostalCode=Request.Form("txtPostalCode")
        objCustomer.Country=Request.Form("txtCountry")
```

```
            objCustomer.Phone=Request.Form("txtPhone")
            objCustomer.Fax=Request.Form("txtFax")
            if objCustomer.AddCustomer then
                Response.Write "New customer added"
            else
                Response.Write "Error adding record"
            end if
        Case "Update"
            objCustomer.CustomerID=Request.Form("txtCustomerID")
            objCustomer.CompanyName=Request.Form("txtCompanyName")
            objCustomer.ContactName=Request.Form("txtContactName")
            objCustomer.ContactTitle=Request.Form("txtContactTitle")
            objCustomer.Address=Request.Form("txtAddress")
            objCustomer.City=Request.Form("txtCity")
            objCustomer.Region=Request.Form("txtRegion")
            objCustomer.PostalCode=Request.Form("txtPostalCode")
            objCustomer.Country=Request.Form("txtCountry")
            objCustomer.Phone=Request.Form("txtPhone")
            objCustomer.Fax=Request.Form("txtFax")
            if objCustomer.UpdateCustomer(Request.Form("OriginalCustomerID")) _
              then
                Response.Write "Customer Updated"
            else
                Response.Write "Error updating customer"
            end if
        Case "Delete"
            if objCustomer.DeleteCustomer(Request.Form("txtCustomerID")) then
                Response.Write("Customer removed")
            else
                Response.Write("Customer could not be deleted")
            end if
    End Select
End If
%>
<FORM Name="frmCustomer" Action="CustomerMaint.asp" Method="Post">
<INPUT Type="Hidden" Name="OriginalCustomerID"
Value=<%=Request.Form("txtCustomerID")%>>
<TABLE Border="1" Cellpadding="2" Cellspacing="2">
    <TR>
        <TD>Customer ID: <INPUT Name="txtCustomerID"
Value="<%=Request.Form("txtCustomerID")%>"></TD>
    </TR>
    <TR>
```

```
        <TD>Company Name: <INPUT Name="txtCompanyName"
Value="<%=Request.Form("txtCompanyName")%>"></TD>
    </TR>
    <TR>
        <TD>Contact Name: <INPUT Name="txtContactName"
Value="<%=Request.Form("txtContactName")%>"></TD>
    </TR>
    <TR>
        <TD>Contact Title: <INPUT Name="txtContactTitle"
Value="<%=Request.Form("txtContactTitle")%>"></TD>
    </TR>
    <TR>
        <TD>Contact Address: <INPUT Name="txtAddress"
Value="<%=Request.Form("txtAddress")%>"></TD>
    </TR>
    <TR>
        <TD>City: <INPUT Name="txtCity" Value="
            <%=Request.Form("txtCity")%>"></TD>
        <TD>Region: <INPUT Name="txtRegion"
Value="<%=Request.Form("txtRegion")%>"></TD>
    </TR>
    <TR>
        <TD>Postal Code: <INPUT Name="txtPostalCode"
Value="<%=Request.Form("txtPostalCode")%>"></TD>
        <TD>Country: <INPUT Name="txtCountry"
Value="<%=Request.Form("txtCountry")%>"></TD>
    </TR>
    <TR>
        <TD>Phone: <INPUT Name="txtPhone"
Value="<%=Request.Form("txtPhone")%>"></TD>
        <TD>Fax: <INPUT Name="txtFax" Value="
            <%=Request.Form("txtFax")%>"></TD>
    </TR>
</TABLE>
<INPUT Type="Submit" Name="cmdSubmit" Value="Add">
<INPUT Type="Submit" Name="cmdSubmit" Value="Update">
<INPUT Type="Submit" Name="cmdSubmit" Value="Delete">
</FORM>
</BODY>
</HTML>
```

Once you have the code in the page, load the page inside of IE. You should have a page with a text field for each field in the Customers table. Fill out the text boxes with some values similar to what I did in Figure 13-10. After filling in the fields, click that Add button.

After clicking the Add button, you should get a message at the top that says, "New customer added." Just to be sure, you can run the SQL Query Analyzer and use a query to see if the new record made it into the database. As you can see in Figure 13-11, the new record has made it to the database.

In the browser, you still have all the text boxes showing the values you just typed in to them. Let's make a change by modifying the Contact Name to a different value, such as "Hailey Spinoza." After making the change, click the Update button. You should receive a message that the customer has been updated, and you can verify this in the Query Analyzer. Finally, as if this is a great surprise, you can press the Delete button to remove this record from the table and, again, verify it with Query Analyzer.

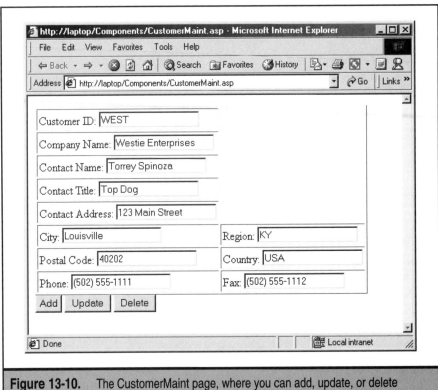

Figure 13-10. The CustomerMaint page, where you can add, update, or delete customers from the Northwind Customers table. Inserts, updates, and deletes flow through a COM component

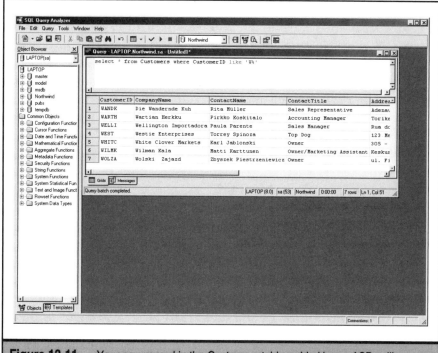

Figure 13-11. Your new record in the Customers table, added by an ASP calling a COM component

Was It Worth It?

You may be looking at this and thinking, "This was an awful lot of code to do for something pretty simple." And, for now, it is. Think back to our original scenario, though. What if, when a new customer signs up, you want to send a page to the salesperson in that area and generate a welcome letter to the customer? That code could be embedded into the cCustomer class in your NWindWeb component. In fact (and here's part of the power), you could add that functionality now and not have to touch your ASP. In fact, even if multiple clients were using this component, you could add that functionality and not have to modify your clients. Realize that some changes would require you to modify your client application, but added functionality within an existing method wouldn't require changes.

The component you wrote isn't the final way you'll write components. First, you want to be calling stored procedures and not using embedded SQL, as you are in this example. Second, as you see in the next chapter, you want to take advantage of Component Services to give you transactions and better scalability. To do this, though, you have to make your component stateless.

Still, you're now calling a compiled component instead of interpreted code, as you have in an ASP, which should be faster, especially with an In Proc component. In addition, multiple clients could use this component, which gives some truly reusable code. By moving the code into components, it helps you separate the business logic from the user interface and gives you reusable components that usually perform better.

SUMMARY

Much more exists to writing about components than was covered in this one chapter. In fact, the entire next chapter continues on this path. Even so, a lot of issues won't be covered. One of the beauties of n-tier development, however, is the capability to separate work and give certain pieces to your experts in each area. If you have someone who is talented with graphics, let her do the UI (certainly not my specialty). Developers can spend their time writing components and implementing the logic that drives the business. Database experts can create stored procedures and triggers.

COM is complicated, but VB hides most of the complexity and makes it as simple as possible. COM is so powerful and does so many things, it can be hard to define. For you, though, COM enables you to create reusable, scalable components written in any language and to use them without worrying about where they're physically located. COM enables you to talk across process boundaries, if needed.

You are beginning to build real, scalable systems. You aren't quite there yet, but COM components form the basis for everything you want to do in your Web application. Nothing you have learned so far is wasted, but you're moving more and more into the middle-tier, while the ASP becomes your UI and makes calls to components that implement the business logic.

CHAPTER 14

COM+ Component Services

In the last chapter, you created a COM component to move some of your business logic into a reusable component. You learned that encapsulating the business rules in components can give you reusability. You also learned that components are compiled, which could lead to some performance gains. By moving functionality into components, you can also update your application easier by updating only the component, which means you needn't touch the various clients that use the component.

All this sounds great, doesn't it? It is great! N-tier development has become a proven software design over the past few years. Still, the way n-tier development was done in the last chapter doesn't take full advantage of what you can do with components. In this chapter, you greatly enhance the functionality of your components by leveraging the services given to you in Windows 2000 by Component Services.

THE NEED FOR COMPONENT SERVICES

Back when I wrote my first client/server program around 1992–1993, the idea of n-tier development didn't exist. My first client/server program was an Access 1.0 application accessing about 20GB data over a 14.4 bps dial-up line. The program was distributed to a 500-person remote sales force all across the United States. Not only was this one of the first client/server programs for this particular customer, but everyone was amazed the program was being used by so many users. In those days, 500 users of a client/server application was a lot.

Today, with the Web, what do you think is a lot of users? 50,000? 100,000? 1,000,000? The Web skews all the numbers you used to talk about, because the sheer number of potential users means your applications must scale to handle a much larger number of users. Obviously, not every application you write needs to scale to 100,000 simultaneous users, but some might, so you want to make sure you design your applications appropriately. As you will soon see, one of the most important issues with Component Services is scalability.

Another one of the major concerns with Component Services is that of transactions. When Microsoft first introduced Microsoft Transaction Server (MTS), one of its goals was to have MTS manage transactions. Unfortunately, MTS was a poorly named product, as it did a lot more than transactions. Transactions are important, though, and Component Services can manage these for you, just as MTS did. Transactions, especially across heterogeneous data sources, can be quite challenging to code manually. Component Services handles these for you transparently and with little code.

Infrastructure Support

One of the reasons Microsoft created MTS, which grew into COM+ Component Services in Windows 2000, is because developers were asking for it. Microsoft performed a study of several high-volume, transaction-intensive applications and found developers spent a great percentage of the time creating and re-creating the same basic infrastructure. The developers were creating custom object pools to try to share a smaller number of objects among a larger number of customers. The developers were creating an architecture to handle transactions across heterogeneous back-end databases. Developers were spending a long time handling threading issues, which can be fraught with danger. Security issues often came into play when dealing with components, and registering components for use on a remote machine could be challenging.

Microsoft saw developers constantly re-creating the same basic infrastructure and decided to provide it to them. All developers have to do now is add in a little code to tap into all this power. Components written in VB can gain such benefits as better threading support, database connection pooling, heterogeneous database transactions, role-based security, and greatly improved scalability.

To tap into this infrastructure support is fairly easy, but to take full advantage of what Component Services has to offer, you must code your components using a stateless model. This is examined in greater detail throughout this chapter.

Exploring Component Services

Adding a component to Component Services is easy, but adding a component into Component Services doesn't do anything other than enable you to see when the component is being used and how many clients are using it. Still, you can explore the Component Services tool and place your NWindWeb DLL under its control now, and then make changes later to take advantage of Component Services.

Click the Start button and choose Programs, Administrative Tools, and then Component Services. The Component Services manager should begin running. On the left-hand side of the program is the console root; under it are three choices. You are only interested in Component Services, so expand that option.

Expanding the Component Services node reveals a Computers folder. With Component Services, you can manage components on many computers. For now, if you expand the Computers folder, the only computer you probably see is My Computer, meaning your local machine. If you expand My Computer, you see two more folders: COM+ Applications and Distributed Transaction Coordinator. For now, let's focus on the COM+ Applications, so expand that node next. You should end up with something similar to what you see in Figure 14-1.

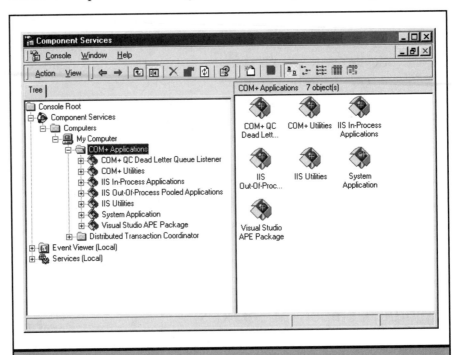

Figure 14-1. The Component Services manager in Windows 2000

Once you expand COM+ Applications, you see a series of icons representing applications, which are explained in a moment. These icons are boxes with spheres in them, and the spheres have a big plus (+) sign on them. If you look over in the right-hand pane, the sphere inside the System Application box may be rotating. This means one or more of the components in that application is being used.

If you expand an application node, such as the IIS Utilities application, you see two folders: Components and Roles. If you then expand the Components folder, you see a list of the components in the application. This is where things get strange. In COM and COM+ terms, a component is the compiled file that contains one or more classes. In Component Services, however, each class is called a component. If you find this a little strange, join the club. Just realize, in Component Services, each component is only a class from a component. If you have a component with multiple classes, not all classes of that component must be added to Component Services. You can add a component with multiple classes later.

The Roles folder is for role-based security, which is discussed in Chapter 15. Be aware that Component Services enables you to integrate your components easily with the built-in security in Windows 2000. This relieves much of the work you once did manually.

Adding a New Application

What is an application? A *COM+ application* is a logical container holding one or more components. In Component Services, an application represents two important boundaries. First, it represents a security boundary. Security is checked every time a call is made in to an application, and all the components in the application can share the same security context. This means you needn't check the security in each component (although you could), but instead, you let the application handle security for you. Second, applications represent process boundaries. All the components inside an application run in process to each other. The application itself is a process and all components in the application are running in that process. Components in other applications run out of process to components in the first application, with one exception, which is discussed in a moment.

There's an oddity about how the Component Services interface lets you work. The oddity started in MTS and, for whatever reason, has been carried forward into Component Services. While in Component Services, if you want to add a new application, you can do so by right-clicking the COM+ Applications node. You must first left-click COM+ Applications to make it the active element, however, and then right-click it. If you don't left-click it first, a right-click only gives you the choice of "New Window from Here." Left-clicking first, and then right-clicking, gives you a New option on the menu and, under that, the choice of Application. Choose to add a new application and you should see the beginning of the Application Installation Wizard, shown in Figure 14-2. You have the choice of installing a prebuilt application or creating a new one. Prebuilt applications are usually used for transferring a finished application from one machine to another, such as from a development to production environment.

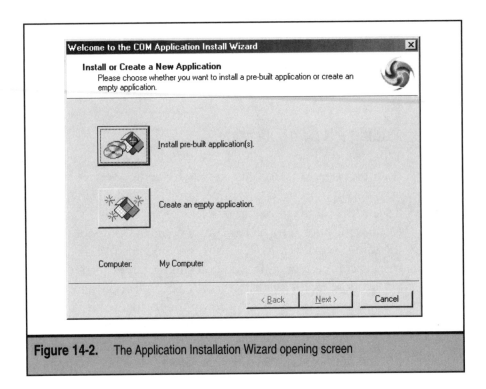

Figure 14-2. The Application Installation Wizard opening screen

For now, you are going to create a new application, so click the
button that says "Create an empty application." The second screen,
shown in Figure 14-3, appears. This screen asks you the name of the
application and what Activation Type you want. The two choices are
Library or Server application. The Library application runs in-process
to the creator's process. This can result in a speed increase but,
typically, is only used for components called by other Component
Services components. In other words, the Library application is
usually used for internal functions rather than components the client
applications need to address directly. For now, leave the option at
Server application, which means this application will have its own
process. Name the new application NWind, although this name
isn't important. You never reference it through code in your client
applications, and the components you place inside don't have to
know the name of the application in which they reside.

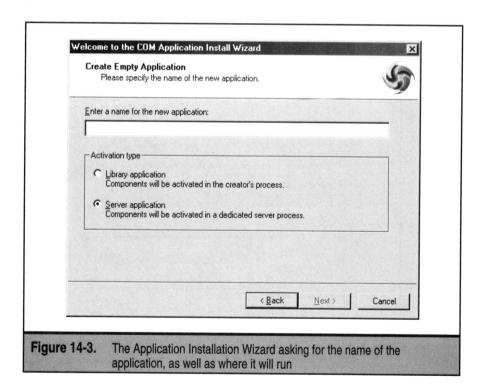

Figure 14-3.   The Application Installation Wizard asking for the name of the
application, as well as where it will run

The next screen in the wizard, shown in Figure 14-4, asks about the Application Identity; specifically, under what security context this application should run. The default is to have the application run as the interactive user, but this isn't always a good idea. If your development machine is the same one on which you are testing this, using the interactive user may be fine. If no one is logged in to the machine on which the application is running, however, no interactive user exists. Specifying a user is generally a better idea. No one has to be logged on that machine and you can control security better. For example, you may have a number of users accessing a Component Services application. These users don't have access to SQL Server, but you have the Component Services application run under the identity of someone who does have access to SQL Server. The components in the Component Services application have access to SQL Server and can return the necessary data to people who normally would be unable to access SQL Server through any other means. This is a great way to control access to certain resources on your system.

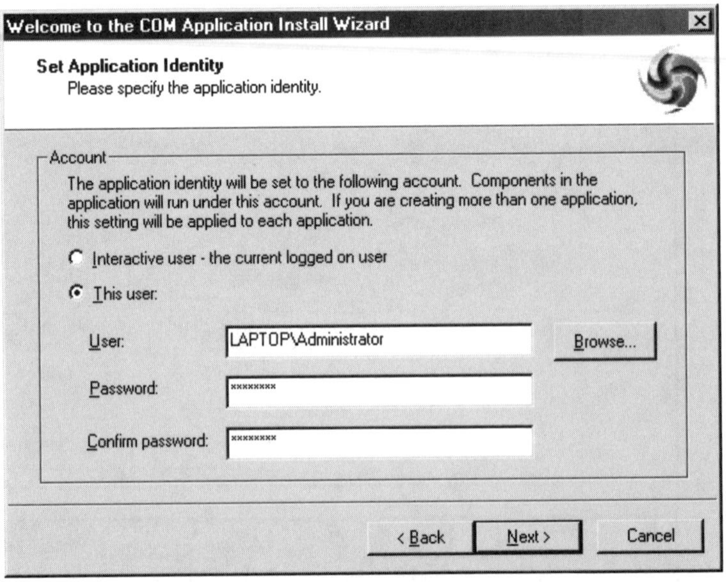

Figure 14-4. The Application Installation Wizard asks about the Application Identity

If you are doing all this work on one machine, you can get by with leaving this as the Interactive user. Otherwise, specify a valid Windows 2000 user and password and then click Next. You get a nice screen saying you are finished, so you can click the Finish button.

Adding Components

You are now returned to the Component Services manager, and you see your new NWind application in the list. If you expand NWind, and then click the Components folder, you can see no components are in the application yet. You can add the components by right-clicking the Components folder, choosing New, and then choosing Component. Remember, you must have the Components folder as the active item or the right-click will show you a different context menu. Once you choose to add a new component, the Component Installation Wizard opens. Click Next to get past the splash screen, and you are then taken to the Import or Install a Component screen, as shown in Figure 14-5. Be aware that bugs continue to persist in the option to import already-registered components, so you should always choose to install new components.

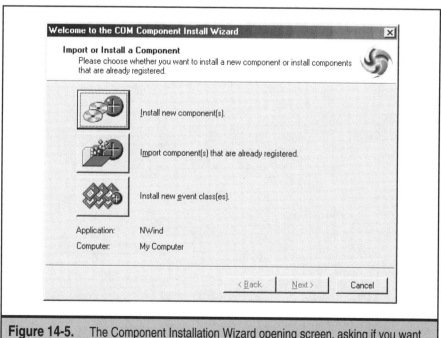

Figure 14-5. The Component Installation Wizard opening screen, asking if you want to import or install a component

On this screen, you have three options: Install new components, Import components that are already registered, and Install new event classes. Event classes aren't covered in this book, so ignore that option for now. Of the first two choices, the second one actually seems to make sense. You know your NWindWeb.dll is already registered on this machine, so to import already-registered components would seem to make sense. And, indeed, it does make sense, except it only works some of the time. This option had unpredictable results in MTS, and the unpredictability made it into Component Services as well, so I highly recommend always using the first choice, Install new components.

If you click the Install new components button, you get a standard file browser window. Navigate to the directory where you compiled the NWindWeb.dll and select that file, and then click the Open button.

Once you click the Open button, the next step of the Component Installation Wizard is shown, as you see in Figure 14-6. This screen shows that one component (what used to be called a class) was found

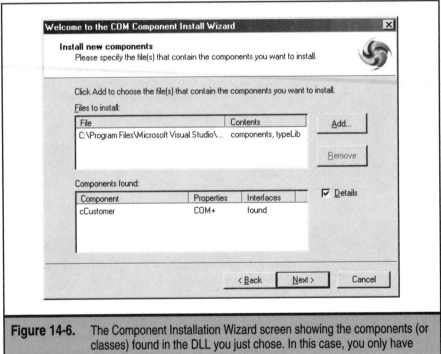

Figure 14-6. The Component Installation Wizard screen showing the components (or classes) found in the DLL you just chose. In this case, you only have one, cCustomer

in the NWindWeb.dll, and this component is called cCustomer. You now know cCustomer will be placed under Component Services control, so you can click the Next button, and you get the ever-popular You are now done screen, so click the Finish button.

Now that the cCustomer component is in Component Services, you can view it in several different ways. Up along the toolbar are five buttons that enable you to change the view or, on the View menu, you can drop down a list of the same five views. If you drop down the View menu and choose Property View, you can see a number of the properties for this component. As Figure 14-7 shows, you can see the CLSID for this component, as well as whether it supports transactions (more on this later), whether it participates in security (which is covered in Chapter 15), and some other properties.

A more interesting view is the Status View. If you change to Status View, at first you only see the component name, but a number of columns appear after the name. Open IE and load the

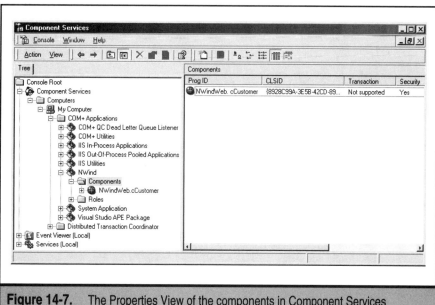

Figure 14-7.   The Properties View of the components in Component Services

same page you used in the last chapter: //localhost/Components/
CustomerMaint.asp. Don't do anything other than load it in the
browser. Go back and look at the Component Services manager.
If you do it quickly, you might see the number one in both the
Objects and Activated columns. Otherwise, you see zeroes in each
column, as shown in Figure 14-8. The zeroes in the Objects and
Activated columns tell you the component has been used recently,
but isn't currently being used. You'll learn more about this later in
the chapter.

USING COMPONENT SERVICES

Now you've created a Component Services application and added your
component into that application. If you view the CustomerMaint.asp
Web page now, you see the numbers changing, which proves

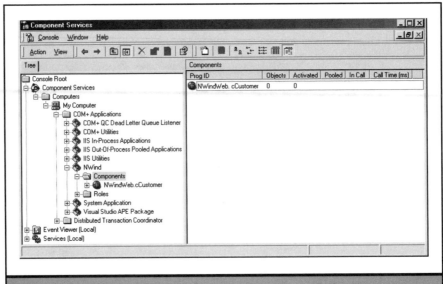

Figure 14-8.   The Status view of the components in Component Services

Component Services is now managing your component for you. But, what advantages are you getting other than being able to see that little sphere spinning? Truthfully, you aren't getting any advantages yet. To get some advantages, you must make some changes to the code in your component. First, let's examine how Component Services can greatly increase the scalability of your application.

Scalability

To show how to get scalability gains from Component Services, you create a new simple component and a standard Visual Basic application with which to test it. Don't worry; I'll get back to NWindWeb.dll soon enough, but for now, I want a simple example to show how Component Services can let your applications scale to a much greater number of users.

In the past, Microsoft had you coding components with properties and methods. You would instantiate the object when the program first started, and then set properties and call methods as needed. In addition, if your component needed to access a database, it often opened the connection when it was instantiated and kept the connection open for the entire time the component was in memory. When your application shut down, your component finally went away, as did any database connections. This wasn't a problem with a small number of users, but think about a busy Web site with tens of thousands of simultaneous users. Can you really afford to have 50,000 copies of your component in memory on the server at one time? Can your database server handle 50,000 simultaneous database connections? Do you have the resources or the licenses for this kind of use of the database?

Obviously, you want to minimize the number of objects and database connections at any given time. You can do this by being smart about when you instantiate objects from your ASPs and when you create database connections within your components.

Still, Component Services offers you an even better way to achieve scalability.

Let's start with a new VB project. Open Visual Basic and choose to create an ActiveX DLL. As you recall, DLLs run in process. Component Services want to work with DLL files because they actually run in process to Component Services itself (technically, inside the application's process). So, you now have a new ActiveX DLL project open and you want to create a new component.

Change the Project name from Project1 to Greetings. This DLL contains one simple class that returns a greeting to the calling routine. Next, change the class name from Class1 to cHello. Leave the other settings the same. Enter the following code into the cHello class module:

```
Dim msName As String

Public Property Get Name() As String
    Name = msName
End Property

Public Property Let Name(psName As String)
    msName = psName
End Property

Public Function SayHello() As String
    SayHello = "Hello there, " & msName
End Function
```

This simple class has one property called Name, and one method called SayHello. You don't do any sort of validation check on the Name property. The SayHello methods simply returns a string that concatenates the strings "Hello there," and msName. You set the Name property, and then call the SayHello method. When you finish this code, compile the DLL, but keep this copy of VB open because you soon make some changes to the DLL.

Open another copy of VB now. Yes, you could add a second project into the first copy of VB, but trust me on this. You want to make sure you're using the compiled copy of the DLL and not some copy running in memory as part of your development environment. In this new copy of VB, tell it you want a Standard EXE as the project type.

Standard EXE projects in VB start out with a form named Form1. This isn't a book about VB, but I show you just enough here to prove the scalability point. On the form, which should already be loaded, create two buttons and one text box. To do this, you can simply double-click the text box icon in the toolbar, and then double-click the button icon twice. VB puts all three on top of each other, but you can drag them around on the form easily enough. Position them in any way you choose. Your form might end up looking something like that in Figure 14-9.

Next, let's make your buttons easier to read, like those in Figure 14-9. Click once on the first button. In the Properties window, change its Name to cmdSetName and its Caption to Set Name. With the second button, click once on it and set its Name property to cmdSayHello and its Caption property to Say Hello. Finally, click once on the text box and set its Name property to txtName. Your form should now look even more like the one in Figure 14-9.

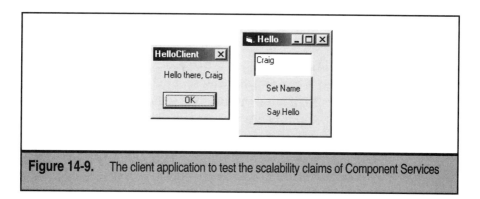

Figure 14-9.   The client application to test the scalability claims of Component Services

Before continuing, you need to add a reference to the DLL you created a few moments ago. Click the Project menu and choose References. The References box then scans through the registry and brings back a list of all the registered components. Scroll down until you find Greetings, check the box next to it, and click the OK button.

Double-click any of the controls now. The code window opens for you and this looks like the code window you've been using for dealing with classes. Even if some code is already there (and there will be), make your code look like this:

```
Dim oHello As Greetings.cHello


Private Sub cmdSayHello_Click()
    MsgBox oHello.SayHello
End Sub


Private Sub cmdSetName_Click()
    oHello.Name = txtName.Text
End Sub


Private Sub Form_Load()
    Set oHello = New Greetings.cHello
End Sub
```

In the client application, you are creating the object as soon as the form is loaded. You are coding this, right now, as a small application. You needn't worry about resource use at this point. Once the object called oHello is created, you can set the Name property when the user clicks the cmdSetName button. When the user clicks the cmdSayHello button, the program pops up a message box that contains the text "Hello there, Craig" or whatever name you assigned to the name property.

Let's compile this extremely complex client application. Place it somewhere within easy reach, such as on the desktop. Run the application. Now verify it works by typing a name into the text box, clicking the Set Name button, and then clicking the Say Hello button. You should end up with a message box similar to that in Figure 14-9, which takes the name you entered and concatenates it to the end of the string "Hello there,".

Add this component to Component Services now. Because one application can have components from different DLLs in it, add this new component to the NWind application. In the NWind application, right-click the Components folder, select New, Component, and then click the Install new components button after advancing into the wizard. Browse to your Greetings.dll and add it into the application. When finished, make sure you are in status view. Your component is now under Component Services and, after the next paragraph, it should look like Figure 14-10.

Next, go to wherever you created the client application, and run it. In fact, run it ten times. Just start launching multiple copies until you have ten of them running. Look at the Component Services manager. You can see, as you do in Figure 14-10, ten copies of the Greetings.cHello are in memory. How scalable is this application? Not very. Imagine if you had thousands of applications instead of ten. Each application has an active copy of the DLL, even though they aren't using it right now! Clearly, this is not what you want.

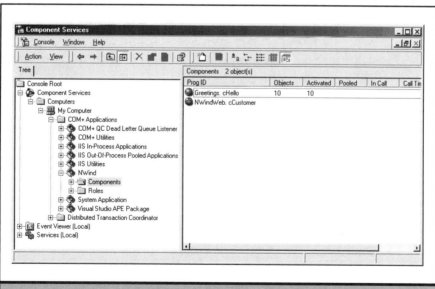

Figure 14-10. Component Services showing you ten copies of your component are in memory at the moment

This is exactly what you have currently with the NWindWeb.cCustomer, though. It's under Component Services control, but you aren't taking advantage of the Component Services infrastructure. Close the ten copies of your test program and go back to the VB code for your Greetings component.

Back in the code for the cHello class in the Greetings component, make this class aware of the Component Services environment in which it will run. First, go to the Project menu, choose References, and add a reference to the COM+ Services Type Library. Once you do this, modify the code in the SayHello method (the only thing you are changing right now) to look like this:

```
Public Function SayHello() As String
    Dim objContext As ObjectContext
    Set objContext = GetObjectContext
    SayHello = "Hello there, " & msName
    objContext.SetComplete
End Function
```

You added one variable called objContext. By the prefix, you can tell it's an object. You set the variable equal to a function called GetObjectContext, which, in a sense, gives your component a handle out to the Component Services environment in which your component will run. You then carry out your work and, at the end, you call the SetComplete method of the context object you created. SetComplete does something important for you, which I discuss in a moment.

It's time to recompile the Greetings.dll. If you still have the test application open in another copy of VB, close it, saving the project as you do. I know it's a pain, but go ahead and close the copy of VB with the test application. Now, recompile Greetings.dll. You get a warning that you are about to overwrite the previous version—that's fine. You may or may not get an error, which tells you permission is denied. If you get this error, and you will eventually, what is it telling you?

Remember back in Figure 14-8, you had two zeros in the status view? Those zeros tell you something important: the component is not serving up any objects at the moment and no clients have connections to it, but the component is still in memory. You see, Component Services loads the structure of the component into memory to use it. To make subsequent calls faster, Component Services leaves the component loaded into memory for a certain period of time, even if the component isn't serving up any objects. Just how long this stays in memory is easy to configure. As long as it is in memory, however, you cannot recompile the DLL. Fortunately, this is easy to fix.

Back in Component Services, right-click the NWind application and choose Properties. Under the Advanced tab, the first box is labeled Server Process Shutdown. The default is three minutes. This says the application stays in memory for three minutes of idle time. After that, the application drops out of memory. Notice you can increase or decrease this number to meet your needs or you can choose never to have it drop out of memory once it's loaded. The current setting of three minutes says the component stays in memory for three minutes after someone has used it, which means you won't be able to recompile for three minutes. So, you can wait for the time-out to occur or you can force it to shut down now. Go ahead and close the Properties dialog box and go back to the Component Services manager. Right-click the NWind application and choose Shut down. This drops the application out of memory immediately and you can now recompile the DLL. Get used to shutting down the application to recompile; this will happen often as you develop COM+ components for Component Services.

Now that you've recompiled your DLL, open another copy of VB and reload the client application. Once VB is open, don't make any code changes, but recompile the application. Run the test application now and notice, at first, things look the same in Component Services: a one appears in both the Objects column and the Activated column. But now, you're about to see things change. Type a name into the text box, click the Set Name button, and then click the Say Hello button. The message box looks the same, but something has changed in Component Services: the Objects column has a number one in it, but the Activated column has a zero. Click OK to clear the message box. Now, click the Say Hello button again (don't click the Set Name button). You get the message box to come back, but your name is gone! Instead, the message box only says "Hello there," and no name follows it. What happened? Well, you changed your code.

You added in a line of code that called the SetComplete method of the context object. This tells Component Services the object is done with its processing, everything worked, and *it can be taken out of memory*. In other words, you told Component Services to drop the component out of memory. Your client, however, has no clue this has happened. That's why you still have the number one in the Objects column: your client application thinks it has a copy of the object but, in fact, it only has a pointer to Component Services. While the Objects column tells you how many clients think they have objects, the Activated column tells you how many objects are actually in memory inside of Component Services.

The Importance of Being Stateless

As you can see, the way you coded your component is to be stateful. You set a property, and then expect that property (in this case, a private module-level variable) to be there anytime you call a method. After the SetComplete method is called, however, the object drops out of memory. On the next call, the component is re-created and now the module-level variable msName is an empty string. Therefore, stateful components and scalability don't mix well.

Making your component stateless requires changes in the component and the client program. Close down the copy of VB holding the client application and go back to the copy of VB holding the component code. This is fairly simple:

1. Get rid of all properties.

2. Modify methods to accept parameters for any needed inputs.

Make the code in the cHello component look like this (and this is ALL the code you should have in the module when you finish):

```
Public Function SayHello(ByVal psName As String) As String
    Dim objContext As ObjectContext
    Set objContext = GetObjectContext
    SayHello = "Hello there, " & psName
    objContext.SetComplete
End Function
```

What has this code done? First, you eliminated the Name property and the private, module-level msName variable. You then added a parameter to the SayHello method. This has the effect of making this component stateless. Instead of depending on the component having the name in memory, you pass in all necessary data with each call. This means your component can be taken out of memory between calls, greatly reducing the load on the server. When you call the SetComplete method, you are telling Component Services you are finished with your work and the component can be dropped out of memory.

Now that you've changed the code in the component, recompile it. Overwrite the existing file and don't forget you must have shut down the other copy of VB. You might have to shut down the application in Component Services.

Open another copy of VB and reload the client application. On the form, delete the Set Name button because you won't need to do this anymore. You can modify the code inside the client application at this point. When you finish, this is ALL the code you should have in your client application:

```
Private Sub cmdSayHello_Click()
    Dim oHello As Greetings.cHello
    Set oHello = New Greetings.cHello
    MsgBox oHello.SayHello(txtName.Text)
End Sub
```

You have now modified the client to pass the name to the SayHello method of the oHello object with each call, rather than relying on a property to be in memory between calls. You also create the object only when you need it, and it falls out of memory when this sub is finished.

Recompile the client application, launch ten copies of the client application, and look at Component Services. Nothing appears to be running on the server and, in fact, nothing is yet! In one of the copies of the client application, type something into the text box and click the Say Hello button. If you are watching Component Services when you do this, you might see the Objects and Activated columns have the number one appear, and then the Activated number will drop to zero. Once you click the OK button on the message box, the Objects column also drops to zero (sometimes after a slight pause).

Did your page seem slow the first time you ran it? Applications usually run noticeably slower when you fire them up for the first time, because Component Services has to load the application and components into memory. Now, however, you can see both the Objects and Activated columns are zero and not blank, indicating the Component Services application is loaded. Test one of the client applications again, and you should see nearly instantaneous results.

On subsequent runs, you usually won't see the Activated column number change, because the component is created and destroyed so quickly, the Component Services UI doesn't have time to update the numbers. Still, the application is working, so you know the component is being called.

Let's carefully examine what is happening, and what this means for your scalability. When you first start your client application, you haven't yet made a call to the component. When the user clicks the Set Name button, you start with the following two lines of code:

```
Dim oHello As Greetings.cHello
Set oHello = New Greetings.cHello
```

This code causes COM+, under the covers, to go out and find the component, instantiate the object, and return a pointer to you. The component is actually created inside a process under Component Services, so even if this component is a DLL, it's out of process to your client. The ramifications of this are discussed later.

With the next line of code, you call the SayHello method and pass in the value that was typed in the txtName text box. Because the SayHello method returns a string, you display the string in a message box:

```
MsgBox oHello.SayHello(txtName.Text)
```

With this call, you are passing the string in the text box into the SayHello method in the component. When the SayHello method is called, the first thing it does is create a Context object to communicate with Component Services:

```
Dim objContext As ObjectContext
Set objContext = GetObjectContext
```

The next line in the component sets the return value to the string "Hello there," and concatenates on the name passed into the component:

```
SayHello = "Hello there, " & psName
```

Finally, you call the SetComplete method of the objContext object. This command tells Component Services you are done with your work and you don't need the component any more, so it can be removed from memory.

```
objContext.SetComplete
```

As you can see from this example, you can support ten simultaneous clients with very little load on the server because the components aren't in memory except exactly when needed. Microsoft calls this *just-in-time activation* and *as-soon-as-possible deactivation*. Remember the idea about when to make the database connection, discussed in Chapter 5? The idea was to have the connection open only when it was needed. That idea is the same here—the component is only in memory when it's needed and it's removed as soon as you finish with it.

Modifying NWindWeb

Now that you know how Component Services handles scalability, let's modify the NWindWeb's cCustomer class to make it stateless, and also add in the code so it can communicate with Component Services. First, make sure you use Project, References to add a reference to the COM+ Services Type Library. Modify cCustomer so it looks like this (and again, this is ALL the code that should be in it):

```
Option Explicit

Const sDBconn = "Provider=SQLOLEDB.1;User ID=sa;" & _
    Initial Catalog=Northwind;Data Source=LAPTOP"

Public Function AddCustomer(ByVal psCustomerID As String, _
    ByVal psCompanyName As String, ByVal psContactName As String, _
    ByVal psContactTitle As String, ByVal psAddress As String, _
```

```
          ByVal psCity As String, ByVal psRegion As String, _
          ByVal psPostalCode As String, ByVal psCountry As String, _
          ByVal psPhone As String, ByVal psFax As String) As Boolean

          On Error GoTo AddError
          Dim cn As ADODB.Connection
          Set cn = New ADODB.Connection
          Dim sSQL As String
          Dim objContext As ObjectContext
          Set objContext = GetObjectContext

          cn.Open sDBconn
          sSQL = "Insert Into Customers Values ('" & psCustomerID & "','" & _
              psCompanyName & "','" & psContactName & "','" & _
              psContactTitle & "','" & psAddress & "','" & psCity & "','" & _
              psRegion & "','" & psPostalCode & "','" & psCountry & "','" & _
              psPhone & "','" & psFax & "')"
          cn.Execute sSQL
          AddCustomer = True
          objContext.SetComplete
          Exit Function
      AddError:
          AddCustomer = False
          objContext.SetAbort
      End Function

      Public Function DeleteCustomer(ByVal psCustomerID As String) As Boolean
          On Error GoTo DeleteError
          Dim cn As ADODB.Connection
          Set cn = New ADODB.Connection
          Dim sSQL As String
          Dim objContext As ObjectContext
          Set objContext = GetObjectContext

          cn.Open sDBconn
          sSQL = "Delete from Customers where CustomerID='" & psCustomerID & "'"
          cn.Execute sSQL
          DeleteCustomer = True
          objContext.SetComplete
          Exit Function
      DeleteError:
          DeleteCustomer = False
```

```
        objContext.SetAbort
End Function


Public Function UpdateCustomer(ByVal psCustomerID As String, _
     ByVal psCompanyName As String, ByVal psContactName As String, _
     ByVal psContactTitle As String, ByVal psAddress As String, _
     ByVal psCity As String, ByVal psRegion As String, _
     ByVal psPostalCode As String, ByVal psCountry As String, _
     ByVal psPhone As String, ByVal psFax As String, _
     ByVal psOriginalCustomerID As String) As Boolean

     On Error GoTo UpdateError
     Dim cn As ADODB.Connection
     Set cn = New ADODB.Connection
     Dim sSQL As String
     Dim objContext As ObjectContext
     Set objContext = GetObjectContext

     cn.Open sDBconn
     sSQL = "Update Customers Set CustomerID='" & psCustomerID & "'," & _
         "CompanyName='" & psCompanyName & "', ContactName='" & _
         psContactName & "',ContactTitle='" & psContactTitle & "'," & _
         "Address='" & psAddress & "',City='" & psCity & "'," & _
         "Region='" & psRegion & "',PostalCode='" & psPostalCode & "'," & _
         "Country='" & psCountry & "',Phone='" & psPhone & "'," & _
         "Fax='" & psFax & "' where CustomerID='" & _
          psOriginalCustomerID & "'"
     cn.Execute sSQL
     UpdateCustomer = True
     objContext.SetComplete
     Exit Function
UpdateError:
     UpdateCustomer = False
     objContext.SetAbort
End Function
```

Now, recompile the component and overwrite the previous version. What you've done here is make your cCustomer class stateless by eliminating all the properties and modifying the methods to accept all the values as parameters to the methods. You've also added in the code needed to talk to Component Services. And you did two other things: you made all the parameters ByVal and you added in a SetAbort command. The ByVal keyword is discussed later in the chapter, when you learn about optimizing this sort of communication. You also learn more about the SetAbort command when transactions are discussed later in this chapter.

Now that you've modified the component and eliminated properties, you need to modify the CustomerMaint.asp page to use the new methods. Open VI and modify the code in CustomerMaint.asp to look like this:

```
<%@ Language=VBScript %>
<HTML>
<HEAD>
</HEAD>
<BODY>
<%
Dim objCustomer
Set objCustomer=Server.CreateObject("NWindWeb.cCustomer")
If Request.Form("txtCustomerID")<>"" Then
      sCustomerID=Request.Form("txtCustomerID")
      sCompanyName=Request.Form("txtCompanyName")
      sContactName=Request.Form("txtContactName")
      sContactTitle=Request.Form("txtContactTitle")
      sAddress=Request.Form("txtAddress")
      sCity=Request.Form("txtCity")
      sRegion=Request.Form("txtRegion")
      sPostalCode=Request.Form("txtPostalCode")
      sCountry=Request.Form("txtCountry")
      sPhone=Request.Form("txtPhone")
      sFax=Request.Form("txtFax")
   Select Case Request.Form("cmdSubmit")
      Case "Add"
         if objCustomer.AddCustomer(sCustomerID, sCompanyName, _
            sContactName, sContactTitle, sAddress, sCity, _
            sRegion, sPostalCode, sCountry, sPhone, sFax) then
           Response.Write "New customer added"
         else
           Response.Write "Error adding record"
         end if
      Case "Update"
```

```
            if objCustomer.UpdateCustomer(sCustomerID, sCompanyName, _
                sContactName, sContactTitle, sAddress, sCity, _
                sRegion, sPostalCode, sCountry, sPhone, sFax, _
                Request.Form("OriginalCustomerID")) then
             Response.Write "Customer Updated"
          else
             Response.Write "Error updating customer"
          end if
       Case "Delete"
          if objCustomer.DeleteCustomer(sCustomerID) then
             Response.Write("Customer removed")
          else
             Response.Write("Customer could not be deleted")
          end if
    End Select
End If
%>
<FORM Name="frmCustomer" Action="CustomerMaint.asp" Method="Post">
<INPUT Type="Hidden" Name="OriginalCustomerID"
Value=<%=Request.Form("txtCustomerID")%>>
<TABLE Border="1" Cellpadding="2" Cellspacing="2">
   <TR>
      <TD>Customer ID: <INPUT Name="txtCustomerID"
Value="<%=Request.Form("txtCustomerID")%>"></TD>
   </TR>
   <TR>
      <TD>Company Name: <INPUT Name="txtCompanyName"
Value="<%=Request.Form("txtCompanyName")%>"></TD>
   </TR>
   <TR>
      <TD>Contact Name: <INPUT Name="txtContactName"
Value="<%=Request.Form("txtContactName")%>"></TD>
   </TR>
   <TR>
      <TD>Contact Title: <INPUT Name="txtContactTitle"
Value="<%=Request.Form("txtContactTitle")%>"></TD>
   </TR>
   <TR>
```

```
    <TD>Contact Address: <INPUT Name="txtAddress"
Value="<%=Request.Form("txtAddress")%>"></TD>
    </TR>
    <TR>
      <TD>City: <INPUT Name="txtCity" Value="
        <%=Request.Form("txtCity")%>"></TD>
      <TD>Region: <INPUT Name="txtRegion"
Value="<%=Request.Form("txtRegion")%>"></TD>
    </TR>
    <TR>
      <TD>Postal Code: <INPUT Name="txtPostalCode"
Value="<%=Request.Form("txtPostalCode")%>"></TD>
      <TD>Country: <INPUT Name="txtCountry"
Value="<%=Request.Form("txtCountry")%>"></TD>
    </TR>
    <TR>
      <TD>Phone: <INPUT Name="txtPhone"
Value="<%=Request.Form("txtPhone")%>"></TD>
      <TD>Fax: <INPUT Name="txtFax" Value="
        <%=Request.Form("txtFax")%>"></TD>
    </TR>
</TABLE>
<INPUT Type="Submit" Name="cmdSubmit" Value="Add">
<INPUT Type="Submit" Name="cmdSubmit" Value="Update">
<INPUT Type="Submit" Name="cmdSubmit" Value="Delete">
</FORM>
</BODY>
</HTML>
```

You've now changed the CustomerMaint.asp to quit calling the properties and, instead, to pass the values of the text boxes in on the method calls. This allows your component to be created only when you call the unit of work you need and to be deactivated as soon as it's finished. In theory, you would be done with the component as soon as the page finished processing on the server because the object variable would fall out of scope. Still, the page has to process after the data is returned from the call, and some pages take a long time to process. Therefore, you are still gaining benefits by destroying the object as early as possible. The scalability of your application is growing rapidly.

Coding Efficiencies

Remember, in the last chapter, the discussion on in-process versus out-of-process components that said out-of-process components require marshalling for data sent from the client to the component and data sent from the component back to the client? Marshalling is slow, in computer terms, so you want to minimize it as much as possible.

"But wait!" I hear you saying, "I'm writing DLLs, which are in-process. I don't have to worry about marshalling." Well, not exactly. You are writing DLLs, and they are in-process, but only to Component Services. Your client applications are external to Component Services. IIS is actually internal to Component Services, but unless your components are in a Library application, you are still running out-of-process to IIS, as shown in Figure 14-11. Therefore, all the issues you normally face with out-of-process components must be considered when designing components that run in Component Services. Even if you don't need the efficiencies seen with the scalability of Component Services so far, you want to take advantage of some of what you've done to minimize marshalling.

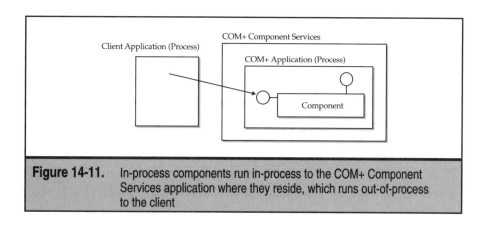

Figure 14-11.   In-process components run in-process to the COM+ Component Services application where they reside, which runs out-of-process to the client

Minimize Marshalling

How do you minimize marshalling? Simple: reduce the number of trips to the component. The easiest way to reduce the number of trips to the component is to do what you just did: eliminate properties and pass everything in the method call. If you want to set five properties, and then call a method, that is a minimum of six (and sometimes up to twelve) round-trips between the client and the component. Each call requires the data to be packaged and unpackaged, and a response to be packaged and unpackaged. Making only one call to a method, and passing all the parameters with the method call, greatly reduces the number of round-trips to the database. So even if you aren't "going stateless," you should consider coding your call the "no property" way.

Don't Pass Objects

Passing objects across process boundaries is expensive. Some objects are much more expensive than others but, in general, avoid passing objects. Instead, pass back strings or numbers wherever possible. I see many developers passing collections back and forth, and collections are generally a great tool, but they're not efficient to pass between processes.

The ADO Recordset, however, has been written with the idea of being passed across processes in mind. While Microsoft discourages passing objects across processes, it says passing the ADO Recordset object is acceptable because tuning has made it more efficient. Is passing a Recordset object or an array better (if you had called GetRows, for example)? Remember the magic answer: it depends. What do you want to do with the data? You might need a recordset and the functionality it provides. Your application design has to determine this.

When I say not to pass objects, I also mean not to raise events across process boundaries. In Web applications, this usually isn't a big deal, because your ASPs aren't event-driven. Still, not raising events across process boundaries is a good idea.

By Value vs. By Reference

Remember your Programming 101 course? Remember passing parameters by value or by reference? On one of my exams, I explained the differences beautifully, but I reversed them. The professor gave me exactly zero points for my answer. I've never mixed them up since then. For those of you who don't remember, let's take a quick trip back to one of those things you should have learned in school.

When you declare a variable, a piece of memory is set aside to hold that variable's value. You only get a pointer to that memory address. When you pass that variable to another routine, you can pass it by value or by reference. By *reference* means you're sending the pointer to the routine you're calling. When the called routine wants to see the *value*, it's looking in the same memory location as the calling routine. If the called routine changes the value of the variable, even if it's using a different variable name, the value is changed in the calling routine as well, because the data has been changed in the one memory location both routines are using. Here's a quick code example in VB to illustrate this point:

```
Sub A()
    Dim x As Integer
    x=5
    B x
    MsgBox x
End Sub


Sub B(y As Integer)
    y=0
End Sub
```

This example starts in *A*. *A* declares a variable, *x*, which sets aside some memory on the computer. *A* sets the value in the memory location of *x* to 5. *A* then calls *B* and passes *x* to *B*. *B* receives the address of *x* and places it in a variable *y*. *B* then changes the value in the memory location that *y* points to, which happens to be the same memory location that *x* points to, to the value of 0. *B* then finishes, so control returns to *A*. The MsgBox function pops up a message box with the value of *x* in it, which is now 0.

You see, in VB, the default is to pass parameters by reference. Why? It's faster. You don't have to set aside a new memory location and copy the value into it. So, for in-process components, it is faster.

But remember, your in-process components are actually running out-of-process to your client, so think about what happens if you pass data by reference, which is the default. Using the previous code example, assume *A* and *B* are in different processes. Different processes can't share the same memory address (technically they can, but this book doesn't go there). When *A* calls *B*, *A* has some memory set aside for the variable *x*. The value in *x* has to be marshalled (bad!) and sent to *B*. *B* then has to create a memory location, pointed to by the variable *y*, and put the passed value in it, and then a response is sent back to *A*, resulting in a round-trip. When *B* changes the value of *y*, the new value has to be marshalled (there's that bad word again!) and sent back to *A*, where the value of *x* is changed, and then a response is sent back to *B*, resulting in another round-trip! *B* then finishes running, and you return to *A*, where the value of *x* has now been changed.

As you can see, by passing parameters by reference, every time a value changes, you have to make a round-trip to the calling component to change the memory space there. This isn't at all efficient. Figure 14-12 shows what happens with passing variables by reference if the called routine is in-process or out-of-process to the calling routine.

If you look at the code examples of the components after you made them stateless, you'll notice I added the ByVal keyword in front of all the parameters. Passing parameters by value forces the called procedure to set aside new memory and put a copy of the variable in there. Now, when the value is changed in the called procedure, it only changes the value in the memory location for that procedure. It has no effect on the variable in the calling procedure.

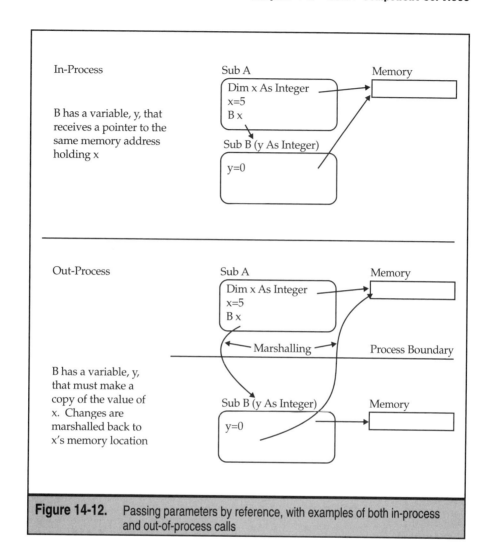

Figure 14-12. Passing parameters by reference, with examples of both in-process and out-of-process calls

Let's modify the earlier code example by adding in only the ByVal keyword:

```
Sub A()
    Dim x As Integer
    x=5
    B x
    MsgBox x
End Sub
```

```
Sub B(ByVal y As Integer)
    y=0
End Sub
```

When *A* calls *B*, *B* sets aside a new memory location, referenced by *y*, and puts a 5 in it. When *B* changes *y* to 0, it has no effect on the memory location for *x* back in *A*. When you return, therefore, the message box shows 5 as the value of *x*. If *B* is in a different process from *A*, this means you needn't marshal changes back to *A*. You gained efficiency. Figure 14-13 shows what passing values look like for both in-process and out-of-process calls.

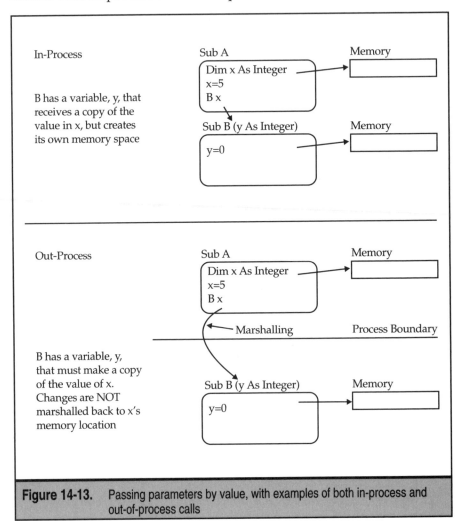

Figure 14-13.   Passing parameters by value, with examples of both in-process and out-of-process calls

NOTE: The rule of thumb: pass all parameters ByVal unless you positively can't avoid it.

Pooling

I can hear some of you asking one of two related questions:

▼ Isn't constantly connecting and disconnecting to the database inefficient?

▲ Isn't continually creating and destroying these objects inefficient?

The answer to both of these questions is, of course, "Yes," but... Remember back in Chapter 5 when you learned about database connection pooling and where to connect to the database? Well, Component Services makes use of database connection pooling so, as long as you are connecting to the same database with the same user name and password, you can take advantage of database connection pooling, with no code needed on your part.

As for the objects, Component Services added something MTS didn't have: object pooling. In *object pooling,* an object actually can be returned to a pool, so subsequent requests can be handed an already created object, instead of having to take the long (in computer terms) time to create a new object from scratch. While object pooling can significantly increase performance, Microsoft says object pooling doesn't work today with VB components, so to take advantage of this feature, you must write your components in C++, or wait for Visual Basic 7, which will support more than just apartment-model threading.

Transactions

Back in NT 4, Microsoft called most of the functionality discussed in this chapter Microsoft Transaction Services. I've gone on for a number of pages about what Component Services can do for you, but haven't discussed transactions yet. The simple reason is that Component Services, like MTS, can do many things for you besides transactions. Still, transactions are important and you should know how they work. The good news here is most of the code you need has already been written.

First, you need to describe a transaction. Simply put, a transaction is an all-or-nothing operation. Think about the Space Shuttle. Before each launch, they go around the various stations in mission control, and each station has to say "Go." If the flight surgeon, communications, and engines stations all say "Go," but the weather station says "No go," then they don't go. Mission control isn't a democracy: it's unanimous or they don't launch.

The classic (and, therefore, boring) computer example is always that of transferring money. If you have two accounts, checking and savings, and you want to transfer money between them, you must make sure you subtract from one account and add to another. Doing either part of this isn't enough. You must make sure you do both parts or neither part.

Say you want to move $100 from savings to checking. You could first subtract the money from the savings account. Before you have time to add the money to the checking account, the system crashes. When the system restarts, the savings account is down by $100, but the checking account is unchanged. This might make the bank happy, but the customer is definitely not happy.

To avoid this, let's assume you add the $100 to the checking account first. But now, before you can subtract the money from savings, the computer crashes. When the computer comes back up, the customer is quite happy because he has an extra $100. The bank, of course, wouldn't be happy with this scenario.

Enter the concept of a transaction. Both the subtraction of $100 from savings *and* the addition of $100 to checking must occur, or neither one occurs. This is accomplished by first writing the changes to logs and asking the database if it can make the changes. If the database says it can, it's in effect signing a contract. Once you tell it to go ahead, even if the machine crashes before it can make the changes, once the machine comes back up it will go ahead and make the changes. If you make the changes to the logs, and then the database responds that it can't make one of the changes (the person might not have $100 in his savings account), then you roll back the changes and they are removed from the logs without ever having actually been applied to the real tables.

The ACID Properties

No discussion of transactions is complete without discussing the ACID properties: atomicity, consistency, isolation, and durability. All real transactions must have the ACID properties and, let's face it, you're here to write real transactions.

Atomicity   *Atomicity* is the concept that you should do one thing and do it completely, or don't do it at all. In the bank example, both the credit and debit must occur, or neither will occur. Both the debit and credit together represent one atomic unit of work.

Consistency   *Consistency* says your data will always be in a consistent state. You won't take $100 out of savings and wait two days before putting the $100 in checking. At the end of the transaction, the $100 will be out of the saving account and into the checking account or, if the transaction fails, no money is moved at all, so the data is still consistent.

Isolation   *Isolation* helps you avoid dirty reads. *Dirty reads* are when you see inconsistent data. For example, you know subtracting money from savings and adding money to checking are two separate operations against the database. With isolation, however, you should never see one without the other. You should never see the savings account down by $100 without seeing the corresponding $100 increase in checking.

Durability   Durability refers to the capability to survive failures. Say you move the $100 from savings to checking. Right now, the data is only in the log file(s). You want to commit the transaction, and the database is now committed to rolling the changes forward into the base tables. Before the database can complete its work, though, someone trips over the power cord and the machine goes down. When the computer comes back up, the data is rolled forward into the tables; in other words, the transaction was durable. If, on the other hand, you've only made one part of the transaction, such as the change to the savings account, when the computer comes back up, that change will be rolled back out of the log, having never touched the underlying table.

But How Do I Code Transactions?

One of the nice things about Component Services is it handles a lot of the transaction work for you. With ADO, you could write your own transactions by using the BeginTrans, CommitTrans, and RollbackTrans methods of the ADO Connection object. However, Component Services can handle all of this for you through the use of your friends, SetComplete and SetAbort.

NOTE: Don't use BeginTrans, CommitTrans, and RollbackTrans if you plan to use Component Services. Let Component Services handle your transactions for you.

Why let Component Services handle your transactions for you? Here's a more complex scenario than this book has. Imagine you need to interact with some corporate data. To do a transaction, you have to add a record to SQL Server, delete a record from Oracle, and update a record in DB2. Could you code all this with the ADO Connection object's BeginTrans, CommitTrans, and RollbackTrans? Yes, but what a pain this would be. Instead, Component Services can use the Distributed Transaction Coordinator (DTC) to synchronize distributed, or heterogeneous, transactions. In other words, Component Services can make all these different database engines work together in one logical transaction. The DTC is doing most of the work for you, and Component Services uses it to handle all transactions. Notice the DTC only works with data sources that support OLE Transactions or X/Open XA-compliant transactions, but most of the databases available today support one of these two types of transactions.

NOTE: In MTS, if you tried to run a transaction and the DTC wasn't running, you got a bizarre error message that "Method '~' of object '~' failed." In Component Services, however, the transaction seems to fail normally.

You currently have a component that does inserts, updates, and deletes to the database. You don't need to have it doing transactions, but go ahead and flip the switch, and force it to use transactions. To do this, simply right-click the cCustomer component in the NWind application in the Component Services manager and choose Properties. Once in properties, click the Transactions tab, and you should see what is shown in Figure 14-14.

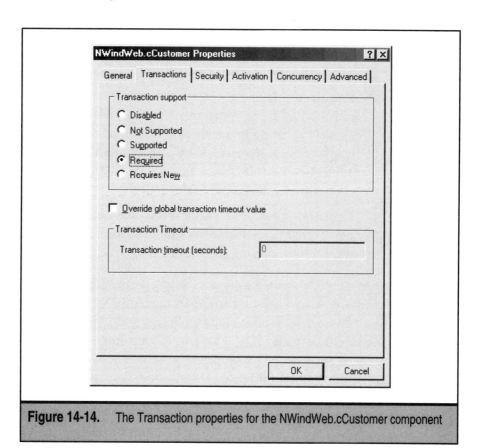

Figure 14-14. The Transaction properties for the NWindWeb.cCustomer component

A number of choices are listed on this tab. Let's examine what these choices mean:

▼ **Disabled**   Choosing this option makes the component run like it's not under Component Services control. It won't receive any Component Services benefits.

■ **Not Supported**   This option says the component won't participate in a transaction, even if it's created by a component in a transaction. This is the default when you first add a component to Component Services.

■ **Supported**   This is the "Hey, I'm flexible" choice. It says, if the component is created by another component that's in a transaction, it will join in the transaction. If it's created by a component (or outside client) that isn't in a transaction, it will run without a transaction. It simply doesn't care.

■ **Required**   This choice says the component must run in a transaction. If the component is created by a component already running in a transaction, it joins the already-running transaction. If it's created by a component that isn't already in a transaction or if it's the first object created by an external client, it will start a new transaction.

▲ **Requires New**   No matter what, this object is going to start a new transaction. It doesn't matter if the caller is already in a transaction, this object will create a new, separate transaction.

Let's flip the switch on your component to Required, and then click OK. You can fire up the CustomerMaint.asp page now and add a new record. Update it as well, if you'd like. Now, go back to Component Services. If you look in the left-hand "explorer" pane, you see that under My Computer, you have a folder for COM+ Applications and a folder for Distributed Transaction Coordinator. If you expand the Distributed Transaction Coordinator node, you see two choices. Click the Transaction Statistics node and you should have something similar to what you see in Figure 14-15. This shows you are actually running transactions being managed by Component Services and the Distributed Transaction Coordinator.

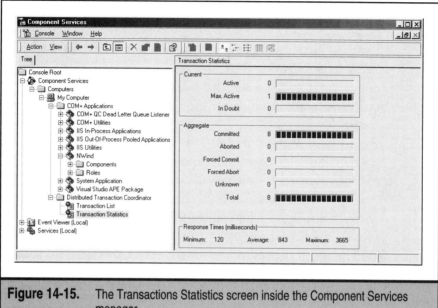

Figure 14-15. The Transactions Statistics screen inside the Component Services manager

With this screen showing in Component Services, add or update some records. Notice how, after a brief pause, the total number of transactions starts to climb. This proves you're using transactions, even though at this point, you probably don't need them. You can even force your earlier cHello component to use transactions, even though it isn't doing any database work.

Extending Transactions

Not only can Component Services handle heterogeneous transactions, but multiple components can participate in one logical transaction. If one component starts a transaction, and then calls another component, the called component may, depending on its transaction setting, become part of the transaction started by the calling component.

Let's go back to the banking example, but change it slightly. Say you want to transfer money from a money market account to a checking account. The money market account is a strange enough animal that you've built a completely separate class to mimic a money market account. So, you have two classes: a cChecking class and a cMoneyMarket class. Whether they are compiled into the same or separate DLLs doesn't matter. You can assume, regardless of how they are physically compiled, both are in the same Component Services application. Further, assume the designer has built a third component, cCustomer, that handles all customer actions. If a customer wants to transfer money from a money market account to checking, you call a TransferMMtoChecking method and pass in the amount of the transfer. This TransferMMtoChecking method then instantiates objects of type cChecking and cMoneyMarket. In cMoneyMarket, it calls a Withdrawal method and, in cChecking, it calls a Deposit method. Both these methods have database code in them that form one logical transaction, but the code is spread over two distinct components.

The secret here is for the first object, cCustomer, to create a new transaction, and for the cChecking and cMoneyMarket objects to participate in that transaction. The transaction setting for the root object, cCustomer, should be Required or Requires New. The transaction setting for cChecking and cMoneyMarket should be Supported or Required (but not Requires New).

The secret to having other objects participate in this transaction is in how you call them. In the past, you always created objects using code like this:

```
Dim objCustomer as Greetings.cCustomer
Set objCustomer = New Greetings.cCustomer
```

With components in Component Services that you want to participate in transactions, however, you cannot call them using this syntax. I don't mean calling them from the client, but when one Component Services component calls another. If you call one component that will then call other components and enlist them in the current transaction, you have to use the CreateObject method, as such:

```
Dim objCustomer as Greetings.cCustomer
Set objCustomer = CreateObject("Greetings.cCustomer")
```

The CreateObject method is necessary to make the called components join in the same transaction as the calling component. Back in the MTS days, you had to use a method of the Context object called CreateInstance. You can still use this or, now with Component Services, you can use CreateObject. The key point here is you cannot use the New keyword as you've been doing.

Why can't you use New? Understand what happens when your client application creates a component in Component Services: Component Services creates the component, but it also creates a Context object to go along with it. This Context object is what you talk to when you make the call to GetObjectContext. This Context object is like a helper object joined to the object you just created: it keeps track of whether the object is in a transaction, where it is in a transaction, and whether it has succeeded or failed in that transaction. When one Component Services object creates another one, if you use New, the new object cannot participate in the transaction because you don't take the information from the calling object's Context object and send it to the called component's Context object. If you use CreateObject, however, the calling object sends the context information to the called object's Context object, so the called object can participate in the transaction.

Here's how this works. Call these components cCustomer, cMoneyMarket, and cChecking, just described, create two tables in the Northwind database, and then add a record to each one. Feel free to create the tables in a different database if you prefer, but don't forget to modify the database connection string you see later. Use Query Analyzer to run the following code:

```
CREATE TABLE [dbo].[Checking] (
      [CustomerID] [int] IDENTITY (1, 1) NOT NULL ,
      [Balance] [money] NOT NULL
) ON [PRIMARY]
GO


CREATE TABLE [dbo].[MoneyMarket] (
      [CustomerID] [int] IDENTITY (1, 1) NOT NULL ,
      [Balance] [money] NOT NULL
) ON [PRIMARY]
GO


ALTER TABLE [dbo].[Checking] WITH NOCHECK ADD
```

```
          CONSTRAINT [PK_Checking] PRIMARY KEY   CLUSTERED
          (
                  [CustomerID]
          )  ON [PRIMARY]
GO


ALTER TABLE [dbo].[MoneyMarket] WITH NOCHECK ADD
          CONSTRAINT [PK_MoneyMarket] PRIMARY KEY   CLUSTERED
          (
                  [CustomerID]
           )  ON [PRIMARY]
GO


Insert Into Checking (Balance) Values (500)
GO


Insert Into MoneyMarket (Balance) Values (200)
GO
```

You've created two tables between which you can transfer money. You want to create a simple component with three classes: cCustomer, cMoneyMarket, and cChecking. cCustomer acts as the root of your transaction. Call the cCustomer.TransferMMtoChecking method. This method will create objects from cMoneyMarket and cChecking, and call either Deposit or Withdrawal methods to move money.

Start a new Visual Basic ActiveX DLL project. Make sure you choose Project, References, and add references to both the COM+ Component Services Type Library and the Microsoft ActiveX Data Object 2.6 Library (or higher). You start with one class. Rename this class to cCustomer. Create two more classes (click Project, Add Class Module) and name them cChecking and cMoneyMarket.

Place the following code into cCustomer:

```
Public Function TransferMMtoChecking(ByVal pcAmount As Currency) _
   As Boolean
      On Error GoTo TMCerr
      Dim objContext As ObjectContext
      Dim Checking As cChecking
```

```
    Dim MoneyMarket As cMoneyMarket


    Set objContext = GetObjectContext
    Set Checking = CreateObject("Banking.cChecking")
    Set MoneyMarket = CreateObject("Banking.cMoneyMarket")
    MoneyMarket.Withdrawal pcAmount
    Checking.Deposit pcAmount
    TransferMMtoChecking = True
    objContext.SetComplete
    Exit Function
TMCerr:
    objContext.SetAbort
    TransferMMtoChecking = False
End Function
```

Notice you are creating the Checking and MoneyMarket objects using the CreateObject syntax, so the components can join in the transaction started with the cCustomer component.

Next, place this code in cChecking:

```
Public Sub Deposit(ByVal pcAmount As Currency)
    On Error GoTo DepErr
    Dim cn As ADODB.Connection
    Set cn = New ADODB.Connection
    Dim objContext As ObjectContext
    Set objContext = GetObjectContext
    Dim sSQL As String
    cn.Open "Provider=SQLOLEDB.1;User ID=sa;Initial Catalog=Northwind;Data
    Source=LAPTOP"
sSQL = "Update Checking set Balance=Balance+" & _
        pcAmount & " where CustomerID=1"
    cn.Execute sSQL, , adCmdText + adExecuteNoRecords
    objContext.SetComplete
    Exit Sub
DepErr:
    objContext.SetAbort
    Err.Raise Err.Number, , "Deposit failed"
End Sub
```

Finally, add the following code to cMoneyMarket:

```
Public Sub Withdrawal(ByVal pcAmount As Currency)
    On Error GoTo WithdrawalErr
    Dim cn As ADODB.Connection
    Set cn = New ADODB.Connection
    Dim rs As ADODB.Recordset
    Dim objContext As ObjectContext
    Set objContext = GetObjectContext
    Dim sSQL As String

    cn.Open "Provider=SQLOLEDB.1;User ID=sa; & _
        Initial Catalog=Northwind;Data Source=LAPTOP"
    sSQL = "Select Balance from MoneyMarket where CustomerID=1"
    Set rs = cn.Execute(sSQL, , adCmdText)
    If rs(0) <= 0 Then
        objContext.SetAbort
        Exit Sub
    End If
    sSQL = "Update MoneyMarket set Balance=Balance-" & _
        pcAmount & " where CustomerID=1"
    cn.Execute sSQL, , adCmdText + adExecuteNoRecords
    objContext.SetComplete
    Exit Sub
WithdrawalErr:
    objContext.SetAbort
    Err.Raise Err.Number, , "Withdrawal failed"
End Sub
```

The cChecking and cMoneyMarket code is similar. If you look, you see both have an error handler, and a call in there to the SetAbort method of the Context object. What is SetAbort? Remember, SetComplete tells Component Services everything succeeded and the component can be taken out of memory. SetAbort tells Component Services you didn't succeed and the component can be taken out of memory. So, either SetComplete or SetAbort can cause your component to be destroyed. But, like going around mission control for a shuttle launch, SetComplete is a "go" but SetAbort is a "no go." Then raise an error, so you drop into the error handler in the root object (cCustomer) and also call SetAbort there. SetAbort tells Component Services to roll back any changes that were made during the course of this transaction.

To summarize, SetComplete does two things: first, it says if the component is in a transaction, its work has succeeded and can be committed. Second, SetComplete says the component can be removed from memory. SetAbort says the work of the component failed and the transaction can be rolled back. It also says the component can be removed from memory.

The cMoneyMarket class also has some code to check the balance of the money market account to make sure you can transfer the money. If you don't have enough money, you call the SetAbort method, and then exit from the sub.

Name the project Banking, and then compile the Banking.dll into the directory of your choosing. Once you compile the DLL, add the DLL to Component Services, in the NWind application. After adding the three components to Component Services, set the transaction setting of all three to Required.

Launch another copy of Visual Basic and start a new Standard EXE. This will be your client program. Choose Project, References, and add a reference to the Banking component you created. Place a button on the form and double-click that button. In the code window, enter the following code:

```
Private Sub Command1_Click()
    Dim Customer As Banking.cCustomer
    Set Customer = New Banking.cCustomer
    If Customer.TransferMMtoChecking(200) Then
        MsgBox "Transaction Succeeded"
    Else
        MsgBox "Transaction Failed"
    End If
End Sub
```

The code here creates a Customer object (of type Banking.cCustomer), and then calls the TransferMMtoChecking method and passes in the value of 200. If the transfer works, you get a message that the transaction succeeded. Otherwise, you're notified the transaction failed.

You're almost there, but before running the transaction, open Query Analyzer and type in the following two queries:

```
select * from Checking
select * from MoneyMarket
```

Run these queries and you should wind up with what you see in Figure 14-16. This shows the current balance of the Checking and MoneyMarket tables and proves you are starting with $500 in the Checking account and $200 in the Money Market account.

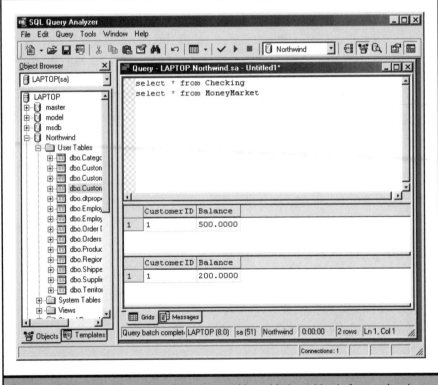

Figure 14-16. The data in the Checking and MoneyMarket tables before you've done any work

Look at the Transaction Statistics screen in Component Services again and note the total number of transactions that have been run. Finally, you're ready: start the client project you just created and click the button. Only do this one time! Check the Transactions Statistics screen and make sure the number of transactions has increased by one. Go back to the Query Analyzer and rerun the queries. As you can see in Figure 14-17, you've successfully moved the money from the MoneyMarket table to the Checking table. Even though this took two components and two SQL statements, you only ran one transaction.

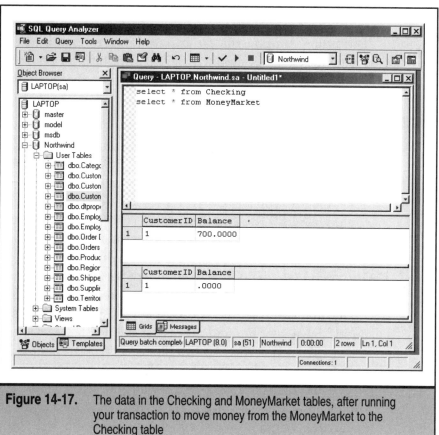

Figure 14-17.   The data in the Checking and MoneyMarket tables, after running your transaction to move money from the MoneyMarket to the Checking table

On the client program, press the button again. You should get a message that the transaction failed. Why? You didn't have enough money in the MoneyMarket table to move the funds. If you look at the Transaction Statistics in Component Services, the number of aborted transactions should have climbed by one. If you rerun the queries in Query Analyzer, you can see neither value has changed. This is exactly what you should have expected. If you hadn't been using transactions, the withdrawal from the money market account would have failed, but the deposit to the checking account would have succeeded, in effect, creating money for this individual.

DISTRIBUTION

One of the things Component Services does for you is to make distributing components easier. Two kinds of distribution occur: moving the entire Component Services application from one computer to another, and registering the components on the client machine.

Distributing an Application

Moving an application from one machine to another is a fairly simple process. At this point, you have an NWind application that contains five components. You've set the transaction property on several of these. Imagine you had done all this on a development server. How would you move this to a production server?

You could copy the DLLs to the production server, go to the production server, and run Regsvr32.exe on each DLL to register it. You could then go into the Component Services manager, create a new application called NWind, and then register all the components. Finally, you could set the appropriate transaction settings. If this all sounds like a very manual process, it is. Fortunately, Component Services gives you an easier way to do it.

In Component Services, right-click on an application and choose Export, and then click next on the welcome screen of the COM Application Export Wizard. On the first real screen of the wizard, type in the pathname and the filename of the package you want to export. In the example in Figure 14-18, I told Component Services to

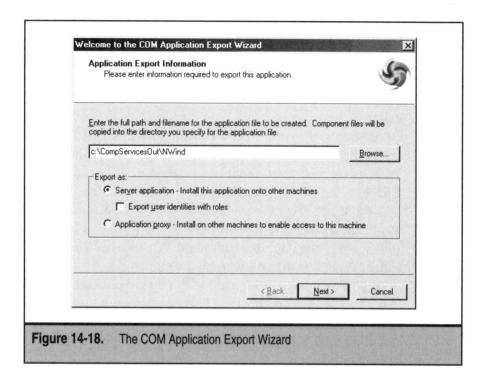

Figure 14-18. The COM Application Export Wizard

export to the C:\CompServicesOut directory, into a file called NWind. When you click next, Component Services exports everything you need into this directory. Component Services adds a .MSI extension to the name of your file, so the actual file written out is NWind.msi.

If you look at the C:\CompServicesOut folder now, you see two files: the NWind.msi file and an NWind.MSI.cab file. The MSI file is a Microsoft Installer file, which creates the NWind application with the components already registered in it. You only have to run this file on the target server and all the work previously mentioned will be done for you.

Or, you could go to the production server, launch the Component Services manager, expand down to the COM+ Applications node, and right-click. Choose New, Application, and when the wizard comes up, choose to install a prebuilt application. Then point the file browser to the MSI file, and the installation is done for you.

Registering on Client Machines

Next, assume you have the components all registered in a Component Services application sitting on an applications server somewhere. You want the ASPs on your Web server to be able to call the components. You know for the ASPs to be able to call the components, the component information must be in the registry on the Web server. But you don't want the components to run on the Web server, you want them to run on your application server. The trick is to get the information in the registry on the Web server that tells the Web server the physical location of the component is on the application server. You could go to the Web server and manually edit the registry, but I don't recommend this approach. Instead, use the same export wizard you were just using.

If you look back in Figure 14-18, you see one of the choices is to export an application proxy. This option creates an MSI file you can run on the Web server; in this case, that adds all the necessary keys into the registry so the ASPs can call the components on the remote application server.

NOTE: Don't run the application proxy on the machine that will actually be hosting the components.

SUMMARY

Again, a lot of territory was covered in this chapter. You learned how to make your components and, therefore, applications much more scalable. You made your components stateless, so you can take advantage of the just-in-time activation and the as-soon-as-possible deactivation provided to you by the Component Services architecture.

You learned how to make the components more efficient by passing parameters by value and by minimizing marshalling as much as possible. Don't forget to minimize the passing of objects as well.

Next, you learned how Component Services could work with the Distributed Transaction Coordinator to manage transactions. You even wrote a transaction that crossed three components and two SQL calls, but you didn't have to write any of the transactional code yourself. Instead, you let Component Services handle the transaction for you.

Finally, you learned about distribution and how to move Component Services applications from one machine to another, as well as how to enable servers to call the components on remote servers.

Component Services is powerful. It does a lot of the infrastructure work for you, so you needn't worry as much about coding for scalability and transactions. As long as you make your components stateless and include the necessary calls to the Context object, you're well on your way to much more scalable systems.

One last note: Some people ask about load balancing of components. In other words, can you put the component on three machines and have it created and run on the machine with the least use at any given time? The answer is "No," for now. Microsoft has promised load balancing in Component Services "in a future release."

CHAPTER 15

Wrapping Up: Scalability and Security

I've covered a variety of topics in this book: you've seen how ASPs work, and how to access databases through technologies such as ADO, English Query, and ADO MD. You've seen the Visual InterDev tools, both the tools to work with the database and the design-time controls that enable you to build data-driven pages without programming. In the last two chapters, you saw how to increase the scalability and speed of your applications by breaking out your business logic into COM+ components, and then using COM+ Component Services to make your applications more scalable and to handle transactions.

What else is left? First, you can squeeze more scalability gains from your applications. You haven't learned about load balancing yet or looked at Web applications that don't use the Session object. You also need to perform some load testing to see how your applications handle the stress.

The most glaring hole so far, however, is security. You learn about two major kinds of security: encryption and application security. Encryption can be used on a public site, but data back and forth is encrypted so customers can send sensitive information, such as credit card numbers. Encryption is at a lower level than your code, so using encryption typically doesn't require any code changes on your part. Application security is where you restrict access to your application, or parts of it, to particular users. This application security can extend to your middle-tier and on to SQL Server on the back-end.

HANDLING HEAVY LOADS

An entire chapter was spent looking at what COM+ Component Services could do for you. One of the major benefits is the capability to achieve huge scalability gains through Component Services's just-in-time activation and as-soon-as-possible deactivation. This is true whether or not the components are actually running transactions. You can tune more than your components for scalability, however.

Clustering and Network Load Balancing

One of the areas for improvement in scalability is in IIS and Windows 2000. With Windows 2000 Advanced Server and Datacenter Server versions, Microsoft includes two related technologies: Clustering and Network Load Balancing. *Clustering* is intended to provide fail-over support, so if one machine fails, another machine can pick right up with the work of the one that failed, with no loss of data and no visible service interruption to the client. *Network Load Balancing* (*NLB*) provides better scalability and high availability for any TCP/IP services, including IIS.

Clustering is a tool for high availability and, without NLB, is mainly intended for database servers, mail servers, and other similar services. Clustering works on the concept of providing redundant boxes that share storage. The purpose of the boxes in the cluster is not to share the load. In fact, in a two-computer cluster, one box is idle except for monitoring the status of the primary computer. If the primary computer fails, the second, or *fail-over* server takes over the job of the primary and accesses the shared storage, so nothing is lost.

If you add in NLB, you have a tool that enables you to share the processing load across the servers in a cluster. With NLB, all incoming requests go to all the machines in the cluster, but only the intended recipient processes the request. This way, different servers can be responding to different clients concurrently, which can greatly increase the performance and reduce response time for clients. In addition, multiple machines can respond to the same client, such as when the client is retrieving all the graphics on a page. The different graphics can all come from different servers, yielding better performance for the client. To the client, the cluster holding the Web servers, often called a Web farm, looks like one computer because the client only needs to contact one IP address. Each machine in the cluster actually has a separate IP address, however, and NLB handles this translation for you. Again, from a client standpoint, the cluster looks like one machine and, as a developer, you needn't modify how you build your ASPs.

NLB enables you to tune the boxes in the cluster. Each server can specify the percentage of the load it will handle or the load can be evenly distributed. NLB works by each server more or less "volunteering" to take on a unit of work, which is a benefit over older, "round-robin" technologies, which sent each new request to the next server in the cluster. Round-robin technologies usually didn't realize when one server in the cluster went down, so they continued sending traffic to that server. With NLB's model, the servers must volunteer, so this problem is eliminated. NLB doesn't currently distribute work based on the CPU utilization of the various servers, however, so a very busy server could possibly volunteer to handle a request while another server sits fairly idle. This isn't a common occurrence, however, because the busy server has less time to spend volunteering for more work.

Session State and Scalability

The capability to use Network Load Balancing can mean great gains in the performance and scalability of your application, but there is one drawback: the IIS Session object only exists on the server where it was originally created. Therefore, if the client makes the first request to Server1 in the cluster, the Session object is created only on that machine. With the second request, Server2 may decide to handle that request. Guess what? The Session object doesn't exist on that server, so this starts a new Session object that's empty. Two solutions exist to this problem and, naturally, each has its pros and cons. The first option is to turn on client affinity. The second option is not to use Session objects at all.

TCP/IP Client Affinity

With Network Load Balancing, you can turn on an Affinity parameter. The first option is None, which says all requests coming in can be picked up by any box. This option renders use of the Session object useless because you cannot guarantee the same server that initially created the Session object will handle the next request from that user.

NOTE: Client affinity is sometimes called a *sticky connection* because it remembers what server you were using and redirects you there. Don't confuse this with a *sticky site*, which means the site wants to draw you back again and again over time.

The second option is the default, and is the most common option for applications that use a Session object. The option is Single and says NLB will send all requests from the same IP address to the same server in the cluster. This option works well for single clients accessing an application because it directs the user to the same server each time, so you can use the Session object to maintain state.

What are the drawbacks to using Single client affinity? The first drawback is, if you have a number of users behind a single proxy server at their site, all those users will look to NLB as one user. Therefore, all those users will be directed to the same server in the cluster, which can destroy most of the scalability gains you wanted. The second drawback is if one of the users is at a location that employs multiple proxy servers. This means some of the requests from the user may have different IP addresses, which means different servers may pick up the various requests.

So, multiple users behind a single proxy server will all use the same server. Users behind multiple proxy servers may be directed to different servers at different times, so there's the potential they could wind up losing state by being directed to a server that doesn't contain their Session object.

To handle the problem of people behind multiple proxy servers, there's the third affinity setting: Class C. Class C affinity says NLB will direct any IP address from a Class C IP address range to the same server in the Web farm. Even if clients are behind multiple proxy servers, they are sent to the same server as long as their proxy servers are all in the same Class C address space, which is usually the case. If the person is behind several proxy servers in different Class C address spaces, you can't do anything for them using affinity.

You still have a problem if people are behind multiple proxy servers that have different Class C addresses (not likely) and you still aren't getting good load balancing if most of your clients are behind the same proxy because all those requests still need to be handled by one server. Affinity tends to work for smaller server farms running fairly simple applications. Complex applications can be problematic, though, because all the traffic from one company or ISP could wind up running on one machine. What do you do? The answer is to do with your ASPs exactly what you did with your components: make them stateless.

Sessionless ASPs

You can create an ASP that is sessionless. In fact, you can create an entire application that is sessionless. This has the advantage of not having to create and maintain the Session object for each user. Even without load balancing, this can boost performance. With sessionless applications and NLB, you can get the full benefit of load balancing because a different machine in the cluster can handle each request.

To create a sessionless ASP in a normally stateful IIS application, simply add the following line of code to the top of the page:

```
<%@ EnableSessionState=False %>
```

In fact, the "@" symbol indicates this is a directive to the IIS engine, so the first line of your ASP usually looks like this:

```
<%@ Language=VBScript EnableSessionState=False %>
```

Assume the previous line is in the first ASP a new user calls. Normally, when a new user calls an ASP, you process the Session_OnStart sub in Global.asa. Calling an ASP that doesn't enable session state won't process the Session_OnStart. It also won't create a Session object or send a SessionID cookie down the client. Finally, a page with this line won't be able to make any calls to the session object.

Create a new Web project in Visual InterDev and call it Stateless. Make this your Global.asa:

```
<SCRIPT LANGUAGE=VBScript RUNAT=Server>

Sub Session_OnStart
    Session("Name")="Westie Enterprises"
```

```
End Sub
</SCRIPT>
```

Now, create a Default.asp and add in the following code:

```
<%@ Language=VBScript %>
<HTML>
   <BODY>
      The name is: <% =Session("Name") %>
   </BODY>
</HTML>
```

It doesn't get more simple than this. View Default.asp in IE, and you can see the name is "Westie Enterprises" as you set in the Global.asa file.

Now, let's make a modification to Default.asp. Change the first line to this:

```
<%@ Language=VBScript EnableSessionState=False %>
```

Save the page and refresh the browser. You get a Type Mismatch error on the word Session. That's because, as a sessionless page, this page cannot access the Session object. In fact, as the first page in this application, no Session object exists yet.

Sessionless Applications

As you see, you can make an individual ASP stateless. You can also make an entire application stateless. Disabling session state for an entire application means you don't have to put the EnableSessionState=False directive in each ASP. This also means no page can access a Session object, the Session_OnStart code won't be called, and no SessionID cookie is sent to the client. Now our ASPs are acting like normal Web pages: each request is seen as a brand new request. The server doesn't "remember" the person was there before.

To make an entire application sessionless, open the Internet Information Services manager and expand the Default Web Site node so you can see the virtual directories. Right-click the Stateless application you just created and choose Properties. The Virtual

Directory tab has a number of sections on it, one of which is Application Settings. In the Application Settings section, click the Configuration button. The Application Configuration dialog box opens. Click the App Options tab. As you can see in Figure 15-1, the first check box is labeled Enable session state and under it is a text box with the default timeout for this application. In this case, the default is set to 20 minutes. You can change that value or uncheck the check box, and you have a sessionless, or stateless, application. Go ahead and make the Stateless application sessionless by checking this box.

Why would you make an ASP application sessionless? One word: scalability. Even if you aren't using NLB, sessionless applications perform better, because the server doesn't have to track session information. How much better the application performs is hard to measure. Without NLB, the difference is probably small at low loads. At higher loads, you save the memory on the server usually taken up

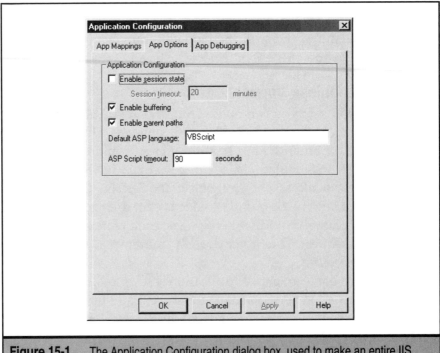

Figure 15-1. The Application Configuration dialog box, used to make an entire IIS application sessionless, or stateless

by the Session objects, so the scalability gains are probably larger as the load increases.

With NLB, it's easy to see how quickly you could achieve scalability gains. With sessionless applications, you no longer have to worry about client affinity. Instead, the requests are distributed over the servers in the cluster and you needn't worry about redirecting a user to the same server every time. Using Network Load Balancing, sessionless IIS applications, stateless components in COM+ Application Services, and stored procedures in SQL Server generally gives you the most scalable Web applications you can achieve with today's technology. There are still ASP performance tips (such as leaving buffering turned on), ADO tricks, VB component techniques, and numerous parameters in Windows 2000 and SQL Server 2000 that can be tuned, all of which can affect performance and scalability. Still, you have seen most of the major techniques used to make your Web application more scalable.

If my application is sessionless, how do I maintain state?

The obvious question is how to handle state in a Web application if the application is sessionless. Several variations exist on the same theme: in one way or another, you have to maintain state on the client or, most often, on both the client and the server. How you do this depends on your needs.

Take, for example, Yahoo!'s personal Web sites. If you go to http://my.yahoo.com, you can get a page you can customize. After creating an account, you can set up the stocks you want to see, the news categories, how many stories in each category, the colors of your page, and many other features. Then, you can have the browser automatically sign you in each time you visit the page.

NOTE: Yahoo! doesn't use Microsoft technology for its Web servers. Still, it's the most popular site to demonstrate the kind of functionality you want to showcase.

After setting up a personal page and getting it exactly the way you want it, you can go to any other computer and log in to the my.yahoo.com site. After entering your name and password, the page comes up exactly the way you set it up, with the news, stocks, and colors you chose. How can Yahoo! do this?

One option, which is actually used by some sites, would be to push all this information down to the client in a giant cookie. For example, you could store the stock, news, and color preferences on the client's hard drive. Each time the user goes to the site, you read all the cookie information and format the page accordingly. Viola! You don't have to store anything in a Session object.

The drawback to the "everything in a cookie" approach is, if the user goes to a new machine, that cookie doesn't exist! The user would have to set up the page again, from scratch. Doing this each time you moved to another computer could dissuade people from using your site. So Yahoo!, and sites like it, use a different technique: they store your username (and sometimes password) in a cookie, but all the other information is stored in a database on the server.

It shouldn't shock you that in a stateless application, you maintain state between calls by writing information to a database or a text file on the server. Then, you use cookies to determine the user on every call. If you must have someone log in, you maintain a job on the server that records whether someone has logged in and the time of her last request. If the person submits a request, but it has been too long since her previous request, you can redirect her to the login screen.

Here's a quick example. Use the SQL Server Query Analyzer to enter and execute the following script:

```
CREATE TABLE [dbo].[CustProd] (
    [CustomerID] [nchar] (5) COLLATE SQL_Latin1_General_CP1_CI_AS NOT NULL ,
    [ProductID] [int] NOT NULL
) ON [PRIMARY]
GO


ALTER TABLE [dbo].[CustProd] WITH NOCHECK ADD
    CONSTRAINT [PK_CustProd] PRIMARY KEY  CLUSTERED
    (
        [CustomerID],
        [ProductID]
    )  ON [PRIMARY]
GO
```

```
Insert Into CustProd Values ('ALFKI',1)
Insert Into CustProd Values ('ALFKI',2)
Insert Into CustProd Values ('ALFKI',3)
Insert Into CustProd Values ('ALFKI',4)
Insert Into CustProd Values ('ALFKI',5)
GO
```

Here you are creating a simple table named CustProd, which, in effect, joins the Customers and Products tables. You don't create the relationships between the tables because you want to keep the example simple. After creating the table and a primary key, you are going to add five records to the new table. These records show the customer with a CustomerID of ALFKI likes products 1–5.

Now, in the Stateless application, create a new ASP called CustPreferences.asp. This file will be the page that shows a particular customer's favorite items and the quantity in stock. Enter the following code into the ASP:

```
<%@ Language=VBScript %>
<HTML>
<BODY>

<%
Dim sName
Dim cn
Dim rs
Dim sSQL
Dim vRecords
Dim x

If Request.Form("txtUserName")<>"" Then
    Response.Cookies("UserName")=Request.Form("txtUserName")
    Response.Cookies("UserName").Expires=Now()+30
End If
sName=Request.Cookies("UserName")
If sName="" Then
%>
    <FORM Name="frmCookie" Action="CustPreferences.asp" Method="post">
        User Name: <INPUT Name="txtUserName"><br>
        <INPUT Type="submit">
    </FORM>
```

```
<%
else
        Set cn=Server.CreateObject("ADODB.Connection")
        cn.Open "Provider=SQLOLEDB;Password=;User ID=sa;" & _
            "Initial Catalog=Northwind;Data Source=laptop;"
        sSQL="Select ProductName, UnitsInStock from Products, CustProd " & _
            "Where CustProd.ProductID=Products.ProductID and " & _
            "CustProd.CustomerID='" & sName & "'"
        set rs=cn.Execute (sSQL,,adCmdText)
        vRecords=rs.GetRows
%>
Welcome, <% =sName %>, here are your favorite products:
<TABLE Border="1">
        <TR>
            <TH>Product</TH>
            <TH>Inventory</TH>
        </TR>
        <% For x=0 to Ubound(vRecords,2) %>
        <TR>
            <TD><% =vRecords(0,x) %></TD>
            <TD><% =vRecords(1,x) %></TD>
        </TR>
        <% Next %>
    </TABLE>
<%
End If
%>
</BODY>
</HTML>
```

This ASP does several things. First, it looks to see if the user has
sent up a value in a text box. If he has, the ASP saves the value to a
cookie on the client machine. If the user hasn't passed up a value, the
ASP goes and looks for a value in the cookie. If no value is found, the
ASP displays a simple form that asks the user to enter a User Name.
After the user enters the name, you save that name out to the cookie.
Now, when the page checks, the page does find the value in the
cookie, and it uses that value to query the CustProd table, joined to
the Products table, and pulls back the product names and number of
units in stock for the products this person has identified.

Load this ASP in IE. You should be prompted to enter a username. Enter ALFKI and press the Submit button. You should now see a page similar to that in Figure 15-2. So far, there isn't anything spectacular. Close the browser (and, if you're a skeptic, feel free to reboot your machine). Open the browser again and reload the page. Using the cookie, the ASP should automatically log you in and show your products to you. How? The Web application has stored those preferences in a database. In fact, you can go to another machine, enter ALFKI when prompted, and see those same values.

Storing preferences across time is usually done on the server side, although it can be done on the client. In this case, you have a totally sessionless application that can still store state information, thanks to a database. Storing the information in a database gives you the capability to remember preferences across time and across different machines.

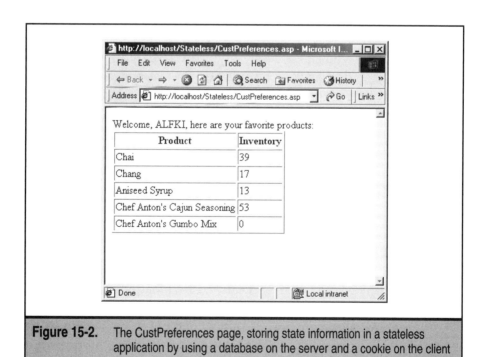

Figure 15-2.   The CustPreferences page, storing state information in a stateless application by using a database on the server and a cookie on the client

But, what if my client doesn't support cookies?

All modern browsers support cookies, but they also let the user choose not to accept cookies. If the user chooses, for whatever reason, not to accept cookies, what can you do? The only real answer, of course, is to use hidden fields.

Sticking with the previous example, let's look at how you would handle this in a cookieless environment as well. First, the user would always see the box asking her for a username because the cookie would never exist. Second, you would use that username in the query without asking for it from the cookie, like this:

```
sName=Request.Form("UserName")
```

And then, when the page was rendered, you would add a line like this:

```
<INPUT Type="Hidden" Name="UserName" Value="<% =sName %>">
```

This line would have to be put into each page, so the username is passed back to the server with each request. This is nothing new, but it shows you can use the standard HTML hidden fields to maintain state on the client, if the client doesn't accept cookies. This can not only be helpful for creating stateless applications, but you can also use this approach in other places. This is a great debugging technique because you can view the source and see what the variable values were when the page was generated.

Load Testing

How will your application perform under heavy loads? Can it handle 5,000 simultaneous users banging away on the pages? Where are the bottlenecks? Most important, how can you test this?

Microsoft provides a tool called the *Web Application Stress* (*WAS*) tool. This tool is free and can be downloaded from Microsoft at http://webtool.rte.microsoft.com/. This tool enables you to simulate many users from one client machine to test your application's performance under heavy loads. The tool not only runs test scripts, but it can also record performance statistics of the database server using the Windows 2000 performance monitor (a piece of which is built into WAS.)

WAS enables you to record an interactive session with your application as you work with it in IE. You can then modify the script, of course. You can simulate a large number of users and, if you want, each can log in with a different username and password (more on security later in this chapter). These simulated users can fill out forms, retrieve data, and perform other functions. You can monitor the responsiveness of IIS, the ASPs, and SQL Server. When the test is over, you can look at statistics and see how many times each page was requested, the average load time of each page, and how many HTTP errors (404 file not found, and so on) you received. You can watch the WAS monitor during the test to see any of the statistics you are used to viewing with the Performance Monitor.

WAS has some other great features. You can run tests from a number of client machines, but have them all controlled by, and reporting their results to, one master client. You can throttle the bandwidth to simulate modem access. You can even create your own VB/VBScript applications to run and customize tests.

Using WAS, you can determine how scalable your application is. If, under heavy loads, you notice the same pages timing out over and over, you know you must go in and tune those particular pages. If you notice overall response time slows down too much under heavy loads, you may need to add servers to an NLB cluster, up the horsepower on the database server, and so on depending on where you see the problems. Overall, WAS can be a valuable tool for validating the performance of your application under a variety of loads.

WEB SITE ENCRYPTION

When it comes to security, you should know about two kinds: encryption and application security. Let's start with *encryption*, which is the process of scrambling the data on one end and unscrambling it on the other end to keep it safe. Web users don't want to see their credit card numbers stolen any more than anyone else, so encryption algorithms are used to make transferring data across the Internet safe.

You should also know about *Secure Sockets Layer* (*SSL*) technology, both how it works and how you can use it with your Web applications. A nice benefit of SSL is it operates at a lower level than your applications, so the encryption is being done for you after you generate the HTML stream, but before it's sent to the client. This means you needn't change any of the code in your application.

Encryption and SSL

Encryption is simply a means to scramble data on one end and unscramble it on the other. Encryption software uses mathematical functions to modify the data into an unreadable form, using a key. This key is what tells the formula exactly how to scramble the data. When the scrambled data arrives at its destination, another key is used to unscramble the data and reassemble the original message. Many of these encryption algorithms are public knowledge; knowing the formula doesn't help you crack the encrypted messages.

When I talk about the keys used to determine how to scramble and unscramble the data, size equals strength. The bigger the key, the longer it would take to break the message using a brute-force attack (trying every possible combination). The keys used are measured in bits, and each bit increase doubles the strength of the key. Currently, a 128-bit key is considered secure because it would take so long to break with the brute-force method, the message would probably be worthless by the time the message was broken. Understand that this changes over time; as processors get faster and faster, it takes less and less time to break a key of a particular size, so larger and larger keys are needed as the hardware progresses.

The U.S. government regulates key size. It classifies encryption as munitions, so exporting keys that are "too powerful" is considered arms smuggling. You may have seen sites that offer 128-bit versions of certain software and you have to promise you don't live in certain countries deemed unfriendly to the United States.

Symmetric Cryptography

Cryptography is the science of codes. For this book, I say encryption software uses cryptographic techniques to encrypt and decrypt data. This may be oversimplified, or some people may have different opinions on the meanings of the words, but this definition will suffice for this book.

Symmetric cryptography is easy to understand: the same key is used both to encrypt and to decrypt a message. For example, imagine you want to create a secret code and do so by shuffling around the letters of the alphabet, so *A* is replaced by *R*, *B* is replaced by *K*, and so forth. If you wanted to send a note to another person, the phrase "Buy this book" might appear as "Kal smqe knnz."

The recipient of this message would have to decode (or decrypt) it using the same key you used to encrypt it. He would have to know that a *K* is really a *B*, and an *N* is really an *O*, and so forth. In other words, he uses the same key to decrypt the message that you used to encrypt the message. Figure 15-3 shows what symmetric cryptography looks like.

Symmetric cryptography is easy to understand, and it's easy to implement in computer algorithms. Unfortunately, two major problems occur with symmetric cryptography:

▼ You must get the key safely to the other party, meaning no one else can see it while it's in transit.

▲ You must be sure the other party won't share the key with anyone else.

Because the key must be kept secret, symmetric cryptography is often called *secret key cryptography*. This means the key used to generate encrypted messages must be kept secret because it's the same key used to decrypt the messages at the other end. Therefore, symmetric encryption isn't enough, by itself, to make the Web secure for sensitive information. It's used as part of SSL, but not before some other things happen first.

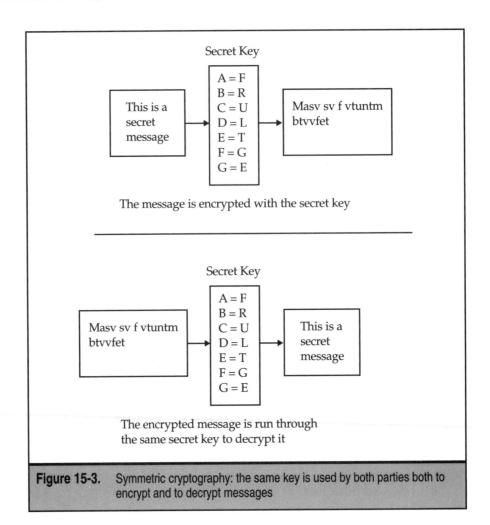

Figure 15-3.   Symmetric cryptography: the same key is used by both parties both to encrypt and to decrypt messages

Asymmetric Cryptography

To get around the two problems you saw with symmetric cryptography, let's examine another technique: asymmetric cryptography. *Asymmetric cryptography* is a little harder to picture because a pair of keys are generated. One key is the public key and the other key is the private key. The public key is just that: public. You can publish the public key on your Web page, include it at the bottom of an e-mail, and let anyone, anywhere, see it. The private key, on the other hand, is never given to anyone.

The reason you can let anyone see your public key is, even if someone uses it to encrypt a message for you, the public key cannot decrypt that message! Even the person who creates the message for you and encrypts it with your public key cannot decrypt it. The only person in the world who can decrypt that message is the holder of private key generated as part of the pair of keys. The public key encrypts the message, and then the private key decrypts it.

Because the public key cannot decrypt messages it encrypts, it's safe to share with the entire world. This gets around the two problems you can have with symmetric cryptography because you needn't worry about getting the key to them without others seeing it, and anyone who has the key is free to share it with anyone else.

To carry out a two-way conversation with asymmetric cryptography, both parties must generate their own public key/private key pairs, and then give each other their public keys. For example, if Alex and Torrey wanted to carry out a secure conversation using asymmetric cryptography, both Alex and Torrey would generate a public key/private key pair. Alex would give a copy of his public key to Torrey, and Torrey would give Alex a copy of her public key. If Alex wants to send Torrey a message, he creates the message, and then encrypts it with Torrey's public key. At this point, no one, including Alex, can decrypt the message, unless that person has the matching private key. Because Torrey is the only one with the private key that complements her public key, she is the only one who can decrypt the message. When the message arrives at Torrey's computer, she uses her private key to decrypt the message. After she creates her reply, she encrypts it with Alex's public key. Now, Alex is the only one who can decrypt the message. Figure 15-4 shows how asymmetric cryptography works, where Alex is using Torrey's public key to encrypt messages for her, and Torrey is using Alex's public key to encrypt messages for him.

Is there any bad news to asymmetric cryptography? Of course— the usual complaint—it's slower than symmetric cryptography. Encryption of any kind slows Web applications because the packets must be encrypted before they are sent, and then decrypted when they're received. Asymmetric cryptography is typically much slower than symmetric cryptography, in computer terms.

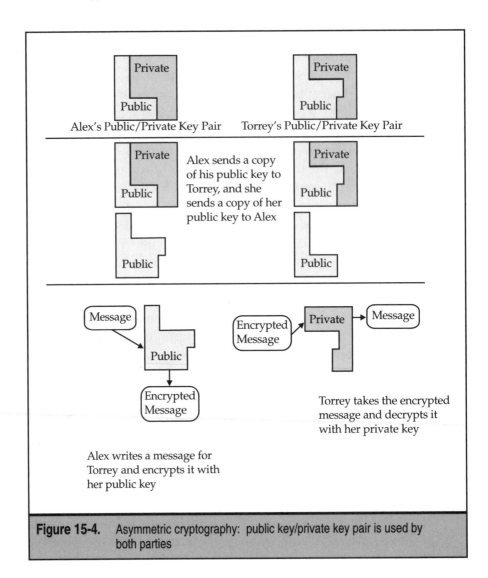

Figure 15-4.   Asymmetric cryptography: public key/private key pair is used by both parties

Digital Signatures

Another use of asymmetric cryptography exists, which is this: it enables digital signatures. If you have lain awake at night worrying about how digital signatures work, fret no longer. Digital signatures are basically a reversal of roles for the public and private keys. If Alex wants to sign something electronically, he encrypts it with his private key. Anyone, anywhere in the world, with his public key can decrypt the message and verify that Alex is the creator. Only Alex has the private key that is coupled with his public key, so if the signature can be properly decrypted with his public key, it had to come from the private key, which means Alex created it. Digital signatures are also used in SSL as a way to verify you are talking to the intended server.

How SSL Works

Now that you know about symmetric and asymmetric cryptography, as well as digital signatures, you can learn how SSL works. I won't go into all the details, but I want to give you a high-level view so you can understand what happens every time you connect to a Web server using encryption.

First, your browser makes a request. Instead of using the standard HTTP protocol, secure communications uses HTTPS, or Secure HTTP. You might not have noticed, but when you access a secure site, the URL in your browser starts with https://. When you try to connect to a secure site, the site responds with what is called a *digital certificate,* which ties a particular company (or individual) to its public key. These certificates are granted by companies called *Certificate Authorities* (CA) and are your assurance these are legitimate businesses.

NOTE: Don't trust every CA by default. In IE, if you click Tools, Internet Options, and then the Content tab, you see a Certificates area. In that area, click the Certificates button, and then click the Trusted Root CA tab. This is a list of the CA your browser already trusts. Two of the biggest are VeriSign (http://www.verisign.com) and Thawte (http://www.thawte.com).

The digital certificate presents you with the server's public key and some other information to make you feel good. As a natural skeptic, however, you decide the certificate is not good enough. Yes, you now have the server's public key, but anyone can get a copy of that. The server also had the digital certificate, but maybe that was stolen. So, you challenge the server to prove it is who it says it is.

The server now generates a random message and sends it to you. It then encrypts a message digest of the random message and sends it to you. A *message digest* is similar to a checksum of the message; it is a one-way algorithm that creates a mathematical summary of the message. The digest is then encrypted with what? The server's private key. So you, as the client, decrypt the encrypted digest with the server's public key (so right now, it's acting like a digital signature). You had the original random data, and now you have a decrypted digest of the random data. You run your own message digest algorithm on the original random data. Finally, you compare your message digest on the original data with the message digest you decrypted from the server. If they match, you know the server has the private key that matches the public key you were sent, and you can feel confident you are talking to the site, and not some phony site.

After you are convinced you are talking to the real server, you, as the client, generate a secret key. If you are saying, "Secret key? That's symmetric cryptography," then go to the head of the class. Remember the two problems with symmetric cryptography? You generate a secret key, and then you encrypt it with the server's public key. Now, who is the only person in the world who can decrypt it? The server is the only one that can decrypt this secret key because the server holds the private key and uses this private key to decrypt the message holding the secret key. You have the same secret key at both the client and server. Did you get it there safely? Yes, because it was encrypted with the server's public key. Is the server going to share it with anyone? No, because the secret key is only stored in memory on both the client and server. After you close this session on the server or close the browser on the client, this secret key will be gone. You then encrypt all messages going both directions using this secret key.

Why is a secret key created? In other words, why do you revert to symmetric cryptography? Simple: symmetric cryptography is faster than asymmetric cryptography. You got around those two problems you had earlier with symmetric cryptography by sending the secret key using asymmetric cryptography. You could continue using asymmetric cryptography, but symmetric is just as safe (now) and it's faster. Figure 15-5 shows this process in action.

Setting Up SSL in IIS 5.0

To set up SSL in IIS 5.0, you need to request a certificate from a CA, and then install that certificate on your Web server. Then, you need to set up an application to use that certificate. The bad news is a

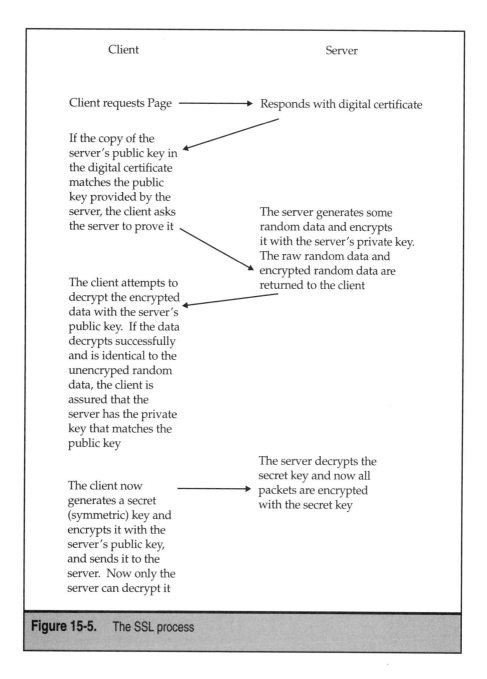

Figure 15-5. The SSL process

number of steps are involved in the process. The good news is no coding changes are required in the application.

NOTE: When I talk about obtaining a certificate from a Certificate Authority, you might wonder if you need Certificate Server loaded in Windows 2000. You don't. Certificate Server would actually let you create your own certificates, and because anyone can create certificates, you don't want your browser automatically accepting certificates. Certificate Server is well beyond the scope of this book.

The First Step: Creating the Key Request

To begin the process of setting up SSL on your server, you have to request a certificate from a CA. To do this, start the Internet Information Services manager and expand the node for your computer. Right-click the node for Default Web Site and choose Properties, and then click the tab for Directory Security. You see three sections, as shown in Figure 15-6. You want the Secure communications section, so click the Server Certificate button. This starts the Web Server Certificate Wizard. The first screen of the wizard is a welcome screen; go ahead and click the Next button.

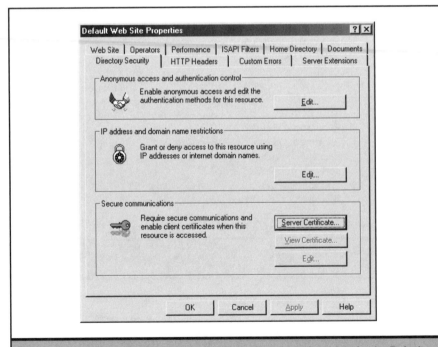

Figure 15-6. The Directory Security tab of the Properties dialog box for the Default Web Site

NOTE: Make sure you right-click and choose Properties for the Default Web Site. If you try this for any of the virtual directories, the Server Certificate button will be disabled.

The first real screen of the Web Server Certificate Wizard shows three choices, as you can see in Figure 15-7. For now, you are creating a new certificate, so leave the first choice selected. After clicking the Next button, the next screen, shown in Figure 15-8, asks if you want to do a delayed or an immediate request. The delayed request creates the request in a file you can use to make the request to a CA, so choose the first option (the second may be disabled, as it is in Figure 15-8).

After clicking the Next button again, you are prompted to name your certificate. You can name your certificate anything you want, as I did in Figure 15-9. You are also asked to choose a bit length. Notice, the larger the key, the more secure it is. As you can imagine, however, the larger the key is, the slower your performance will be. You already know that encryption of any kind slows down the application, so it's always going to be a tradeoff of security and

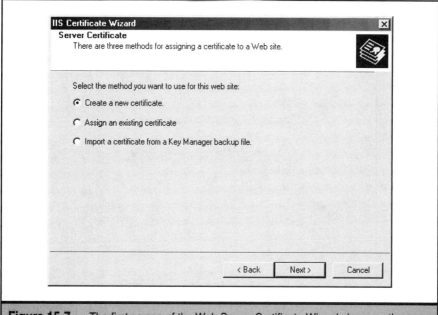

Figure 15-7.   The first screen of the Web Server Certificate Wizard gives you three choices for adding a certificate to your site

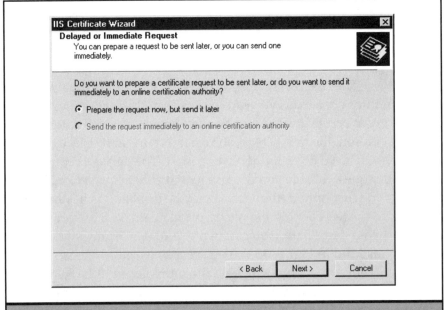

Figure 15-8. The next screen asks if you want to make an immediate or a delayed request

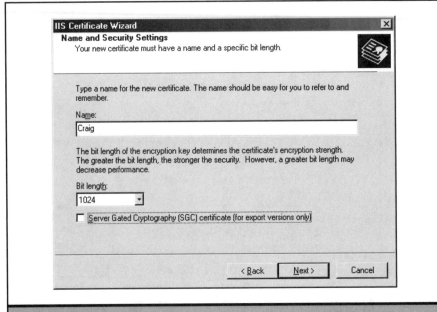

Figure 15-9. The Web Server Certificate Wizard asks you to name the certificate and pick a bit size for the encryption key

speed. Not many people are willing to give you their credit card numbers without any security on the site, but they won't be able to give you their credit card numbers if your site keeps timing out! Once you name the certificate and choose a bit size for the key, click the Next button to advance.

The next screen asks you for your Organization and your Organizational Unit. These values end up being stored as part of the certificate, so make them reasonable, as I did in Figure 15-10. Other than having these values as part of the certificate, there's nothing magical about the values you choose here. When you've made your entries, click the Next button.

The next screen asks for your site's common name: this is where you must be careful. If the site is on the Internet, this should be your common DNS name (such as www.osborne.com) and, if it is on an intranet, the common name should be the name of the server. In Figure 15-11, you can see I set the common name to that of my server. The common name should be the DNS name of your server for Internet servers, or the server name for intranet servers. If the

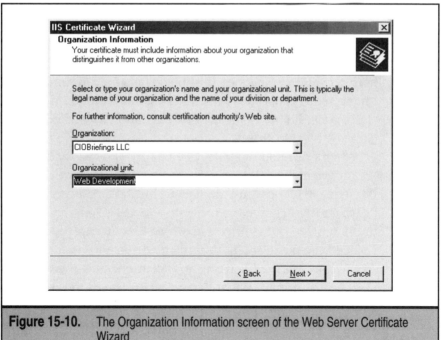

Figure 15-10.   The Organization Information screen of the Web Server Certificate Wizard

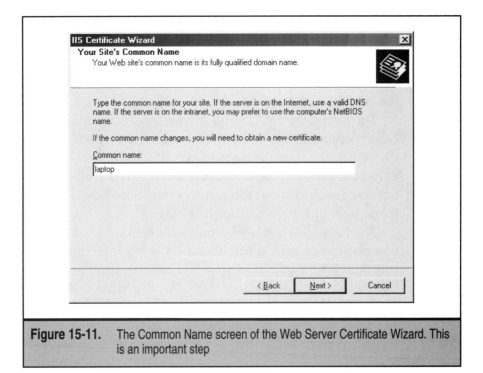

Figure 15-11.   The Common Name screen of the Web Server Certificate Wizard. This is an important step

server name changes later, I would have to create a new certificate. Go ahead and fill in the common name and hit the Next button.

The Geographical Information screen of the wizard is next. Be careful here, as well: you cannot abbreviate, as you can see in Figure 15-12. I have seen certificates fail to perform if the person abbreviates the state name. Fill in the Country, State, and City information, and then click the Next button.

After a number of steps, you're almost done with the key request creation. The final screen asks you for the filename in which to store the request. Choose any name and location you prefer, but realize it'll be easier if you leave the file with a ".txt" extension because the file that's written out is only a text file. As you can see in Figure 15-13, I placed the file in the root of my C: drive and named it "craig.txt." After choosing the file name and location, click the Next button and you see a summary page. Verify the information is correct, and then click the Next button. Finally, you are on the final, see you later screen and you can click the Finish button.

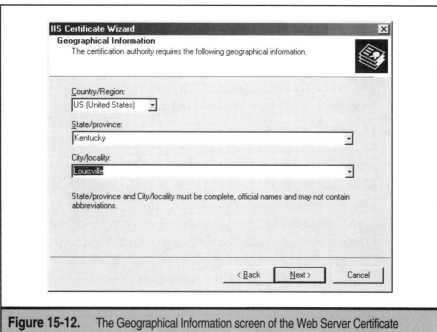

Figure 15-12.   The Geographical Information screen of the Web Server Certificate Wizard. Be careful here: you cannot abbreviate any of the names

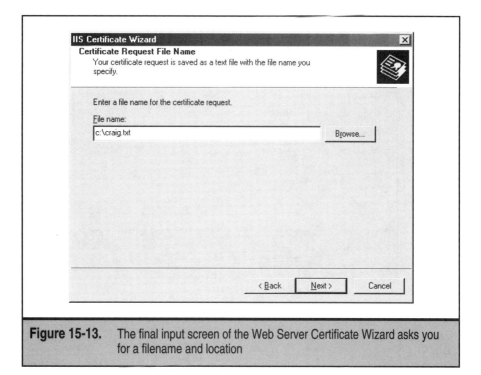

Figure 15-13.   The final input screen of the Web Server Certificate Wizard asks you for a filename and location

If you now open the text file you created, you can see what a key request looks like. This is pretty much what a key looks like. Believe it or not, that block of text has most of the information you entered while using the Web Server Certificate Wizard. Figure 15-14 shows you what my key request looks like. What you want to do now is copy the entire block of text into the clipboard because you're going to paste it into a Web page soon.

The Second Step: Requesting a Certificate

Now that you've created a certificate request, you need to obtain a certificate. Several CAs offer temporary certificates (with no assurances) for testing purposes. I'm using VeriSign for this one, but this isn't an endorsement for any one company over another.

In IE, I'm going to http://www.verisign.com. VeriSign changes its site frequently, so I always look for the word "free." At press time,

Figure 15-14. The Key Request, stored in a text file. You must copy that block of text and paste it into a Web page to get a certificate

a link to free trials for a Web server certificate is on VeriSign's home page. After filling out some information, you are taken into a series of screens. First, you are asked to generate a *Certificate Signing Request* (*CSR*). This is what Microsoft calls *a key request* and it's what you just did in the previous section. Paste your key request into the designated area as shown in Figure 15-15, and then click the Next button (or image, in this case).

After entering your key request, the site pulls most of the information back out, such as the Common Name, Organizational Unit, and so on. You are then asked to enter a number of other fields, such as your name, address, and other contact information. Make sure you get the e-mail address right because your certificate is e-mailed to you. After you enter the required information, read the legal information carefully (I'm sure you will), and then click the Accept button. This is shown in Figure 15-16.

The Third Step: Installing the Certificate

VeriSign will now mail you a certificate that you can install on the Web server. When the e-mail arrives, the certificate is included in it and will look similar to your key request. The way to install the certificate is, once again, to right-click the Default Web Site node in the Internet Information Services manager, choose Properties, and then select the Directory Security tab. Now, click the Server Certificate button again and, after passing the welcome screen, your next page will be the Pending Certificate Request screen, as seen in Figure 15-17. You want the first option, which installs the pending certificate. Click the Next button.

The next screen asks you to enter the filename and path of the file holding the certificate. VeriSign sent you an e-mail, so copy only the lines in the e-mail that are actually the certificate and paste them into a new text document. For example, I am opening Notepad, pasting in the certificate, and saving the file as c:\cert.txt, as you

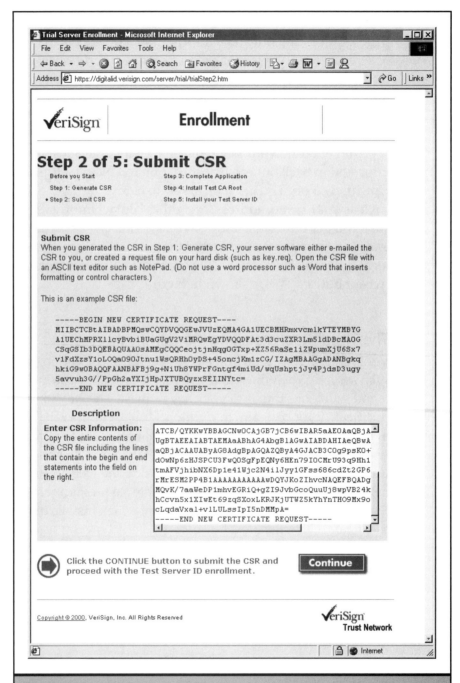

Figure 15-15. Entering your certificate request on the VeriSign site

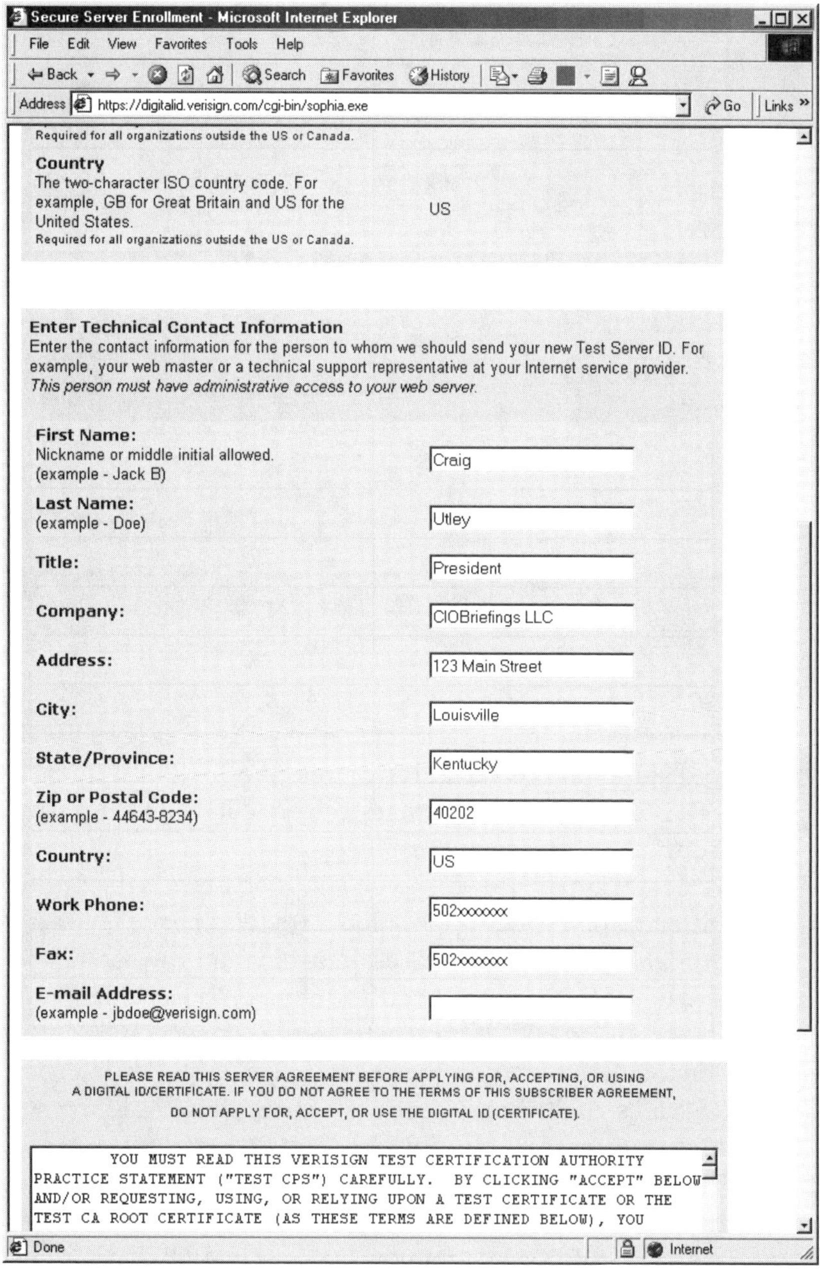

Figure 15-16. The VeriSign certificate process requires you to enter contact information to fulfill the certificate request

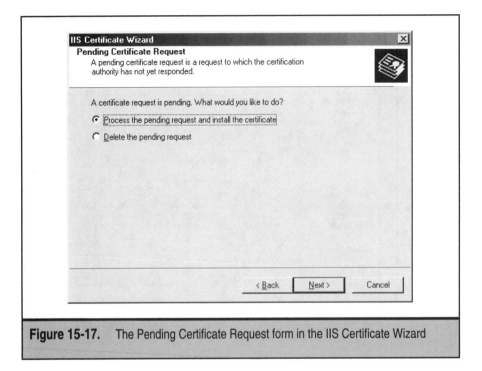

Figure 15-17.   The Pending Certificate Request form in the IIS Certificate Wizard

can see in Figure 15-18. Back in the wizard, choose the file where you stored the certificate and press the Next button.

After seeing the summary screen, click Next and then click Finish. Your certificate is now installed.

How do you use SSL now? The good news is the certificate is installed for all your applications. You don't have to use it, but it is available. Try entering this address in your browser but, be careful, and notice the protocol is HTTPS: https://localhost/adotest/callsp.asp. By specifying HTTPS, you get a secure connection. When you try to connect, however, you receive the warning shown in Figure 15-19. This tells you the browser doesn't trust this CA. Remember, the test certificate is for testing only and doesn't contain any assurances. Therefore, the browser cannot verify the site is safe. It's possible to download a small file from VeriSign that tells your browser to trust the test certificate but, for now, just put up with the warning message. We know the site is safe, so click Yes.

Figure 15-18.   The certificate in a text file. More will be in the e-mail that comes back, but copy this code and save it in a file

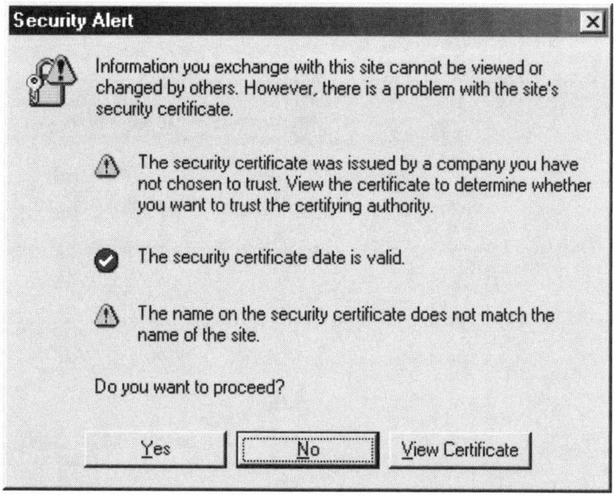

Figure 15-19.   The warning dialog box that says you are trying to connect to a secure site that cannot be verified as safe

NOTE: If you do not get this warning message box, your browser security may be set too high. Click on the Tools menu and choose Internet Options. On the Security tab, lower your security to Medium or Medium-low and you should be able to run this demonstration.

Once you click Yes to go ahead and communicate with this site, the page loads as it always did, but the packets came to you encrypted and you decrypted them on your end. You can tell you are connected to a secure site not only by the "https:" in the address bar, but also by the gold lock that appears in the status bar. The browser, with the page loaded in it and the gold lock in the status bar, can be seen in Figure 15-20.

The way this is set up now, you can access a virtual directory with or without a secure connection. You could simply remove the *s* from https and connect to the site without a secure connection. But what if you want to force a secure connection? To do this, you must choose an option on the particular virtual directory. Right-click the ADOTest virtual directory in the Internet Information Services manager and choose Properties. Three buttons are in the Secure

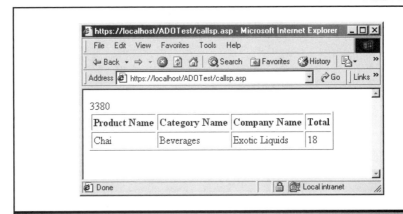

Figure 15-20. The CallSP.asp loaded into the browser using SSL. Notice the address starts with "https:" and a lock icon is in the status bar

communications area on the Directory Security tab. These three buttons are disabled unless you have already installed a certificate, which you just did. Click the Edit button, and a Secure Communications dialog box appears, as show in Figure 15-21. The first check box asks if you want to require a secure connection (using SSL). Check this box. Don't worry about the 128-bit box, as you may or may not have 128-bit support on your machine. Click the OK button and then click the OK button to close the Properties dialog box. A new dialog box appears, showing a series of folders under your virtual directory, and asking which of those folders should inherit the new security settings you created. In this situation, it doesn't matter, so click the OK button on this dialog box.

Now, try to open http://laptop/adotest/callsp.asp (notice this isn't using HTTPS). You set the application to accept only secure communications and attempts to connect to it using only HTTP result

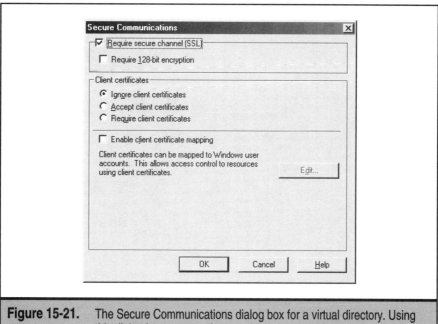

Figure 15-21.   The Secure Communications dialog box for a virtual directory. Using this dialog box, you can force a site to accept only secure connections

in an error, as seen in Figure 15-22. If you change the address to https://laptop/adotest/callsp.asp, however, you can connect with no problems.

You set up secure communications with your Web server and you didn't have to make any code changes to take advantage of encryption. Now people can feel comfortable sending you their credit card information, trading their stocks through your service, or whatever you're trying to accomplish.

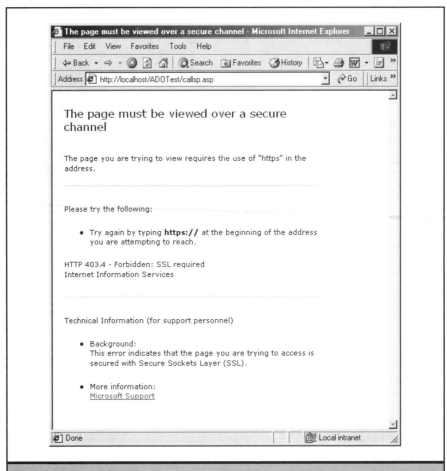

Figure 15-22.   Attempting to connect to a secure site with the standard HTTP protocol results in this error message in IE

APPLICATION SECURITY

Here's a news flash: IIS is integrated with Windows 2000. Okay, that probably didn't surprise you much, but it means, among other things, you can limit access to the files in your Web application. This means you can restrict certain files to certain people or, more often, to members of specific Windows 2000 groups. Instead of securing only individual files, you can secure entire applications to be used only by certain users, which is more often the case. These user permissions can flow into the components and, if you want, on to the database. The good news is you have a lot of places to apply security, but this can be a two-edged sword: I've seen people tie themselves in knots trying to apply too much security, scattered all over every corner of their application.

When I discuss security, I'm not talking about SSL. You can have SSL in the loop or not; it doesn't really matter, except when you send the username and password. This is discussed in more detail in the next section.

Logging In

Although I haven't discussed this yet, every Web application in this book has had you logging in to run the application. You haven't noticed it because all your applications so far have enabled anonymous access and they have also been set to use Windows authentication. Either one of those is enough for you now. Just understand that Windows 2000 doesn't want anyone on the system who hasn't logged in, just like most operating systems. Therefore, even anonymous users have to log in.

Most Web sites, of course, don't require you to enter a username and password to use them. The Web sites you've built so far don't require the user to log in explicitly but, behind the scenes, IIS is logging them in. By default, the username under which an anonymous Web user logs in is IUSR_<servername>, so on my main machine for this book, the user is IUSR_laptop.

It's possible to force the user to log in with an actual NT userid and password, and it's also possible to have the user's token passed to the Web server so she can be automatically logged in under her already existing context. You can see that setting in a moment, but realize that, for this to work, the client browser must be Internet Explorer.

To see these various choices to force someone to log in, let's use the Internet Information Services manager to right-click the Stateless virtual directory and choose Properties. Now, return to the Directory Security tab. The first section on this tab is labeled Anonymous access and authentication control. Click the edit button to open the authentication methods dialog box shown in Figure 15-23. Notice that, by default, the Anonymous access and Integrated Windows authentication boxes are checked, and the Basic authentication box is not checked. In this screenshot, Digest authentication is disabled. Let's examine what each one means:

▼ **Anonymous access** Anyone can use this application. The user is actually logging in as IUSR_<servername> without realizing it. The user doesn't have to enter a username or password. Any browser can use this authentication method.

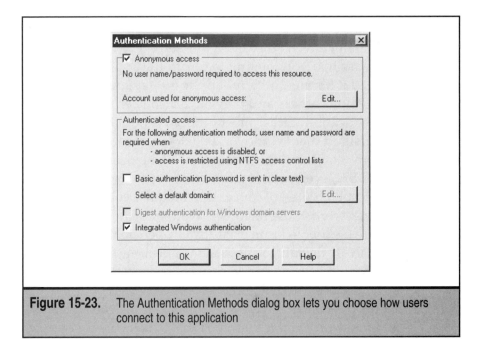

Figure 15-23. The Authentication Methods dialog box lets you choose how users connect to this application

- **Basic authentication** Basic authentication forces a user to log in using a username and password. The information is sent as clear text, however, which means anyone watching the packets could view the username and password as long as they move across the Internet. Nearly any browser can use this authentication method. The username used must be a valid Windows 2000 user.

- **Digest authentication** Like Basic, Digest can be used by most browsers, and it prompts the user for a username and password. Digest, however, encrypts the password with a one-way hash algorithm. The drawback is that a clear-text version of the password must exist on the server. Digest has the advantage of being able to work across proxy servers and firewalls. This feature is only available in IIS 5.0. The user name used must be a valid Windows 2000 user.

- ▲ **Integrated Windows authentication** Integrated authentication works by performing a cryptographic exchange between the browser, which must be IE, and the server, which must be IIS 5.0. The user isn't prompted for a username and password because this is done automatically for you. While secure, Integrated authentication doesn't work over proxy servers.

Notice that, by default, both Anonymous access and Integrated Windows authentication are on. Either works fine for your applications so far, but let's turn off both Anonymous and Integrated authentication, and turn on Basic. When you turn on Basic authentication, you get a warning that you will be sending the information as clear text. As you can imagine, this can be a problem because you are having people transmit their passwords in an unencrypted manner. If your site is using SSL, then the packet containing the password will be encrypted, and that will cover you here. Don't worry about this for now, though. In the Stateless application, you have turned on Basic authentication only. Click the OK button to close out the dialog boxes and, in the browser, call up the

CustPreferences.asp (http://localhost/stateless/custpreferences.asp). You receive a box asking you to log in, which is something you haven't seen before. Figure 15-24 shows you the standard username and password box, which appears when you choose either Basic or Digest authentication. Enter your username and password and press OK. The CustPreferences page should load normally. You have now been validated against the server and you can now use the application normally.

Why might you want to force people to log in, using either Basic, Digest, or Integrated authentication? Imagine you have an intranet site that has some human resources pages, and one of those pages lets you change someone's salary. You can bet if you left this page accessible to just anyone, eventually some of the employees would be making large salaries. So, you might want to restrict certain pages to certain individuals.

Setting Individual Page Permissions

You can restrict individual pages simply by setting the file permissions in the directory using standard Windows 2000 permissions. You can restrict any file to individual users, or users in particular groups. For example, with the salary update page, you could restrict it to use by members of a Senior Managers group.

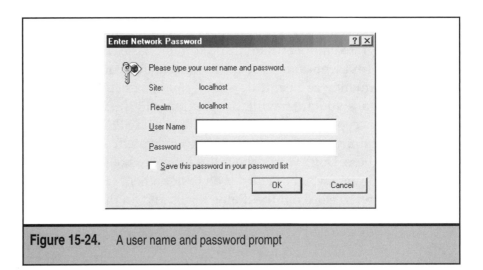

Figure 15-24. A user name and password prompt

To see how to change the permissions on any particular file, simply use the Windows Explorer to find the file, right-click it, and choose Properties. There is a Security tab on the Properties dialog box, shown in Figure 15-25. Here, you can add and remove the users and groups that have access to any file, and the permissions they have to that file. This way, you can control which users have access to which files in your application.

NOTE: To set per-file permissions, you must be using NTFS as your file system. NTFS has many other advantages as well; most people using Windows 2000 are using NTFS already. If you aren't, you should consider moving to NTFS.

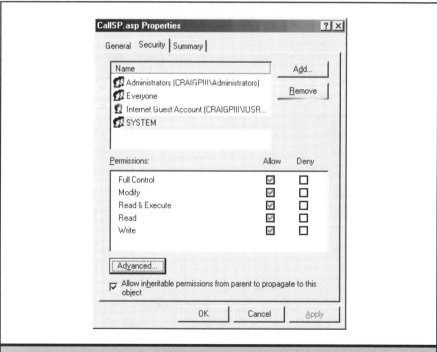

Figure 15-25.   The Security Properties for the Call.asp file. You can use these settings to control access to the individual files in your Web application

Notice in Figure 15-25 that the Internet Guest Account (IUSR_<servername>) has permissions to this file. If you remove the Internet Guest Account, you must use something other than Anonymous authentication for this application. If you leave Anonymous authentication turned on, all users will log in as the IUSR_<servername> user, and they won't be able to run this file.

COM+ Component Security

In the previous two chapters, you built COM+ components, and then integrated them into COM+ Component Services. Handling component security before MTS/Component Services wasn't a lot of fun, requiring the permissions to be set through DCOM or coded into the component. Now, Component Services provides a security framework for you, with role-based security that (surprise!) ties into Windows 2000 security.

COM+ Application and Component Security

Open the Component Services manager and expand the nodes so you can see the NWind application you created earlier. Right-click NWind and choose Properties. Under the Security tab, notice the first section, labeled Authorization, doesn't have a check in the Enforce access checks for this application box, as you can see in Figure 15-26. By default, security is turned off on a COM+ application, which means anyone can have access to it. Remember, COM+ applications represent both a process boundary and a security boundary. With security, the access check is performed when the user makes a call to any component in the COM+ application. Check this box to turn on security for the NWind application. Two options exist for the security level. The first simply checks security when the user makes a call into the application. Security isn't checked again at the component level, which means you cannot check security information from the ObjectContext object associated with an individual object. The default is to perform checks at the application and component level, and pass the necessary security information to the ObjectContext object. Leave this as it is, and click the OK button.

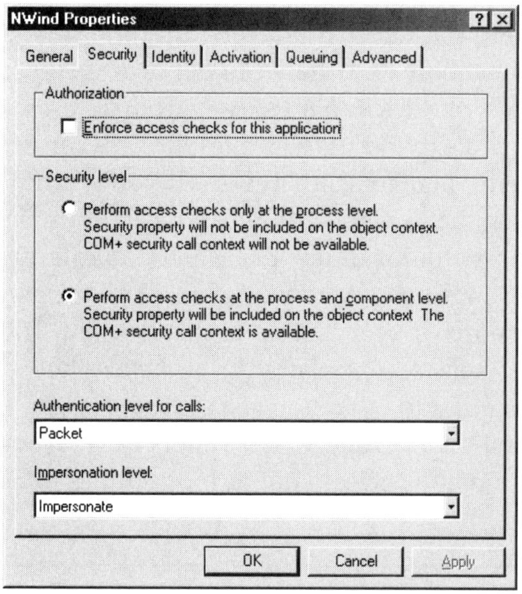

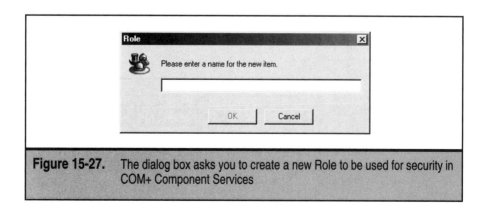

Figure 15-26. The Security tab of the NWind Properties dialog box. By default, security is turned off at the COM+ application level

Security is turned on, but you don't have any roles defined yet. In the Component Services manager, if you expand the NWind application, you can see a Roles folder under it. Left-click the Roles folder, and then right-click it and choose New, Role. A dialog box like that shown in Figure 15-27 is presented, asking you to enter a

Figure 15-27. The dialog box asks you to create a new Role to be used for security in COM+ Component Services

name for the role. Enter the word Tellers and click OK. Now, create a second role called Managers. Assume you have certain duties at the bank that only Managers can perform, so you should segment your bank employees into these two groups.

If you expand the Roles folder, you can see the two roles you just created: Managers and Tellers. If you expand both of these, you can see each has a Users folder under it. Left-click and then right-click the Users folder under the Managers role, and choose New, User. This brings up a standard Users and Groups dialog box, showing the groups or users set up in this domain. To make things easy, simply select Administrators and click the Add button. It should look similar to what you see in Figure 15-28. Click OK and then add the Users group to the Tellers Role. When you finish, COM+ Component Services should look similar to Figure 15-29.

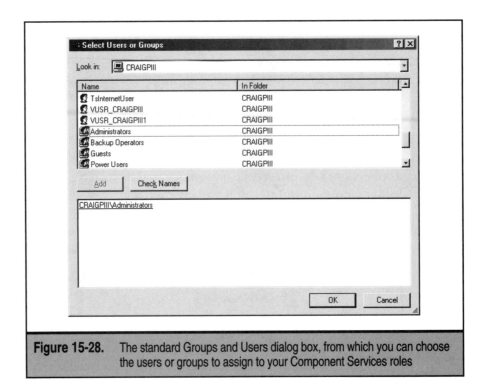

Figure 15-28. The standard Groups and Users dialog box, from which you can choose the users or groups to assign to your Component Services roles

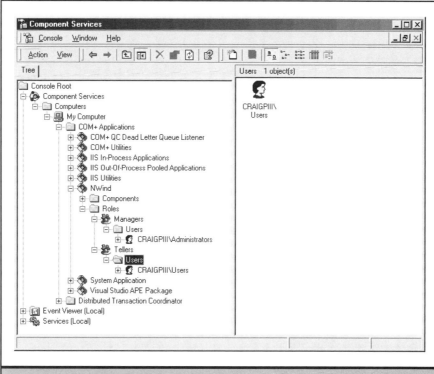

Figure 15-29.   The Component Services manager, showing your new roles and the users assigned to those roles

At this point, you have created two roles and assigned groups to them. You need to do one more thing: you need to assign permissions to the components in the application. Expand the NWind components folder and left-click, and then right-click the Banking.cCustomer component, choose Properties, and then click the Security tab. As Figure 15-30 shows you, the component participates in the access checks by default. This is the default setting for any component, but it's meaningless unless you turn security checks on for the application. Note that in this dialog box you see two roles, which happen to be the same two roles you just created. If you want to check only the Managers role, only people with a username who happen to belong to the Administrators group could run this component.

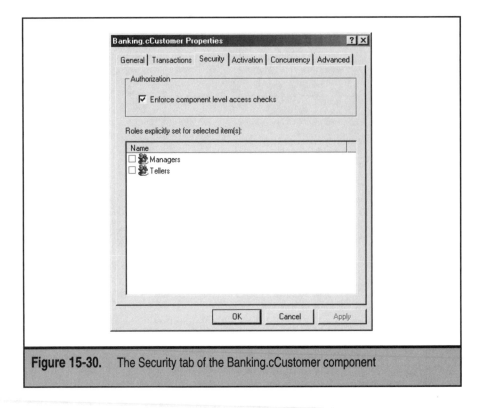

Figure 15-30. The Security tab of the Banking.cCustomer component

Now, imagine this component will be called over the Web. If you said that only people in the Administrators group can call the component, what type of security would your Web application need? Obviously, anonymous won't work, because the IUSR_<servername> isn't in the Administrators group. Therefore, you would have to use Basic, Digest, or Integrated security to get a "real" username and password from the user. If that user happens to be in the Administrators group, she could create an object from the cCustomer component. If she isn't in the Administrators group, her call would fail.

Component-to-Component Security

Assume you log in to a Web application with a user name that happens to be in the Administrators group, such as "HaileySpinoza."

You call the cCustomer component and pass the security checks. The cCustomer component calls the cBanking component, but what if cBanking is in another application entirely? Who does the application holding cBanking see as its caller? The cBanking application doesn't see "HaileySpinoza" as the caller but, instead, sees the application with cCustomer as the caller! Remember the discussion on the Identity of an application? Well, if you create a COM+ application and leave the identity as the default, the identity of any running COM+ application is the interactive user. If no one is logged on, though, there isn't an interactive user. Therefore, I recommended before that you make the identity a valid username and password. You need to do this for security reasons. You could create a new user for a particular COM+ application. You could then have other COM+ applications that only give rights to that user. In effect, you can create COM+ applications that can only be called by other COM+ applications and are unavailable to the outside world.

If your head is spinning, just remember this: You can check security every time you cross COM+ application boundaries. Therefore, if one application calls another, security will be checked in the called application. It will see the calling application as its caller and, therefore, the calling application must have the identity of a user who can see the called application.

Let's assume a user calls a component, named CompA, in COM+ application AppA. AppA has security turned on, but the user has all the necessary credentials, so you let them use CompA. CompA calls another component, CompB, in a different application, called AppB. When AppB is first accessed, it looks and sees CompA calling it. If CompA has an identity that has permissions to CompB, the call goes through to the component. Otherwise, the call fails. If you want to know, in CompB, who first called CompA, don't worry. You can identify that caller, as you see in a moment.

Method Security   You can set up role-based security all the way down the method level. If you expand a component, and then the Interfaces folder, and then the interface name that appears, there will be a Methods folder. Expand that and you can see all the methods in a component. Right-click a method and choose the Security tab, and you can assign roles all the way down to individual methods. For example, you could create a component that allows any user to add or remove items from inventory, but there might also be a method that lets you adjust inventory. Management is afraid if everyone can use the Adjust method, people will remove items, and then they'll adjust the inventory to cover the theft. Therefore, only people in certain roles can call the Adjust method.

How Do You Find out the Real Caller?   If you are down in CompB, you see AppA as your caller. What if, for auditing purposes, you want to know the "real" user who started this process? The ObjectContext object has a SecurityProperty object in it that you can access. You can make a call to this SecurityProperty object's GetOriginalCallerName or GetDirectCallerName methods to see exactly who the original caller was to the root object. This is true no matter how far down the chain you happen to be with your component. Don't use the old GetDirectCreatorName or GetOriginalCreatorName; these were used in MTS, but have unpredictable results in Component Services.

SQL Server Security

Entire chapters, or maybe even an entire book, can be written on SQL Server security. It wouldn't make for the most fascinating reading, but it is an extensive topic, and one where I only scratched the surface. I cover only the security pieces you may have to interact with as the developer of a Web application, talking to SQL Server 2000 on the back-end.

Authentication Modes

SQL Server 2000 includes two Authentication modes: Windows Authentication and Mixed. Windows Authentication mode enables users to use a trusted connection. In other words, Windows 2000 validates the user and passes the token information to SQL Server automatically. The user doesn't have to log in again to SQL Server. This is often friendlier for users, but it requires more setup in SQL Server. For example, while writing this book, I had one machine with Windows Authentication and another machine with Mixed Authentication. The machine with Windows Authentication required that for every new object I created, I also went in and set the user permissions on it. With Mixed security, I could add a username and password to the OLE DB connection string that had system admin privileges in SQL Server, so I didn't have to set permissions on each object in SQL Server.

The database connection string is different depending on what kind of security you're using. If you want to use standard SQL Server security, you add a username and password to your connection string. If you want to use Windows authentication, you add the following value to your connection string and leave out the username and password:

```
Integrated Security=SSPI;
```

Connecting to SQL Server

Your goals in connecting to SQL Server are to make it automatic. This is fairly easy to do, as it's handled by the connection string you build, and then ADO opens the connection for you. If you're using Mixed security and want to have SQL Server log you on, you build a connection string with User Name and Password values, and you're either given access to SQL Server or you aren't.

With Windows Authentication mode, however, it is trickier. If you go with an ASP with a connection string in it that's using Windows Authentication, the objects in SQL Server you're trying to access must have granted permissions to the proper user. If the Web application is set up to use Anonymous authentication, then the SQL Server objects must give permissions to the IUSR_<servername> user. If, on the other had, you're using Basic, Digest, or Integrated security on the Web application, you need to make sure all the individual users have the proper permissions to the objects.

If you extend this to a more robust application, you now have components sitting inside COM+ Component Services applications. If you're using standard SQL security, you only include the username and password in the database connection string inside the component. If you're using Windows authentication, however, you must make sure the COM+ application has an identity other than the interactive user, and whatever identity it uses has been given permissions to the proper SQL Server objects. Realize SQL Server is seeing the COM+ application as the user, and not the user who originally started the application.

SUMMARY

As I wrap up talking about how to build Web applications, you have looked at two things usually done toward the end: you lock everything down with security and you perform load testing. Don't get me wrong: security is critical in many applications and you should design for it up-front. As you have seen in this chapter, however, you usually don't have to write much, if any, code to secure your Web applications.

First, you learned how to squeeze even more scalability out of your systems. You looked at Network Load Balancing and you learned about sessionless Web applications to boost performance even higher. You learned about the Web Application Stress tool as a way to simulate heavy loads on your Web application using one to a few clients.

You saw how to set up SSL on your server. This is a process with many steps, but the end result is a Web application that can be run with encrypted packets flying back and forth, ensuring the safety of the data sent. People will be comfortable sending you information, and you can respond with data that they are assured no one else can see as it crosses the Internet.

You learned how to set the authentication modes on your Web application. This doesn't have anything to do with encryption but, instead, limits who can run your applications. Limiting access to your applications provides you with the capability to write one Web application, but gives different users access to different pieces.

Finally, you learned about the security in COM+ Component Services and how the role-based security makes it easy for you to restrict access to the components and even methods within the components. You learned how the security works across COM+ application boundaries and why the identity of the applications is so important.

Securing a Web application is a deep, complex subject. You can dive into IIS and Windows 2000 security, and you can examine COM+ Component Services security. You can also work with the security in SQL Server 2000. These choices alone could be books in themselves.

I hope you've enjoyed it.

PART V

Appendixes

APPENDIX A

Internet Information Services ASP Object Model

One of the great strengths of Internet Information Services (IIS) is it provides a comprehensive object model to enable you to access many of the inner workings of IIS. These objects provide a mechanism to perform such actions as writing output to the HTML stream, to retrieve information passed up from forms or on the address line, to write cookies to the user's hard drive, and to call COM components, such as the ActiveX Data Objects.

The object model is shown in Figure A-1. As you can see, many of the objects are independent of each other. This isn't a hierarchical object model used in many Microsoft products.

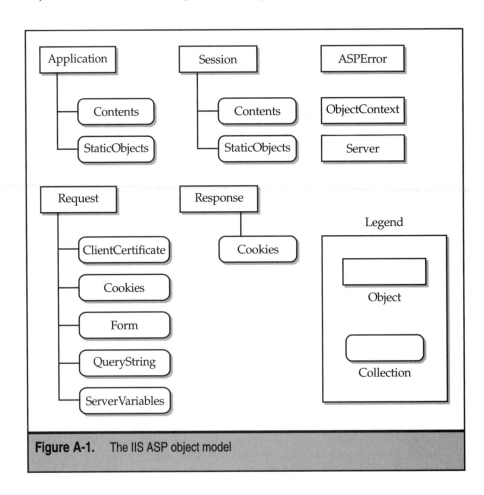

Figure A-1. The IIS ASP object model

THE APPLICATION OBJECT

The Application object is available to all the users of a Web application, and you can use it to share information among all the users. Because the Application object is accessible to multiple users, you should place locks on it before you begin updating its values.

Properties, Methods, Collections, and Events

The Application object contains the following properties, methods, collections, and events:

Properties

None

Methods

Contents.Remove	This method deletes a single item from the Application's Contents collection. The item must be identified by an index number or the name of the item.
Contents.RemoveAll	This method removes all the items from the Application's Contents collection.

Collections

Contents	The Contents collection contains all the items added to the Application object through script code. These are usually called application variables or application-level variables.
StaticObjects	The StaticObjects collection contains all the items added to the Application object through the <OBJECT> tag.

Events

Application_OnStart	This event fires when the application is first started. The application is started when the first user access any ASP file in the application. The application does not shut down unless the application or the entire server is shut down.
Application_OnEnd	This event fires when the application or server is stopped gracefully. This event can be used to write out variable values so they can be restored when the Application_OnStart event fires the next time.

THE SESSION OBJECT

The Session object a "per-user" object. While only one Application object is shared by all users, one Session object exists for each user in the application. One user cannot see the values in another user's Session object.

Properties, Methods, Collections, and Events

The Session object contains the following properties, methods, collections, and events:

Properties

CodePage	The CodePage property controls the code page used to generate the page. A CodePage describes the character set to be used. The default is ANSI code page 1252, which has the character set for American English and several European languages.

Properties

LCID	The LCID represents the locale. For example, you could set the LCID to 2057, which happens to be Britain. Now, functions such as FormatCurrency show the pound symbol (£) instead of the dollar sign ($).
SessionID	The SessionID is a number that uniquely identifies each session on a server. This number is passed back and forth between the client and the server to ensure the user is always returned to the session with his information in it.
TimeOut	The TimeOut property determines how long the session should remain on the server after the last request. Because HTTP is stateless, the server doesn't know if the user has disconnected, so it measures the time between requests. Once the TimeOut is reached, the server closes down the session.

Methods

Abandon	The Abandon method destroys the session object immediately.
Contents.Remove	This method deletes a single item from the Session's Contents collection. The item must be identified by an index number or the name of the item.
Contents.RemoveAll	This method removes all the items from the Session's Contents collection.

Collections

Contents	The Contents collection contains all the items added to the Session object through script code. These are usually called session variables or session-level variables.
StaticObjects	The StaticObjects collection contains all the items added to the Session object through the <OBJECT> tag.

Events

Session_OnStart	This event fires when the session is first started. The session is started when a user first accesses any ASP file in the application. Each user has her own session, which shuts down after a certain period of inactivity.
Session_OnEnd	This event fires when the session drops out of memory. This can happen when the session timeout is reached or when Session.Abandon is called.

THE ASPERROR OBJECT

The ASPError object contains a number of properties that hold information about the last error that occurred in an ASP page. You get an ASPError object by calling the Server.GetLastError method.

Properties, Methods, Collections, and Events

The ASPError object contains the following properties, methods, collections, and events:

Properties

ASPCode	This property returns a string containing the error code generated by IIS.
Number	This property contains the long integer error code from a COM component.
Source	This property returns the line of source code that caused the error, if available. This is usually available in ASP files because ASP files are interpreted.
Category	This property identifies if the error was an internal ASP error, an error in the scripting language, or an error in an object.
File	This property is the name of the ASP that was being processed when the error occurred.
Line	This property returns the line number of the ASP that caused the error.
Column	This property returns the column number on the line of the ASP that caused the error.
Description	This property returns a string that is a short description of the problem.
ASPDescription	This property returns a string that is a more complete description of the problem, if available.

Methods

None

Collections

None

Events

None

THE OBJECTCONTEXT OBJECT

The ObjectContext object lets you either commit or rollback a transaction that the page has initiated in COM+ Component Services. IIS runs most of its functions in COM+ Component Services, so your ASP can get access to the Component Services engine. To use this, you must set the @Transaction directive in your ASP.

Properties, Methods, Collections, and Events

The Object Context object contains the following properties, methods, collections, and events:

Properties

None

Methods

SetAbort	The SetAbort method tells COM+ Component Services something in the transaction has failed and it needs to rollback all the processing done by this transaction.
SetComplete	The SetComplete method tells COM+ Component Services everything in the transaction has succeeded and all the changes made can be committed.

Collections

None

Events

OnTransaction Abort	If the transaction is aborted, IIS calls a Sub OnTransactionAbort routine in the ASP.
OnTransaction Commit	If the transaction completes successfully, IIS calls a Sub OnTransactionCommit in the ASP.

THE REQUEST OBJECT

The Request object is used to retrieve information that came up from the client browser with the HTTP request. For example, the user may be submitting cookie information or data via an HTML form.

Properties, Methods, Collections, and Events

The Request object contains the following properties, methods, collections, and events:

Properties

TotalBytes	The TotalBytes property returns how many total bytes were received from the client in the request.

Methods

BinaryRead	This method retrieves all the raw data sent to the server in the HTTP Post request. This is for low-level access and isn't often used.

Collections

ClientCertificate	This collection contains the values in a client certificate, which are usually used in applications that need a high degree of security.
Cookies	This collection contains the values stored in cookies on the client machine. These may be persistent cookies (written to the hard drive) or cookies that are only stored in memory.
Form	This collection contains the values passed up from an HTML form.

Collections

QueryString	This collection contains the values passed in an HTTP query string, which appears on the address line as a question mark and the data after it.
ServerVariables	This collection contains the values of certain environment variables, such as all the HTTP headers sent by the client or the IP address of the client.

Events

None

THE RESPONSE OBJECT

The Response object is used to send output to the client. This can include writing information into the HTML stream or giving the browser instructions, such as forcing it to request a new page.

Properties, Methods, Collections, and Events

The Session object contains the following properties, methods, collections, and events:

Properties

Buffer	This property controls whether page buffering is enabled. IIS defaults to page buffering being true, which means nothing is sent to the client until the entire page has finished processing, or until the Flush or End methods are called. Turning on buffering can improve performance.

Properties

CacheControl	The CacheControl property determines whether proxy servers can cache the output of the ASP. The default is "Private," which tells proxy servers not to cache the output. Setting the value to "Public" allows proxy servers to cache the page.
Charset	This property appends the name of the character set to the content-type header in the response object.
ContentType	This property specifies the type of content in the response. The default is "text/HTML."
Expires	This property tells the browser how long it can cache the page. To disable caching, set this value to negative one (-1).
ExpiresAbsolute	This property sets an absolute date and time for a page to be expired from the client cache.
IsClientConnected	This property checks to see if the client is still connected and awaiting a response. You can check this before embarking on a long-running process to make sure you aren't wasting precious processor cycles.
Pics	This property sets the PICS ratings for your site for such values as sex and violence.
Status	This property represents the value returned by the server. For example, you could set this to "404 File not found."

Methods

AddHeader	This method adds an HTML header to the response.
AppendToLog	This method can be used to write information to a log file. To use this, you must enable the URI Stem option on the ASP application.
BinaryWrite	This method writes data to the HTTP output without performing any character conversion on it. This is one method to dump binary data to a custom program over HTTP.
Clear	This method clears anything in the buffer.
End	This method stops the processing of the ASP and returns any buffered output.
Flush	This method sends any buffered output to the client immediately.
Redirect	This method actually sends a message to the client browser, telling it to request a new page. This used to be the only method to redirect a user to a new page, but it required a round-trip between the server and client. The Server.Transfer can be a better alternative.
Write	The Write method sends string information into the HTTP output.

Collections

Cookies	Using this collection, you can set cookie values on the client computer.

Events

None

THE SERVER OBJECT

The Server object provides access to some of the functions on the server. This object is most often used to access COM components, such as ADO.

Properties, Methods, Collections, and Events

The Session object contains the following properties, methods, collections, and events:

Properties

ScriptTimeout	This property sets the amount of time a script can run before timing out. The default is 90 seconds.

Methods

CreateObject	CreateObject is used to create an instance of a COM object.
Execute	Execute calls another ASP, processes it, and then finishes processing the calling page. In many ways, the called ASP acts like a called procedure.
GetLastError	This method returns an ASPError object holding the information about the last error.
HTMLEncode	This method HTML encodes a string. For example, the string " Is your salary <50k" would be converted to "Is your salary < 50K."
MapPath	This method returns the physical path of the virtual directory passed in as an argument.

Methods

Transfer	This method moves processing to another ASP. The processing doesn't return to the calling ASP. This is often a better alternative than the older Response.Redirect.
URLEncode	This method URL encodes a string. For example, the string "Mat O'Neal" is changed to "Mat+O%27Neal."

Collections

None

Events

None

APPENDIX B

ActiveX Data Objects
Object Model

ADO is not technically part of IIS; instead, it's part of what Microsoft calls the Microsoft Data Access Components (MDAC). You can always find the latest MDAC at http://www.microsoft.com/data. You will want to visit this site often, as MDAC updates occur frequently. Unfortunately, MDAC seems to get "broken" on a regular basis by other components and service packs.

The object model is shown in Figure B-1. As you can see, many of the objects are independent of each other. This is not a hierarchical object model used in many Microsoft products.

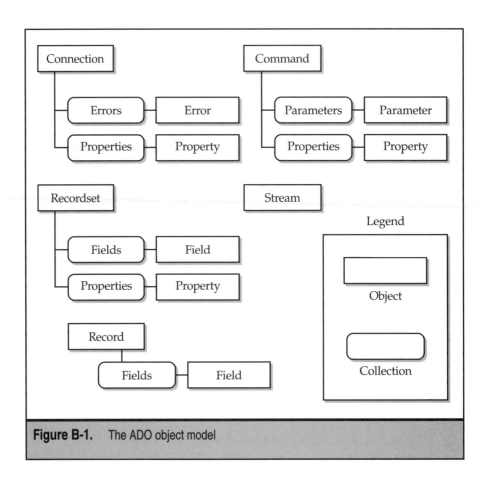

Figure B-1. The ADO object model

THE CONNECTION OBJECT

The Connection object is used to connect to the database server. It also has the capability to execute statements against the server.

Properties, Methods, Collections, and Events

The Connection object contains the following properties, methods, collections, and events:

Properties

Attributes	This property can be set so aborting or committing a transaction automatically starts a new one, if the provider supports that functionality.
CommandTimeout	Determines how long a command, issued with the Execute method, runs before timing out.
ConnectionString	The Connection object uses this to connect to the database.
ConnectionTimeout	Determines how long a connection is attempted before timing out.
CursorLocation	Determines if the cursor is to be created on the client or server.
DefaultDatabase	Sets a default database for the Connection object.
IsolationLevel	Used for transactions. This can enable you to see dirty reads, for example.

Properties

Mode	Determines how the connection is opened, such as for read-only or read/write. You can also use a mode that denies all others access to the resource.
Provider	The OLE DB provided to be used by the connection.
State	Indicates whether the connection is opened or closed.
Version	The version of ADO.

Methods

BeginTrans	Starts a transaction, provided the database supports it.
Cancel	Cancels an asynchronous query.
Close	Closes an open connection.
CommitTrans	Commits a pending transaction.
Execute	Executes a statement against the database. This statement is passed into the Execute method.
Open	Opens a connection. The connection string can be passed into the Open method call or set in the ConnectionString property.
OpenSchema	Returns schema information, such as the tables in the data source, and the columns within the tables.
RollbackTrans	Tells ADO to cancel the transaction and roll back any changes.

Collections

Errors	A collection of zero to many Error objects returned from the data source or ADO itself.
Properties	A collection of zero to many Property objects. These dynamic properties are provided by the different data providers.

Events

BeginTransComplete	Called after the BeginTrans method starts a transaction.
CommitTransComplete	Called after the CommitTrans method is done.
ConnectComplete	Called after a connection is made to the data source.
Disconnect	Called after a connection is stopped.
ExecuteComplete	Called after a command, run with the Execute method, is finished.
InfoMessage	Called whenever an error is encountered during a connection operation.
RollbackTransComplete	Called after the RollbackTrans method is done.
WillConnect	Called before the connection starts.
WillExecute	Called before a command is executed. This enables you to cancel a pending execution.

THE COMMAND OBJECT

The Command object is used to execute command against the data source. It works well when interacting with stored procedures.

Properties, Methods, Collections, and Events

The Command object contains the following properties, methods, collections, and events:

Properties

ActiveConnection	Represents the connection to the data source. This can be a Connection object or a connection string.
CommandText	The command to be executed. This can be a SQL string, table name, or the name of a stored procedure.
CommandTimeout	The number of seconds a command runs before timing out.
CommandType	The command type can be text (a SQL string), a table, a stored procedure, unknown (the default), or a file.
Name	The name of the command object.
Prepared	Indicates whether to save a temporary stored procedure on the server.
State	Indicates whether the connection is opened or closed.

Methods

Cancel	Cancels an asynchronous query.
CreateParameter	Creates a Parameter object to be included in the Parameters collection.
Execute	Executes a statement against the database. This statement is contained in the CommandText property.

Collections

Parameters	A collection of Parameter objects. Each Parameter object maps to a parameter in a stored procedure.
Properties	A collection of zero to many Property objects. These dynamic properties are provided by the different data providers.

Events

None

THE RECORDSET OBJECT

The Recordset object is used to obtain records from the data source. It can open recordsets directly or receive the recordset as the return of a Connection or Command object's Execute method.

Properties, Methods, Collections, and Events

The Recordset object contains the following properties, methods, collections, and events:

Properties

AbsolutePage	Indicates the page number of the current record. The number of records per logical page is controlled by the PageSize property.
AbsolutePosition	Indicates the ordinal number of the current record in the recordset.
ActiveCommand	Contains the Command object used to create the recordset. If no Command object was used, a Null is returned.
ActiveConnection	Contains the Connection object used by the recordset. If no Connection object was used, a Null is returned.

Properties

BOF	Returns a true if the current record position is on the "beginning of file" marker.
Bookmark	Returns a value to identify the current record uniquely.
CacheSize	This indicates the number of records to cache in local memory. The default is one.
CursorLocation	Determines if the cursor is created on the client or the server.
CursorType	Determines which one of four types of cursors is created. Not all data sources support all types.
DataMember	This property interacts with data-bound controls, indicating the data member that will be retrieved from the data source.
DataSource	Used by data-bound controls and is usually set to a Data Environment command.
EditMode	Indicates the current edit status, such as none, edit in process, delete, and so on.
EOF	Returns a true if the current record position is on the "end of file" marker.
Filter	A string that filters the current recordset, acting much like a SQL where clause.
Index	Returns the name of the index used to create the Recordset object.
LockType	Indicates the type of locks in place on the data. Not all data sources support all types of locks.

Properties

MarshalOptions	Indicates whether to marshal all records or just modified records.
MaxRecords	The maximum number of records to return.
PageCount	The number of pages in the recordset.
PageSize	The number of records to place on each page in the recordset.
RecordCount	The number of records in the recordset. This is not accurate until all the records have been accessed.
Sort	A string holding one or more fields on which to sort, and whether to sort ascending and descending.
Source	Returns a string that represents the current source, such as a SQL string, Command, or Connection object. Can also be set to a string, Command, or Connection object.
State	Indicates whether the object is opened or closed.
Status	Indicates the status with regard to batch updates or bulk operations.
StayInSync	Indicates whether a hierarchical recordset's child records should be changed as the parent changes.

Methods

AddNew	Adds a new, blank record to the data source. The cursor and lock types must support this.
Cancel	Cancels an asynchronous query.
CancelBatch	Cancels a pending batch update, which enables you to update many records at once.

Methods

CancelUpdate	Cancels changes made to the current record.
Clone	Creates a copy of the current recordset.
Close	Closes the current recordset.
CompareBookmarks	Compares two bookmarks and returns whether they are equal, and the relative position of the first to the second.
Delete	Deletes the current record.
Find	Searches the current recordset for a record matching the criteria. If none is found, you stop on the EOF (or on the BOF, if you were searching backwards).
GetRows	Retrieves all the records into an array.
GetString	Retrieves all the records into a string.
Move	Moves a specified number of records in the database. A negative number moves you backward.
MoveFirst	Moves to the first record in the recordset.
MoveLast	Moves to the last record in the recordset.
MoveNext	Moves to the next record in the recordset.
MovePrevious	Moves to the previous record in the recordset.
NextRecordset	Closes the current recordset and opens the next one. Some commands can return multiple recordsets.
Open	Opens the recordset.

Methods

Requery	Refreshes the data in the recordset by rerunning the query that first created the recordset.
Resync	Refreshes the data for the records in the recordset but, unlike the Requery method, it doesn't show new records.
Save	Saves the recordset in a file or Stream object. The format can be binary or XML.
Seek	Finds records that match certain criteria. Can only be used on server-side cursors, but can take advantage of indexes.
Supports	Determines whether a particular provider supports certain cursor options.
Update	Updates the underlying data with the new values.
UpdateBatch	Writes multiple pending updates to the base table in one large batch.

Collections

Fields	A collection of Field objects representing the fields in a row of the recordset.
Properties	A collection of zero to many Property objects. These dynamic properties are provided by the different data providers.

Events

EndOfRecordset	This event is fired when the user attempts to move past the end of a recordset.
FetchComplete	This event is fired after the fetch is completed in an asynchronous query.

Events

FetchProgress	This event fires occasionally during a long-running asynchronous query and reports how many records have been retrieved to that point.
FieldChangeComplete	Called after a field value has been changed.
MoveComplete	Called after a move has been made.
RecordChangeComplete	Called after one or more rows are changed.
RecordsetChangeComplete	Called after the recordset is changed (for example, with a Resync, AddNew, and so forth).
WillChangeField	Called before a field value is changed.
WillChangeRecord	Called before one or more rows are changed.
WillChangeRecordset	Called before the recordset is changed (for example, with a Resync, AddNew, and so forth).
WillMove	Called before a move is made.

THE RECORD OBJECT

The Record object represents a row in a recordset, or a file or folder in a file system.

Properties, Methods, Collections, and Events

The Record object contains the following properties, methods, collections, and events:

Properties

ActiveConnection	Contains the Connection object used by the recordset. If no Connection object was used, a Null is returned.

Properties

Mode	Indicates the permissions for modifying the data.
ParentURL	A string that points to the parent of the current record. This is used when the record represents a file or directory in a file system.
RecordType	Indicates the type of record, such as a simple record or a COM structured file.
Source	Indicates where this record came from. It may point to a Recordset object, for example.
State	Indicates if the object is open or closed.

Methods

Cancel	Cancels an asynchronous query.
Close	Closes the current Record object.
CopyRecord	Copies a file or folder to a different location.
DeleteRecord	Deletes a file or a folder and all its subfolders.
GetChildren	Returns a Recordset object where the rows represent the files and folders of the folder represented by the Record object.
MoveRecord	Moves a file or folder to another location.
Open	Opens an existing Record object or creates a new file or folder.

Collections

Fields	A collection of Field objects representing the fields in a row of the record.
Properties	A collection of zero to many Property objects. These dynamic properties are provided by the different data providers.

Events

None

THE STREAM OBJECT

The Stream object represents a stream of binary or text data.

Properties, Methods, Collections, and Events

The Stream object contains the following properties, methods, collections, and events:

Properties

Charset	Indicates the character set that will be used to translate the stream. The default is "Unicode."
EOS	True, if you are at the "end of stream" marker.
LineSeparator	Indicates the binary character used to separate lines in a text stream.
Mode	Indicates the permissions for modifying the data.
Position	A long that indicates the position within the stream, in bytes.
Size	A long that indicates the size of the stream, in bytes.
State	Indicates whether the object is open or closed.
Type	Indicates if the stream is text or binary.

Methods

Cancel	Cancels an asynchronous query.
Close	Closes the current Stream object.
CopyTo	Copies a specified number of bytes or characters to another stream.
Flush	Makes sure all changes to the stream are moved into the underlying source data.
LoadFromFile	Loads a file into a Stream object.
Open	Opens a stream of binary or text data.
Read	Read a specified number of bytes from a binary stream.

Methods

ReadText	Read a specified number of characters from a text stream.
SaveToFile	Saves the binary stream contents to a file.
SetEOS	Makes the current position the End of Stream marker.
SkipLine	Skips one line when reading the stream. The default line separator is adCRLF.
Write	Writes data to a binary stream.
WriteText	Writes text to a text stream.

Collections

None

Events

None

THE ERROR OBJECT

The Error object represents an error returned from a data source.

Properties, Methods, Collections, and Events

The Error object contains only the following properties:

Properties

Description	A string that contains a short description of the error.
HelpContext	A long value that represents a topic in a help file that contains information about the error.
HelpFile	The name of the help file that contains information about the error.
NativeError	The error code returned by the provider.
Number	A number that uniquely identifies the Error object.

Properties

Source	Indicates the name of the application or object that generated the error.
SQLState	A five-character string that indicates the error. This is an ANSI SQL standard error code.

THE PARAMETER OBJECT

The Parameter object represents a parameter in a Command object. The parameter is a parameter in either a stored procedure or parameterized query.

Properties, Methods, Collections, and Events

The Parameter object contains only the following properties and methods:

Properties

Attributes	Indicates if a parameter is signed, nullable, or can accept long binary data.
Direction	Indicates if the parameter is an input, output, input/output, or return value parameter.
Name	Indicates the name of the Parameter object.
NumericScale	Indicates the number of decimal places used to resolve numeric values.
Precision	Indicates the maximum number of digits that can be used to represent a numeric value.
Size	Indicates the maximum size of a parameter object, in characters or bytes.
Type	Represents the data type of the parameter.
Value	This is the value assigned to the parameter on input parameters, or the returned value on output parameters.

Methods

AppendChunk	Used to add a large binary or text value to the Parameter object.

Collections

Properties	A collection of zero to many Property objects. These dynamic properties are provided by the different data providers.

THE FIELD OBJECT

The Field object represents a column of data in a record or recordset.

Properties, Methods, Collections, and Events

The Field object contains only the following properties and methods:

Properties

ActualSize	This property returns the actual length of a field's value.
Attributes	Indicates special attributes about the field. For example, is the field the primary key, is it nullable, and so forth.
DefinedSize	Indicates the maximum size a field can be.
Name	The name of the Field object.
NumericScale	Indicates the number of decimal places used to resolve numeric values.
OriginalValue	Shows the value of the field as it was before any changes were made.
Precision	Indicates the maximum number of digits that can be used to represent a numeric value.
Status	Indicates if the field was successfully added or deleted, or if it returned an error, such as a data overflow.
Type	Returns the data type of the field.

Properties

UnderlyingValue	Returns the current value from the database. If the record was changed after the field was retrieved, this value may not be what is in the field.
Value	This is the value assigned to the parameter on input parameters, or the returned value on output parameters.

Methods

AppendChunk	Used to add a large binary or text value to the Field object.
GetChunk	Returns the contents of a field with a large binary or text value.

Collections

Properties	A collection of zero to many Property objects. These dynamic properties are provided by the different data providers.

APPENDIX C

ActiveX Data Objects Extensions Object Model

A   *ctiveX Data Objects Extensions (ADOX)* is an object model that was added after ADO was released. *ActiveX Data Objects* (*ADO*) cannot assume a relational database as the source, so it doesn't naturally have any concept of tables, columns, and other relational constructs. ADO is powerful because it can handle almost any type of data, but most data is, in fact, relational, so many developers were disappointed when ADO didn't automatically fill in a collection of tables, along with the fields in each table and other schema information.

ADOX attempts to handle these shortcomings of ADO by supplying objects to handle schema information and manipulation (see Figure C-1). In addition, it includes objects designed to work with the security features of the database, such as roles and permissions.

THE CATALOG OBJECT

The Catalog object contains a series of collections that describe the data source schema.

Properties, Methods, Collections, and Events

The Catalog object contains the following properties, methods, collections, and events:

Properties

ActiveConnection	Indicates the standard ADO Connection object or connection string used to connect to the data source.

Methods

Create	The Create method creates a new Catalog object; it can create a new database if the data provider supports such creation.

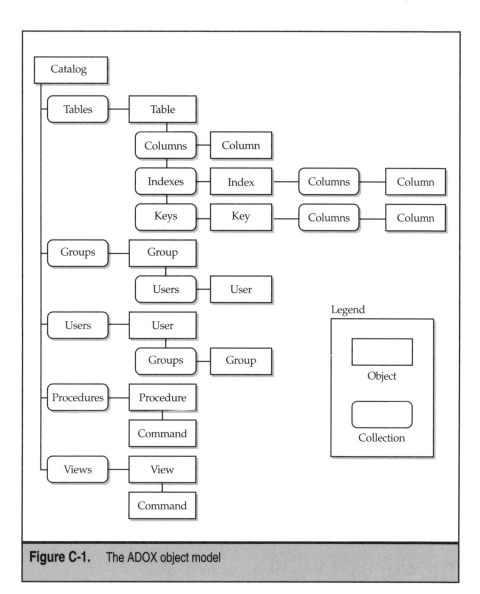

Figure C-1.   The ADOX object model

Methods

GetObjectOwner	Returns the name of the owner of an object in the Catalog.
SetObjectOwner	Sets the owner of a particular object in the Catalog.

Collections

Groups	A collection of zero to many Group objects representing user groups used in security.
Procedures	A collection of zero to many Procedure objects representing the stored procedures in the database.
Tables	A collection of zero to many Table objects representing the tables in the database.
Users	A collection of zero to many User objects representing the users in the database.
Views	A collection of zero to many View objects representing the views in the database.

Events

None

THE COLUMN OBJECT

The Column object represents a column in an index, table, or key.

Properties, Methods, Collections, and Events

The Column object contains the following properties, methods, collections, and events:

Properties

Attributes	Describes whether the column is fixed length and whether it's nullable.
DefinedSize	Indicates the maximum size of the column, in characters.
Name	The name of the column.
NumericScale	Indicates the number of decimal places used to resolve numeric values.
ParentCatalog	Indicates the Catalog acting as the source for this column.
Precision	Indicates the maximum number of digits that can be used to represent a numeric value.
RelatedColumn	Returns the name of the related key in the related table, if this column is a key column.
SortOrder	Indicates the sort order of this column, if this column is an index column.
Type	Returns the data type of the column.

Methods

None

Collections

None

Events

None

THE GROUP OBJECT

The Group object represents a group account that has been granted permissions in the database.

Properties, Methods, Collections, and Events

The Group object contains the following properties, methods, collections, and events:

Properties

Name	The name of the Group.

Methods

GetPermissions	Returns the permissions for a particular group on a particular object.
SetPermissions	Sets the permissions for a particular group on a particular object.

Collections

Users	A collection of zero to many User objects representing the users defined in the database.

Events

None

THE INDEX OBJECT

The Index object represents an index in the database.

Properties, Methods, Collections, and Events

The Index object contains the following properties, methods, collections, and events:

Properties

Clustered	Returns a Boolean indicating whether the index is clustered.
IndexNulls	Indicates if records with null values in indexed fields have index entries.
Name	The name of the index.
PrimaryKey	Returns a Boolean indicating whether this is a primary key index.
Unique	Returns a Boolean indicating whether the index values must be unique.

Methods

None

Collections

Columns	A collection of zero to many Column objects representing the columns in the index.

Events

None

THE KEY OBJECT

The Key object represents a primary, foreign, or unique key on a table.

Properties, Methods, Collections, and Events

The Key object contains the following properties, methods, collections, and events:

Properties

DeleteRule	Indicates what to do if the primary key is deleted. For example, the rule can be cascading deletes, setting values to Null, and so forth.
Name	The name of the key.
RelatedTable	Indicates the name of the related table if the key is a foreign key.
Type	Indicates if the key is a primary, foreign, or unique key.
UpdateRule	Indicates what to do if the primary key is updated.

Methods

None

Collections

Columns	A collection of zero to many Column objects representing the columns in the key.

Events

None

THE PROCEDURE OBJECT

The Procedure object represents a stored procedure in the database.

Properties, Methods, Collections, and Events

The Procedure object contains the following properties, methods, collections, and events:

Properties

Command	Indicates the standard ADO Command object used to create or execute the procedure.
DateCreated	The date the procedure was created.
DateModified	The date the procedure was last modified.
Name	The name of the stored procedure.

Methods

None

Collections

None

Events

None

THE TABLE OBJECT

The Table object represents a table in the database.

Properties, Methods, Collections, and Events

The Table object contains the following properties, methods, collections, and events:

Properties

DateCreated	The date the table was created.
DateModified	The date the table was last modified.
Name	The name of the table.
ParentCatalog	Returns or sets the Catalog object acting as the source for this table.

Properties

Type	Indicates the type of table, such as table, system table, temporary table, and so on.

Methods

None

Collections

Columns	A collection of zero to many Group objects representing user groups used in security.
Indexes	A collection of zero to many Procedure objects representing the stored procedures in the database.
Keys	A collection of zero to many Table objects representing the tables in the database.

Events

None

THE USER OBJECT

The User object represents a user account that has been granted access privileges.

Properties, Methods, Collections, and Events

The User object contains the following properties, methods, collections, and events:

Properties

Name	The name of the user.

Methods

ChangePassword	Changes the password for the specified user account.
GetPermissions	Returns the permissions for a particular user on a particular object.
SetPermissions	Sets the permissions for a particular user on a particular object.

Collections

Groups	A collection of zero to many Group objects representing the groups to which this user belongs.

Events

None

THE VIEW OBJECT

The View object represents a view in the database.

Properties, Methods, Collections, and Events

The View object contains the following properties, methods, collections, and events:

Properties

Command	Indicates the standard ADO Command object used to create or modify the view.
DateCreated	The date the view was created.
DateModified	The date the view was last modified.

Properties

Name   The name of the view.

Methods

None

Collections

None

Events

None

APPENDIX D

ActiveX Data Objects Multidimensional Object Model

While ADO was originally designed to handle data in nearly any format, it still assumed a rather two-dimensional view of the data. Multidimensional data, such as that generated by Analysis Services, required a new object model, so ADO MD was born.

Unlike ADO and ADOX, ADO MD is extremely hierarchical because of the nature of multidimensional data. Two main areas of ADO MD exist: the first enables you to navigate the structure of a multidimensional cube, and the second lets you work with cellsets, which are returned records from a cube (see Figure D-1).

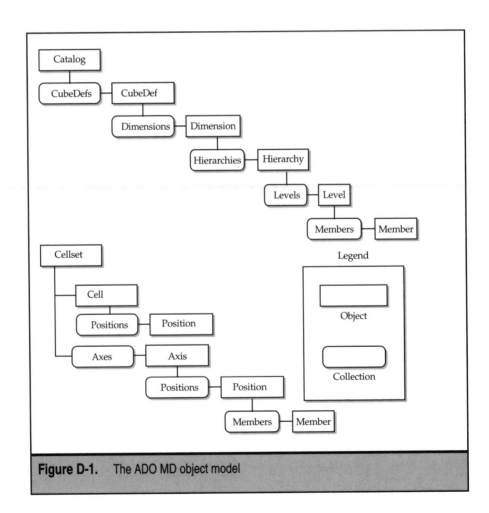

Figure D-1. The ADO MD object model

THE AXIS OBJECT

The Axis object represents one of the axes of a cellset, containing members of one or more dimensions.

Properties, Methods, Collections, and Events

The Axis object contains the following properties, methods, collections, and events:

Properties

DimensionCount	The number of dimensions on the axis.
Name	The name of the axis.

Methods

None

Collections

Positions	A collection of zero to many Position objects representing a point on an axis.

Events

None

THE CATALOG OBJECT

The Catalog object represents the schema information for the underlying multidimensional data provider.

Properties, Methods, Collections, and Events

The Catalog object contains the following properties, methods, collections, and events:

Properties

ActiveConnection	A standard ADO Connection object used to connect to the multidimensional data provider.

Properties

Name	The name of the catalog, or database, to which a connection is established.

Methods

None

Collections

CubeDefs	A collection of zero to many CubeDef objects representing the cubes in the database.

Events

None

THE CELL OBJECT

The Cell object represents an individual cell in a cellset. A cell is at the intersection of multiple axes.

Properties, Methods, Collections, and Events

The Cell object contains the following properties, methods, collections, and events:

Properties

FormattedValue	The value of a particular cell, formatted according to the data type.
Ordinal	Uniquely identifies a cell in a cellset.
Value	The unformatted value of an individual cell.

Methods

None

Axes

A collection of zero to many Axis objects representing the axes making up this cell.

Positions

A collection of zero to many Position objects representing the position in the axes to make up this cell.

Events

None

THE CELLSET OBJECT

The Cellset object represents records that have been returned from a cube, similar to a recordset in ADO. It's a collection of Cell objects or other CellSet objects.

Properties, Methods, Collections, and Events

The CellSet object contains the following properties, methods, collections, and events:

Properties

ActiveConnection

A standard ADO Connection object to which the cellset belongs.

FilterAxis

Returns an Axis object representing an axis used to slice the data.

Item

Returns a Cell object from the cellset using its coordinates.

Source

The query that created the cellset.

Properties

State	Indicates if the CellSet object is opened or closed.

Methods

Close	Closes the open CellSet.
Open	Opens the CellSet, executing the query to return records.

Collections

Axes	A collection of zero to many Axis objects representing the axes in the cellset.

Events

None

THE CUBEDEF OBJECT

The CubeDef object represents a cube in the database.

Properties, Methods, Collections, and Events

The CubeDef object contains the following properties, methods, collections, and events:

Properties

Description	Returns a string describing the cube.
Name	The name of the cube.

Methods

None

Collections

Dimensions   A collection of zero to many
                                Dimension objects representing
                                the dimensions in the cube.

Events

None

THE DIMENSION OBJECT

The Dimension object represents a dimension within a cube.

Properties, Methods, Collections, and Events

The Dimension object contains the following properties, methods,
collections, and events:

Properties

Description   Returns a string describing the
                                dimension.

Name   The name of the dimension.

UniqueName   Returns an unambiguous name
                                for the current dimension.

Methods

None

Collections

Hierarchies   A collection of one to many Hierarchy
                                objects representing the hierarchies in
                                the dimension.

Events

None

THE HIERARCHY OBJECT

The Hierarchy object represents a hierarchy within a dimension.

Properties, Methods, Collections, and Events

The Hierarchy object contains the following properties, methods, collections, and events:

Properties

Description	Returns a string describing the hierarchy.
Name	The name of the hierarchy.
UniqueName	Returns an unambiguous name for the current hierarchy.

Methods

None

Collections

Levels	A collection of zero to many Level objects representing the levels in the hierarchy.

Events

None

THE LEVEL OBJECT

The Level object represents a particular level within a hierarchy in a dimension.

Properties, Methods, Collections, and Events

The Level object contains the following properties, methods, collections, and events:

Properties

Caption	The text caption used to display a level.
Depth	Returns the number of levels between the current level and the root of the hierarchy.
Description	Returns a string describing the level.
Name	The name of the level.
UniqueName	Returns an unambiguous name for the current level.

Methods

None

Collections

Members	A collection of zero to many Member objects representing the members of the level.

Events

None

THE MEMBER OBJECT

The Member object represents an individual member within a level of the hierarchy.

Properties, Methods, Collections, and Events

The Member object contains the following properties, methods, collections, and events:

Properties

Caption	The text caption used to display the member.
ChildCount	Indicates the number of members for which this member is a parent.
Children	Returns a Members collection with a Member object for each child member for this member.
Description	Returns a string describing the level.
DrilledDown	Returns a Boolean, with a True meaning no children exist.
LevelDepth	Indicates the number of levels between this member and the root of the hierarchy.
LevelName	Returns the name of the level of this member.
Name	The name of the member.
Parent	Returns a Member object of the parent member of this member.
ParentSameAsPrev	A Boolean that indicates if the parent of this member is the same as the parent of the preceding member.
Type	The type of the current member, such as normal or measure.

Properties

UniqueName   The unique name for this member.

Methods

None

Collections

None

Events

None

THE POSITION OBJECT

The Position object represents set of one or more members that define a point on an axis.

Properties, Methods, Collections, and Events

The Position object contains the following properties, methods, collections, and events:

Properties

Ordinal   Uniquely specifies a point along
                              an axis.

Methods

None

Collections

None

Events

None

APPENDIX E

HTML Introduction

lmost everything you do on the Web ends up as HTML on the client. Complex applications can access data from multiple databases, call COM+ components scattered on various machines, and crunch and manipulate data in the most extreme contortions. At the end of the day, however, the server sends simple HTML back to the client.

This appendix presents a quick introduction to HTML—basically, just enough so you can dive into this book. This introduction is aimed at people who have never seen HTML or who need a better grasp on tables and forms, two of the most important topics to building Web applications.

THE BASICS OF HTML

HTML is the acronym for *Hypertext Markup Language*. HTML is a computer language, but it isn't a programming language. Instead, it was built to have text that preserved formatting from one machine to another, regardless of the hardware or operating system of the computer. This means HTML was built to be portable, or capable of running on any platform. In addition, HTML gives you the capability to link to other information in a nonlinear way. Anywhere in the document, you can click a link and be taken to a specific page. You needn't follow one page to the next; instead, you can jump around as you want.

Just as HTML isn't a programming language, it's important to note that HTML is not case-sensitive. In other words, the following commands are the same: <FORM>, <Form>, and <form>.

Building HTML documents is fairly simple. On your computer, right-click the desktop and choose New, and then choose Text Document. Name the new document MyFirst.htm. You receive a warning that you are changing the file extension, but go ahead and click OK. Now, double-click the file.

Congratulations! Internet Explorer starts and shows that you've just created a blank HTML page. That was pretty simple. Now, in Internet Explorer, click the View menu and choose Source. Notepad opens, and there won't be anything in it. Type the following line:

```
This is my first HTML page
```

Now, in Notepad, click File and then click Save. You needn't close Notepad, so just save the file. Now, click back on Internet Explorer and then click the Refresh button. You should see a screen similar to that in Figure E-1.

This actually does show you something about HTML. A browser displays almost any text it finds as regular text. The key here is the word "almost." You can put special text in the browser that won't be displayed as text but, instead, acts as commands to the browser, telling it how to display the text.

Tags

While "tags" may sound like a bad name for a wrestling tag team, *tags* in HTML are what you use to control the output. You should still have

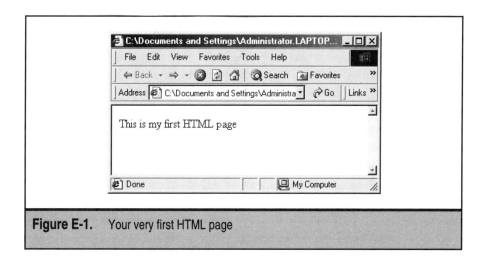

Figure E-1.   Your very first HTML page

Notepad open with the test for MyFirst.htm in it. If not, in IE, click the View menu and choose Source again. Modify the one statement you have in the document to look like this:

```
<H1>This is my first HTML page</H1>
```

Now, save the page and click the Refresh button in the browser. Instead of displaying the <H1> and </H1> as text, the sentence now appears in a large, bold font, as shown in Figure E-2.

The <H1> and </H1> didn't display because they are tags. Tags tell the browser to display the text in a certain way. In this case, <H1> told the browser to start displaying the text in "Heading 1" fashion, which happens to be big and bold. The </H1> tag said to stop displaying the text as a heading 1. In fact, the <H1> and </H1> are the same tag, with the </H1> representing the closing of the <H1> tag.

The Two Tag Types

Two types of tags exist: elements and containers. *Element* tags are only single items; they place something on the page, but they don't

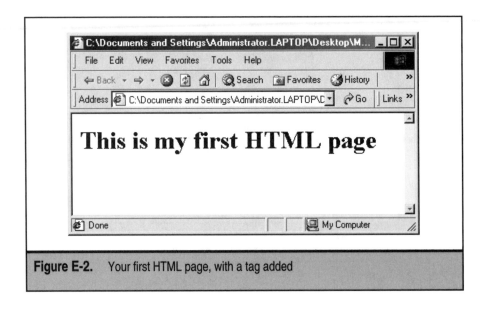

Figure E-2.   Your first HTML page, with a tag added

have a closing tag, as you saw with the <H1> tag. Modify your page to contain the following code:

```
<H1>This is my first HTML page</H1>
<HR>
The tag above represents a horizontal line
```

Now, save the page and refresh your browser. Notice the <HR> tag became a horizontal line. <HR> stands for horizontal rule and it places a horizontal line on the screen. This is an example of an element tag; it doesn't have a closing tag because it simply puts an element on the screen, as shown in Figure E-3.

In contrast, *container* tags do have closing tags because they contain things. For example, the previous <H1> tag contains the text "This is my first HTML page" and you have to tell it where to close. Everything in between will be formatted using the <H1> tag.

Before you go further, you might have two questions. First, how do you know if a tag is an element or a container? Unfortunately, the usual answer is "experience." Literally hundreds, if not thousands, of

Figure E-3.   An HTML page with a container tag and an element tag

books are available on the subject of HTML, and thousands of Web sites exist. Never hesitate to look up a tag to see whether it is an element or a container.

The second question you may have is, "Who decides what the <H1> should look like?" The short answer is the browser manufacturer. A standards body called the *World Wide Web Consortium* (*W3C*) generally determines how a browser should render the <H1> tag, but the actual font and font size are left up to the browser manufacturers.

Attributes

Most tags let you place attributes on them. These attributes can give the browser further directions on how to work with the tags. For example, the <HR> tag puts a horizontal line on the page. What if you didn't want the line to go all the way across? Because that <HR> tag has the Width attribute, you can set the *Width* attribute to a percentage to tell the line to take up only a certain percentage of the page. You can also enter a number of pixels if you want to specify an exact size for the line.

The heading tags also accept attributes. For example, there's an *Align* attribute you can use if you want to align the text to the center or to the right. The default is the left, so you normally don't specify left alignment, but you could.

Putting an attribute on a tag is easy. For example, look at the following two lines:

```
<H1 Align="Center">This is a test</H1>
<HR Width="50%">
```

Notice the values for the attributes are enclosed in double quotes. This is the way the HTML standard is written, but most browsers don't care if you enclose the values in double quotes. The only time it's required is if a space is in the value.

Formatting Text

One of the primary goals of HTML is to preserve the formatting of text across multiple platforms. When it comes to HTML, the browser is what is doing the work. As long as browsers are built so they know how to render the HTML, the HTML file can be sent anywhere because HTML is all text. Normally, formatting is stored as binary data, but HTML must store all the formatting as regular text to be portable. This is why you have tags; they act as instructions to the browser on how to format text.

Headings

You can format the text in the document in numerous ways. You've already seen Heading 1. Six levels of headings exist: <H1> to <H6>. To see what some of these look like, modify the code in MyFirst.htm to the following:

```
<H1>This is my first HTML page</H1>
<H2>I am now learning about headings</H2>
<H3>This is the third level of headings</H3>
<HR>
The tag above represents a horizontal line
```

After saving this page and refreshing the browser, the page should look something like Figure E-4. You can see each level of heading is smaller than the previous one. This is expected. Some are bold and, if you keep going, some will be italicized. Again, this is mostly up to the discretion of the browser manufacturers.

Text Formatting

You can also apply formatting to regular text. For example, you can bold, italicize, or underline text. To bold text, you use the <B> tag.

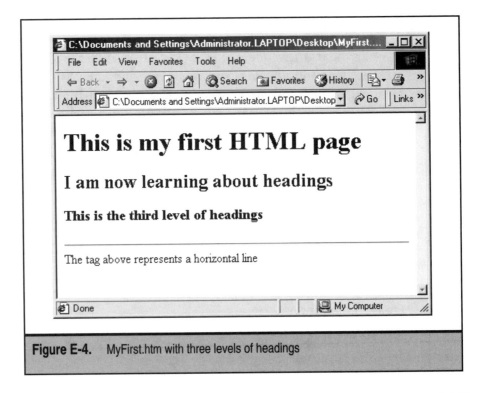

Figure E-4.   MyFirst.htm with three levels of headings

Italicizing is done with the <I> tag. If you guessed that <U> was for underlining, go to the head of the class. Modify your MyFirst.htm to contain the following code:

```
<H1>This is my first HTML page</H1>
<H2>I am now learning about headings</H2>
<H3>This is the third level of headings</H3>
<HR>
<U>The tag above represents a horizontal line</U>
```

If you save this page and view it in the browser, the last sentence is now underlined. But why stop there? Tags can be nested, so you could put another tag inside the <U> tag. Modify the page again, so the code looks like this:

```
<H1>This is my first HTML page</H1>
<H2>I am now learning about headings</H2>
<H3>This is the third level of headings</H3>
<HR>
<U>The tag <I>above</I> represents a <B>horizontal line<B></U>
```

Now, look at Figure E-5 to see what this should look like. The entire last line will be underlined, the word "above" will be italicized, and the words "horizontal line" will be in bold.

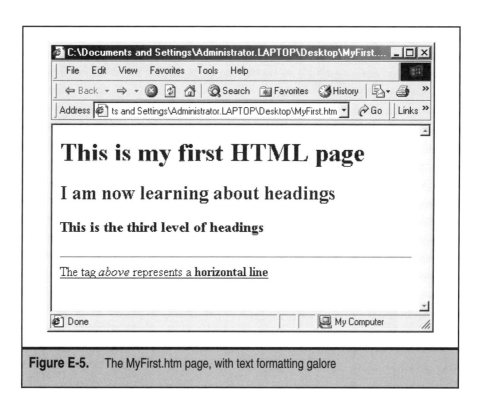

Figure E-5. The MyFirst.htm page, with text formatting galore

White Space

One thing HTML does is collapse white space. White space is any tab, extra spaces, or even carriage-return/line feeds between lines. For example, modify your MyFirst.htm to contain the following code:

```
<H1>This is my first HTML page</H1>
<H2>I am now learning about headings</H2>
<H3>This is the third level of headings</H3>
<HR>
This is the first paragraph.


This is the second paragraph.
```

If you view this in the browser, however, you can see the white space is removed and the line "This is the second paragraph" appears on the same line as the sentence claiming to be the first paragraph. You can see this in Figure E-6.

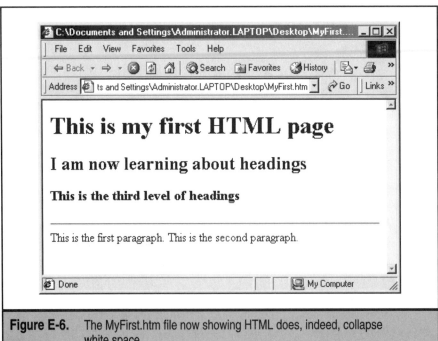

Figure E-6.   The MyFirst.htm file now showing HTML does, indeed, collapse white space

Obviously, this isn't what you want to have happen, so you need to tell the browser where you want the white space and what you want it to look like. Not surprisingly, there are tags to do this. In fact, people use two different tags to do this on a regular basis. The first is the <P> tag, which is actually a container. The <P> stands for paragraph and is used for two purposes: first, it inserts a carriage return/line feed and, second, you can apply formatting to individual paragraphs because the <P> tag is a container. The other common tag is an element tag, <BR>, which simply enters a carriage return. To see how these work, modify your MyFirst.htm page to contain the following code:

```
<H1>This is my first HTML page</H1>
<H2>I am now learning about headings</H2>
<H3>This is the third level of headings</H3>
<HR Width="40%">
<P Align="Center">This is the first paragraph.</P>
<P>This is the second paragraph.<BR>
It contains multiple lines.<BR>You can even
type lines like this.</P>
```

Now, save this page and view it in IE. Figure E-7 shows you what to expect in the page. If you want to add white space and have it preserved so your document looks just as it did when you typed it, you can use the <PRE> container tags.

Adding Hyperlinks

Anyone who surfs the Web for more than a few minutes quickly discovers *hyperlinks,* those pieces of text or graphics you can click to jump to another page. Adding hyperlinks is simple, as it is simply another tag. The tag is commonly referred to as the *anchor tag,* and is <A>. The anchor tag is a container, but what it contains is the text or graphic that acts as the link. To make the anchor tag work, you have to add an HREF attribute. Examine the following line:

```
<A HREF="http://www.osborne.com">Osborne McGraw-Hill</A>
```

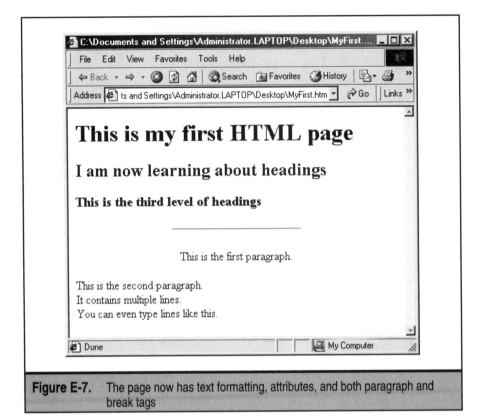

Figure E-7. The page now has text formatting, attributes, and both paragraph and break tags

Notice what's here: you have the <A> tag, with an HREF attribute. The HREF points to http://www.osborne.com. However, between the opening and closing <A> tags, you see the words Osborne McGraw-Hill. These words will act as the link. Anything between the opening and closing <A> tags is displayed to the user, and the user can click these words to jump to the site reference in the HREF attribute. To see this in action, modify MyFirst.htm to look like this:

```
<H1>This is my first HTML page</H1>
<H2>I am now learning about headings</H2>
<H3>This is the third level of headings</H3>
<HR Width="40%">
<A HREF="http://www.osborne.com">Osborne McGraw-Hill</A><BR>
<A HREF="http://www.microsoft.com">Microsoft</A>
```

Here, you have added two links: one to Osborne, and one to Microsoft. The first link has multiple words in it, while the second link has one word. The <A> tag can span as much text as you want, from one character to your entire page. See Figure E-8 to see how the page should appear.

The Basic Structure of an HTML Document

So far, your HTML document has been unstructured, but that hasn't stopped it from working. One of the nice things about HTML is browsers tend to be forgiving. No required structure exists for an HTML document, but there's a generally accepted standard. This standard looks like this:

```
<HTML>
    <HEAD>
    </HEAD>
    <BODY>
    </BODY>
</HTML>
```

The <HTML> tags tell the browser the document to follow is HTML. As you know, the browser figures it out fine if these tags don't exist but again, you're going for a well-structured page here. The <HEAD> tags enclose the header section. The header section can be used to give special commands to the browser. For example, you can have a page automatically go to another page after a certain amount of time.

The <BODY> tags represent the body of the page. This is normally where the vast majority of your HTML resides. So far, everything you've written would go in the body section of the page.

TABLES

When it comes to building Web applications, tables are commonly used to display data. Tables enable you to create a grid on the page in which to display data. Tables are also commonly used to help

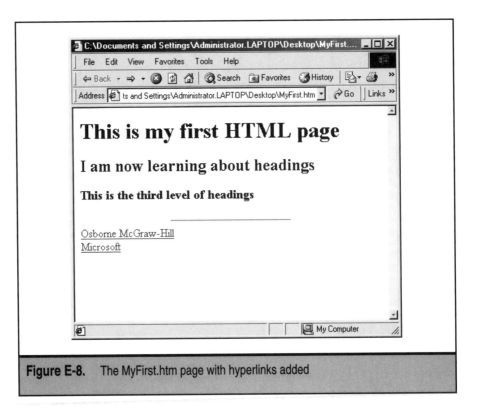

Figure E-8. The MyFirst.htm page with hyperlinks added

format a page. While HTML is great at formatting text, it isn't good at positioning text. Tables can overcome many of the formatting issues.

Building a Grid

When it comes to creating an HTML table, you start with the <TABLE> tag. This tag doesn't, by itself, display anything on the screen for the user to see. However, it tells the browser it's about to start displaying information in a row and column format.

NOTE: All the tags you use in the table are containers, and you should be careful to close all of them. Some browsers, most notably Netscape Navigator, won't display *anything* in a table unless all the tags are properly closed.

Because just putting in the <TABLE> tag doesn't display anything, you need some additional tags. After creating the table, you need to create a row, which you do with the <TR> tag. The row, by itself, still doesn't display any data, so you need to add at least one cell into the row, which you do with the <TD> tag. <TD> stands for table data and represents a cell within the table.

Look at the following code snippet:

```
<TABLE>
   <TR>
      <TD>This is data in a cell!</TD>
   </TR>
</TABLE>
```

This is the basic structure of a table. You have the <TABLE> tags and, within those, you have one or more <TR> tags. Within each <TR> tag, you have one or more <TD> tags. Modify your MyFirst.htm to look like this:

```
<H1>This is my first HTML page</H1>

<TABLE Border="1">
   <TR>
      <TD>Row 1, Cell 1</TD>
      <TD>Row 1, Cell 2</TD>
   </TR>
   <TR>
      <TD>Row 2, Cell 1</TD>
      <TD>Row 2, Cell 2</TD>
   </TR>
</TABLE>
```

The page should look like what you see in Figure E-9. This isn't an exciting table, but notice a few things about it. First, you can see the grid lines, because in the <TABLE> tag you added an attribute called *Border*. If you'd left this out, or set it to zero, no grid lines would have been visible.

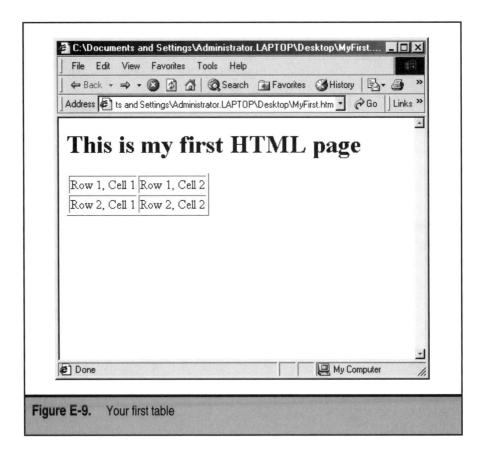

Figure E-9. Your first table

Second, the table matched up the cells into columns, but no law says one row must have the same number of columns as other rows. You'll examine this in a moment.

Finally, notice the cells happen to be just large enough for the text. If you type more text in one cell, that cell will grow to accommodate the text, until it takes up 100 percent of the viewing area, after which the text will wrap. You can specify cell widths with a *Width* attribute on the cell or you can set a Width attribute for the whole table.

Modify your code to examine two things. First, you'll expand the text in one of the cells and you'll also add a third cell to the second row. Make your code look like this:

```
<H1>This is my first HTML page</H1>

<TABLE Border="1">
```

```
<TR>
   <TD>Row 1, Cell 1 is now longer</TD>
   <TD>Row 1, Cell 2</TD>
</TR>
<TR>
   <TD>Row 2, Cell 1</TD>
   <TD>Row 2, Cell 2</TD>
   <TD>Row 2, Cell 3</TD>
</TR>
</TABLE>
```

Figure E-10 shows you what you will see. Notice row 1 cell 1 has stretched to accommodate the longer text. This isn't a problem because row 2 cell 1 stretches to match it. However, notice also that row 2 now has three cells. The browser can no longer match up the columns, but it does the best it can. To fix this, you can add an attribute to row 1

Figure E-10.   Your table, now changed by the longer text and the addition of a third cell to the second row

cell 2 to tell it to take up two columns. Modify only one line of your program, the line that is the cell for row 1 cell 2, by changing it to this:

```
<TD Colspan="2">Row 1, Cell 2</TD>
```

This tells the cell to span the equivalent of two columns. This will make the table look much better. There's also a *Rowspan* attribute that will allow a cell to span multiple rows.

Using Tables for Layout

One of the most common uses for tables is to achieve some layout control over your page. You still use the same three tags, but you usually specify a fixed width for some of the page. For example, modify the code in MyFirst.asp to the following:

```
<TABLE Height="90%">
   <TR Valign="Top">
      <TD BgColor="Silver" Width="120">
         <A HREF="http://www.osborne.com">Osborne</A><BR>
         <A HREF="http://www.microsoft.com">Microsoft</A><BR>
         <A HREF="http://www.ciobriefings.com">CIOBriefings</A>
      </TD>
      <TD>
         <H1>News Flash!</H1>
         Today, our company stock soared on reports...
         <H1>Company Picnic Next Week</H1>
         Don't forget the company picnic next week...
      </TD>
   </TR>
</TABLE>
```

This is a simple table, with only one row and two cells. But, even with this simple example, you see how you can lay out a page. The final result is shown in Figure E-11.

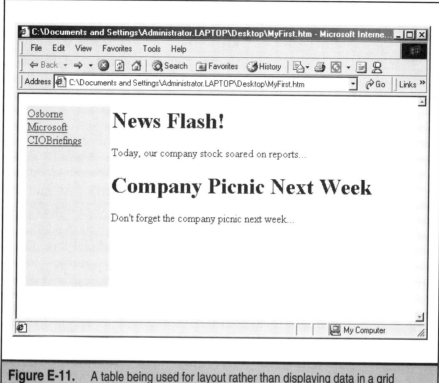

Figure E-11. A table being used for layout rather than displaying data in a grid

HTML FORMS

Now that you've seen the basics of how HTML works and how tables are created, it's time to tackle one other area critical to building Web applications: HTML forms. Even though the purpose of HTML was to provide a portable way to preserve text formatting, the original creators of HTML knew, at some point, they would need a way to get data from the client back to the server. To accomplish this, they added a series of tags that give users elements in which they can enter information. The page then has a way to send this information to the server and have a program on the server act on it.

The <FORM> Tag

Just as the <TABLE> tag told the browser a table was about to be created, the <FORM> tag tells the browser a form is about to be created. Unlike the <TABLE> tag, however, certain attributes of the <FORM> tag are required to make it work. The two most important attributes are the Action and Method attributes.

The *Action* attribute tells the form to what program on the server it needs to pass its information. Remember, HTML isn't a programming language and, therefore, it cannot, by itself, process any information. With forms, you create the form in HTML, but a program must be on the server that will accept the user input and act on it. This program on the server can be a compiled program written in a language like C++ or Java, or it can be a script file like a Perl script or, as you will use here, it can be an Active Server Page.

The Action attribute may contain only the name of the program but, usually it contains the entire URL. For example, your Action attribute might look like this:

```
Action="http://www.ciobriefings.com/ProcessData.asp"
```

In this case, there's an Active Server Page named ProcessData.asp on the CIOBriefings site (www.ciobriefings.com). The data will be passed to the CIOBriefings site into a script called ProcessData.asp.

The second important attribute is the *Method* attribute. Several values exist for this, but the main two you will deal with are Post and Get. Both *Post* and *Get* values send data to the server so, in many instances, you will be fine with either one. The difference is in how the data is sent. The Get method appends the data on to the URL. You have probably seen this before—when you go to a site and look up to see the address looks extremely complicated—with a series of strange characters and numbers in it. The Get method is often limited to returning 1,024 or 2,048 characters. The browser imposes this limit, so it may vary from one browser manufacturer to another or even from one version to another.

The Post method, on the other hand, is able to pass back a much larger number of characters because it passes the data "under the covers," so to speak. The data makes it to the server, just as it did with the Get method, but the user doesn't see the data appended to the URL.

You might be asking why anyone would use the Get method if it's restricted to 1,024 or 2,048 characters. The answer is you may want to be able to save that exact page. To illustrate, open IE and go to http://www.microsoft.com/search. In the search box, enter the string "ado md" without the double quotes. When you click the search button, the search engine prepares a page with the results. If you look at the address, it now looks something like this:

```
http://search.microsoft.com/us/SearchMS25.asp?so=RECCNT&qu=ado+md&boole
an=ALL&i=00&i=02&i=04&i=06&i=08&i=01&i=03&i=05&i=07&i=09&p=1&nq=NEW
```

Where did all this come from? This is the data you are sending to the server. Because you can see it on the address line, this is obviously using the Get method. If you were using the Post method, all you would see is this:

```
http://search.microsoft.com/us/SearchMS25.asp
```

The data would still be sent to the server, but it wouldn't be visible on the address line. If you like the results of this query and want to save a link to the results, you could do so if the page was using the Get method because you would be saving the page name and all the data (the stuff after the question mark). If the page was using the Post method, however, you wouldn't be able to save a link to the exact results. Instead, you'd be saving a link to the search page, but with no data attached. You would only get the page asking you to enter a search string.

In this example, feel free to use either the Post or the Get method. I use the Get method so you can see the data on the address line.

Adding Form Elements

Once you create the form using the <FORM> tag, you need to add some elements to it for the user to do anything. A variety of elements use the same tag, which is the <INPUT> tag. To add a single-line text box, you can add the <INPUT> tag or you can add the Type attribute to it. If you use the Type attribute, the tag would look like this:

```
<INPUT Type="text">
```

You also want to add a *Name* attribute, which lets the server know to pass up the data to all your form elements. Your final tag would look something like this:

```
<INPUT Type="text" Name="txtUserName">
```

Modify your MyFirst.htm file to contain the following code:

```
<HTML>
    <BODY>
        <FORM Method="Get" Action="http://localhost/TestForm.asp">
            UserName: <INPUT Type="text" Name="txtUserName">
        </FORM>
    </BODY>
</HTML>
```

If you view this in the browser, it should look like Figure E-12. This isn't the most exciting page you've ever seen, but now there's a textbox in which you can type information, something you haven't had before.

As mentioned earlier, other types of elements can be created with the <INPUT> tag. For example, you can add radio buttons, check boxes, and password boxes. *Password boxes* look just like text boxes, but anything you type into them appears as a series of asterisks. To add a password box, you simply add the <INPUT Type="password"> tag into your code—and, of course, give it a name.

Radio buttons are the controls that allow only one of a list of possible choices. For example, if someone asks you for your salary range, you cannot be in more than one range at a time. Therefore, it might be valid to ask for the salary range using radio buttons (often called *option*

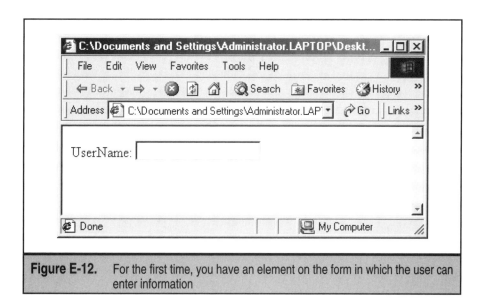

Figure E-12.   For the first time, you have an element on the form in which the user can enter information

buttons). For radio buttons, the tag is <INPUT Type="radio"> but there's a catch: how does the browser know which buttons belong in a logical group? If you have three buttons asking for your salary range, how does the browser know only one button can be on at a time? The answer is simple: just give all the radio buttons the same name.

On the subject of radio buttons, how does the server know which one was chosen? The easiest way is to give each radio button its own Value attribute. The *Value* attribute is what is actually passed to the server, regardless of the text the user sees to identify the button. You see this in a code example in a moment.

For check boxes, zero to many of them can be chosen at a time. To add a check box, the code is as simple as <INPUT Type="checkbox">. Each check box would have a different name, of course.

Modify your MyFirst.htm page to contain the following code, and then save it and view it in the browser:

```
<HTML>
    <BODY>
        <FORM Method="Get" Action="http://localhost/TestForm.asp">
            UserName: <INPUT Type="text" Name="txtUserName"><BR>
            Password: <INPUT Type="password" Name="txtPassword"><BR>
```

```
        <BR><BR>
        Your Annual Salary:<BR>
        <INPUT Type="radio" Name="Salary" Value="1">
           Less than $50,000<BR>
        <INPUT Type="radio" Name="Salary" Value="2">
           Between $50,000 and $100,000<BR>
        <INPUT Type="radio" Name="Salary" Value="3">
           Greater than $100,000<BR>
        Your Hobbies:<BR>
        <INPUT> Type="checkbox" Name="chkSD"
           Skydiving<BR>
        <INPUT> Type="checkbox" Name="chkMB"
           Mountain Biking<BR>
        <INPUT> Type="checkbox" Name="chkUWBW"
           Underwater Basket Weaving<BR><BR>
      </FORM>
   </BODY>
</HTML>
```

Your page should now appear similar to the page in Figure E-13. You now have a textbox, a password box, radio buttons, and check boxes.

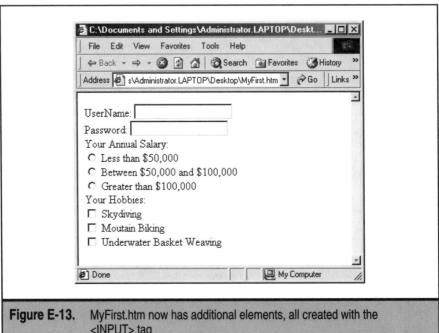

Figure E-13. MyFirst.htm now has additional elements, all created with the <INPUT> tag

You can add other elements that don't use the <INPUT> tag. For example, you may want to add a list box, or a drop-down list box, depending on an attribute you set. A list box lets you select one, or more than one, choice from a list. For example, you can show a list of the states and have the person select one. The list box is created with the <SELECT> tag. Each item in the select box is further surrounded by an <OPTION> tag, however. Like the radio buttons, you can add a Value attribute that will pass a different value to the server than what is shown to the user. For example, you may show the user a product description, but pass back to the server only the product code.

Finally, a multiline text box enables the user to enter a large block of text and use the enter key to add blank lines in the text. The tag for this is the <TEXTAREA> tag, but be careful: this is a container tag. If you forget to close it, the rest of your page will appear in the text box.

Modify your MyFirst.htm page to contain the following code:

```
<HTML>
  <BODY>
    <FORM Method="Get" Action="http://localhost/TestForm.asp">
      UserName: <INPUT Type="text" Name="txtUserName"><BR>
      Password: <INPUT Type="password" Name="txtPassword">
      <BR><BR>
      Your Annual Salary:<BR>
      <INPUT Type="radio" Name="Salary" Value="1">
         Less than $50,000<BR>
      <INPUT Type="radio" Name="Salary" Value="2">
         Between $50,000 and $100,000<BR>
      <INPUT Type="radio" Name="Salary" Value="3">
         Greater than $100,000<BR><BR>
      Your Hobbies:<BR>
      <INPUT Type="checkbox" Name="chkSD">
         Skydiving<BR>
      <INPUT Type="checkbox" Name="chkMB">
         Mountain Biking<BR>
      <INPUT Type="checkbox" Name="chkUWBW">
         Underwater Basket Weaving<BR><BR>
      Choose your State:<BR>
```

```
        <SELECT Name="State">
            <OPTION Value="KY">Kentucky</OPTION>
            <OPTION Value="OH">Ohio</OPTION>
            <OPTION Value="KY">Indiana</OPTION>
        </SELECT><BR><BR>
        Comments:<BR>
        <TEXTAREA>Enter your comments here</TEXTAREA>
    </FORM>
  </BODY>
</HTML>
```

This page should end up looking similar to what is shown in Figure E-14. Some added <BR> tags are added to help make the page more readable.

Submitting the Page

At this point, you could work with the page, entering data, checking boxes, and choosing a value from the list. But then what will you do? Remember, the idea behind HTML forms is to get the data to the server. You've set the page up to do this, by giving it a Method of Get and an Action of http://localhost/TestForm.asp, but there's no way actually to submit the form right now. How do you tell it to take the data and send it to the server?

The answer is you need to add a Submit button. Remember your friend, the <INPUT> tag? Well, the <INPUT> tag has a type of submit that adds a button to the form, which then calls the page on the server.

First, however, you need to create the TestForm.asp. Don't worry if you don't understand this code, as you will by the time you finish

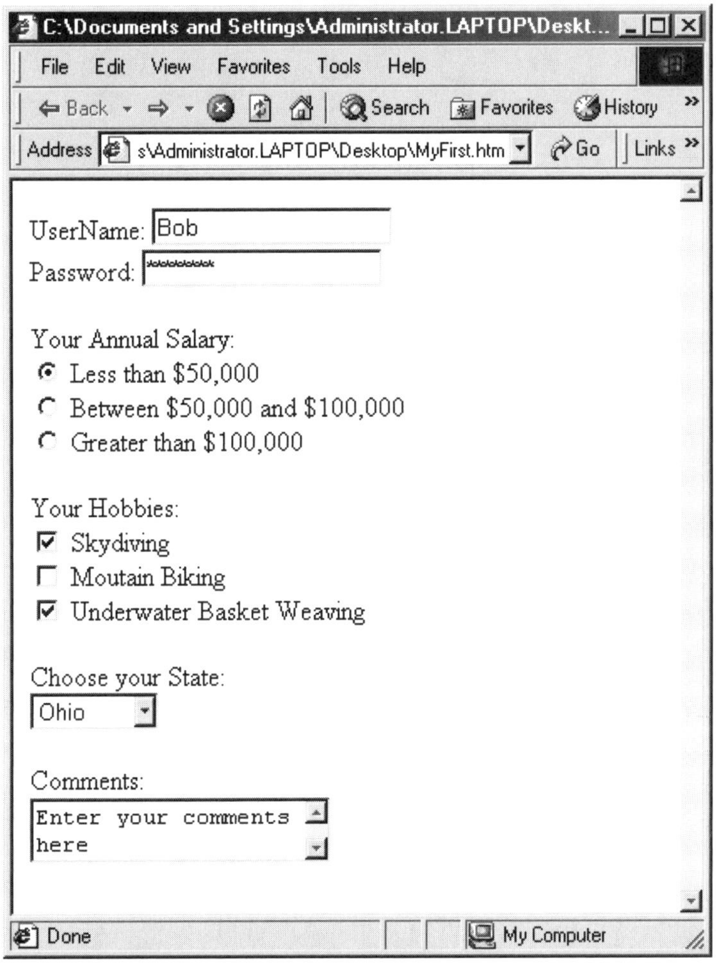

Figure E-14.   MyFirst.htm now has a variety of elements and is ready to be submitted

this book. For now, just create a new file and type in the following code. The information about where to save it follows the code:

```
<%@ Language="VBScript" %>

<H1>Data sent via the Get method:</H1>
<%
For Each vKey in Request.Querystring
    Response.Write vKey & " - " & _
        Request.Querystring(vKey) & "<BR>"
Next
%>
<BR><HR><BR>
<H1>Data sent via the Post method:</H1>
<%
For Each vKey in Request.Form
    Response.Write vKey & " - " & _
        Request.Form(vKey) & "<BR>"
Next
%>
```

After entering this code, save the file with the name TestForm.asp, and then save it in the root of your Web server. Usually, this is c:\inetpub\wwwroot. If you don't have this directory and don't know what to do, you can modify the Action attribute back in MyFirst.htm to point to a site where the file exists. If you have problems, set your Action attribute to:

```
Action="http://www.ciobriefings.com/TestForm.asp"
```

Now, modify your MyFirst.htm page to include the submit button. Your new code should look like this:

```
<HTML>
    <BODY>
        <FORM Method="Get" Action="http://localhost/TestForm.asp">
            UserName: <INPUT Type="text" Name="txtUserName"><BR>
            Password: <INPUT Type="password" Name="txtPassword">
            <BR><BR>
```

```
        Your Annual Salary:<BR>
        <INPUT Type="radio" Name="Salary" Value="1">
           Less than $50,000<BR>
        <INPUT Type="radio" Name="Salary" Value="2">
           Between $50,000 and $100,000<BR>
        <INPUT Type="radio" Name="Salary" Value="3">
           Greater than $100,000<BR><BR>
        Your Hobbies:<BR>
        <INPUT Type="checkbox" Name="chkSD">
           Skydiving<BR>
        <INPUT Type="checkbox" Name="chkMB">
           Mountain Biking<BR>
        <INPUT Type="checkbox" Name="chkUWBW">
           Underwater Basket Weaving<BR><BR>
        Choose your State:<BR>
        <SELECT Name="State">
           <OPTION Value="KY">Kentucky</OPTION>
           <OPTION Value="OH">Ohio</OPTION>
           <OPTION Value="KY">Indiana</OPTION>
        </SELECT><BR><BR>
        Comments:<BR>
        <TEXTAREA>Enter your comments here</TEXTAREA><BR>
        <INPUT Type="submit">
      </FORM>
   </BODY>
</HTML>
```

You have now added the submit button to the bottom of the page. When you click the submit button, the browser takes the data and manipulates it so it can be sent. This involves taking the element name and setting it equal to the value to be passed. For example, if you type "John Doe" in the User Name field, the actual name of this field is txtUserName. The server passes up the following:

```
txtUserName=John+Doe
```

Where did the plus (+) sign come from? URLs cannot contain any spaces, so spaces are replaced with a plus sign. In addition, special characters such as question marks, apostrophes, and commas are not allowed, so the browser replaces them with special numbers, preceded by a percent sign. Multiple fields are then separated with an ampersand. So, if you type "Mike O'Neal" in the User Name field, and then you type "secret" in the password box, this is what is sent to the server:

```
txtUserName=Mike+O%27Neal&txtPassword=secret
```

If you are using the Get method, you'll see this in the address line. If you are using the Post method, you won't. But the data gets to the server regardless.

Now, run your page. When you fill in the data and press the Submit button, you should notice the resulting page simply parrots what you entered. This simple ASP works for any form, as it only looks at a list of the elements passed up and their values. Notice check boxes have the value of "on" when they are passed up.

SUMMARY

To be a Web developer, you have to know HTML. This appendix only scratches the surface, but it covers perhaps the most important topics: tables and forms. Don't let this be your only introduction to HTML, however. Find a book that can help you learn HTML because many more tags and attributes haven't been mentioned, and you should also learn about more advanced areas, such as cascading style sheets and client-side scripting.

APPENDIX F

VBScript Introduction

VBScript is one of the two main languages used in Active Server Pages. The other is JScript, which is often called JavaScript and sometimes ECMAScript. VBScript is more common for server-side scripting because many more people know its parent language, Visual Basic (or Visual Basic for Applications). Because this appendix is a primer for VBScript, I assume you are just starting on this book and want to know the basics of VBScript before you get started.

This appendix takes a quick view of a few topics in VBScript, such as declaring variables, the looping and conditional constructs, and building functions. In no way is it intended to replace a book on VBScript and, if you are going to build Active Server Pages for a living, a good reference book on VBScript will be most helpful. Also, you can check out http://msdn.microsoft.com/scripting for a complete VBScript (and JScript) reference. This appendix also assumes you at least know what a variable is and how computers work in general.

DECLARING VARIABLES

VBScript is a weakly typed language. This simply means all variables are of the variant data type. If you are a Visual Basic programmer, you've been told over and over that variants are bad. They take up a lot of memory and are slow relative to strong data types, like an integer or string.

A variant can take on any data type, at any time. For example, the following is a snippet of VB code:

```
'VB code
Dim sSQL As String
sSQL = "Select CompanyName from Customers"
sSQL = 12
```

In this case, you use the Dim keyword to declare a variable. If you're keeping score, Dim is short for Dimension, which means the computer should set aside some memory to hold the value of this variable.

In VB, which has strong data types, you would have a problem with the previous code. You declared sSQL as a string data type. Therefore, when you set it to the string "Select CompanyName from Customers" you are in good shape. When you try to set it to 12, however, you would run into a problem because, in this case, 12 is a numeric value.

In VBScript, however, the only data type is a variant. Your VBScript code would look like this:

```
'VBScript code
Dim sSQL
sSQL = "Select CompanyName from Customers"
sSQL = 12
```

Now, notice that when you Dim a variable, you don't put a data type after it. sSQL is now a variant and can hold a string or a number. In fact, the previous code is perfectly legal in VBScript.

When you declare variables in VBScript, the variable name must start with an alphabetic character, which means any letter *A-Z*. The variable cannot start with a number or an underscore. Variables cannot have any spaces, periods, question marks, or most other special characters. The limit on a variable name is 255 characters. If you cannot create a meaningful variable name in less than 255 characters, please consider what you are doing and try again.

VBScript is not case-sensitive. In other words, the variables sSQL, sSql, and ssql are all the same in VBScript. This is not true in many other programming languages.

Option Explicit

In VBScript, you don't have to declare variables, which may seem like a great idea. For example, the following block of code is perfectly legal:

```
Dim x
x=x+1
y=x+1
```

In this example, you Dim x on the first line. The VBScript language interpreter sets aside some memory for x and gives it a blank value. The second line takes x and adds one to it. Because x was a blank value, the VBScript interpreter sees that as being the same as zero, so after the second line, the value of x will be 1. Now, on the third line, the VBScript interpreter sees the variable y. Having never seen it before, it decides to set aside space for use by y. The value of y will now be x+1, which equates to 2.

Not declaring variables makes life easy . . . or does it? In college, I remember the professor saying you should always declare your variables. Now, here's a real-world example that might convince you better than simply saying you should do it.

A developer working for me, whom I'll call Chris, called me into his office because he was stumped. He had been working on an Active Server Page, full of VBScript, for about an hour. He was pulling data from a database, manipulating it a bit, and displaying it on the Web page. No matter what Chris did, he couldn't get the FirstName field to display. He showed me there really was a value for it in the database, and then Chris showed me his code. He was pulling the value out of the database and storing it in a variable called sFirstName. Then, many, many lines of code later, Chris was printing out the variable . . . sFName. As a fresh set of eyes, I noticed it right away, and I've been telling this story for three years.

Why tell this story? Part of it is to make fun of Chris, but the real reason is because he could have typed in two little words that would have caught this mistake the first time he ran it. Those two words are "Option Explicit." Typing Option Explicit in your VBScript forces you to declare all your variables. I cannot recommend Option Explicit highly enough.

CONDITIONALS

Conditional, or decision, constructs in VBScript are fairly straightforward. The most common one by far is the simple If statement. In VBScript, the If statement has several different formats. Examine the following block of code:

```
If x=5 then y=10
```

This statement says if the variable x has a value of 5, then assign the value of 10 to the variable y. This is a perfectly valid VBScript If statement, but you see it written this way much more often:

```
If x=5 Then
    y=10
End If
```

Why would someone go to this amount of work if the first example is valid? What if you needed to do more than just assign he value of 10 to y? What if you also needed to assign the variable z a value? You cannot perform multiple operations with the first syntax, but you can put as many lines of code as you want between the If and End If statements in the second syntax, as such:

```
If x=5 Then
    y=10
    z=20
End If
```

You can now see two things happen when x has the value 5. What if you need something else to happen if x wasn't equal to 5? The answer is to use the Else statement, as shown here:

```
If x=5 Then
    y=10
    z=20
Else
    y=0
    z=0
End If
```

Now, you can see that if x is equal to 5, y will be set to 10 and z will be set to 20. If x is any value other than 5, however, y and z will both be set to 0.

What if you need to check more than just one value? In other words, what if you need to do something when x was 5, something else when it was 7, and something else when it was anything else? You can have nested If statements, like this one:

```
If x=5 Then
    y=10
    z=20
```

```
ElseIf x=7 Then
    y=3
    z=1
Else
    y=0
    z=0
End If
```

An alternative structure exists to this because the logic can get rather hard to follow if you are searching for a large number of cases. The Select Case statement enables you to specify a large number of conditions in an easy-to-read structure. Examine the following block of code:

```
Select Case x
    Case 5
        y=10
        z=20
    Case 7
        y=3
        z=1
    Case 20
        y=50
        z=100
    Case Else
        y=0
        z=0
End Select
```

In this code, the value of x is examined when the Select Case x line is encountered. The program then finds the matching case and executes the code in that block. If x is 20, for example, it sets y to 50 and z to 100. If no cases match, you fall into the Case Else portion of the statement and execute those lines of code.

LOOPS

Loops are a way of repeating sections of code for a fixed number of iterations, or until a condition becomes true or false. Several loops are available in VBScript: the Do…Loop, the While…Wend loop, the For…Next loop, and the For Each loop.

The Do…Loop

The dominant and most flexible loop is the *Do…Loop* syntax. Four variations of this loop exist:

1. Do While…Loop
2. Do…Loop While
3. Do Until…Loop
4. Do…Loop Until

Take the first variation and examine the following block of code:

```
Do While x<10
    'code goes here
    x=x+1
Loop
```

This block of code will run as long as the value of x is less than 10. Assume as you enter the loop, the value of x is 1. The first time through, the lines of code represented by the comment "code goes here" will be executed, and then the value of x will be incremented by 1. Now, x is equal to 2. Is x less than 10? Yes, so you repeat the loop. Eventually, x will be 9. Because x is less than 10, you run the code and then press the x=x+1 line. Now, x goes to 10, and when you examine the value, you see x is no longer less than 10, and you drop out of the loop and continue the execution.

Now, what if before you got to this loop, the value of x was 15? The Do While x<10 line will see x is *not* less than 10, and you will skip over the loop, having never executed anything in it.

If, instead, you use the Do…Loop While syntax, it will work somewhat differently. Examine the following code

```
Do
    'code goes here
    x=x+1
Loop While x<10
```

Now, assume x is zero when you enter the loop; this loop will run the same as before. However, what if the value of x is 15? The While condition is not checked until after the loop code has been executed one time. Therefore, with this syntax, you are guaranteed to have the loop code execute a minimum of one time.

The Do Until...Loop and Do...Loop Until work in almost exactly the same way. The difference is the Do While loops *while a condition is true*. The Do Until loops *until a condition becomes true*.

The While...Wend Loop

The While...Wend loop is a holdover from the older days of Visual Basic. It works just like the Do While variation of the Do loop. The syntax would look like this:

```
While x<10
    'do code here
    x=x+1
Wend
```

That's all there is to the While...Wend loop. Given the flexibility of the Do loop, you don't see the While loop used often any more, but it's still perfectly valid.

The For...Next Loop

Both the Do and While loops require you to increment or, at least change, the conditional variable inside the loop. In the previous examples, the variable x is being checked as the loop condition, and inside the loop, the value is being incremented by one each time. The For...Next loop, however, can automatically increment a variable for you. If you want to run some code a fixed number of times, you can do that easily with a For...Next loop. Look at the following code snippet:

```
For x=1 to 10
    'do code here
Next
```

Unlike the Do and While loops, the value of x before you enter the loop is unimportant. Here, you start the loop by assigning x the value of 1. Then, you perform the code inside the loop. When you press the word Next, x automatically increments by one and you check the conditional, which in this case is: is x now greater than or equal to 10? Normally, you would repeat this loop ten times but, sometimes, the value of x can be changed inside the loop.

You needn't accept the automatic increment of one each time through the loop. You can add the word Step to the For statement to change the amount of the increment. For example, to increase by two each time, the code would look like this:

```
For x=1 to 11 Step 2
```

The For Each Loop

A relatively new loop in the Visual Basic and VBScript languages is the For Each loop. This is designed to loop through a collection and examine each value, regardless of the number of elements. For now, consider a collection to be similar to an array; it can have multiple values inside it, accessed with an index number.

Often times, when working with collections, you create a number of objects. You don't know how many objects exist and you don't care. You simply need to loop through all of them to display or process them in some way. The For Each statement does just that. The code for the For Each looks like this:

```
For Each x in Request.Form
    'perform operations on x
Next
```

With the For Each, x takes on the value of each individual object in the collection, one at a time. You can then reference that object's properties and methods as needed.

FUNCTIONS AND SUBS

Unlike many languages, VBScript has two types of procedures: the Function and the Sub. These two work almost identically, except the Function can return one value and the Sub doesn't return a value. Both Functions and Subs can accept parameters.

Sub stands for *subprocedure*, or *subroutine*, or *subfunction*, depending on who you believe. The idea behind a Sub is to create a reusable block of code that doesn't need to return a value. For example, you might want a Sub that logs information into a text file for you occasionally. Your code might look something like this:

```
'some generic processing
If nRecordCount=0 Then
   Log "No records found"
End If
...


Sub Log(sMessage)
   'open text file
   OutFile.Write sMessage
   'close text file
End Sub
```

Notice the Sub doesn't have to return any value. It does its work and the previous code can continue processing. Notice that when the Sub is called, you don't put parentheses around the value you are passing to the Sub, in this case, the string "No records found".

A Function, on the other hand, does return a value. Therefore, when you call it, you must have the return value stored in a variable. Look at this code:

```
x=5
y=SqrIt(x)
...


Function SqrIt(nNumber)
   SqrIt=nNumber * nNumber
End Function
```

Functions return values by setting the name of the Function to the value to be returned. In the previous snippet, the value of SqrIt will be returned to the variable y. After this code runs, x will still have the value of 5, and y will have the value 25.

Unlike many languages, when the Function name is set to the value to return, the value is not returned immediately. Instead, you continue executing the code in the Function until you reach the End Function statement or an early exit occurs with the Exit Function command.

BUILT-IN COMMANDS

Perhaps one of the greatest challenges in learning any new language is finding out the built-in functions and commands to perform certain operations. Almost all languages have an If statement, but the format varies from one language to another. VBScript has a number of built-in commands and functions that can make your programming job much easier.

Date/Time Functions

VBScript has several built-in date and time functions. For example, examine these three lines of code:

```
x=Date()
y=Time()
z=Now()
```

Given these three lines, what would the values of x, y, and z be? The Date function returns only the date, and the exact format depends on the settings in Windows on that particular machine. For x, you might get something back like "8/20/2000". For y, you will retrieve only the current time, so it might be in the format "11:36:32 AM". The Now() function returns the date and time, so z would look like this: "8/20/2000 11:36:32 AM".

A series of built-in commands can also extract information from date and time values. For example, the DatePart function can return information, such as only the year, or the day, or the day of the year, the week of the year, and so forth. The DateAdd function enables you to add or subtract days, months, seconds, hours, and so on. If you need to know the exact day that is 180 days from today, you can do so.

String Manipulation

One of the most common things you will have to do is work with strings. VBScript lets you concatenate strings with the ampersand symbol. Examine the following code snippet:

```
x="Hello"
y="Craig"

z=x & ", " & y
```

In this code, the value of x is concatenated with a string that has a comma, and then a space. Finally the string held in y is concatenated onto that. Once done, the string held by z is "Hello, Craig".

Concatenating strings is easy enough, but you will need to perform other functions against strings. For example, examine the following lines of code:

```
sSentence="This is a sentence inside a variable"
x=Left(sSentence, 12)
y=Right(sSentence, 10)
z=Mid(sSentence, 2, 5)
nSentenceLength=Len(sSentence)
```

First, you create a string named sSentence and assign a sentence to it. You use the Left function to pull out the first 12 characters; Left starts at the left-most character, and then retrieves the number of characters specified in the second argument. Therefore, the value of x will be "This is a se".

The Right function retrieves characters at the end of the string. The number of characters to return is specified in the second argument. Therefore, the value of y is "a variable".

The Mid function pulls out part of a string. It starts with the character you specify in the second argument, and then retrieves the number of characters you specify in the third argument. Starting with the second character and pulling a total of five characters total will give z the value of "his i".

Finally, if you need to know how long a string is, simply use the Len function. This will return the total number of characters, including spaces. In this case, the variable nSentenceLength will be 36.

SUMMARY

Again, this appendix covers only the basics. If you've never programmed before in your life, grab a book on basic programming concepts, such as variables, loops, and so on. Most people reading this book have some programming experience, however, so this appendix simply attempts to show the basics of the major VBScript constructs. For a full VBScript reference, you can check out http://msdn.microsoft.com/scripting.

INDEX

References to figures and illustrations are in italics.

 A

Active Server Pages
 applications, 40-44
 and CGI, 14
 Chili!Soft ASP, 21
 compared to how HTML works, 26
 "compile-free" technology, 20-21
 creating a simple ASP, 32-34
 directory browsing and default documents, 38-39
 how the engine processes code, 34-37
 and IIS, 14, 19-21
 include files, 40-44
 making the connection on each ASP, 142-145
 moving to ASP+, 385-387
 and scripting languages, 20
 sessionless, 500-501
 See also ASP+
ActiveX controls, 12-14
ActiveX Data Objects, 120-155
 Command object, 158-180, 570-571

D

▼ E

▼ F

W

X